Reading & Learning Strategies

QUICK REFERENCE GUIDE FOR TEACHING GOALS

Reading & Learning Strategies

MIDDLE GRADES THROUGH HIGH SCHOOL

Second Edition

Susan Davis Lenski
Illinois State University

Mary Ann Wham, Emerita
University of Wisconsin-Whitewater

Jerry L. Johns, Emeritus
Northern Illinois University

KENDALL/HUNT PUBLISHING COMPANY
4050 Westmark Drive Dubuque, Iowa 52002

www.kendallhunt.com

Books by Jerry L. Johns

Basic Reading Inventory (8th ed.)

Secondary & College Reading Inventory
  (two editions)

Literacy for Diverse Learners (edited)

Handbook for Remediation of Reading Difficulties

Informal Reading Inventories: An Annotated
  Reference Guide (compiled)

Literacy: Celebration and Challenge (edited)

Spanish Reading Inventory

Book Team

President & Chief Executive Officer: Mark C. Falb

Vice President, Director of National Book
  Program: Alfred C. Grisanti

Editorial Developmental Manager: Georgia Botsford

Prepress Project Coordinator: Sheri Hosek

Prepress Editor: Ellen Kaune

Design Manager: Jodi Splinter

Designer: Deb Howes

Books by Jerry L. Johns and Susan Davis Lenski

Improving Reading: Strategies & Resources (3rd ed.)

Celebrate Literacy! The Joy of Reading and Writing (with June E. Barnhart, James H. Moss, and
  Thomas E. Wheat)

Language Arts for Gifted Middle School Students

Improving Writing: Resources, Strategies, Assessments

Teaching Beginning Readers: Linking Assessment and Instruction (2nd ed.) (with Laurie Elish-Piper)

Author Information for Correspondence and Workshops

Susan Davis Lenski
Illinois State University
Campus Box 5330
Normal, IL 61790
E-mail: sjlensk@ilstu.edu
309-438-3028

Mary Ann Wham
1974 Wedgewood Way
Rockford, IL 61107
E-mail: wham.maryann@mcleodusa.net
815-877-0528

Jerry L. Johns
Consultant in Reading
2105 Eastgate Drive
Sycamore, IL 60178
E-mail: jjohns@niu.edu
815-895-3022

Ordering Information

Phone 800-247-3458, ext. 4 or 5   Fax 800-772-9165
www.kendallhunt.com

Previously titled *Reading & Learning Strategies for Middle & High School Students*

Selected resources from chapters may be reproduced for noncommercial
educational purposes without obtaining written permission from the publisher.
These resources have a permission line at the bottom of the page.

Cover and interior photos: comstock.com

CONTENTS

PREFACE

Purpose of This Book

Reading & Learning Strategies: Middle Grades through High School (2nd ed.) is a user-friendly, practical book grounded in solid knowledge about reading. It is intended for use in undergraduate and graduate secondary and content area reading courses as well as for workshops and inservice programs for teachers in middle and high schools. Reading teachers and specialists will embrace it as a valuable resource for their personal libraries.

Unique Characteristics

The characteristics of *Reading & Learning Strategies: Middle Grades through High School* (2nd ed.) that make it a content book that is different from the ones already on your shelves are as follows.

- Straightforward organizational scheme
- Clear writing
- Useful strategies
- Helpful examples
- Content area examples
- Reproducible classroom resources

Content Area Strategies

There is at least one content area example for each strategy presented in this book; many strategies have examples gleaned from more than one subject. We tried to vary the content examples in each chapter so that you could see for yourself how to apply the strategies to your classroom instruction. However, there will be strategies with examples from middle and high school subjects other than your own. For those strategies that have examples from other subject areas, we urge you to adapt the strategies to fit your particular content and classroom. Virtually all of the strategies presented in this book can be applied to each of the subjects taught in schools.

Word to the Wise Teacher

Please use and adapt these strategies to make your instruction more responsive to the needs of your students. Through your thoughtful and conscientious use of this book, we know that your students will become more effective readers and learners—the base for knowledge learned throughout their lives.

How to Use This Book

Take a few minutes to get acquainted with *Reading & Learning Strategies: Middle Grades through High School* (2nd ed.).

A **Quick Reference Guide** is placed on the inside front cover and continues on page i. Beneath each chapter title are three to five goals for students.

Go Ahead—choose a specific goal and find it on the page number listed.

You will see that each chapter is arranged in the same format.

- Overview
- Numbered section heading
- Boxed student learning goal
- Background information
- Numbered teaching strategies

There is a **numbered section** heading (e.g., 2.1 Creating Interest).

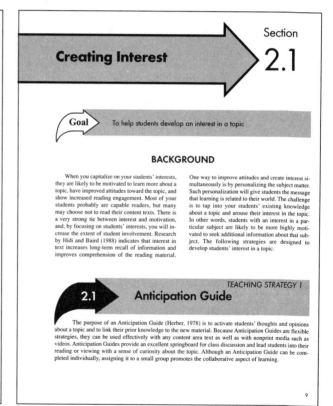

The **goal** for the section is identified in the box.

Background information is given to aid in reaching the goal.

Teaching strategies form the heart of this book. These strategies are carefully described and use examples from various content areas. For each goal, you will find one or more strategies.

Resources are listed with some sections as a reference tool.

Technology Tips provide website addresses pertinent to some sections. Please note that websites are accurate at the time of publication. We cannot guarantee how long these sites will remain online.

 denotes **Directions and Examples.**

 denotes **Group Activities.**

Appendix Material

Appendix A lists various professional organizations by subject to help you find a network of content area specialists in your field.

Appendix B provides you with information on ways to determine readability of texts using readability formulas both manually and with computer software.

Susan Davis Lenski is an Associate Professor at Illinois State University (ISU) where she teaches undergraduate and graduate courses in reading and language arts.

Dr. Lenski brings 20 years of public school teaching experience to her work as a professor and writer. During her years as a middle school teacher, Dr. Lenski developed a program that integrated reading instruction with content area subjects. In recognition of Dr. Lenski's program, the International Reading Association presented her with the Nila Banton Smith Award, a national award given each year to one secondary teacher who has been instrumental in infusing reading into the content areas.

As a professor, Dr. Lenski has been actively engaged in research and writing. She was awarded the Outstanding Researcher Award for the Illinois State University College of Education for her work on reading and writing from multiple sources. She has co-authored seven books, one of which is *Improving Reading: A Handbook of Strategies* (with Jerry L. Johns).

Mary Ann Wham is Professor Emerita at the University of Wisconsin-Whitewater. She has taught undergraduate and graduate courses related to reading and the language arts. Prior to her position in Whitewater, Dr. Wham was director of the Rockford College Reading Clinic in Rockford, IL, where she worked with middle and high school students involved in reading improvement.

Dr. Wham is a former member of the editorial board of *The Reading Teacher* and has served on the Board of Directors of the Mid-Western Educational Research Association. She has conducted inservices and workshops for practicing teachers and has made frequent presentations at regional and national reading conferences. Dr. Wham has contributed a number of articles to reading journals regarding effective classroom literacy instruction. Currently she is an adjunct professor at Northern Illinois University.

AUTHORS

Jerry L. Johns, Distinguished Teaching Professor Emeritus of Northern Illinois University, is the 2002–2003 president of the International Reading Association. He has been recognized as a distinguished professor, writer, and outstanding teacher educator. He has taught students from kindergarten through college and serves as a consultant and speaker to schools and professional organizations.

Dr. Johns is a past president of the Illinois Reading Council, College Reading Association, and Northern Illinois Reading Council. He has received recognition for outstanding service to each of these professional organizations and is a member of the Illinois Reading Council Hall of Fame. Dr. Johns has served on numerous committees of the International Reading Association and was a member of the Board of Directors. He has also received the Outstanding Teacher Educator in Reading Award from the International Reading Association. He recently received the Champion for Children award from the HOSTS Corporation for leadership and making a difference in the educational development of students.

Dr. Johns has been invited to consult, conduct workshops, and make presentations for teachers and professional groups throughout the United States and Canada. He has also prepared nearly 300 publications that have been useful to a diverse group of educators. His *Basic Reading Inventory* is widely used in undergraduate and graduate classes as well as by practicing teachers. Dr. Johns coauthored *Improving Reading: Strategies and Resources* (3rd ed.), *Teaching Beginning Readers* (2nd ed.), and *Strategies for Content Area Learning: Vocabulary, Comprehension, and Response. Fluency: Questions, Answers, and Evidence-Based Strategies* is his fifteenth book.

ACKNOWLEDGMENTS

We are grateful to colleagues, teachers, and other professionals who have assisted us with the preparation of this book. Our special thanks go to Georgia Botsford, our superb editor, for her help and friendship; to Fran Lenski, copyeditor extraordinaire; to Annette Johns for her helpful input; and to Fred Wham for his continued support.

A number of teachers and graduate students were willing to share their resources, provide content examples, react to drafts of our writing, and assist in various ways that strengthened the book. We are pleased to acknowledge the excellent assistance of these wonderful individuals.

Deb Askelson, Northern Illinois University
Jennifer Bolander, Illinois State University
Linda Bookout, Streator District #44
Kathy Byron, University of Wisconsin-Whitewater
Heather Carlson, Northern Illinois University
Dawn Cavanaugh, Sycamore High School
Nancy Drake, University of Wisconsin-Whitewater
Becky Eloe, Glen Westlake Middle School
Mary Engleken, Wheeling District #21
Lou Ferroli, Rockford College
LaVonne Knapstein, Wheeling District #21
Ken Kubycheck, Elgin District #46
John Liedtke, Jefferson Middle School
Janelle Lone, University of Wisconsin-Whitewater
Peggy Nink, Streator District #44
Janet Pariza, Northern Illinois University
Marsha Riss, Metcalf Laboratory School
Marilyn Roark, Palatine, Illinois
Anne Marie Rubendall, Sycamore District #427
J. Suzanne Oliver Sheets, Westview Elementary School
Ellen Spycher, Illinois State University
Carolyn Strzok, Huntley Middle School
Christine Wolff, Wheeling District #21
Roslyn Wylie, Illinois State University

Sue, Mary Ann, and Jerry

Chapter 1

LEARNING WITH TEXTS

OVERVIEW

Reading is an essential skill in our society. We encounter print in all aspects of our lives, and we often take being able to read for granted. This morning, for example, you may have read the newspaper during breakfast. If you watched morning television, you may have encountered print during commercial breaks or as a moving text at the bottom of the screen. If you drove to work, you probably read road and street signs, and during work you constantly made use of print by reading memos, letters, students' papers, and so on. Reading is one of the fundamental skills for the 21st century.

Reading as a Sociocultural Activity

We rely on the printed word because so much of what we learn is through language. Reading and writing are complex cognitive processes whose development is facilitated by social interactions in cultural contexts. This sociocultural view of reading and writing implies that literacy learning is acquired and developed through purposeful transactions with texts in meaningful social groups. These transactions are literacy events from which the reader or writer can apply strategies that support independent processing. On the surface, reading and writing may seem to be solitary acts, but in reality they are learned and practiced through social

1

interactions. As students engage in reading and writing, they construct meaning in language-oriented situations (Wertsch, 1991). When students read, they rely on their backgrounds of language-rich situations for knowledge about the content of texts, ways texts are organized, vocabulary and concept knowledge, and intersecting texts; all of this knowledge about language is present as students read. In addition, language (and consequently reading and writing) is grounded in social interactions (Vygotsky, 1978).

Sociocultural views of reading also posit that learning and construction of meaning is contextual. Understanding reading from a sociocultural perspective involves viewing readers as constructing meaning within a specific social context (Bean, 2000; Bloome & Egan-Robertson, 1993). From this perspective, schools and classrooms are contexts in which students develop reading competencies through interactions with language, instructional practices and settings, peers, and other features that constitute a learning environment. Comprehension of texts becomes a complex activity because it involves readers negotiating their background knowledge and the phonemic, syntactic, semantic, and pragmatic elements of a text as they construct an understanding of what they read. This complexity deepens as students move into secondary schools where there is a greater demand for content area reading that requires more sophisticated background knowledge and vocabulary.

Difficulty of Content Area Texts

Many students, however, have difficulty comprehending content area texts. The National Assessment of Education Progress (NAEP) data indicate that the majority of secondary readers (60%) are able to read at a basic level, but only 5% are able to read and interpret informational text, and these results have remained stable over the past 20 years (Donahue, Voelkl, Campbell, & Mazzeo, 1999). Furthermore, the achievement gap between students from minority backgrounds and students from European-American backgrounds is widening and is becoming a national concern (Rand Study Group, 2002).

There are a number of reasons why older students have difficulty reading complex texts such as science, history, and math books. First, most students have had few experiences reading informational texts. Elementary schools typically emphasize narrative text over informational text (e.g., Duke, 2000). Furthermore, despite two decades of research on reading comprehension, the National Reading Panel (2000) reported that content area teachers generally do not teach the strategies that students need to use when reading textbooks. That may be because many teachers don't know which strategies help students comprehend informational texts (Spor & Schneider, 1999). Some students, therefore, do not comprehend complex texts, and most teachers are not providing the instruction necessary for them to do so.

Another reason why secondary students have difficulty reading content area texts is that the texts students encounter in the middle grades through high school are far more complex than content texts in the earlier grades. Furthermore, some teachers believe that when students are faced with more difficult texts they should be able to read without difficulty. This assumption seems logical, but it is unrealistic. An analogy illustrates how complex skills need to be taught. Imagine that you (or a son, daughter, or friend) learned how to do a front dive from a one-meter diving board. You might be able to do a front dive on a higher board without much trouble. But being able to dive does not automatically mean you can accomplish a more difficult one—say a back somersault. To learn this new skill, you would have to learn a new set of more complicated physical moves.

The same principle holds true with content area reading. As students progress through the grades, they encounter more difficult texts and need more than basic reading skills, especially in the content areas. For example, read the following passages from an elementary science textbook and a high school biology textbook.

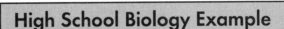

Elementary Science Example

Growing Green Plants

You've probably eaten many different kinds of seeds. Beans, peas, and corn are seeds. So are nuts such as acorns. You know apples and oranges have seeds. But you probably don't know that some pine cones have seeds. Perhaps you've puffed on a dandelion and blown some of the seeds away. What might have happened to the seeds?

From Science and technology: Changes we make. (1985). San Diego, CA: Coronado, p. 202.

High School Biology Example

Flowering Plants May Appear Very Different

Flowering plants are divided into two large classes—the monocots and the dicots. In monocots, the embryo contains a single cotyledon. The monocots include grasses and grain-producing plants such as wheat, rice, and corn—the chief food plants of the world. The pasture grasses that feed cattle, another source of human food, are also monocots. Without monocots, the human population never could have reached its present state.

From BSCS Biology: An ecological approach. (1998). Dubuque, IA: Kendall/Hunt, p. 330.

In the elementary passage, notice that the vocabulary is simple, the sentences are short, the text is personalized, and the ideas are basic. As you look at the example from the high school science text, you'll notice the complexity of the language and thoughts. Students need to have more highly developed reading skills to read this text, skills that do not necessarily come without instructional intervention.

Learning with Text in Content Areas

Although students will use many methods to learn in your subject area, reading is one of the skills they should have in order to learn the content that you teach. When you want students to learn about polymers, for example, you might tell them the information, or you could ask students to read from their textbooks to learn. The beauty of reading is that it's so versatile. When we want to learn about something, we can read brochures, manuals, websites, books, and so on. When we read, it's not necessary to read every word or even every page. We are in control of the information flow. We can speed up, slow down, or stop at any time. Reading, therefore, should be one of the primary tools you use to help students learn with texts.

As students read informational text, however, they need to approach it in a different manner than they do fictional text. Readers need to take a specific stance toward text when they read to learn. Rosenblatt (1978, 1994) theorized that readers read for different purposes, and as they read, they adopt a stance toward that text. The stance a reader could take varies across a continuum from efferent to aesthetic. When reading informational text to learn, readers approach text from an efferent stance. (In contrast, readers of fiction typically read from an aesthetic perspective.) According to transactional theory, whether or not readers approach informational texts from an efferent stance has an impact on the depth of their comprehension.

Teachers tend to spend much more time explaining to students how to read fictional text from an aesthetic viewpoint than they do instructing students on ways to read informational text (Ogle & Blachowicz, 2002). For example, elementary teachers spend a great deal of time teaching students how to read novels, explaining how to identify the plot, setting, theme, and characters. Many teachers also give students the opportunity to respond to the story through discussions and writing. However, few teachers help students approach informational text, especially content area texts, from the efferent stance. Students are frequently left on their own to try to construct meaning as they read.

Reading Comprehension

The goal of reading is comprehension. Reading comprehension can be defined as the "process of simultaneously extracting and constructing meaning through interaction and involvement with written language" (Rand Study Group, 2002, p. 11). Reading comprehension, therefore, involves a reader, a text, and reading activities set in a larger sociocultural context. Comprehension is the construction of meaning by readers who actively use their minds to construct their own individual understandings. These meanings are constructed using the readers' background knowledge; moreover, because every learner's background knowledge is different, every person's construction of meaning is unique. Furthermore, readers bring with them to each reading event their linguistic ability, vocabulary knowledge, motivations, interests, and purposes.

The second aspect of reading comprehension is the demands of the texts—characteristics that make texts easy or difficult for particular readers. Some of the text characteristics that affect difficulty and accessibility are the familiarity of topic content, predictability, repetition of words, inter-

est level, language and genre, rhyming words, number of words per page and layout of the words, illustrations, high-frequency words, size of print, length of book, and complexity or structure of the text. Reading also entails interactive processes. As readers approach text, they employ a variety of processes, such as setting and revising purposes, making and confirming predictions, drawing inferences and conclusions, summarizing, evaluating the veracity of the text, and forming opinions. Finally, knowledge is not constructed in a vacuum. Readers construct meaning using their background knowledge, but they also construct meaning in concert with other people. The figure that follows illustrates the connections between the reader, text, and context.

Content Area Strategies

When students read and write, they use strategies either to make sense of text while reading or to produce text while writing. A strategy is a sequence of cognitive steps to accomplish a specific goal (Collins, 1998). Even though all students use

Reader

Text

Context

strategies to some extent, students who experience difficulty with reading and writing apply strategies differently than do good readers and writers. Proficient readers and writers selectively and flexibly apply a vast array of strategies to every reading or writing event (Pressley, 1995). In contrast, students who are experiencing difficulty with reading and writing typically use fewer strategies and their strategy use tends to be rigid rather than flexible. The judicious, flexible use of strategies when reading and writing, therefore, is a prime characteristic of expert readers and writers and should be an instructional goal for every teacher.

Comprehension strategies can be defined as "specific, learned procedures that foster active, competent, self-regulated, and intentional reading" (Trabasso & Bouchard, 2002, p. 177). Although some readers "figure out" strategies for themselves, most students need to be taught reading strategies explicitly because they are much more likely to learn how to be strategic readers with instruction (Trabasso & Bouchard, 2002). Reading and writing strategies can be acquired intuitively from experience or can be learned deliberately through instructional interventions (Lenski & Nierstheimer, 2002).

For instructional interventions to be effective, teachers need to model the strategies in authentic situations (Duffy, 2002). For this type of instruction to occur, teachers need to know that reading is an interaction between the reader, the text, and the activity, and they need to know how to select appropriate strategies to facilitate comprehension. Unfortunately, most secondary teachers have not had training in teaching reading strategies, nor can we assume that teachers who have been taught strategies in preservice programs automatically use them in their classrooms (Jackson & Davis, 2000; Nourie & Lenski, 1998). Also, the teachers who teach strategies tend to design strategy lessons using traditional teacher-centered instruction (Stevens, 2001).

Self-regulated Reading

The impact of strategy instruction is limited by the extent to which students become self-initiating: whether they internalize the strategies that they learn (Alexander & Murphy, 1998). Research indicates that students are more likely to use strategies if they need to know them for meaningful reading tasks (Allington, 1994; Guthrie, 1996). Isolated strategy instruction does not help students know when to use certain strategies as they experience a variety of reading texts. How students learn to use strategies independently has been a matter of debate, but in a summary of strategy instruction, Pressley (2002) concluded that the explicit teaching of strategies embedded in natural learning contexts is more likely to become internalized by students. Therefore, models of strategy instruction should emphasize learning a repertoire of strategies and their flexible orchestration, as students and teachers co-construct strategy learning situations (Collins, 1998).

Cultural Diversity

Students from the majority culture come to school with what Bourdieu and Passeron (1977) have termed "cultural capital"; that is, these students possess culturally valued advantages as a result of family backgrounds or life experiences. Cultural capital is respected and reproduced in schooling, and in the United States, the cultural capital of the European-American middle class is given greater value in schools than the cultural capital of other groups, even in schools that have students predominantly from minority races (Banks & Banks, 2001).

Cultural capital influences and is influenced by school-based knowledges. Reading and writing, school-based knowledges, are cultural practices. These cultural practices can be considered a secondary discourse (Gee, 1993). To explain, most children acquire language, their primary discourse, through natural social interaction with adults (Holdaway, 1979). However, secondary discourses such as reading and writing in content areas may not be similar to a student's primary discourse and need to be learned in order for students to be successful in school. For example, students from the mainstream culture have had many more experiences with expository textual patterns than students from minority cultures; when students listen to adults talking, they hear information through a series of factual statements that are linked together. Conversely, students from some minority cultures have heard very few of these types of discussion patterns (Au, 1993).

Some students from minority cultures, therefore, may be unfamiliar with the discourse that predominates in schooling. Just as readers interpret reading tasks based on social and cultural influences, the decisions that teachers make about instruction are embedded in their cultural contexts. Gay (2000) states that teachers must make adaptations to cultural settings in order to be culturally responsive and, therefore, to begin to face the achievement gap between students in the majority culture and students in minority cultures. When children have not acquired the discourse of schools, they need instructional support and may need more explicit instruction in the discourse of schooling before they will become successful (e.g., Delpit, 1992). Instructional implementations, therefore, need to be studied in different cultural contexts and adapted to fit cultural needs.

Content Area Comprehension

The primary purpose of strategy instruction in content areas is for students to learn their content by reading print materials. However, having the ability to read content texts is just the beginning. "Although teachers may focus their content area instruction on helping students understand the material, an important concurrent goal is helping students learn how to become self-regulated, active readers who have a variety of strategies to help them comprehend" (Rand Study Group, 2002, p. 14). Embedding reading strategies within content

area instruction can help students learn content and it can increase their ability to use strategies in other contexts (NRP, 2000; Brown, 1997; Pressley, El-Dinary, Gaskins, Schinder, Bergman, Almasi, & Brown, 1992).

In response to the lack of literacy progress of middle and secondary students, the International Reading Association appointed a Commission on Adolescent Literacy. This Commission developed a position statement delineating what adolescents "deserve" in order to become literate adults. Among its recommendations, the Commission wrote that adolescents deserve instruction that builds both the skill and the desire to read increasingly complex material, that adolescents need well-developed repertoires of reading comprehension strategies, and that adolescents deserve expert teachers who model and provide explicit instruction in reading comprehension across the curriculum (Moore, Bean, Birdyshaw, & Rycik, 1999).

As content area teachers incorporate reading and learning strategies into their instruction, they will empower their students to take charge of their learning. What an exciting occurrence! As a teacher, your goal is for students to become knowledgeable in your subject and to use the subject area you teach as one lens through which to view the world. As students learn your subject and how to learn with text, they will be better equipped to become lifelong learners.

Chapter 2

PROMOTING READING ENGAGEMENT

OVERVIEW

Promoting reading engagement is one of the biggest challenges for content area teachers. Content area teachers have had their enthusiasm for their subject thwarted when they realize that their students have not done their assigned reading (Mathison, 1989). Teachers' questions are met with blank looks, and class discussions lack the insights that can only occur by completing reading assignments. Teachers' concerns about students' reading (or lack of it) are justified. A report from the National Assessment of Educational Progress (NAEP, 1997) found that 56% of students age 13 and 47% of students age 17 reported reading 10 or fewer pages per day. It appears that many students will do almost anything to avoid reading a chapter of text (Vacca & Vacca, 2002). In order to avoid

their text assignments, students may resort to memorizing class notes, reading summaries, or hoping for a test that requires little or no understanding of the text material.

Teachers, of course, want students to read the text and related materials in order to extend their learning and enhance their knowledge. That behavior is more likely to occur if students are engaged learners. "The phrase *engaged reading* refers to the fusion of cognitive strategies, conceptual knowledge, and motivational goals during reading" (Guthrie & Knowles, 2001, p. 159). If learning is to be meaningful, engagement, intrinsic motivation, personal interest, and other factors must be an important part of the instructional process (Verhoeven & Snow, 2001). Reading engagement doesn't just happen. It is facilitated by a combination of factors that include those just mentioned as well as your students' previous experiences in other classrooms as well as in life (Afflerbach, 1996).

Guthrie and Knowles (2001) have provided seven principles that can serve as a solid foundation to help promote engaged and motivated readers. We will describe briefly each of these principles.

1. *Conceptual theme*. Organize instruction around broad interdisciplinary themes in which skills, strategies, and content are integrated. Teachers often recognize this principle as thematic instruction.

2. *Real-world interactions*. Students are given opportunities to interact "with tangible objects, events, and experiences related to a conceptual theme by observing, manipulating, and recording" (Guthrie & Knowles, 2001, p. 167). Science and social studies teachers may see ways to make some immediate connections to their content areas.

3. *Self-direction*. Teachers help students gradually assume responsibility for their reading by assisting them in selecting a topic, text, tasks, questions, and multimedia for reading and learning about the conceptual theme.

4. *Interesting texts*. Teachers need to make available a wide variety of reading materials. These include, but are not limited to, texts, newspapers, magazines, reference materials, electronic databases, websites, and literary works. A key aspect of this principle is that the materials encompass a wide range of difficulty. Appendix B contains an explanation of one way to estimate the difficulty of printed materials.

5. *Cognitive strategies*. Teachers need to provide well-designed instruction. Such instruction usually includes explaining, modeling, coaching, peer discussions, guided and independent practice, and student self-reflection.

6. *Social collaboration*. During a conceptual theme and at other appropriate times, students work together in a variety of ways: whole group, small groups, and partners. According to Vygotsky (1978), learning is a social process that is enhanced by peer interaction. Peers can provide essential feedback and encouragement as well as a sense of team spirit.

7. *Self-expression*. Teachers support students in articulating their understanding of what they have read "in ways that are personally and culturally relevant to them and their audiences" (Guthrie & Knowles, 2001, p. 172). This principle, while important, has a limited evidence base in empirical research. A study by Oldfather and Wigfield (1996) found that intrinsic motivation could be enhanced by activities involving self-expression. Written, oral, and artistic self-expression are options that should be available to your students.

The strategies presented in this chapter should be thoughtfully adapted and integrated into your curriculum. McCombs and Barton (2001, p. 77) note that the kinds of solutions needed to enhance student motivation and engagement in reading must go "beyond the technical domain (e.g., the content, standards, curriculum) and organizational domain (e.g., management structures, decision-making strategies, policies) to focus on the personal domain (e.g., beliefs, assumptions, interpersonal relationships)." Student engagement can be promoted when you consider reading to be both cognitive and affective and both solitary and social (Verhoeven & Snow, 2001).

Creating Interest

Goal To help students develop an interest in a topic

BACKGROUND

When you capitalize on your students' interests, they are likely to be motivated to learn more about a topic, have improved attitudes toward the topic, and show increased reading engagement. Most of your students probably are capable readers, but many may choose not to read their content texts. There is a very strong tie between interest and motivation, and, by focusing on students' interests, you will increase the extent of student involvement. Research by Hidi and Baird (1988) indicates that interest in text increases long-term recall of information and improves comprehension of the reading material.

One way to improve attitudes and create interest simultaneously is by personalizing the subject matter. Such personalization will give students the message that learning is related to their world. The challenge is to tap into your students' existing knowledge about a topic and arouse their interest in the topic. In other words, students with an interest in a particular subject are likely to be more highly motivated to seek additional information about that subject. The following strategies are designed to develop students' interest in a topic.

TEACHING STRATEGY 1

2.1 Anticipation Guide

The purpose of an Anticipation Guide (Herber, 1978) is to activate students' thoughts and opinions about a topic and to link their prior knowledge to the new material. Because Anticipation Guides are flexible strategies, they can be used effectively with any content area text as well as with nonprint media such as videos. Anticipation Guides provide an excellent springboard for class discussion and lead students into their reading or viewing with a sense of curiosity about the topic. Although an Anticipation Guide can be completed individually, assigning it to a small group promotes the collaborative aspect of learning.

Directions and Examples

1. Identify the major concepts that you want your students to learn from text materials and think about what your students may already know or believe to be true about the topic. For example, when beginning a chapter on pollution in your text, think about your students' existing knowledge related to pollution and about the concepts you want them to learn from the text. You might consider the following aspects of the chapter to be important:

   The implication of human activities on the environment.
   The major types of pollution and their impact on human health.
   The effects of acid rain on people, plants, water, and materials.

2. Create four to six statements relating to the major concepts of the text. The most effective statements are those about which students have some knowledge but do not have complete understanding. Write the statements on the chalkboard or an overhead transparency and present the Anticipation Guide to your students, as in the following example.

   _____ 1. Because of water pollution, some fish do not have enough oxygen to survive.

   _____ 2. Most pollution is caused by legal, everyday activities such as brushing your teeth.

   _____ 3. The coal producing factories in the Midwest are responsible for much of the acid rain.

   _____ 4. Every year more than 40,000 people in the United States die from diseases related to air pollution.

3. Explain to students that they are about to read a new section of text. Then say the following:

   Before you read the text, I want you to respond to a series of statements based on the text material. As you read the statements, put a check mark next to those that you believe to be true or with which you agree.

4. After students have completed the Anticipation Guide, proceed with class discussion. Urge students to share their opinions about the validity of the statements based on their prior knowledge. Then have students read their texts.

5. A math Anticipation Guide follows.

Math Example

Anticipation Guide

Directions: Below are some statements about bank loans from your math text. Read each statement carefully and place a check mark in front of those statements with which you agree or believe to be true. Be prepared to defend your thinking when we discuss the statements.

_____ 1. To get a loan from a bank, you may have to pay interest at the time the loan is made.

_____ 2. Sometimes banks discount loans.

_____ 3. Some banks lend money on a discount basis rather than on an interest basis because they make more money that way.

_____ 4. Some loan repayment schedules require increasing payments each month.

2.1   People Search

TEACHING STRATEGY 2

People Search (Hemmrich, Lim, & Neel, 1994) is a strategy designed to promote collaboration among the students in your classroom. It uses an interview technique for implementation and creates interest in a topic as it increases students' motivation to learn more about a topic. Additionally, it supports social interaction and helps foster positive attitudes toward learning. This interaction among students is a source of enjoyment and is an excellent way to introduce a new unit of study. It has also been used effectively as a way of reviewing concepts developed during a topic of study.

TECHNOLOGY

T I P

Pitsco's Ask An Expert

Ask An Expert is a comprehensive list with links and information about contacting professionals who will answer students' questions.

www.askanexpert.com

Directions and Examples

1. Decide on the topic or theme of your People Search. This strategy can be implemented as a way of introducing a new course, as the beginning of a unit, as an introduction to a new chapter of study, or as a review technique.

2. Prepare 10 to 20 relevant statements or questions about the topic. If you are introducing a new subject to your students, your statements might be more general. For example, if you are beginning a study of the United States government, you might use the following statement.

   Find someone who . . .
   can name the vice president of the United States.

   If, however, you are continuing a unit of study about the United States government, your statements might be more specific. An example of this type of statement follows.

   Find someone who . . .
   can name the main job of the vice president.

3. Duplicate copies of the People Search and distribute a copy to each student.

4. Tell students they are to walk around the room and interview their classmates to find someone who can answer the questions or perform the required tasks. Tell them that once someone has answered a question or responded to a statement in the appropriate space, they are to ask the person to sign his or her name next to the answer. Remind them that they must have as many different signatures as possible.

5. Set a time limit of 10 to 15 minutes for completion of the People Search.

6. Have students share the success of their People Search at the end of the allotted time. This can be done as a whole class activity or in small groups.

7. The following examples are based on a geography text and a history text.

Geography Example

People Search

Find someone who . . .   Name

1. knows the name of an economic system in which
   businesses and factories are owned by individuals.   _____

2. knows to which nation most of Canada's exports go.   _____

3. can name the three major river systems of Latin America.   _____

4. knows the country of the *mestizos*.   _____

5. can identify Pablo Neruda's "claim to fame."   _____

History Example

People Search

Find someone who . . .   Name

1. is of Native American descent.   _____
2. has visited a state on the west coast.   _____
3. knows someone who immigrated to the U.S.   _____
4. knows what discrimination means.   _____
5. is friends with someone of another race.   _____
6. has visited another country besides Canada.   _____
7. is friendly to everyone.   _____
8. knows the definition of stereotype.   _____
9. would like to know a person of another race.   _____
10. would like to learn about the diversity of the U.S. _____

2.1

TEACHING STRATEGY 3

Problematic Situation

Mathison (1989) suggests that asking students to solve a paradox or a problem is one of the primary elements in sparking students' interest about a topic. A Problematic Situation (Vacca & Vacca, 2002) promotes lively classroom discussions as it compels students to delve into their prior experiences and share their knowledge with their classmates, thus increasing their interest in a topic. As teachers, you can design problematic situations specifically related to a particular text. By creating a problem to be solved, you can develop an exciting and imaginative introduction to text material. This particular strategy provides an avenue for arousing students' natural curiosity and prepares them for texts in which a problem/solution scenario exists or can be developed by the teacher.

Directions and Example

1. Identify a topic from your text about which you can develop a problematic situation for students to analyze. Prepare a short paragraph describing the problem using an example from your content area or use the example that follows. The following example has been developed for a geography class.

Geography Example

Problematic Situation

The year is 1946 and you are a citizen of Argentina. Your country is ruled by a dictator whose name is Juan Peron. He has maintained power by creating labor unions, schools, and new industries. His wife, Eva Peron, has helped him by encouraging workers to give money to the government's programs. However, with his power as a dictator, Peron has taken control of the press, businesses, labor unions, and the army. Sometimes people are arrested and killed without cause. If people are seen as enemies of the government, they frequently "disappear." Some opposition to the Perons is developing. People you know have reason to believe that the Perons are stealing money that the workers have given to the government. But life is better than it used to be. Although you are poor, you're not as poor as you once were because you have a job.

2. Place students into mixed ability groups and read the problematic situation to them. Then present a written copy of the problem to each group of students. This may be done by distributing a handout or by writing the problem on the chalkboard or an overhead transparency. An example of a problem follows.

   A revolution or a coup against the Perons is developing. You have been asked to join the effort to overthrow the Perons, whom you have come to believe are corrupt. What will you do? Will you continue to live as you are, knowing that some of your money is being misused? Or will you become part of the revolt that is brewing? Upon what will you base your decision? How will it impact your family? What will happen if you decide not to join the revolt and the revolution is successful?

3. Instruct students, within their groups, to generate possible solutions to the problem. Tell them to imagine that they are the persons facing the dilemma in the problematic situation. Be sure to provide them with enough information so that they will focus their attention on the key concepts within the text as they discuss and develop their solutions. One possible solution follows.

   I think I'll take my family and leave the country. I can't stand living where dishonest people rule. I want my family to be safe and my children to grow up in an environment that gives them good values.

4. Have each group record all of their responses as they discuss them. As students make their lists, encourage them to discuss the merits and difficulties of each presented solution, as in the following example.

   Leaving the country is not going to be easy. Where will we go? How will we get extra money for travel?

5. Encourage whole class sharing of the solutions after the small groups have completed their assigned task. After completing a Problematic Situation, students are ready to read their texts and supplement their existing information with additional material.

6. Ask students to read the text passage, looking for information that supports their solutions during reading. Encourage students to modify their proposed solutions if they discover new information that influences their original decisions.

7. Have the class discuss the merits of each group's revised solutions.

2.1 ▶ Story Impressions

TEACHING STRATEGY 4

Story Impressions (Denner & McGinley, 1986) is a prereading strategy primarily designed to create interest in upcoming narrative text. It can, however, be used with expository text. Story Impressions involves your students in using key concepts from the story or passage in order to develop their impressions of how these elements will fit together. In addition to creating interest, this strategy helps students develop anticipatory outlooks about the text that will be confirmed or modified as they read. When students write their Story Impressions, they become interested in how the author will use the words in the actual text.

Directions and Examples

1. Explain to students that the purpose of this activity is to look at a series of words taken from the text and to determine whether they can predict how the author will use the words in the selection.

2. Identify and write a list of words on the chalkboard or an overhead transparency. The following words have been taken from the poem "To Be of Use."

people	fires	task	clean	food
forward	satisfies	fields	worth	real
haul	used	work	patience	effort

3. Ask students to brainstorm the ways that the words might be used in a poem. For example, one student might say:

   People might work in their fields for food.

4. Direct students to write their own selections incorporating words from the Story Impression list. They may choose to write a poem or a short narrative paragraph using the words. Ask them to underline all of the words their Story Impressions include. After completing their stories, students might enjoy sharing their writing in small groups as in the following example.

   People work with patience if they have a task that compels them to move forward. They'll even haul food for a living or fight fires in the fields. Hard work is worth the effort, particularly if it's clean work and satisfies your soul. It's satisfying to be involved in real work and, even if it's difficult, you get used to it.

5. Have students read the author's version and compare their Story Impressions with the actual piece.

6. Story Impressions can also be used with expository text. The following key words are taken from a geography text. The section describes Great Britain and its monarchy. The directions for implementation are the same as for narrative text. Students may find a Story Impression using expository text to be more difficult because they need to rely primarily on their prior knowledge. However, you will find, through a whole class discussion of the words, that many of your students have a surprising depth of knowledge.

Geography Example

Story Impression

Key Words

constitutional monarchy   prime minister
king or queen   House of Commons
British Parliament $40 million
House of Lords   public functions
aristocrats   loyalty

Written Example

British Parliament has two parts: the House of Lords and the House of Commons. The members of the House of Lords are called aristocrats. The Parliament is led by the prime minister. Great Britain is called a constitutional monarchy because it has a king or queen. I think they mainly appear at public functions and, even though it costs Great Britain about $40 million a year to support them, there is a strong sense of loyalty to them among many of the English people.

2.1

Picture Books

TEACHING STRATEGY 5

Picture books, alphabet books, wordless books, narrative picture books, and expository picture books can be used in the content areas to increase motivation, help students understand concepts, appeal to visual learners, and provide easier reading materials for students who struggle with reading (Carr, Buchanan, Wentz, Weiss, & Grant, 2001). Generally, books read aloud to middle and high school students should contain provocative issues and moral dilemmas to stimulate critical thinking, promote thoughtful discussion, and help students collaborate in the construction of meaning (Carr et al., 2001; Richardson, 2000). Fortunately, a bibliography of picture books for secondary content area teachers has been compiled (Carr et al., 2001) to provide possible resources. In addition, Tiedt (2000) offers many ideas for using picture books with older students.

Directions and Example

1. Survey the bibliography to locate a particular picture book that may be appropriate for a topic in your curriculum. Other books may be recommended by colleagues or librarians in your school system.

2. After selecting a book, read it to determine whether it is appropriate for the topic or unit being taught.

3. Decide whether the book should be read aloud or offered to students for independent reading. For example, *Starry Messenger* (Sis, 1996) tells the story of Galileo "in simple language but with rich illustrations" (Carr et al., 2001, p. 152). Reading it aloud to students may help them appreciate this talented individual. The book also contains some of the words written by Galileo on the perimeters of the pages, and it might be a useful introduction to the world of this scientist.

4. By sharing quality picture books with students, along with your genuine pleasure in such books, you help students expand their opportunities for learning.

5. A list of books especially appropriate to use in selected content areas (adapted from Carr et al., 2001) follows.

LANGUAGE ARTS

Ada, A.F. (1997). *Dear Peter Rabbit*. New York: Aladdin.

Alexander, L. (1992). *The fortune tellers*. New York: Bantam Doubleday Dell.

Base, G. (1992). *The sign of the seahorse*. New York: Harry Abrams.

Brumbeau, J. (1999). *The quilt maker's gift*. Duluth, MN: Pfeifer-Hamilton.

Celsi, T. (1992). *The fourth little pig*. Austin, TX: Steck-Vaughn.

Conrad, P. (1996). *The rooster's gift*. New York: HarperCollins.

Dragonwagon, C. (1992). *Alligator arrived with apples*. New York: Aladdin.

Grimes, Nikki. (1999). *My man Blue*. New York: Scholastic.

Heller, R. (1990). *Merry-go-round*. New York: Grosset & Dunlap.

Heller, R. (1991). *Up, up and away*. New York: Grosset & Dunlap.

Heller, R. (1995). *Behind the mask*. New York: Scholastic.

Hepworth, Cathi. (1992). *Antics!* New York: G.P. Putnam's Sons.

James, S. (1991). *Dear Mr. Blueberry*. New York: Aladdin.

Johnson, P. (1999). *Old Dry Frye*. New York: Scholastic.

Lowell, S. (1992). *The three little javelinas*. New York: Scholastic.

Macaulay, D. (1990). *Black and white*. Boston: Houghton Mifflin.

Martin, R. (1992). *The rough-face girl*. New York: Putnam & Grosset.

Rohmann, E. (1994). *Time flies*. New York: Scholastic.

Scieszka, J. (1991). *The Frog Prince continued*. New York: Puffin.

Scieszka, J. (1992). *The stinky cheese man*. New York: Viking.

Scieszka, J. (1994). *The book that Jack wrote*. New York: Viking.

Scieszka, J. (1998). *Squids will be squids*. New York: Viking.

Sheldon, D. (1990). *The whales' song*. New York: Puffin.

Talbott, H. (1999). *O'Sullivan stew*. New York: G.P. Putnam's Sons.

Tobias, T. (1998). *A world of words*. New York: Lothrop, Lee & Shepard.

Trivizas, E. (1993). *The three little wolves and the big bad pig*. New York: Aladdin.

Viorst, Judith. (1994). *The alphabet from Z to A*. New York: Aladdin.

Wiesner, D. (1992). *Tuesday*. New York: Trumpet Club.

Willard, N. (1991). *Pish, posh, said Hieronymus Bosch*. San Diego, CA: Harcourt Brace.

Yolen, J. (1992). *Encounter*. San Diego, CA: Harcourt Brace.

MATHEMATICS

Demi. (1997). *One grain of rice*. New York: Scholastic. (math concepts)

Pinczes, E.J. (1993). *One hundred hungry ants*. New York: Scholastic. (math concepts)

Pinczes, E.J. (1995). *A remainder of one*. New York: Scholastic. (math concepts)

Scieszka, J. (1995). *Math curse*. New York: Viking. (math concepts)

SCIENCE

Cherry, L. (1993). *The great kapok tree*. San Diego, CA: Harcourt Brace. (ecology)

Hart, T. (1994). *Antarctic diary*. New York: Macmillan/McGraw-Hill.

Heller, R. (1994). *How to hide a crocodile*. New York: Grosset & Dunlap.

Heller, R. (1995). *How to hide a parakeet*. New York: Grosset & Dunlap.

Keller, L. (2000). *Open wide, tooth school inside*. New York: Henry Holt. (dental care)

Livingston, M. (1991). *Sea songs*. New York: Scholastic.

Martin, J. (1998). *Snowflake Bentley*. Boston: Houghton Mifflin.

Sis, P. (1996). *Starry messenger: Galileo Galilei*. New York: Farrar, Straus & Giroux.

Van Allsburg, C. (1990). *Just a dream*. Boston: Houghton Mifflin. (ecology)

SOCIAL STUDIES

Baillie, A. (1994). *Rebel*. New York: Ticknor & Fields.

Bartone, E. (1993). *Peppe the lamplighter*. New York: Scholastic. (European immigrants)

Bouchard, D. (1993). *If you're not from the prairie*. Vancouver, BC: Raincoast Books. (geography)

Bridges, R. (1999). *Through my eyes*. New York: Scholastic. (African American, school integration)

Bunting, E. (1990). *The wall*. New York: Clarion. (Vietnam War)

Bunting, E. (1991). *Fly away home*. New York: Clarion. (the homeless)

Bunting, E. (1995). *Smoky night*. San Diego, CA: Harcourt Brace. (African American, Watts riots)

Bunting, E. (1996). *Going home*. New York: HarperCollins. (Mexican family, farm laborers)

Cech, J. (1991). *My grandmother's journey*. New York: Bradbury Press. (European immigration)

Cooney, B. (1996). *Eleanor*. New York: Puffin. (biography of Eleanor Roosevelt)

Cordova, A. (1997). *Abuelita's heart*. New York: Simon & Schuster (Mexican and Native American cultures)

Der Manuelian, P. (1991). *Hieroglyphs from A to Z*. New York: Scholastic. (Egyptian hieroglyphs)

Goble, P. (1992). *Love flute*. New York: Bradbury Press. (Native American culture)

Harness, C. (1992). *Three young pilgrims*. New York: Aladdin. (the Mayflower)

Harness, C. (1998). *Ghosts of the White House*. New York: Simon & Schuster. (U.S. presidents)

Harness, C. (1998). *Mark Twain and the queens of the Mississippi*. New York: Simon & Schuster. (steamboat era)

Heide, F., & Gilliland, J. (1990). *The day of Ahmed's secret*. New York: Scholastic. (North Africa)

Hoffman, M. (1991). *Amazing Grace*. New York: Dial Books for Young Readers. (African American)

Houston, G. (1992). *My great-aunt Arizona*. New York: Scholastic. (early 20th century)

Howard, E.F. (1991). *Aunt Flossie's hats*. New York: Scholastic. (African American)

Isadora, R. (1991). *At the crossroads*. New York: Scholastic. (African American)

Johnson, J.W. (1995). *Lift ev'ry voice and sing*. New York: Scholastic. (African American culture)

Kalman, B. (1998). *Colonial times from A to Z*. New York: Crabtree. (alphabet reference book)

King, M.L., Jr. (1997). *I have a dream*. New York: Scholastic. (African American)

Krensky, S. (1991). *Children of the earth and sky*. New York: Scholastic. (Native American)

Layne, S.L. (1998). *Thomas's sheep and the great geography test*. Gretna, LA: Pelican. (geography)

Lied, K. (1997). *Potato*. Washington, DC: National Geographic Society. (Depression era)

McKissack, P., & McKissack, F. (1994). *Christmas in the big house, Christmas in the quarters*. New York: Scholastic. (slave era)

Mitchell, M.K. (1993). *Uncle Jed's barbershop*. New York: Scholastic. (African American)

Mochizuki, K. (1993). *Baseball saved us*. New York: Scholastic. (Japanese American)

Moore, Y. (1992). *A prairie alphabet*. Montreal, Quebec: Tunda Books. (prairies)

Myers, W.D. (1993). *Brown angels*. New York: HarperCollins. (African American)

Myers, W.D. (1997). *Harlem*. New York: Scholastic. (African American)

Nicholson, D.M. (1998). *Pearl Harbor Child*. Honolulu, HI: Memorial Museum Association. (World War II era)

Polacco, P. (1990). *Just plain fancy*. New York: Dell. (Amish)

Provensen, A. (1990). *The buck stops here*. New York: Trumpet Club. (U.S. presidents)

Rice, J. (1990). *Cowboy alphabet*. New York: Pelican. (U.S. West)

Ringold, F. (1991). *Tar beach*. New York: Scholastic. (African American)

Rumford, J. (1998). *Island-below-the-star*. Boston: Houghton Mifflin. (Polynesian explorers)

Rylant, C. (1994). *Something permanent*. New York: Harcourt Brace. (Depression era)

Say, A. (1993). *Grandfather's journey*. Boston: Houghton Mifflin. (Japanese American)

Siegelson, K. (1999). *In the time of the drums*. New York: Hyperion. (Gullah, slave ships)

Sisulu, E. (1996). *The day Gogo went to vote*. Boston: Little, Brown. (South Africa)

Stanley, S. (1998). *Monkey Sunday: A story from a Congolese village*. New York: Farrar, Straus & Giroux. (Africa)

Stewart, S. (1997). *The gardener*. New York: Farrar, Straus & Giroux. (Depression era)

Tarbescu, E. (1998). *Annushka's voyage*. New York: Clarion. (European immigration)

Uchida, Y. (1993). *The bracelet*. New York: Philomel. (Japanese American)

Williams, S.A. (1992). *Working cotton*. San Diego, CA: Harcourt Brace. (African American)

Yolen, J. (1992). *Encounter*. San Diego, CA: Harcourt Brace.

Promoting Positive Attitudes

 To help students develop positive attitudes toward content area topics

BACKGROUND

Attitudes have been defined as "those feelings that cause a reader to approach or avoid a reading situation" (Readence, Bean, & Baldwin, 2001, p. 128). Attitudes toward reading are connected with feelings about reading. It stands to reason that students' feelings about reading will probably correlate positively with the amount of reading they are willing to do. By providing activities for students that are enjoyable as well as challenging and manageable, you can encourage students to have positive attitudes toward reading and your content area. For learning to occur within your classroom, students need to have positive attitudes about themselves as learners and must believe that they are capable of succeeding academically (Graves, Juel, & Graves, 1998).

The old adage "nothing succeeds like success" can be applied to your classroom. Try to offer activities to your students that virtually ensure some successful experiences in the course. Students must experience success in the vast majority of activities in which they participate if they are to progress academically (Brophy, 1986).

Activities that allow students to participate in aspects of self-expression can help develop positive attitudes toward a content area. Written, oral, and artistic self-expression activities are all avenues that promote students' sense of being valued within their classrooms. Marzano (1992) has presented four ways that teachers can promote positive attitudes among students. They include instilling in students feelings of acceptance, providing a classroom that is comfortable and orderly, involving students in activities that they value, and explaining with clarity what you expect them to do.

Positive attitudes often go hand in hand with self-awareness and self-expression. By providing students with experiences that acknowledge that their feelings and opinions are important, you are empowering them as learners. The following strategies are designed to build positive attitudes toward content material while communicating to students that you value their thoughts and opinions.

2.2

TEACHING STRATEGY 6

Writing an Autobiography

This strategy, Writing an Autobiography (Countryman, 1992), can easily and effectively be applied to any content area. All students bring some sort of history to every subject. For example, in social studies, all students have experienced interactions with other people; in history, all students have families with a unique personal background; and in math, everyone has a math autobiography because all of us use math in our everyday lives.

Writing an autobiography enhances engagement among students because it enables them to assume more responsibility for what goes on in their classrooms. Even students for whom mathematics may have been a negative experience feel empowered as they write about themselves in relationship to the subject matter. Suddenly, the impersonal world of mathematics becomes one that engenders feelings. Students often are surprised to find that their classmates share many similar experiences and attitudes toward a subject (Countryman, 1992).

Another benefit of this strategy is that teachers learn about their students in a personal, individual way. For example, autobiographies reveal information about confidence levels, self-esteem, and attitudes. Most important, autobiographies bring laughter into the classroom as students share their experiences. When learning becomes engaging, teachers are on their way to producing learners who are enthusiastic and willing to be active participants in the academic journey.

TECHNOLOGY

Biographies

Over 20,000 short biographies from the Cambridge Dictionary of Biography can be searched. There are also more lengthy biographies with pictures and video clips based on the programming from the nightly Arts & Entertainment series.

www.kennedy-center.org

T I P

Directions and Example

1. Introduce and discuss the idea of writing autobiographies. Tell students that an autobiography is an author's account of his or her own life. Use the following example or adapt it to fit your content area.

   Today we are going to focus on one aspect of your life—your experience with mathematics. I want you to tell me about your successes with math. How have they been important in your life? Consider what you like about learning math. What do you not like? If you could teach this class for one day, what would you teach your classmates? What would you personally like to learn this year in the area of mathematics?

2. Model writing your own content area autobiography and read it to the class. In addition to being presented with a model, your students will enjoy knowing that you, too, have feelings about your experiences with your content area.

3. Give your students ample time to complete their autobiographies. Perhaps one class period can be devoted to writing rough drafts and another period used for revisions.

4. Place students in small groups after the autobiographies have been completed. Ask them to share their autobiographies with their group members. Some of your students may be comfortable sharing their writing with the entire class.

5. Collect the autobiographies and read them if you wish to gain insights about your students and their attitudes toward the subjects you are teaching. An example of a mathematics autobiography follows.

Mathematics Example

Autobiography

When I was in junior high school, I sort of liked math. I liked it because everything made sense and seemed to fit together very neatly. Then I met Mrs. Brynwood in eighth-grade algebra. Nothing has been the same for me since then as far as math is concerned. I still don't get the abstract principles that she tried to teach us. And besides, who needs to know the value of x in real life? Last semester, however, I took geometry from Mr. Phillips. He is cool and so is his class. He really makes learning fun, and if I didn't get it, he figured out a different way to help me understand it.

If I could teach this class for one day, I would teach the students how to figure out the cost of going to college. Like how do you know how much you should pay for tuition? And if you only go part-time do you just pay a percentage of the tuition? These are things I'd like to learn about this semester.

TEACHING STRATEGY 7

2.2 Opinionnaire/Questionnaire

Opinionnaire/Questionnaire (Reasoner, 1976) is designed to examine students' attitudes and experiences related to selected issues. In addition to encouraging students to examine their own attitudes towards a subject or event, this strategy enables students to interact with their classmates as they interview them. Opinionnaire/Questionnaire is another strategy that promotes social interaction among your students, thereby helping to promote positive attitudes toward learning while developing interest and increased motivation.

Directions and Example

1. Look over your text and identify ideas or events on which you wish to focus your instruction. Write a series of questions designed to tap students' opinions, attitudes, and prior knowledge related to the subject.

2. Use an example from your content area or the following example. It is designed to generate information about students' attitudes towards the Holocaust in a high school literature class reading *Anne Frank: Diary of a Young Girl* (1995) and studying the Holocaust in world history.

3. Tell students that they are going to survey their classmates to find out their opinions and knowledge about the topic.

4. Provide all students with a copy of the Opinionnaire/Questionnaire and ask them to interview their classmates.

Literature and History Example

Opinionnaire/Questionnaire

Directions: Respond to the following questions. You may choose more than one response to each question.

1. What words would you use to describe concentration camps?
   _____ death factories   _____ relocation facilities
   _____ hard labor camps   _____ historical fiction
   _____ jails   _____ punishment
   _____ other

2. Why do you think that the Nazis hated Jewish people?
   _____ They were afraid of them.
   _____ The Nazis felt superior to the Jews.
   _____ Nazis were just naturally mean.
   _____ The Nazis didn't hate the Jews. They were just following orders.

3. Which of the following statements do you believe to be true?
   _____ Auschwitz was the largest Nazi-operated camp.
   _____ One hundred individuals were reduced to ashes each day.
   _____ Prisoners who worked hard were allowed to go free.
   _____ There was usually enough food to go around in the concentration camps.
   _____ Blue-eyed blonds were spared.

5. Divide the class into small groups and ask them to share and compare their responses.

6. Ask each group to write a summary for each part of the Opinionnaire/Questionnaire, incorporating elements of summary writing.

7. Collect the summaries and develop a class summary or book that can be reviewed at the end of the unit. Students will enjoy seeing how their attitudes and knowledge have changed during their course of study.

TECHNOLOGY

T I P

This Day in History

Choose the month and day to learn about events that happened throughout history.

www.historychannel.com

TEACHING STRATEGY 8
2.2 Sustained Silent Reading (SSR)

Sustained Silent Reading (Berglund & Johns, 1983; Hunt, 1970; Ivey & Broaddus, 2000, 2001) encourages students to read self-selected materials during a designated time in the school day. Many research studies have shown relationships between the amount of reading students engage in and reading achievement (see Pearson & Fielding, 1991, for a review). Teachers should provide students with ample opportunities to engage in self-selected reading in and out of school. A recent study by Ivey and Broaddus (2001) found that over 60% of middle school students in their study valued independent reading. Such reading has been referred to as free reading, silent reading, or Sustained Silent Reading. Teachers may need to work with colleagues to help establish workable Sustained Silent Reading programs.

 ## Directions

1. Begin by telling students that they will be given an opportunity to choose something that they would like to read and to read it for a specified period of time. Invite students to suggest possible names for the reading period. Johns and Lenski (2001) list many names that have been used to characterize the period (e.g., Drop Everything and Read [DEAR], Read in Peace [RIP], Students and Faculty All Read Independently [SAFARI]).

2. Have students develop a procedure for selecting a name for the SSR period. Once a name is selected, designate a specific time when everyone will participate in the SSR period.

3. Help students establish a set of procedures and guidelines that will characterize the SSR period. Some possible items could include selections from the following list.

   - Find a comfortable place to read.
   - Have more to read than you think you will need.
   - Have your materials with you.
   - Stay quiet and read during the entire time.

4. Begin SSR with a period that is relatively short and increase the time as students demonstrate a readiness to read for longer periods. When students ask to continue reading after the time is up, you may want to consider increasing the SSR period in the near future.

5. Model the process by reading your self-selected materials as students engage in their reading. Be prepared for students to ask you about what you are reading.

6. Allow students to achieve their own purposes during the period. Refrain from quizzing students or turning the period into a lesson of some sort.

7. Have materials available for students who do not have anything to read or who run short of materials before the period ends. Ivey and Broaddus (2001) found the ten most popular types of reading materials were the following (beginning with the most popular).

   - Magazines
   - Adventure books
   - Mysteries
   - Scary stories
   - Joke books
   - Animals (informational books)
   - Comic books
   - Series books
   - Sports (informational books)
   - Books about people their age

8. Encourage students to find materials for their independent reading in the public library, a bookstore, the school library, or at home.

Arousing Curiosity for Topics

Goal To help students become curious about content area topics

BACKGROUND

After you have determined the important concepts in the text that you are asking your students to read, ask yourself *why* they would want to read it. You want to spark your students' curiosity about the subject matter. When your students' curiosity about a topic is aroused, they will naturally become interested in the topic and begin to consider adding new information to what they already know. Building a bridge between new and known material is a necessary element for comprehension.

The text that you are asking your students to read must be manageable, not too difficult and not too easy (see Appendix A for estimating textbook difficulty). Arousing your students' curiosity will help them develop questions about the topic and seek answers to their questions as they read. When students actively seek information, they naturally use cognitive strategies, one of the hallmarks of an engaged reader. The following strategies are designed to arouse your students' curiosity about a topic as they become interested in the topic.

TEACHING STRATEGY 9

2.3 Creating Sentences

Creating Sentences is a strategy that uses some of the vocabulary words that will be encountered in the text in order to arouse students' curiosity. Students will become curious about the text when they make predictions about the text's contents. In addition to motivating students to read the upcoming text and to determine the accuracy of their predictions, Creating Sentences encourages students to think about the relationships among a variety of words from the assigned selection.

Directions and Examples

1. List the important vocabulary words for the text selection on the chalkboard or an overhead transparency. Pronounce each word. These words should be core words from the selection and should be able to be defined by their use in the selection. The following example is based on a biology text.

heart	circulates	arteries	oxygen
pumps	blood vessels	cells	veins

2. Ask students to select pairs of words from the list and, for each pair, to create a sentence that they think might appear in the text.

3. Pick several students to write their sentences on the chalkboard or an overhead transparency. Ask them to underline the words that they have included from the list. Some examples follow.

   1. The <u>heart</u> is a muscle that <u>pumps</u> blood.
   2. Blood <u>circulates</u> through our <u>blood vessels</u>.
   3. <u>Arteries</u> carry blood toward the heart, and <u>veins</u> carry blood away from the heart.
   4. <u>Cells</u> in the body store <u>oxygen</u>.

4. Ask students if anyone disagrees with any of the sentences. Encourage discussion about these sentences.

5. Have students read their textbook selection to verify the accuracy of their sentences. Then have students evaluate each sentence through class discussion and, if there are any incorrect sentences, invite a student to offer a corrected sentence. In this example, students will find that sentence 3 needs to be modified. The new sentence might read as follows: <u>Arteries</u> carry blood away from the heart, and <u>veins</u> carry blood toward the heart.

6. Ask for additional sentences based on the information that has been presented in the text.

7. Students may wish to record the sentences in their notebooks for further study.

2.3 Probable Passages

TEACHING STRATEGY 10

Probable Passages (Wood, 1984) is a writing strategy that is very similar to Possible Sentences in that it involves students in making predictions about their upcoming reading assignment. However, Probable Passages focuses on larger sections of text. One of the attributes of this strategy is that it lends itself well to both narrative and expository writing. It also can be used effectively for a collaborative effort among small groups of students.

Directions and Examples

1. Determine the main concepts in the text selection that you have chosen for your students to read. Then decide if the text has an identifiable organizational pattern such as problem-solution or cause-effect.

2. Identify key words within the selection and categorize them under the text structure labels. The following example is based on a text selection about Africa. The organizational pattern found in the selection is cause-effect.

Cause	**Effect**
Olaudah Equiano	best
captives	capable
died	healthiest
Africans	disaster
journey	strong
freedom	youngest

3. Write the words on the chalkboard or an overhead transparency and explain to your students that you have placed the words in categories according to the text structure.

4. Then provide students with the cause portion of the text selection leaving blanks for the words under the cause label above. Have students fill in the blanks of the first part of the Probable Passage by selecting words from the cause list, as in the following example.

   Captured _____ were branded with hot irons and transported as _____ on filthy shelves stacked from floor to ceiling. They were given little food or water on the _____ across the Atlantic. As many as 20 percent of the slaves _____ during the crossing. _____ _____ described this horrible experience in a book he wrote about his life. He proved luckier than most African slaves. In time, he was able to buy his _____.

5. Provide students with the effect portion of the Probable Passage. Write an opening sentence that suggests the contents of the second part of the text passage or the effect. An example follows.

   Africa suffered as a result of the practice of slavery.

6. Ask students to select words from the effect list and write a paragraph, such as the following one, about the effects of slavery on Africa.

   Africa suffered as a result of the practice of slavery. Although some Africans grew wealthy, the slave trade was a <u>disaster</u> for the country. The people who were sold as slaves were the <u>youngest</u> and <u>healthiest</u> workers from the region. When a continent loses its most <u>capable</u> and <u>best</u> young people, it is difficult for it to remain <u>strong</u>.

7. Direct students to read the actual selection.

8. Ask students to edit their work in order to correct any contradictory statements or add any missing information.

9. An example of a Probable Passage using a literature text follows. In this example the text structure categories have been grouped according to the elements of the story (setting, characters, problem, and resolution).

Literature Example

Probable Passage

Directions: Place the key words below into the appropriate categories. Then read the incomplete Probable Passage and see if you can place the appropriate word or words in each blank. After reading the story, make any necessary changes in your passage.

Key Words

Bellevue Hospital	complicated convalescence	bumbled
operating room	operating jitters	surgery
Dr. George Walters	guilt	appendectomy
Mr. Polansky	responsibility	

Categories

Setting	Characters	Problem
Bellevue Hospital	Dr. George Walters	operating jitters
operating room	Mr. Polansky	surgery
		appendectomy
		bumbled

Resolution

complicated convalescence
guilt and responsibility

Incomplete Probable Passage

This story takes place in the _____ at _____. Two doctors, _____, and the narrator are about to perform an _____ on _____. Suddenly the narrator, who is the chief surgeon, develops a bad case of _____.

Although the _____ is _____, the operation is completed. As a result, however, the patient endures a _____ and the surgeon is left with feelings of _____.

2.3 **Character Quotes**

TEACHING STRATEGY 11

Character Quotes (Buehl, 2001) is a strategy that motivates students to analyze the personality traits of characters in a literature selection and sparks their curiosity about the selection. Students enjoy becoming "amateur psychiatrists" as they attempt to describe the type of person who could voice the selected comments.

Directions and Example

1. Preview a story or novel to identify several quotations by a character that illustrate different elements of his or her personality. Select quotations that will encourage students to develop varying descriptions of what kind of person this character might be. Write each quotation on a separate slip of paper or note card as in the following example from a short story.

   > I guess all of you want to make just as much of yourselves as you can.

   > Now eat as much as you want, Boyd. I want to see you get filled up.

   > Boyd, Johnny has some suits that are a little too small for him and a winter coat. The coat's not new, of course, but there's lots of wear in it still. And I have a few dresses that your mother or sister could probably use. Your mother can make them over into lots of things for all of you.

   > There are many little boys like you, Boyd, who would be very grateful for the clothes someone was kind enough to give them.

   > Don't think I'm angry, Boyd. I'm just disappointed in you, that's all. Now let's not say anything more about it.

   > I'll bet he's strong though. Does he . . . work?

2. Organize students into cooperative groups with three or four students in each group. Give each group a different quotation to consider. Each group then has the responsibility to generate as many words as possible that might describe this character. For example, students might use some of the following words to describe the character: condescending, prejudiced, generous, curious, and self-serving.

3. Ask a member from each group to read a quotation to the entire class and share the list of qualities and traits that he or she associated with the character. Write these qualities on the chalkboard or an overhead transparency as they are presented. Then tell students that all of the quotations were uttered by the same individual.

4. Assist the students in making some generalizations about this character or individual. Have the students work again in their cooperative groups to write a preliminary "personality profile" of this character by using the qualities and traits listed by the entire class. The summary should contain four or five statements that integrate important qualities from the list. An example of a personality profile for a character from this short story is presented on the next page.

Personality Profile

The character whose words we analyzed seems to mean well, but she sounds very self-serving and smug. She speaks to Boyd in a condescending manner and seems to assume that he needs her help. We get the impression that she doesn't really know him but is making judgments about him perhaps because of the way he is dressed or the color of his skin. We think she probably believes that she is doing the "right thing" when, in fact, her comments are very insulting.

5. Direct students to begin reading the story, novel, or other text assignment. After completing their reading, they can return to their "personality profiles" to discuss what new qualities or traits they might add. Students can also discuss how they would change the profiles to make them better match the true nature of the character.

2.3   Classroom Libraries

TEACHING STRATEGY 12

"A critical factor in literacy engagement is access to books" (Verhoeven & Snow, 2001, p. 4). A well-designed, functional classroom library can contribute to the overall quality of students' learning experiences. Unfortunately, a study conducted by Fractor, Woodruff, Martinez, and Teale (1993) revealed that the percentage of classrooms with a library decreased rather dramatically from kindergarten (72% had libraries) to fifth grade (about 26% had libraries). In middle and high schools, there are many classrooms without libraries. While *school* libraries certainly exist, they do not provide the ready access of a classroom library. Ivey (1999) notes that, by middle school, students who struggle in reading can be inspired by getting the right books into their hands. In addition, Langer (2001, p. 177) contends that "literature can play a central role in students' intellectual, social, and personal development." Content area teachers often have favorite materials that relate to a particular theme or unit. Making them part of a classroom library can increase their accessibility to and use by students.

 ## Directions and Example

1. Survey your classroom(s) and identify locations that might function as a library. Strive to be both creative and realistic as you allocate space.

2. Identify materials you have that would be appropriate for the library. A science teacher might have a series of small books that are biographies of scientists. There might also be some science fiction titles and books on easy-to-do experiments.

3. Enlist the assistance of colleagues and your students to identify additional materials and ways to obtain them. Realize that establishing a library takes time and can evolve over the years.

4. Develop a system for how materials are checked out and maintained.

5. Try to secure materials that students like to read. Not every piece of material in the library needs to relate to your content area. Ivey and Broaddus (2001) surveyed over 1,700 middle school students with an interest checklist and found the following types of materials to be of interest. Students could check more than one item. The following types of books and related materials are listed from high (77%) to low (20%). It seems clear that even the lowest rated item is of interest to a fair percentage of students.

- Magazines
- Adventure books
- Mysteries
- Scary stories
- Joke books
- Animals (informational books)
- Comic books
- Series books
- Sports (informational books)
- Books about people their age
- Fantasy
- Science fiction
- Newspapers
- Poetry books
- Biographies
- Picture books
- History (novels/chapter books)
- Science books
- History (informational books)
- Other specific topics

6. Consult other research studies that may offer insights for your library but rely on your observations of students as your primary source of information.

7. Consider establishing a time for free reading as part of your class time. Over 60% of students in the Ivey and Broaddus (2001) study responded positively to free reading as part of class time.

TECHNOLOGY TIP

Teens Read and Write Book Reviews

Find a Favorite Teenage Angst page where students can read book reviews and write comments at:

www.grouchy.com

Find interviews with authors, book reviews, a newsletter, and message boards where teens can post comments on books, related school issues, and original poetry and short stories at:

www.teenreads.com

Section
2.4

Encouraging Motivation

 **Goal**   To help students become motivated to learn

BACKGROUND

Motivation is a key component of reading engagement. It is enhanced by challenge, choice, and collaboration. Educators and researchers agree that, if we can motivate students to learn, we increase the chances that they will view academic achievement as a worthy pursuit. The "Ten Commandments of Motivation" (Irwin & Baker, 1989) are presented below to help you as you plan lessons in your content area.

1. Never give a reading assignment without thinking about how to motivate your students.
2. Never use reading as a form of punishment.
3. Increase the rewards and decrease the effort needed to complete an assignment.
4. Give students some choices about what they read.
5. Follow reading assignments with activities that allow students to work together and to use what they've learned.
6. Give students a purpose for reading.
7. When possible, use reading material related to students' interests.
8. Show students how the material relates to real life.
9. Be enthusiastic about the reading material.
10. Provide for success!

The strategies in this section are designed to motivate students to participate actively in their learning.

TEACHING STRATEGY 13

2.4 ▶ K-W-L

K-W-L (Ogle, 1986) is designed to engage students in becoming active learners as it motivates them to purposefully seek information from their texts and other sources. It can be used effectively as a prereading strategy because it activates students' prior knowledge about a subject and also helps them organize their thoughts and questions before they begin to read. K-W-L involves three basic steps: determining what students already **K**now about a topic; determining what they **W**ant to learn about a topic; and, after reading, assessing what they have **L**earned about the topic. This strategy lends itself well to follow-up activities such as the construction of graphic organizers and summary writing. Blachowicz and Ogle (2001) also present some variations of K-W-L that extend and expand the original strategy.

 ## Directions and Example

1. Introduce the K-W-L strategy prior to assigning a reading selection with a new unit of study. Explain to students that, when they begin to study new material, it is important to determine prior knowledge or what they already know about the material. Use an example from your content area or use the following example. In this example, the new topic is the country of Cuba from a geography text.

2. Ask students to brainstorm what they know about the topic as you record the information under **K.** The following list is an example of sentences describing what students know about Cuba.

Cuba

K	W	L
Cuba is 90 miles from Miami.		
Castro is the dictator.		
The government is communist.		
They grow sugar.		

3. Ask students what they would like to know about the topic. Some of their questions will arise from curiosity and others from a real desire to know more about the country. Record their questions under the **W** portion of the graph. The following list is an example of questions students asked about Cuba.

Cuba

K	W	L
Cuba is 90 miles from Miami.	What language do Cubans speak?	
Castro is the dictator.	What is Cuba's major industry?	
The government is communist.	What is the capital of Cuba?	
They grow sugar.	Why are so many Cubans leaving Cuba?	

4. Direct students to read the selection. When they have completed their reading, they are ready to return to the chart and record the answers to their questions in the column labeled **L** as in the following example. For unanswered questions, students should place question marks on the chart.

Cuba

K	W	L
Cuba is 90 miles from Miami.	What language do Cubans speak?	Spanish
Castro is the dictator.	What is Cuba's major industry?	sugar cane
The government is communist.	What is the capital of Cuba?	Havana
They grow sugar.	Why are so many Cubans leaving Cuba?	?

5. Involve students in follow-up activities designed to extend their learning. Questions that were not answered in the **W**ant to know column provide opportunities for further reading and research.

2.4 ▶ Decisions!

TEACHING STRATEGY 14

Activities that students find particularly motivating are those that relate to their lives and the lives of people they know. Students must make decisions throughout their lifetimes. This particular activity ties decision-making to their course work and encourages them to link their personal experiences and knowledge to the text. Being able to make personal connections to information greatly increases comprehension and long-term memory of the material.

Directions and Example

1. Examine your text and determine what information can be incorporated into situations that students might actually experience.

2. Write several short vignettes that incorporate elements of the text material. For example, in a government class studying the United States Constitution, you might think about the fifth amendment and write the following vignette.

Rose Slender was accused of murdering her husband. She was tried and acquitted (found, in the jury's opinion, not to have murdered her husband). Three years later, her former mother-in-law found more evidence of Rose's guilt. She demanded that Rose be tried again. Rose's lawyer said that a retrial was unconstitutional.

3. Duplicate and distribute handouts for each of your students. One handout will contain the vignettes, and the other will be a response sheet for recording information regarding students' opinions and decisions. An abbreviated example of a response sheet follows.

Social Studies Example

Response Sheet

City of Red River Courts

Case	Who is the case against?	What part of the United States Constitution is involved?	How does the amendment apply to the case?	What is your decision?
1.	Rose Slender	fifth amendment	can't be tried again for the same crime	Rose Slender doesn't have another trial.
2.				

4. Have students read each vignette and respond to the questions on the response sheet. Students may wish to work in pairs for this activity.

5. Ask them to record their decisions on the appropriate response sheet. After students have completed their work, divide the class into groups of three or four students and ask them to discuss their decisions with their group members.

6. An example of Decisions! from a career development course follows.

Career Development Example

Decisions!

Directions: The following scenarios from your text focus on work behaviors that may affect career development. Read each scenario and decide if the individual's behavior is positive or negative. Then decide what effect the behavior will have on future success in the workplace. Record your answers on the sheet labeled Apex Toy Company. The first one is done for you.

1. Lucretia never comes to work early and never stays a minute beyond quitting time at 5:00 p.m. She will not take any work home with her. Also, Lucretia makes sure to use every minute of her allotted lunchtime and never misses a coffee break regardless of her workload.

2. Although Charlie works on a word processor with a spell checker, he always carefully reads over his work for possible errors before submitting it to his boss.

3. Marcia could not solve a customer's problem. Rather than asking a fellow employee for assistance, Marcia told the customer that she was sorry and suggested that the customer seek assistance in another department.

4. Although Maria is a member of a team working on a project, she prefers to do most of the work herself rather than consulting her team members. She is sure that this will provide quality control and will enable her team to present an excellent final product.

Response Sheet

Apex Toy Company

Name of Employee	Behavior Exhibited	Positive/Negative Trait	Effect on Future
1. Lucretia	clock watcher	negative	may indicate lack of commitment
2.			
3.			
4.			

TEACHING STRATEGY 15

Structured Question Guide and Process Sheet

The Structured Question Guide and Process Sheet (Crawley & Mountain, 1995) serves as a motivational tool as students draw on their prior knowledge, form generalizations, and discuss those generalizations with their classmates. When engaging in the activities of this strategy, students use cognitive skills such as predicting, observing, inferring, analyzing, and making deductions (Crawley & Mountain, 1995).

 ## Directions and Example

1. Decide on a unit of study and determine the aspects of the unit that are important and will be of interest to your students.

2. Think of a question that relates to the topic and use it as you develop your Structured Question Guide. Use an example from your content area or the following example from a biology text. In this example, students are about to begin a unit in biology on the effects abusive substances and activities have on the body. This example is based on the following question:

   What effects do you think the listed substances and activities have on your body?

3. Select key words from a chapter with a cause-effect text pattern. List the key words under column A.

4. Tell students to list the effect of each key word in column B. Ask them to note the seriousness of the effect in column C.

Biology Example

Structured Question Guide

Directions: In your biology text, we are reading about substance and activity abuses. What effects do you think these substances and activities have on your body? Use your prior knowledge to rate (1 through 6) the seriousness of their effects, with 1 representing the most harmful effects and 6 representing the least harmful effects. You may wish to add additional abusive substances and activities to the list.

A Substances/Experiences	B Effects	C Ratings
alcohol	impaired judgment	2
tobacco	increased heart rate	4
sleep deprivation	hallucinations	3
narcotics	depression	1
sedentary lifestyle	weight gain	5
other _____		

5. After students have completed the Structured Question Guide, divide the class into groups of three or four students so that they can compare their answers. They should use the Process Sheet to guide their discussions. The following is an example of a Process Sheet.

Biology Example

Process Sheet

- How do your answers compare with your group members' answers?
- Did any of your group members list additional harmful substances or abusive behaviors?
- Did all of your group members list the same harmful effects? Were there any effects that were different?
- Compare the ratings listed in column C. Were the ratings different among your group members? Why do you think your ratings were different?

6. After discussion, students should prepare a written summary of the results obtained by their group members.

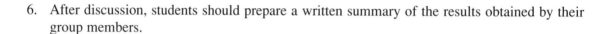 **TECHNOLOGY**

Why Files

Every two weeks an article is posted that focuses on current science topics in the news. You can use these articles with students to generate discussions in the classroom.

www.whyfiles.org

TIP

TEACHING STRATEGY 16

2.4 ▶ Draw, Read, Attend, Write (DRAW)

DRAW (Agnew, 2000) is a motivational comprehension strategy based on teacher-prepared questions related to some text (an article, selection, or chapter). A variety of questions are typed on a sheet of paper, duplicated, and distributed to students. The questions on one sheet are cut apart and used for the strategy. An overview of DRAW is presented below.

D: Draw—Different students or groups draw questions from the master sheet that was cut apart.

R: Read—Students read the material upon which the questions are based and write their answers on the sheet containing all the questions.

A: Attend—The teacher asks the student (or group) who drew the first question to read the question, answer it, and explain how the answer was determined. Class members then discuss the answer and arrive at a consensus. Students are encouraged to make notes on their sheets that contain all the questions.

W: Write—When all the questions have been asked, answered, and discussed, students put away their question sheets and the teacher collects the individual question slips. Several questions are drawn to make a quiz. Each question is then read aloud, and the students write their answers on a clean sheet of paper. Students may then hand in the quiz to be graded.

Agnew (2000) mentions numerous benefits of using the DRAW strategy. Among them are helping readers who struggle understand the content, encouraging full class participation, encouraging thinking on various levels, and involving students in learning from each other.

Directions and Example

1. Select the text from which to construct the questions. Create literal (factual), inferential (implicit), and application questions to reflect the main ideas, themes, and information in the text. Type the questions and reproduce sufficient copies for students. The following example is from a middle school unit on the Holocaust.

2. Take one sheet of questions and cut it into strips so each question is on a separate strip of paper. Distribute a copy of the full set of questions to each student. Have students form small groups or work with a partner. In this example, the class contained 24 students and the sheet contained 12 questions; therefore, the teacher decided to use partner grouping.

3. Hold up the strips of paper containing the questions and say something like the following. (Adapt what you say to the particular situation.)

    Before you begin reading the section in your text that deals with the Holocaust, I will have each group draw one question and answer it. You should write out your answer and be prepared to share and discuss it with the entire class.

Social Studies Example

Directions: You or your partner will be asked to answer one of the following questions. When the questions are discussed in class, you should take notes on all the responses. After our discussion is concluded, some of these questions will be used for a quiz. You will not be able to refer to this sheet during the quiz, so pay attention to the answers and discussion.

1. What group of people was the central focus of the Holocaust?
2. In what country did the Holocaust mostly take place?
3. What does *Holocaust* mean?
4. Why were people persecuted during the Holocaust?
5. How were the people persecuted during the Holocaust?
6. What is the name of the person generally associated with the Holocaust?
7. During which war did the Holocaust occur?
8. How would you feel if this happened to you and your family?
9. Do you think something like this could ever happen to you in the United States?
10. What happened to a particular ethnic group in the United States in the 1940s? Why were these people treated this way?
11. Do you think certain groups of people in the United States are persecuted today because of their ethnic origins? Who are they? Why does this happen?

4. After the questions have been drawn, have students read the assigned portion of text (silently or orally with their partners) and answer the question. When students have finished, ask the group that drew the first question to read and answer it. Have students explain their answers and possibly refer to the text to support their answers. The factual questions are among the easiest to link with a specific part of the text. Once a consensus is reached through discussion, the other students should write the answers on their sheets containing all the questions.

5. Proceed through the remaining questions in a similar manner. Some of the higher-level questions may promote discussion and debate. The final question in the example may lead to considerable discussion, as more than one group may be identified. The responses to the "why" part of the question may also vary, depending on the particular group identified.

6. When all the questions have been answered and discussed, collect the question strips, have students put away their sheets containing all the questions, and ask students to prepare a clean sheet of paper for a quiz.

7. Decide how many questions to use for the quiz. You or students could draw the number of questions needed. You or a student should read each question aloud as many times as necessary, and students should write their answers. The completed quizzes may be handed in for a grade.

8. Variations of this strategy include dividing the class into two teams and having future quizzes include questions containing important information from earlier material.

2.4 ► Electronic Texts

Electronic texts "are moving closer to the mainstream of reading and writing" (Reinking, 2001, p. 198). Such texts can be thought of as "a unique configuration of symbol systems, technologies, contents, and situations of use" (Reinking, 2001, p. 200) that can help teachers promote engagement, motivation, and enjoyment in reading. There is some evidence (Tobias, 1988) that using digital texts can help students learn expository content. The Internet, e-mail, CD-ROM encyclopedias, and a wide variety of CD-ROMS are now available to help teachers support their teaching. A problem may be that some teachers are challenged to address an area with which they themselves are not fully comfortable. The reality, however, is that this technology will continue to grow and influence how reading is done.

Directions and Example

1. Take stock of your current knowledge about computer technology in general. How would you rate your knowledge and use on the following continuum?

none	a little	some	quite a bit	a lot

2. If you have at least a little knowledge of computers, think about how you use them as a teacher. Do you keep records or grades on a computer? Do you use the computer to type students' assignments, tests, and examinations? Do you use computer simulations, the Internet, and a variety of CD-ROMS in your content area? Rate your overall instructional use on the following continuum.

very low	low	some	quite a bit	a lot

3. Select at least one area where you would like to gain additional knowledge to strengthen instruction in your content area using computer technology. Be realistic and begin within your comfort zone.

4. Talk with colleagues or technology resource people in your school or school district to gain insights and to help achieve your objectives. These objectives may include special classes, small group assistance, or one-on-one instruction. Printed resources may also be available. Be willing to devote sufficient time to your objectives and expect some frustrating moments. Several resources are provided on the next page. You may wish to explore some of them.

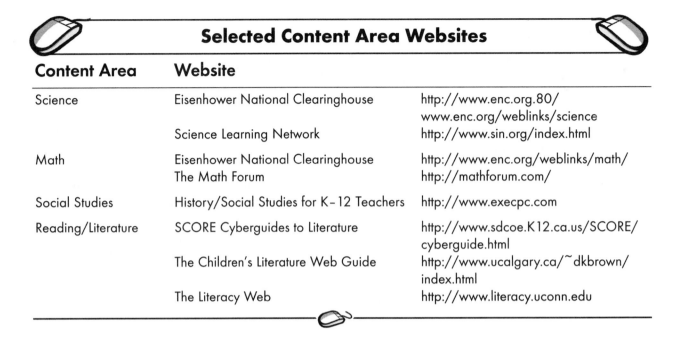

Selected Content Area Websites

Content Area	Website	
Science	Eisenhower National Clearinghouse	http://www.enc.org.80/ www.enc.org/weblinks/science
	Science Learning Network	http://www.sin.org/index.html
Math	Eisenhower National Clearinghouse	http://www.enc.org/weblinks/math/
	The Math Forum	http://mathforum.com/
Social Studies	History/Social Studies for K-12 Teachers	http://www.execpc.com
Reading/Literature	SCORE Cyberguides to Literature	http://www.sdcoe.K12.ca.us/SCORE/ cyberguide.html
	The Children's Literature Web Guide	http://www.ucalgary.ca/~dkbrown/ index.html
	The Literacy Web	http://www.literacy.uconn.edu

Lesson Plans and Searches by Grade Level

AskERIC Lesson Plans by Subject
http://www.askeric.org/Virtual/Lessons/

This collection contains more than 2,000 unique lesson plans that have been written and submitted to AskERIC by teachers from all over the United States and the world.

Lesson Plans Page
http://www.lessonplanspage.com/

To find lesson plans that match your criteria, simply begin by selecting a subject or search for specific topics.

The Gateway
http://www.thegateway.org

Search by grade level (K–College) and subject. You can also browse keywords and subject.

Searchopolis
http://www.searchopolis.com/

This directory and search engine is organized for students in the elementary grades, middle grades, and high school.

Chapter 3
BUILDING VOCABULARY

OVERVIEW

Most content area teachers recognize the strong relationship between vocabulary knowledge and comprehension of text. They know that if their students have a well-developed content vocabulary, they will understand written materials within their content area more easily. Consequently, many teachers spend a portion of time with vocabulary instruction. Vocabulary knowledge has become a strong focus of research among educators during the past two decades. No longer do we believe that memory is built sequentially from an accumulation of facts. Rather, meaning relies on the interrelatedness between words and ideas (Nagy & Scott, 2000).

Knowing words actually involves four different vocabularies: speaking, writing, reading, and listen-

ing. Speaking and writing are expressive vocabularies, while reading and listening are receptive vocabularies (Baumann & Kame'enui, 1991). In order for a word to be used in expressive vocabulary, it must be adequately learned so that it is retained in memory and easily retrieved in speaking and writing. The Word Storm strategy (Klemp, 1994) facilitates word retention and understanding. By contrast, our receptive vocabulary involves associating a meaning with a given label when we read text or listen to conversation (Kame'enui, Dixon, & Carnine, 1987). Effective vocabulary instruction will develop students' vocabularies in all four areas.

As a content specialist, you must determine which vocabulary words your students need to learn in order to comprehend their textbooks. Once

45

you have decided on the words that are important to teach, it is necessary to select methods for instruction. Regardless of the particular strategy selected, class discussion of the new words should always be conducted in order to help students process the meanings of the words more deeply. As you teach students new words, it is important that you teach not only the denotative, or general meaning of the words, but also the connotative definitions. Connotative definitions are the range of meanings a word may have, determined by the specific context in which it occurs (Readence, Bean, & Baldwin, 2001). Providing opportunities for class discussion often facilitates students' understanding of the connotative definitions of words.

In order to be effective, vocabulary instruction must be meaningful. A basic premise of effective instruction in any area is that students need to relate new information to what they already know. This principle is equally applicable to vocabulary instruction. Not only is it important for students to understand the meaning of a word, but they must also develop ownership of the word by interacting with it in some individual and personal way (Blachowicz & Fisher, 2000). Strategies that activate prior knowledge focus on semantic relatedness and involve presenting new words in relation to words of similar meaning. Relating new words or concepts to those already within the learner's schema or background knowledge allows the learner to develop a personal connection. Strategies such as Semantic Feature Analysis (Johnson & Pearson, 1984) and the Knowledge Rating Scale (Blachowicz, 1986) focus on activities that require students to think deeply about words and relate to them on a personal level.

Because different methods of teaching words are appropriate in different circumstances, there is no one best method for teaching new words. "Vocabulary instruction should vary according to the context of instruction and the nature of the words being taught and learned" (Blachowicz & Fisher, 2000, p. 504). For example, if you are a science teacher and wish to teach your students the meanings of a few key words, you might choose to use a definitional approach. This approach involves presenting selected words prior to asking your students to read the text and directing them to categorize the words as they compare their properties and characteristics. List-Group-Label (Taba, 1967) and Concept of Definition Maps (Schwartz & Raphael, 1985) are two strategies that facilitate this process.

A goal of effective instruction is to help students experience enjoyment and satisfaction as they build their vocabulary knowledge. This goal can be achieved by developing activities that allow students to play with words through word games linked to content topics. Challenging students to complete a Magic Square provides an opportunity for collaboration and enjoyment among students as it fortifies links to their background knowledge.

A final major component of effective vocabulary instruction is to help students increase their vocabulary knowledge independently. Effective instruction in this area will include many activities that are student directed as well as some that are teacher directed. When you involve students in class discussions that incorporate new vocabulary and provide opportunities for students to apply the newly acquired vocabulary to a different situation, you are helping students become independent learners. All vocabulary instruction should help students develop the ability to acquire new vocabulary independently.

Different methods of teaching words are appropriate in different circumstances, and different word learning activities result in different levels of word knowledge (Nagy & Scott, 2000). This chapter is designed to present strategies that help students link new words to what they already know, understand relationships among words, and develop their existing vocabularies.

Linking Vocabulary to Background Knowledge

Section 3.1

Goal To help students link vocabulary to their background knowledge

BACKGROUND

Effective vocabulary instruction involves assisting students in relating new vocabulary to what they already know. Helping students make ties to new vocabulary words that are personally meaningful aids in long-term retention of the words. Additionally, relating new vocabulary to previous experiences frequently leads to increased retention and usage (Blachowicz & Fisher, 2000). There are a variety of simple strategies that can be used in your classroom to help students make these personal ties. One such strategy, developed by Gipe (1979), guides students as they read a short passage that uses an unknown word in a defined context. After reading the passage, students are asked to respond in writing to a question or statement with information from their personal experience that further develops the meaning of the unknown word. For example, if the new word were *barbarian,* you might ask students to write down something a barbarian might do if he or she came to their home for dinner.

Making this personal tie enhances students' ability to remember the meaning of a new vocabulary word.

Students should be active participants in creating semantic connections between their prior knowledge and new vocabulary. Asking themselves "What do I already know about these words?" should be their first strategic step when new vocabulary is introduced. As they preview an upcoming reading selection, they can also ask themselves "What do I see in this selection that gives me a clue to what these words might mean?" Encourage your students to make preliminary predictions about the relationship between the new words and the topic of their content reading selection. These predictions demonstrate for students the semantic relatedness of words and concepts and underscore the fact that vocabulary learning is a crucial element in understanding textbook material (Blachowicz & Fisher, 2000).

TEACHING STRATEGY 1

3.1   Knowledge Rating Scale

The Knowledge Rating Scale (Blachowicz, 1986) is a prereading activity designed to introduce a list of potentially unknown content words to your students. The Knowledge Rating Scale uses a survey format to have students determine their knowledge of a word or concept. As students complete the survey and participate in class discussions, they become aware of how much they already know about the subject to which the words are related. Additionally, using a Knowledge Rating Scale activates students' existing background knowledge and helps them begin to forge links with the new vocabulary concepts. As their teacher, you will be able to gauge the depth of your students' existing knowledge and note what areas need special attention during your instruction.

Directions and Example

1. Select a list of important vocabulary words from a new unit or a chapter of text. Prepare a handout for each of your students that lists the vocabulary words followed by three columns labeled *Know It Well, Have Heard/Seen It,* and *No Clue*.

2. Divide the class into mixed ability groups of three or four students to provide students with opportunities to share their diverse background knowledge.

3. Have students consider each word on the Knowledge Rating Scale and place an X in the appropriate column next to the word. Ask students to look carefully at each word. Tell them that, if they think that they can define the word, they should place an X in the first column under *Know It Well*. If they have heard of the word or have seen it, but are unsure of its meaning, they should place an X in the second column under *Have Heard/Seen It*. If it is totally unfamiliar, they should place an X in the third column labeled *No Clue*.

Government Example

Knowledge Rating Scale

	Know It Well	Have Heard/Seen It	No Clue
interdependence		X	
refugee	X		
nuclear proliferation		X	
international laws		X	
ethnic intolerance	X		
religious intolerance	X		
chemical weapons			X
biological weapons			X
United Nations	X		
human rights		X	

4. After students have completed the Knowledge Rating Scale, ask them to write sentences using the words they have marked in the *Know It Well* column.

5. Lead the class in a discussion about the words for which students have composed sentences. As students read the chapter in the following days, direct them to add definitions for unknown words and confirm or, if appropriate, change the sentences they have for known words.

3.1   Exclusion Brainstorming

TEACHING STRATEGY 2

Exclusion Brainstorming (Blachowicz, 1986) is a strategy designed to guide students as they think about what they already know about concept words related to a particular topic. It is a user-friendly technique, easy to implement, and easy for students to understand. Additionally, it accommodates reluctant readers and those students who may be unfamiliar with the topic.

 ## Directions and Example

1. Place the title of a selection or a topic on the chalkboard or an overhead transparency. Use an example from your content area or use the following example from a world history text.

2. Underneath the topic or title, list a mixture of words or phrases—five that are related to the topic, five that are not related to the topic, and five that are ambiguous. List the words in random order. An example follows.

Topic: Chernobyl
Mixture of Words and Phrases

Kiev	rain forests	radiation
illness	energy	exposure
greenhouse effect	death	accident
meltdown	global warming	world climate
nuclear power	thyroid cancer	conservation

3. Ask students to eliminate those words and phrases that they think are not related to the topic or would not be included in a selection about the topic. Ask students to explain their decisions. In this example, students should eliminate the following words and phrases.

Words Unrelated to the Topic

greenhouse effect	conservation
global warming	rain forests
world climate	

4. Next, ask students to choose the words and phrases that they think are most likely to appear in the selection and that are related to the topic. Once again, be sure to ask students to explain their decisions. An essential component of any brainstorming activity is for students to explain why they think the way they do (Blachowicz, 1986). In this example, the words and phrases related to the topic are listed below.

Words Related to the Topic

Kiev	accident
nuclear power	radiation
meltdown	

5. Have students choose those words and phrases that are somewhat ambiguous. The words and phrases that are ambiguous are listed below.

Ambiguous Words

thyroid cancer	death
illness	energy
exposure	

6. Assign the related reading selection and ask students to look for the vocabulary words as they read. Direct students to make particular note of the ambiguous words and phrases to see if they can determine how they are used in the selection.

7. After students have completed the reading assignment, discuss the meanings of the ambiguous vocabulary words and how they relate to the selection. Encourage students to share their knowledge about the meanings of the words. For any words that are still unknown, ask students to determine their meanings by using their dictionaries and the contexts in which the words are presented.

TECHNOLOGY

SAT Vocabulary Words

Visit the interactive site for learning advanced English vocabulary words for the SAT.

www.vocabulary.com

T
I
P

3.1   List-Group-Label

TEACHING STRATEGY 3

List-Group-Label (Taba, 1967) was originally developed as an aid to students encountering technical vocabulary in science and social studies classes. This strategy, which emphasizes word relationships, is based on the idea of organizing words and concepts into categories as a way of linking them to previously learned terminology. Additionally, it activates students' prior knowledge when they brainstorm words related to the topic. List-Group-Label is a three-part strategy that consists of listing, grouping and labeling, and follow-up discussion.

Directions and Example

1. Select a concept that you wish to clarify from a chapter in your content textbook.

2. Ask students to brainstorm all of the words they can think of that are related to the topic. Record students' responses on the chalkboard or on an overhead transparency. Select an example from your content area or use the following example from a science text. Below is a list of words brainstormed by students studying earthquakes.

faults	tremors	tidal waves	rocks
epicenter	seismologists	magnitude	plates
California	death	warning systems	South Carolina
seismic waves	destruction	cracks	Richter scale

3. Ask students to decide if any of the words can be grouped together. Invite students to share their reasoning as they present a possible grouping. One student might say that the following words should be grouped together because they all deal with things or people that warn about an earthquake.

> warning systems
> seismologists
> magnitude
> Richter scale

4. Divide the class into groups of three or four students and ask them to place all of the words into categories. Remind them that the words they place together must have something in common. This is the grouping portion of the activity.

5. Ask students to title or label each group in order to indicate the shared relationship of the words within the group, as in the following example.

Locations	Indicators	Elements	Aftermath
California	warning systems	rocks	death
South Carolina	seismologists	plates	destruction
	Richter scale	faults	tidal waves
	magnitude	cracks	
		tremors	
		seismic waves	

6. After students have completed their categorizations, have the class discuss their categories and share reasons for placing words together. This is the discussion portion of the activity.

7. Students are now ready to read the chapter on earthquakes in their text. This activity will provide you with information about your students' background knowledge and can guide the depth of your instruction.

8. Encourage students to add words to their categories or move words from one category to another as they read.

Defining Words

Goal To help students learn the meanings of words

BACKGROUND

When teachers give their students a list of seemingly unknown words and ask them to find the words in dictionaries, write down definitions for them, and use the words in sentences, they are not involving their students in a meaningful instructional activity. Too often, students will comply with the instructions, complete the exercise, and immediately forget the definitions for which they have arduously searched. In other words, no personal connection to the new words is being forged through participation in this activity. Teachers need to help students define and categorize these new words and assist students in making personal connections. Every content area has vocabulary that is unique to its subject matter. These special and technical vocabulary terms provide the framework for learning the information specific to a particular subject.

It is impossible for teachers to predict all of the words that their students will need to know in order to gain meaning from a text selection. Stahl (1986) has developed three guidelines for determining which words may need special instruction.

First, decide how important each word is to understanding the text. If the word is one that will probably not be encountered again, that word can be ignored. For example, in *Exploring Art* (1992, p. 180), the following sentence appears: "This work was done with quick drying *duco* paint." Although the word *duco* may not be in the students' vocabu-

lary, it is not a word that is necessary to teach because it does not affect the meaning of the passage. If, however, comprehension of the material hinges on understanding a particular word, it is important to select this word for special instruction. In the sentence "When applied thickly, oil paint is *opaque*," it might be necessary to teach the word *opaque* because it is important for understanding the meaning of the sentence.

Second, try to decide if students can figure out the meaning of the word through the context in which it is presented. If the word is well defined in context it is not imperative that you teach it. The following example taken from *Biology* (1981, p. 42) defines *theory:* "If an hypothesis continues to generate successful predictions, it may be promoted to the status of a *theory*. A theory is any hypothesis that is supported by many observations." If, however, the text does not clearly define the word, you may wish to select the word for teaching.

Third, decide how much time you need to spend teaching a particular word. If the word represents a concept that is not within students' understanding but is closely related to a known word, it can be taught relatively easily by providing examples that establish the connection. For example, the word *parsimonious* may be an unfamiliar word to many of your students. However, the word *stingy* is one that most of them will recognize. Making the

53

connection between the two words for your students will assist them in learning and remembering the meaning of *parsimonious*. Discussion may motivate them to pursue further vocabulary exploration as they become more conscious of new words (Stahl, 1986).

3.2   Possible Sentences

TEACHING STRATEGY 4

Possible Sentences (Moore & Moore, 1986) is a strategy designed to help students anticipate the meaning of a passage before they begin reading. Through the construction of sentences based on key words selected from the passage, students are able to use their prior knowledge to make predictions about the meaning of their upcoming reading assignment. Then, as students read, they determine the accuracy of their predictions about the selected key words.

 ## Directions and Example

1. Identify 10 to 15 words in conjunction with a reading assignment. Select words that students should understand in order to adequately comprehend the text selection. Be sure to choose some words that will be familiar to the students as well as some that may be new but are important to the meaning of the selection. Select words from your content area or use the following words from a current events article.

doses	terrorists
vaccinations	spread
extinct	vaccine
exposure	government
protection	outbreak
stockpile	virus
smallpox	epidemic

2. Ask students either individually or in small groups to select at least two words from the list and write one sentence that might "possibly" occur in the reading passage. As they write their sentences, students are predicting how the words might appear in the text passage.

3. After students have completed several sentences, ask them to read their sentences aloud as you write them on the chalkboard exactly as given. Continue until all the words on the list have been used in sentences. The following are examples of sentences that might be constructed using the words listed above.

   1. The <u>government</u> may try to stop the <u>spread</u> of the deadly <u>smallpox</u> disease.
   2. <u>Vaccinations</u> against the disease would stop an <u>outbreak</u>.
   3. It is frightening to think of <u>exposure</u> to this <u>virus.</u>

4. Next ask students to read the passage silently and evaluate the accuracy of the sentences written on the chalkboard. As they read, students can evaluate their predictions in terms of the information provided by the text.

5. Using the text as a reference, conduct a discussion as each sentence is evaluated. Sentences that are not accurate, according to the text, are either eliminated or changed to reflect the information in the passage. You might choose to use a form such as the one below to aid your students in the evaluation procedure.

> Circle the appropriate evaluation. Is the specific sentence true (supported by the text), false (not supported by the text), or indeterminate (the statement cannot be proved or disproved based on the text)?

| Sentence 1 | True | False | Can't be determined |
| Sentence 2 | True | False | Can't be determined |

6. As students generate new sentences to replace those they have determined to be incorrect, their understanding of the vocabulary terms and their comprehension of the material are extended.

TEACHING STRATEGY 5

3.2 ▶ Magic Squares

The purpose of Magic Squares (Vacca & Vacca, 2002) is for students to match a content term with its definition. Magic Squares provide a challenging yet enjoyable way for students to think about word definitions as they solve a simple math puzzle based on a particular number combination. Magic Squares can be used as an opportunity for students to predict the meanings of new words by seeing the words in context or as a review for important definitions from a chapter of text.

Directions and Example

1. Construct an activity sheet that has two sections, one for content area terms and one for definitions.

2. Direct students to match each term with its definition. As they do this, students consider the numbers denoting the terms as well as the letters denoting the definitions.

3. Instruct students to put the number of a word in the proper space of the Magic Square that is marked by the letter of its definition. For example, the definition of Dali (word 2) is B, a Spanish Surrealist painter, so the number 2 goes in the box labeled B. If students' answers are correct, they will complete a Magic Square. The numerical total will be the same for each row across and each column down in the square. In the following example from an art text, the magic number is 18.

Magic Square

Definitions

A. turning something familiar into something strange
B. Spanish Surrealist painter
C. joining images in impossible combinations
D. Belgian Surrealist
E. art movement based on radical ideas and dream-like images
F. the range from light to dark
G. use of space
H. things are not where they naturally belong
I. surface quality

A	B	C
D	E	F
G	H	I

Content Terms (Answers)

1. Scale
2. Dali
3. Texture
4. Magritte
5. Composition
6. Surrealism
7. Juxtaposing
8. Value
9. Transformation
10. Dislocation

Answers

A (9)	B (2)	C (7)
D (4)	E (6)	F (8)
G (5)	H (10)	I (3)

4. Vacca and Vacca (2002) offer the following patterns for Magic Square compositions (p. 166).

A.

7	3	5
2	4	9
6	8	1

0*   15**

B.

9	7	5
1	8	12
11	6	4

3*   21**

C.

7	11	8
10	12	4
9	3	14

5*   26**

* extra terms needed in answer columns   ** magic number

5. The asterisk in number 4 (* extra terms needed in answer columns) refers to the necessity of adding extra terms to the answer column in order to establish a consecutive order of numbers as in examples B and C. However only 9 of the choices will be used.

TECHNOLOGY

Vandelay Games: Word Gamer's Paradise!

Here's an opportunity to play a variety of word games.

www.powercom.net/internet/

3.2

TEACHING STRATEGY 6

Concept of Definition Map

A Concept of Definition Map (Schwartz & Raphael, 1985) is a strategy designed for teaching the definitions of key vocabulary concepts. Its purpose is to help students develop a rich, in-depth understanding of a concept through the use of a graphic structure. This strategy is particularly effective when introducing a text selection with an important concept that you are especially interested in your students remembering. The Concept of Definition Map focuses on the key components of a concept: its class or category, its properties or characteristics, several illustrations or examples, and an example of a comparison (Schwartz, 1988).

 ## Directions and Example

1. Identify a term or concept from your text that is necessary to teach in order for students to better comprehend the selection. In this example from a science text, students are learning about coelenterates.

2. Write a term on the chalkboard or an overhead transparency and place the term or concept that you wish to teach in the center of the Concept of Definition Map.

3. Guide students in completing the Concept of Definition Map as you ask them the following questions.

   What is a coelenterate? (category of the concept)
   What are some things you know about a coelenterate? (properties of the concept)
   What is an example of a coelenterate? (an example of the concept)
   What is it like? (an example of a comparison)

4. Direct students to use their textbooks and background knowledge for adding information to the Concept of Definition Map.

5. A blank Concept of Definition Map follows the example.

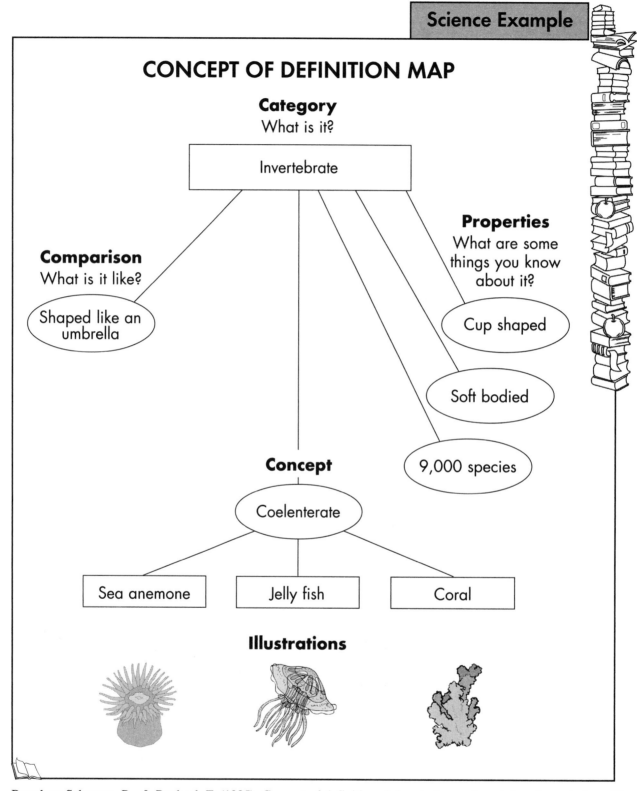

CONCEPT OF DEFINITION MAP

Category
What is it?

Invertebrate

Comparison
What is it like?

Shaped like an umbrella

Properties
What are some things you know about it?

Cup shaped

Soft bodied

9,000 species

Concept

Coelenterate

Sea anemone   Jelly fish   Coral

Illustrations

Based on Schwartz, R., & Raphael, T. (1985). Concept of definition: A key to improving students' vocabulary. *The Reading Teacher, 39,* 198–205.

Name _____ Date _____

Concept of Definition Map

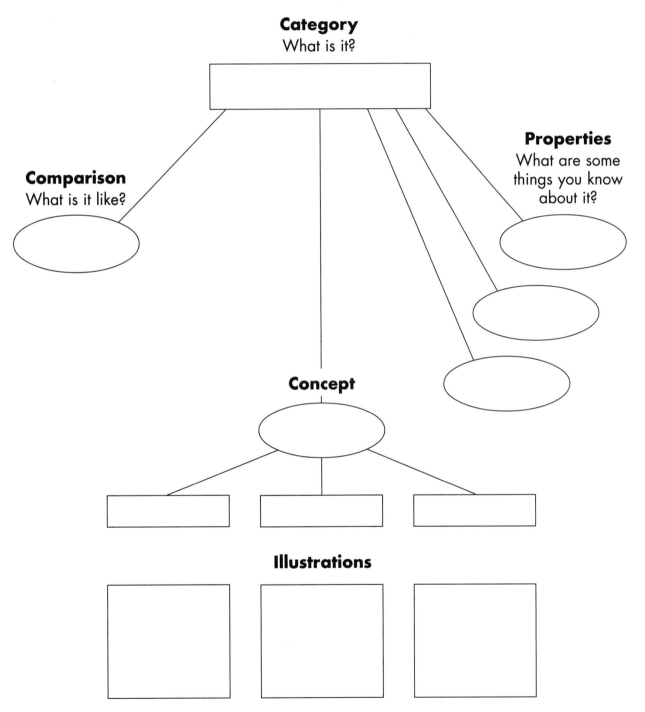

Category
What is it?

Comparison
What is it like?

Properties
What are some
things you know
about it?

Concept

Illustrations

Based on Schwartz, R., & Raphael, T. (1985). Concept of definition: A key to improving students' vocabulary. *The Reading Teacher, 39,* 198–205.

From Susan Davis Lenski, Mary Ann Wham, and Jerry L. Johns, *Reading & Learning Strategies: Middle Grades through High School,* 2nd Edition. Copyright © 2003 by Kendall/Hunt Publishing Company (1-800-247-3458, ext. 4 or 5). May be reproduced for noncommercial educational purposes.

3.2   Four Square

Four Square is a strategy that is easy to implement and is effective in helping students learn the definitions of new words. In Four Square students make personal connections to new words, thus increasing the likelihood that the words will be retained in their long-term memories.

 ## Directions and Example

1. Draw a square with four quadrants on the chalkboard or an overhead transparency.

2. Ask students to select a word from their content text that they consider important or select a word that you want students to learn. Write the vocabulary word in the upper left quadrant.

3. Invite students to suggest an appropriate definition for the selected word. Write the definition in the upper right quadrant.

4. Ask students to suggest words or phrases that they personally associate with the vocabulary word. Write one of the personal associations suggested by students in the lower left quadrant.

5. Next, ask students to suggest a word or phrase that does *not* define the vocabulary word. Write this word or phrase in the lower right quadrant. The following example is from an American government text.

Four Square	
Vocabulary Word détente	**Definition** decrease in tension between countries
Personal Association French for relaxation	**Opposite** strained relations

6. Invite students to develop several Four Square vocabulary examples using words from their text that are important for understanding content material.

3.2 ➤ **Word Storm**

TEACHING STRATEGY 8

Word Storm (Klemp, 1994) combines the use of content area vocabulary with the students' predictions about how the words will be used in context. It is effective as a preteaching activity and will enhance your students' connections with the technical or specialized vocabulary of content area material. Students may work in pairs or in small groups. Encourage students to discuss their responses as they work. Students can determine their answers by drawing on their background knowledge, or they may use a dictionary, glossary, or thesaurus.

Directions and Example

1. Give each of your students a Word Storm sheet with a word in the top space. Assign the words you have selected from your content area so that no more than two groups of students have the same word. Duplication of some words is important, to provide insights into the uses of the words during the discussion phase of the activity. For this example the Word Storm word is *combustion*.

2. Next ask students to write the sentence from the text that contains the word *combustion*. In this case, the sentence is: *Combustion includes many chemical reactions.*

3. For number three, ask students to write some words that they think of when they see the word *combustion*. For this example, the words are *explosion, fire*, and *heat*.

4. Some of the directives on the Word Storm sheet are intentionally ambiguous, which may encourage diverse responses from students. For example, in question four students are asked to think of some different forms of the word given at the top of the page. Students may write down variations of the word. Other forms of the word *combustion* are *combustible, combustibility*, and *combustive*.

5. For question number five, students are to name three people who would be likely to use this word. Possible responses are *firefighter*, *chemist*, and *rocket builder*.

6. Students may not be able to answer some of the questions if the word does not fit neatly into the given prompt. For example, if the word were a noun such as *alphabet*, it would be difficult to answer question six. For this question, students are to think of other words that mean the same thing as the word at the top of the page. A nonanswer is also valuable because it encourages students to think about the various forms of words. In this case, other words that mean the same thing as *combustion* are *flaming, burning*, and *visible oxidation*.

7. For the last directive students are to write a sentence using the chosen word (*combustion*) appropriately. A sentence might be: *Combustion is a chemical reaction that gives off heat and light.*

8. A blank Word Storm sheet follows the example.

Science Example

WORD STORM

1. What is the word?   _combustion_

2. Write the sentence from the text in which the word is used.

   Combustion includes many chemical reactions.

3. What are some words that you think of when you see this word?

   explosion   _fire_   _heat_

4. Do you know any other forms of this word? If so, what are they?

   combustible   _combustibility_   _combustive_

5. Name three people who would be likely to use this word.

   fireman   _chemist_   _rocket builder_

6. Can you think of any other words that mean the same thing?

   flaming   _burning_   _visible oxidation_

7. Write a sentence using this word appropriately. Make sure your sentence tells us what the word means!

   Combustion is a chemical reaction that gives off heat and light.

Based on Klemp, R.M. (1994). Word storm: Connecting vocabulary to the student's database. *The Reading Teacher, 48,* 282.

Name _____   Date _____

WORD STORM

1. What is the word?_____

2. Write the sentence from the text in which the word is used.

   _____

3. What are some words that you think of when you see this word?

   _____   _____   _____

4. Do you know any other forms of this word? If so, what are they?

   _____   _____   _____

5. Name three people who would be likely to use this word.

   _____   _____   _____

6. Can you think of any other words that mean the same thing?

   _____   _____   _____

7. Write a sentence using this word appropriately. Make sure your sentence tells us what the word means!

   _____

TECHNOLOGY

T I P

Word-A-Day

Improve your vocabulary by checking out this Word-A-Day site. Don't be caught verbally unaware!

www.wordsmith.org

3.2   Word Webs

TEACHING STRATEGY 9

Word Webs (Rosenbaum, 2001) are designed to facilitate students' vocabulary development by clarifying and enriching the meanings of known words and introducing students to unknown words. This strategy is designed to integrate the components of effective vocabulary instruction. These components include activating and extending prior knowledge and using context, dictionaries, and the structural or morphemic analysis of a word in order to establish personal meanings (Rosenbaum, 2001). Urge your students to seek out new and interesting words during independent or assigned reading and record them in a journal or notebook for use in their word webs.

Directions and Example

1. Ask students to select an unfamiliar word from their text or vocabulary journal and write it and the page number where it is located in Bubble 1. This example uses the word *heroine* from page 17 in a history text.

2. In Bubble 2, direct students to record the essential part of the sentence from their text containing the word. The text says, "Rosa Parks continues to be a national *heroine*."

3. In Bubble 3, ask students to write the dictionary definition of the new word, using the definition that most appropriately supports the context in which the word is used. The dictionary defines *heroine* as "a female who is endowed with courage and strength."

4. Ask students to use a dictionary or thesaurus to select and record both a synonym and an antonym for the new word and to place them in Bubbles 4 and 5. Rosenbaum (2001) suggests that students may choose to substitute a nonexample for their word rather than an antonym, because some words do not have antonyms. For a synonym of *heroine*, the word *champion* was chosen. The antonym in this example is *coward.*

5. Have students record another form of the new word in Bubble 6. While investigating a new form of the word, students will probably encounter similar roots or affixes. "Not only does this manipulation help the student tap into background knowledge but it also extends new learning" (Rosenbaum, 2001, p. 45). Another form of the word *heroine* is *heroic*.

6. In Bubble 7, ask students to write a phrase, a category, an example, or some personal clue to the word they have selected. The personal clue in this example is another heroine, Joan of Arc. The directions for this entry are flexible and, therefore, may be the easiest part of the web for many students. "Here is another opportunity for active student involvement, conversation with peers or teacher, and integration or elaboration of prior knowledge" (Rosenbaum, 2001, p. 46).

7. The last step in the Word Web is for students to write an original sentence using the word correctly. "This step presents your students with a logical conclusion to the entire activity as it allows them to integrate prior knowledge, new learning and elaborated personal meaning" (Rosenbaum, 2001, p. 46). This sentence will be in Bubble 8. The example sentence is: To become a *heroine*, you have to be a girl and have a lot of courage.

8. A blank Word Web follows the example.

History Example

Word Web

```
        ( 4. champion )    ( 1. heroine-page 17 )    ( 5. coward )

        ( 6. heroic )                              ( 7. Joan of Arc )
```

(2. Rosa Parks continues to be a national heroine.)

(3. a female who is endowed with courage and strength)

(8. To become a heroine, you have to be a girl and have
a lot of courage.)

Based on Rosenbaum, C. (2001). A word map for middle school: A tool for effective vocabulary instruction. *Journal of Adolescent & Adult Literacy, 45*, 44–49.

WORD WEB

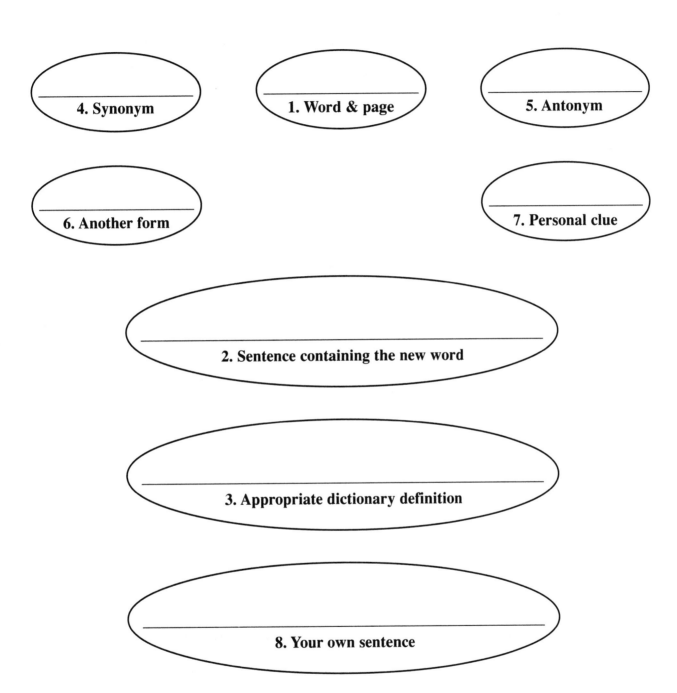

4. Synonym

1. Word & page

5. Antonym

6. Another form

7. Personal clue

2. Sentence containing the new word

3. Appropriate dictionary definition

8. Your own sentence

Based on Rosenbaum, C. (2001). A word map for middle school: A tool for effective vocabulary instruction. *Journal of Adolescent & Adult Literacy, 45,* 44–49.

From Susan Davis Lenski, Mary Ann Wham, and Jerry L. Johns, *Reading & Learning Strategies: Middle Grades through High School,* 2nd Edition. Copyright © 2003 by Kendall/Hunt Publishing Company (1-800-247-3458, ext. 4 or 5). May be reproduced for noncommercial educational purposes.

Section

3.3

Understanding Relationships Among Words

Goal To help students understand the relationships among words

BACKGROUND

The complexity of learning new words is compounded by the variety of word level knowledge that students bring with them to the classroom. Four different relationships representing four different levels of knowledge exist between words or concepts and students' schemata or background knowledge (Herber, 1978). These four relationships are known word/known concept, new word/known concept, known word/new concept, and new word/new concept.

In the first relationship, words represent a concept that students know and can explain. For example, when beginning a history unit on Native Americans in Crisis, many high school students are probably familiar with *Native Americans* and *crisis*. During instruction you will expand their knowledge base and refine these concepts for them.

In the second relationship, new word/known concept, the task is to apply new words to familiar concepts. For example, you might introduce words such as *mobility* and *assimilation*. These words may not be familiar in the context of Native Americans and crisis.

The third relationship requires students to learn a new concept but use a familiar word to describe or talk about it. For instance, the concept *counting coup* will probably be unfamiliar to students even though they may have some background information about tribal warfare.

The final kind of word-learning task is the most complex as it involves both new words and new concepts. You might focus on the Pacific Railroad Act of 1873 and the exodusters—African Americans who moved from the post-Reconstruction South to Kansas in large numbers. Students are unlikely to be familiar with either the word or the concept in this example.

There is a common thread running through all content subjects. All students need a variety of experiences in order to develop and enhance their vocabularies beyond specific content areas. The strategies in this section are designed to provide opportunities for students to use new words in meaningful contexts as they develop a deeper understanding of the relationships among words.

3.3

TEACHING STRATEGY 10

Semantic Feature Analysis

A Semantic Feature Analysis (Johnson & Pearson, 1984) is an effective strategy for helping students visualize the relationships among concepts. This activity helps students as they build bridges between new concepts and known concepts that are already part of their background knowledge. As students complete a Semantic Feature Analysis, they establish conceptual frameworks that help them understand the meanings of the words in new contexts. When students participate in this activity, they analyze words and concepts by identifying and comparing their various properties. Through the use of a matrix or a grid, students will be involved in developing their categorization skills as they determine the similarities and differences between related words. A Semantic Feature Analysis is designed to provide a systematic procedure for establishing categories and developing significant relationships among new words and concepts.

Directions and Example

1. Select a topic or category from your text that you want your students to analyze in some depth. Write the name of the topic on a chart, the chalkboard, or an overhead transparency. To demonstrate the Semantic Feature Analysis, use an example from your content area or use the following example. This particular example focuses on the topic of the art media used by a variety of artists.

2. List terms related to the topic down the left side of the grid. In this example, the names of the artists are listed.

3. List features or properties related to the topic across the top of the grid. In this example, types of art media are listed. The following example is from an art text.

Art Example

Semantic Feature Analysis
Art Media

Artists	print making	water-color	acrylic	oil	sculpture	charcoal
Mary Cassatt						
Henri de Toulouse-Lautrec						
Wassily Kandinsky						
Henri-Charles Manguin						
Georgia O'Keeffe						

4. Discuss each topic word as you read it aloud. Remind students of the definitions of the feature words written across the top of the grid, briefly discussing each one.

5. Guide your students through the matrix. Ask them to decide how each topic word relates to each feature on the top of the matrix. In this particular example, students are to decide if a listed artist used a particular medium. Ask students to place a plus (+) on the grid if the feature relates to a topic word, a minus (–) if it does not, and a question mark (?) if they are unsure.

6. After you have completed this initial phase of the Semantic Feature Analysis, direct students to read the appropriate chapter in their textbooks. In this example, students can also be encouraged to look for the names of additional artists and art media. As they do this, they will expand their vocabulary related to the subject and build their background knowledge.

7. Discuss the selection with the class and add their suggestions to the appropriate areas of the grid. Below is an example of a Semantic Feature Analysis based on a mathematics text.

Mathematics Example

Semantic Feature Analysis

Geometric Figures	Features			
	Convex	Exactly 4-Sided	Contains Right Angle	Contains Straight Line Segments
parallelogram	–	+	?	+
circle	+	–	–	–
obtuse triangle	+	–	–	+
polygon	?	?	?	+
quadrilateral	?	+	?	+
nonagon	?	–	?	+
acute triangle	+	–	–	+
right triangle	+	–	+	+

8. A blank Semantic Feature Analysis Chart follows.

Name _____ Date _____

SEMANTIC FEATURE ANALYSIS CHART

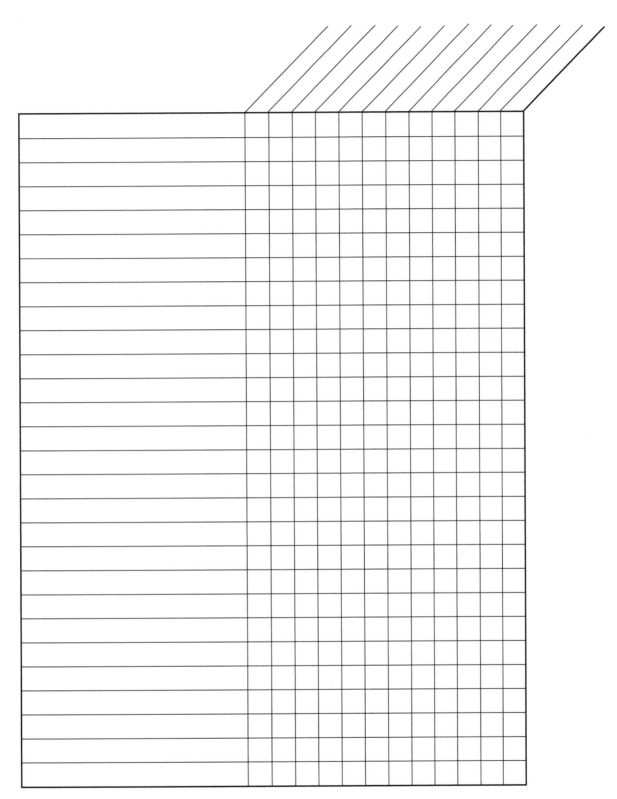

From Susan Davis Lenski, Mary Ann Wham, and Jerry L. Johns, *Reading & Learning Strategies: Middle Grades through High School,* 2nd Edition. Copyright © 2003 by Kendall/Hunt Publishing Company (1-800-247-3458, ext. 4 or 5). May be reproduced for noncommercial educational purposes.

3.3   **Word Sort**

A Word Sort (Gillet & Kita, 1979) requires students to organize and classify words based on their prior knowledge about the words. It is a simple activity that lends itself well to small group collaboration. The object of a Word Sort is to group words into categories according to some shared feature. Word Sorts can be conducted in two ways: closed and open. In a Closed Word Sort, the teacher predetermines the categories for the students and thus establishes the criterion that the words must have in common in order to form a group or category. In an Open Word Sort, there are no predetermined categories and thus no shared characteristics have been decided in advance. Students are asked to decide for themselves what the words have in common and to group them accordingly. Word Sorts can be used before reading as a predictive exercise or after reading as a way of extending understanding of the concepts (Vacca & Vacca, 2002).

Directions and Examples

1. Select 12 to 15 interesting words from a chapter in your content textbook. The words should be ones that you have determined are related to some of the important concepts in the chapter. Write the words on sets of note cards, on the chalkboard, or on an overhead transparency.

2. Divide the class into groups of three or four students. Tell the students that they are going to participate in a Closed Word Sort and are to sort the words according to the categories you have established. If using cards, distribute a set to each group. Use an example from your content area or use the following example from a biology text.

Biology Example

Closed Word Sort

Categories

Animalia	Plantae	Protista

Words to Sort

Animalia	Plantae	Protista
anemone	whisk fern	diatom
bobcat	paramecium	hornwort
horsetail	millipede	dinosaur
lady beetle	trypanosoma	planarian

3. Allow about 10 minutes for students to sort the words. Ask a student from each group to share one of their group's categories. Continue until all categories have been discussed. Invite students to explain why they sorted the words as they did.

4. To conduct an Open Word Sort, tell students to group the selected words into categories by looking for shared traits among them. The former example would be an Open Word Sort if the categories were omitted. In this case, students would need to establish their own categories for the words.

5. Following is an example of words for an Open Word Sort using terms selected from an accounting text.

Words to Sort

accountant	charter	manufacturing business
accounting clerk	corporation	merchandising business
accounting system	fiscal period	partnership
business entity	general bookkeeper	profit
capital	going concern	service business
certified public accountant	loss	sole proprietorship

6. After students have completed the Word Sort, invite a student to share one of the categories. An example follows.

Types of Businesses Operated for Profit

manufacturing business	partnership
merchandising business	sole proprietorship
service business	corporation

TEACHING STRATEGY 12

3.3 Magnet Words

Magnet Words, adapted from Magnet Summaries (Buehl, 2001), has students identify key vocabulary terms from a text selection. As students select their words, they are focusing on the main concepts presented in the chapter. Thus, students are provided with opportunities for enhancing two important skills: their understanding of key vocabulary terms and the relationship of the words to each other. Students work in small groups to identify the Magnet Words, which provides them with the chance to work collaboratively.

 ## Directions and Example

1. Use the idea of magnets as you introduce the concept of Magnet Words to your students. For example, make the following comments.

    Magnets attract metal objects and magnet words attract information or details to them. Look over your text assignment and see if you can identify some Magnet Words that the details in the passage "stick to." Most of the information in each section of your text will be connected to the Magnet Words in that section.

2. After students have completed reading a short selection of text, ask them to suggest possible Magnet Words from the text selection. Initially, students may need you to model selecting the Magnet Words from a selection.

3. Write the Magnet Words offered by your students on the chalkboard or an overhead transparency. The following words were taken from a world history text.

Nile River   pharaohs   society   religion

4. Distribute four note cards to each student and ask students to write one Magnet Word on each card.

5. Ask students to recall some important details from the passage related to each Magnet Word. Write these details beneath the appropriate Magnet Word. As you write them, ask students to follow the same procedure on the appropriate note card.

Nile River	Pharaohs	Society	Religion
shaped Egyptian life	Egyptian kings	nobles	maat
linked diverse lands	immortal	peasants	Osiris
fertile farming	pyramids	slaves	Akhenaton
	first illness		
	middle kingdom		
	second illness		

6. Divide the class into groups of three or four students of mixed ability. Ask students to record additional details from the passage related to each of the Magnet Words.

7. Model writing a short paragraph that incorporates a Magnet Word. Although additional details can be added from the text, students should be sure that the Magnet Word forms the structure of the paragraph. An example follows.

The Nile River shaped Egyptian life. It linked diverse lands from the highlands of eastern Africa to the Mediterranean Sea. The river brought water to Egypt from the distant mountains, plateaus, and lakes of central Africa. When the river receded each year in October, it left behind a rich, wet deposit of fertile black mud perfect for farming.

8. Ask each group of students to share a paragraph using a Magnet Word. Encourage class members to offer suggestions for effectively incorporating other words relating to the Magnet Word into the paragraph.

3.3 ▶ Word Analogies

Analogies provide students with the opportunity to establish relationships between familiar concepts and new ideas. For example, in social studies, students studying the culture of Mexico can compare it with the culture of the United States. Analogies promote creative and divergent thinking. Additionally, using analogies in your vocabulary instruction provides students with a powerful visual framework for comparing two relationships. There are many types of analogies you can use to help students understand the relationships among words. The following types of analogies are recommended for content area instruction (Vacca & Vacca, 1999).

TYPES OF ANALOGIES

Part to whole	battery : flashlight :: hard drive : computer
Cause and effect	fatigue : yawning :: itching : scratching
Person to situation	mother : home :: teacher : school
Synonym	obese : fat :: slender : thin
Antonym	poverty : wealth :: sickness : health
Geography	Chicago : Illinois :: Denver : Colorado
Measurement	pound : kilogram :: quart : liter
Time	March : Spring :: December : Winter

Directions and Example

1. Explain to students that analogies are a comparison of two similar concepts.

2. Model the reasoning process involved in completing an analogy, as some of your students may find this type of thinking difficult. For example, tell students that analogies are like mathematical equations; the sides are balanced. Provide the following sentence and explain to students that it contains an analogy.

   March is to Spring as December is to Winter.

3. Tell students that March is the beginning of springtime and December is the month when winter begins. Therefore, the relationship between March and Spring is similar to the relationship between December and Winter. Then, using colons, write the analogy on the chalkboard or an overhead transparency. Be sure that students understand that the single colon (:) stands for *is to,* and the double colon (::) stands for *as.*

4. Provide students with several other partially completed examples from the list above or use examples from your content area.

5. Encourage students to talk about the relationship in each pair and discuss the type of analogy it is. Model this procedure for them. For example, say the following: Pound is to kilogram as quart is to liter. Pounds and kilograms measure weight and quarts and liters measure capacity.

6. After students are comfortable with the concept of analogies, prepare an analogy exercise using material about which you wish to enhance the depth of their vocabulary and concept knowledge. The following example is from a biology text.

Biology Example

Word Analogies

Directions: See if you can complete the comparisons between a factory complex and a cell.

1. Computer center : product production :: _____ : protein production.
   (nucleus)

2. Electrical outlets and generators : factory energy :: _____ : cell energy.
   (mitochondria)

3. Machines : factory products :: protein synthesis : _____.
   (ribosomes)

4. Boxes : products :: cell packaging : _____.
   (golgi apparatus)

5. Garbage cans : factory garbage :: _____ : cell waste products.
   (lysosomes)

7. Invite students to construct their own analogies using additional material from the chapter.

3.3

TEACHING STRATEGY 14

Classifying Challenge

Classifying words is a thinking skill that supports students' use and exploration of word meanings (Graves, 1986). This strategy is designed to expand students' knowledge of the meanings of unknown words as well as to clarify their existing information about known words.

Directions and Example

1. Find one, two, or three words from your text that may be new to your students. Ideally, these words should be related to a text that students are currently reading or to a theme that is being explored in your classroom. For this example, the word *perpetuity* is used.

2. On small cards, print up to 10 synonyms or associations for each of the new words. These synonyms can be words, phrases, or associations that are familiar to students. Synonyms for *perpetuity* might include *everlastingness, constancy, eternity, infinity, time without end, deathlessness, immortality, and continuity.*

3. Introduce the new words to students by writing them in sentences on the chalkboard or an overhead transparency. A sentence using *perpetuity* could be: The *perpetuity* of public education is based on our country's belief that everyone has the right to be educated.

4. Using the context provided, encourage your students to discuss the meanings of the new words. After the discussion has been completed, provide students with an explicit definition of the new words. The explicit definition of *perpetuity* is time without end or the quality, state, or condition of being perpetual.

5. When the new words have been introduced in this fashion, write each of them at the top of the chalkboard or an overhead transparency as category headings.

6. Distribute the note cards containing the synonyms or phrases to the students. Ask them to discuss with a partner or in a small group the word category to which their synonym belongs. Invite students to come forward and write their synonym under the appropriate word category heading.

7. When all of the synonyms are placed in the appropriate categories, ask students to select one of the new words and write a short descriptive paragraph using as many of the synonyms under their chosen category word as they can. You might say the following to students. "What do the words in this category and its synonyms make you think of? Can you use these words to write a descriptive paragraph of that idea?"

Section

3.4 Developing Independence in Vocabulary Acquisition

Goal ▷ To help students develop independence by extending their knowledge of words

BACKGROUND

There are nearly 400,000 graphically distinct word types in books used in schools. This does not include proper names, of which there are an estimated 100,000 (Nagy & Anderson, 1984). It is estimated that students learn approximately 3,000 new words per year during their school years, and a high school senior's vocabulary contains approximately 40,000 words (Nagy & Herman, 1987). Clearly, the vocabulary learning challenge for students is extensive.

A goal in teaching any subject is for students to become independent learners and eventually assume responsibility for their own learning. However, this will not happen automatically. We must scaffold instruction so that students independently develop the ability to learn from texts and other sources. Scaffolding instruction involves supporting learners as they develop the ability to learn without us. We must provide the necessary support or scaffolds while students develop the confidence to learn independently. It is essential that students

develop the use of strategies that will provide them with the tools they need.

One way in which students learn new words is through using the context in which the word appears. Artley (1975) wrote that it is context, not the dictionary meaning, that gives each word its unique flavor. By teaching students to consider the context as they determine word meanings, you help them further develop their independent vocabulary strategies.

In order for students to develop independence as they increase their vocabularies, they should sometimes be allowed to select the words they wish to learn, define the words in their own terms, and engage in word play so that they gain an appreciation for a versatile vocabulary (Moore, Moore, Cunningham, & Cunningham, 1994). This section will present several strategies designed to assist students in developing independence in extending their word knowledge.

3.4 ▶ Vocabulary Self-Collection

Vocabulary Self-Collection (Haggard, 1986) is designed to promote growth in both the students' general vocabulary and content area vocabulary. This strategy facilitates long-term retention of words that are used in a variety of academic disciplines. Students work in teams to choose the vocabulary words they believe are important to the meaning of a text selection, thus expanding their vocabulary as they assume responsibility for their own learning.

Directions and Example

1. After students have completed reading and discussing an assigned text selection, divide the class into groups of three or four students. Ask students to go through the text selection and identify one word that they think should be studied further by the class. Encourage students to pick words they believe are important to understanding the content. Model the procedure by selecting a word and presenting it to the class.

2. Explain that each group is to choose an individual to present the selected word and its definition.

3. Write the word you selected and those selected by the students on the chalkboard or an overhead transparency. As you record each word, invite students to present its definition from its original context. Use the following example from a history text or an example from your textbook.

   conquistadors: Spanish explorers who claimed new colonies for Spain during the 16th century.

4. Discuss each word's meaning adding whatever information is necessary in order to clarify the definitions. Urge students to draw upon their prior knowledge as well as their textbooks as they verify their definitions. Use the following example as a guide.

   conquistadors: Spanish explorers who crossed the Atlantic to claim new colonies for Spain during the 16th century. They traveled first into the Caribbean islands and along the coasts of Central America and South America. Then they swept through Mexico and south to the tip of South America.

5. Complete the discussion and instruct students to review the list and eliminate words that are duplicates, words they already know, and words that they do not think are important to the comprehension of the text selection.

6. Ask students to define the remaining words and record them in their vocabulary journals or notebooks.

TECHNOLOGY

Thesaurus

Do you need a word? Use *Roget's Thesaurus.* Most of the words in the English language are listed, according to the ideas they express rather than in alphabetical order. You'll never again be at a loss for words.

T I P

www.thesaurus.com

TEACHING STRATEGY 16

3.4 ▸ Polar Opposites

Polar Opposites (Yopp & Yopp, 2001) is a strategy specifically designed to aid students in analyzing characters by studying the language used by poets. It can also be used effectively with prose selections. In this activity, students are asked to analyze characters by rating them on a variety of descriptive dimensions along three-, five-, or seven-point scales. The effectiveness of this strategy is increased when students are asked to justify their responses. In other words, students may not simply rate a character as "weak" rather than "strong"; they also must give reasons for their word choices and cite supporting incidents in the selection (Yopp & Yopp, 2001).

Directions and Example

1. Begin by choosing a character from a text selection students are currently reading. For example, you might use the poem "Sea Fever" by John Masefield. In this poem, a man wishes to return to the sea to experience the gray mist, the wind's song, and the gypsy life.

2. Develop a list of qualities or characteristics that describe this character. The words chosen to describe the character should specifically reflect the character's personality within the text selection. For "Sea Fever," appropriate words would include *yearning, adventuresome, determined, outdoorsman,* and *dreamer.*

3. Think of the opposite of each of the descriptive words. Opposites of these words might include *complacent, timid, reticent, couch potato,* and *realist.*

4. Develop a continuum for each pair of opposites. After students have read the selection, ask them to rate the character by placing a mark on each continuum. Nowhere in the poem does the author use the words that are on the continuum; therefore, students must think about the author's intended meaning when choosing a location on the continuum. Students' responses will vary depending on their impressions of the character. Their choices will contribute to a lively discussion of word meanings and poetic language!

5. A blank Polar Opposites sheet follows.

Literature Example

The author of "Sea Fever" is:

yearning					complacent
adventuresome					timid
determined					reticent
outdoorsman					couch potato
dreamer					realist

Polar Opposites

Characteristics		Characteristics

1. _____ ___|___|___|___|___ _____

2. _____ ___|___|___|___|___ _____

3. _____ ___|___|___|___|___ _____

4. _____ ___|___|___|___|___ _____

5. _____ ___|___|___|___|___ _____

6. _____ ___|___|___|___|___ _____

7. _____ ___|___|___|___|___ _____

8. _____ ___|___|___|___|___ _____

9. _____ ___|___|___|___|___ _____

10. _____ ___|___|___|___|___ _____

Based on Yopp, R.H., & Yopp, H.K. (2001). *Literature-based reading activities* (3rd ed.). Boston: Allyn and Bacon.

3.4 TOAST

Dana and Rodriguez (1992) developed TOAST to provide students with a system for studying vocabulary independently. TOAST is an acronym for Test, Organize, Anchor, Say, and Test. This strategy provides students with the opportunity to learn at their own rate and to choose words to study that seem particularly difficult for them.

 ## Directions and Example

1. **TEST.** After students have completed reading a text selection, choose some words or phrases that you would like them to learn in order to facilitate their understanding of the material. Ask students to make up a set of vocabulary cards that will contain the vocabulary word on one side and the definition and a sentence using the word on the other side. A word from a math text that is important for understanding might be *probability*. It is defined as the likelihood of the occurrence of a specific event. A sentence containing the word follows. In all *probability*, we will have a math quiz on Friday. As a test, students are to examine each word, attempt to define it, and use it in a sentence. They can check for understanding by reading the other side of the card.

2. **ORGANIZE.** Direct students to organize their vocabulary words into categories that will enhance their ability to remember the words and their meanings. For example, students might choose to organize their words semantically or place them into categories based on structural similarities. *Probability*, the sample word, might be placed with other words ending in *-ility,* such as *reliability*.

3. **ANCHOR.** At this point, it is necessary for students to devise some strategy for anchoring the vocabulary words and their meanings into their long-term memories. There are a variety of ways to achieve this goal. Students might choose to work with a partner to teach and test each other, or they might use a tape recorder to tape, listen to, and recite definitions. Another effective tool is to try to find a word that will act as a mnemonic link to the vocabulary word. Perhaps linking the word *probability* to the word *probably* would provide a mnemonic link for this word.

4. **SAY.** This section provides the review component of the procedure. A periodic review of the words is necessary in order not to forget them. Dana and Rodriguez (1992) suggest that students review the words and their definitions 5 to 10 minutes after learning the words, a week later, and once again at a later date.

5. **TEST.** Students should conduct a posttest when they have completed each review, in order to determine their success in learning the words. It can be done in the same way as was the pretest.

6. Encourage students to become familiar with this strategy so that they will use it independently to strengthen their vocabulary knowledge.

Notes and Favorite Strategies

Chapter 4

WORD STUDY

OVERVIEW

Word study is often neglected in content area instruction. Ivey and Broaddus (2001) observed that middle school students with limited word analysis skills rarely get the help they need. In addition, data from the National Assessment of Educational Progress (NAEP) (1997) revealed that approximately 25% of eighth and twelfth graders in the United States were reading below the basic level. As one content area teacher observed, "It's tough for students to comprehend the text when they don't know the words."

Graves (2000) identifies three word-study strategies that are worthwhile teaching: context, word parts, and the dictionary. We will broaden these three areas a bit in this chapter to include foreign words and phrases, glossaries, and in-text aids (e.g., word pronunciations and word meanings in footnotes).

Effective instruction in word study should be based on the following general approach. First, create an awareness of the strategy and help students understand how learning and using the strategy will make them better readers. For example, you should help students understand what context is in a broad sense (e.g., their school, a golf course) and then link it to context as it applies to reading traditional and electronic texts.

Second, define the strategy and model its use. Be alert for how you can use your content area texts and related resources to show students how the strategy can be implemented. You might also be on the lookout for examples in your daily reading that you can model and share with students. It is important to help students understand that the strategies are used in a variety of situations. One effective modeling strategy is to think aloud as you work out the pronunciation of a word or use context to try to determine the meaning of an unknown word.

Third, provide practice in the use of the strategy, preferably by using materials from your content area as well as other experiences that are particularly meaningful for students. For example, if word parts are being presented (e.g., prefixes and root words), reference could be made to what typically occurs in a movie theatre before the main feature (previews).

Finally, invite students to apply the strategy in an authentic reading situation. You may want to alert students by saying something like the following. "When you read pages 243–248 in your text, there are at least 22 words containing prefixes. Remember what you have been learning about prefixes and use that knowledge to help pronounce those words and use the meanings of the prefixes to help you predict the meanings of the words if they are unknown to you."

Rarely are effective lessons on word study one-shot approaches. Instruction may not be particularly lengthy, but it could take place one or two days a week over the course of several weeks, a semester, or the entire school year. Although word study is a foundation for effective reading, developing the strategic behavior necessary for students to generalize and apply what was taught is a major challenge. One way to help students is with verbal prompts and occasionally completing part of the task for them. Gradually, reduce your involvement and have students assume greater responsibility.

Teachers who integrate the above characteristics into carefully developed and powerful lessons on word study will help students become better readers. The essential ingredient is to prioritize the class period so instruction of this sort can become a reality.

Using Context

Goal — To help students use context to anticipate known words and to predict meanings of unknown words

BACKGROUND

There are two major uses of context in reading. One is using the words in a sentence to predict the next _____ (word). By the middle grades, this strategy may be understood and used by students. Use of this strategy while reading often enables students to predict the next word, sometimes before they turn the page in a text. The second major use of context is to predict meanings of words. There are times when the words near an unfamiliar word will provide clues to the unfamiliar word's meaning. The strategies in this section will help students learn to apply these two major uses of context.

TEACHING STRATEGY 1

4.1 ▶ Anticipating Known Words

The student can sometimes use the other words in a sentence to predict an upcoming word. The process may be very natural for some students and unfamiliar to others. Using cues within the text to read fluently and anticipate words is a hallmark of efficient and effective readers. The following strategy represents one way to sensitize students to this important cueing system.

 ## Directions and Examples

1. Begin a discussion with students about the meaning of context. Explore students' perceptions of the word. One student might say that context refers to the circumstances or situations within which something happens. Invite students to suggest some of these situations and list them on the chalkboard or an overhead transparency. Some possible areas follow.

   football game   movie
   pep rally   assembly
   field trip   eating out

2. Select one of the areas and have students describe the context. A football game, for example, would take place on the school grounds and would involve players, officials, spectators, refreshment stands, a band, cheerleaders, and a playing field. Discuss the context in some detail.

3. Use the discussion to present some oral sentences to students and see if they can use their knowledge to fill in missing words. Some possible oral sentences follow.

> The football players on the opposing team were dressed in blue and white _____. (uniforms)
>
> My friends and I sat in the _____. (stands, bleachers, stadium)
>
> At halftime, the _____ played. (band)
>
> My friend Cote plays a _____ in the band. (any of several musical instruments)
>
> When our team scored a touchdown, the crowd _____. (cheered, yelled, screamed, etc.)

4. Take time to discuss the words suggested by students. When more than one word is suggested, discuss whether the words make sense in the context. Help students understand that they are using their knowledge and background experiences to predict words that would make sense in the context of the sentence.

5. Shift the discussion to text and help students understand that they can also use the context of the sentence to predict words that make sense. Stress that good readers make use of context in this way. Several examples from different content areas are provided below.

> The Bedouins live in the Middle _____. (East)
>
> Life in the village revolves around the care of the cattle and other _____. (animals)
>
> The countries of Kenya and Tanzania are located in eastern _____. (Africa)
>
> The animal kingdom can be divided into approximately 20 major _____. (groups)
>
> Roberto Clemente was the first Hispanic player to be elected to the Baseball Hall of _____. (Fame)
>
> Modern society has _____ greatly affected these proud and noble people. (not)
>
> There are three types of _____ vessels in the human circulatory system. (blood)
>
> With each contraction or _____, the heart moves blood throughout the body. (beat)
>
> In a normal adult, the _____ beats about 70 times a minute. (heart)

TECHNOLOGY

T
I
P

Word Connections

Use this list of connections to find various links to word sources on the Internet.

www.lexfiles.com/index-connections

TEACHING STRATEGY 2

4.1   Predicting Words

Predicting Words builds upon the previous strategy and focuses more specifically on texts used in the various content areas. This strategy makes use of modeling and helps students realize the importance of their previous experiences in making predictions about words in text.

Directions and Examples

1. Use this strategy after your students have a general understanding of context developed in Teaching Strategy 1.

2. Tell students that you want to help them understand how to use context cues in their reading to predict words that they already know. Briefly review the students' general understanding of context and how it relates to their lives. Then focus on context as it applies to reading. You might use a personal example or say something like the following.

> Context refers to the environment in which a word is found. For example, the word *STOP* can appear on a sign near a traffic intersection. You can also use context to read the word missing from this traffic sign: *DO NOT _____ (PASS)*. When reading a book or words from a computer screen, the words appear in context. The context is the other words around a particular word.

> When I read, I can sometimes use the context to predict a word. For example, just the other day, I was reading about federal taxes. One of the sentences I began reading was that the federal government sends an income tax (and then I had to turn the page to continue with the text). But before I turned the page, I had already predicted the next word would probably be *form*. I turned the page and, sure enough, I was right. What I saw was the word I had predicted.

> I can also use the other words in a sentence to help me predict words that make sense that are on the same page as the sentence. In that same article about taxes, a sentence began, *Send in any payments due no later than. . . .* I was able to predict that *April 15* would complete the sentence. I was correct. Although I may not always be right, I can use

context to help me predict words that make sense. The words I predicted in these cases are words I know and understand.

3. Invite students to share instances where they have used context to predict a word. One student might share how she used the context to figure out a word in a handwritten note from a friend. Another student might share how he was able to predict a word before turning the page in a novel he was reading.

4. Shift the discussion to your content area and provide written examples on an overhead transparency. Invite students to predict the covered word in each sentence. Write students' predictions on the chalkboard or an overhead transparency. Discuss the predictions and the reasons supporting them. Then uncover the word and have students compare their predictions to the word used in the text. Take time for students to discuss their predictions, especially those that differ from the text. In the first example below, *employment* could also be a suitable word—even though the author did not use it. The discussion should lead to an understanding that some words make sense even if they do not match the word used by the author. Other words suggested by students may be off target. It is important that students share their thinking. Stress that predictions may not always be accurate, but the more that is known about a topic, the greater the likelihood for more accurate predictions. Some possible sentences from different content areas appear below.

The United States' labor force refers to the number of people over 16 who are employed or who are actively seeking _____. (work) [Employment is another word that makes sense.]

Careers in the life sciences can be divided into two professions: _____ and _____. (biology, health) [Only these two words fit in the text consulted.]

Probability is the _____ that something will happen or not happen. (chance) [Possibility and likelihood are other words that make sense.]

How the Gray Panthers started is an _____ story. (interesting) [Entertaining is another word that makes sense.]

A French word that means "summary" of your job qualifications is _____. (résumé) [No other word fits this context.]

Ray gazed down the long _____ towards his locker. (corridor) [Hall and hallway also make sense.]

5. Extend students' understanding by sharing actual examples from your own reading to help them realize that good readers use this strategy. Encourage students to write down examples from their reading and share them with classmates at a designated time. Encourage discussion.

4.1 ▶ Cloze

Cloze refers to sentences or passages containing word deletions in which lines are substituted for words. Students are asked to supply the missing words using context and syntactic clues. Baker and Brown (1984) note that better readers perform at higher levels on Cloze tasks than younger and poorer readers (including students in middle and high schools). Cloze can be used in at least three ways as a teaching technique: 1) a line of standard length is used for each word deleted; 2) lines of various lengths are used to reflect the length of the actual word; and 3) one or more letters of the word are included to provide information about the specific word deleted.

⟵⊕⟶ Directions and Examples

1. Decide which of the Cloze strategies or combination of strategies you will use with students. You might initially select easier deletion patterns using your text or the example below.

   Most reptiles are covered with hard _____ or plates. Some live on land, and some live in _____. All breathe by means of _____. The loggerhead turtle, _____ example, can spend long periods under w_____ before coming _____ for _____.

2. Write the example on the chalkboard or use an overhead transparency with the text enlarged. Invite students to read the text selection silently and try to predict the missing words.

3. After students have read the selection, proceed with one sentence at a time. For the first sentence, invite students to share their predictions. Write their predictions on the chalkboard or an overhead transparency. Be sure to have students share reasons for their predictions. You might ask questions like the following ones.

   - Why did you choose that word?
   - Did any other words in the sentence help you?
   - What did you already know about the topic that may have been useful?
   - Were there any other words you considered initially? What caused you to abandon those words?

4. After several predictions have been shared, have students predict which of the words was used in the first sentence by the author. Then share the actual word (*scales*) and have students reflect on their predictions. Guide students in evaluating their words, so they can determine whether their words were close to the author's word in meaning. Point out any word that is the wrong part of speech or doesn't make sense.

5. Continue with the remaining sentences, using a similar approach. The author's words are *water, lungs, for, water, up,* and *air*. If there is full agreement on a particular word, have a volunteer explain how the context, the length of the line, or a letter helped to predict that particular word.

6. Make the point that good readers use the context, the length of the word, the sense of the sentence, the cues offered by letters, and their background knowledge to help predict words.

7. Invite students to make a short Cloze activity from their text and share it with a partner who makes predictions for the missing words. After discussion, have the students switch roles and repeat the process.

8. Use Cloze from time to time with texts to sharpen students' ability to use context for prediction. Another sample passage is provided below.

> The class Mammalia includes hairy, intelligent, _____-blooded vertebrates. The females have mammary glands that produce m_____ for their y_____g. Mammals _____ two pairs of l_____ and breathe by means of _____. [The author's words are *warm, milk, young, have, limbs,* and *lungs.*]

TECHNOLOGY

T I P

Creating Cloze Exercises

Learn how to make Cloze activities.

www.auburn.edu/~mitrege/knowledge/cloze.html

4.1

TEACHING STRATEGY 4

Predicting Meanings

Predicting Meanings refers to using context to determine the meaning of a word whose meaning is unknown. It is commonly agreed that context determines the meaning of a specific word. But how often does context reveal the meaning of an unknown word to the reader? The answer is that "context reveals meaning far less frequently than has commonly been supposed" (Deighton, 1959, p. 2). The box that follows (based on Deighton, 1959) contains some guidelines to keep in mind, as you develop this strategy with students.

GUIDELINES FOR USING CONTEXT TO REVEAL MEANING

1.   Context reveals meaning for unfamiliar words less often than is commonly supposed.
2.   The experience of the student impacts how well the context is used.
3.   Vocabulary growth through context is a gradual matter.

The above guidelines suggest that you will need to help students learn the common patterns for how context operates (see bulleted list below) and demonstrate to students how they work in text materials used in your content area. Such efforts should help students become more perceptive readers who are able to use this strategy on their own.

 ## Directions and Examples

1.   Context can reveal meaning in a variety of ways. We recommend that you develop separate or unified lessons for each of the following ways that context can reveal meanings for unknown words.

- Definition—an outright definition is provided.
  Lincoln used the word *score* in the Gettysburg Address. *Score* refers to a time period of 20 years.
- Example—examples are cited. The examples often use signal words such as the following ones: *such as, such, like, especially, for example, other, this* or *these* (followed by a synonym), *the way,* or *in that way that* (Deighton, 1959).
  Do you take your hands and arms for granted? If so, you probably never considered just how much these [signal word] *organs* make you different from the typical animal.
- Modifiers—phrases, clauses, or single words. Sometimes the modifier "appears after a linking verb in the position of a predicate adjective" (Deighton, 1959, p. 7).
  She was *consolidating* her gains, making secure her position before moving ahead.
- Restatement—signal words *(that is,* or with a synonym, *in other words, to put it another way, what this means, which is to say)* or mechanical devices (a dash, i.e., parenthetical expressions).
  It is not uncommon for scientists to make a *hypothesis* (a sort of guess) about how to explain an unusual occurrence.
- Appositive—"the unfamiliar word is separated only by commas from the word or phrase which illuminates it" (Deighton, 1959, p. 8).
  A majority of the committee was against the bill so it was pigeonholed, *put aside to be forgotten,* as the committee moved on to another bill.
- Inference—the student must make connections that are not specifically stated. This ability requires an attentive reader who has been taught to look for clues not specifically stated, such as "a sentence that restates a thought or provides an example without use of signal words" (Deighton, 1959, pp. 10–11). In such instances, the student must become a detective of sorts who gathers details, perceives relationships, and makes connections to construct meaning for a particular word.

2. Tell students that they will be learning how context can be used to help determine meanings of unfamiliar words. You might begin with a straightforward example from your content area or use the following example.

> Context refers to the words around a particular word. If the meaning of a word is unknown to you, sometimes the context can help you predict, or guess, the meaning of the word. Context won't work every time, but it is one strategy that you can try. Let's see what you can do with this example.

> In the kitchen there were quarts of almonds, dozens of oranges, pounds of raisins, stacks of biffins, and soup plates full of nuts.

3. Write the above sentence on the chalkboard or an overhead transparency. Have students read the sentence to themselves. Then ask if any words are unfamiliar. It is likely that the word *biffins* will be identified as an unfamiliar word. You might then make the following comments.

> Who can pronounce the word I've underlined? [Call on a volunteer to pronounce the word.] Yes, the word is pronounced *biffins,* but who knows what it means? Can you use the other words around the word to make a prediction or guess about the meaning of the word?

4. Invite students to work briefly with a partner to share their ideas. Then have the entire class share. Possible typical comments from students are presented below.

Sophia: I think the word means some type of food.

Teacher: What makes you think so?

Sophia: Well, there are other foods mentioned in the sentence, and it seems like biffins would also be a food.

Zack: I agree and I think biffins are biscuits.

Teacher: Thanks, Zack, for sharing your idea. Sophia, I just want to point out that you realized that the other items were foods, and you inferred or guessed that biffins would also be a food. Does the context make the meaning of biffins clear?

Zack: I don't think so, but I think buffins are like biscuits. I really don't know, but biffins make me think of biscuits.

Teacher: What do some of the rest of you think? [Other students name various foods. Then the teacher may comment as follows.]

Teacher: We all agree that the word biffins likely refers to something that can be eaten. That knowledge may be sufficient for now but suppose we wanted to be sure?

Josh: You could tell us or we could look up the word in a dictionary.

Teacher: I really don't know what the word means. I guess we'd better look up biffins, if we want to know what the word means.

5. In subsequent lessons, present some of the other ways context can be used to help determine the meanings of unfamiliar words. A few sentences from various content areas are presented below for possible use in such lessons.

> "Here I am, sir!" shouted Mark, suddenly replying from the edge of the quay and leaping at a bound on board the ship.

> The group was very loquacious; they talked incessantly.

> The pocket-handkerchief was taken in and out of the flat reticule at least a dozen times. The woman seemed very nervous.

> Most computers are digital computers, which means that before information goes into the computer it is changed into a code in which groups of digits stand for letters, symbols, and numbers.

> The main component of a computer is a CPU, or central processing unit. It is in the CPU that information and instructions are stored and processed.

> An atlas contains many different kinds of maps.

> In the submarine view port, I could make out the seabed, a rough terrain of deep cracks and giant boulders.

> The submarine edged out of the fissure. (probably no help or limited help from context)

> A bunch of freshly picked kingcups was put in a vase on the dining room table.

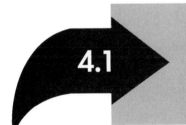

TEACHING STRATEGY 5

4.1 Predictions, Definitions, and Connections

Predictions, Definitions, and Connections invites students to identify an unfamiliar word, place it in context, predict one or more possible definitions of the word, determine the actual definition, and then connect the word to content areas and personal experiences. The strategy encourages students to actively work among themselves to arrive at a definition and make connections.

Directions and Example

1. Identify an important term or concept from your text that is likely to be unfamiliar to students. You could also use the example from social studies that follows.

2. Tell students that you will share a strategy to help them learn the meanings of unfamiliar words and link them to their experiences. Distribute copies of the Predictions, Definitions, and Connections sheet. You might make the following comments.

> I have selected a word from our text that may be unfamiliar to you. I'll write the word on the chalkboard (or overhead transparency), and you write it on your sheet in the proper box. Now turn to page 184 in your text and find the section titled "Statehood at Last" in bold print. Go to the second paragraph in that section and you will find the word. Please write the sentence containing the word in the second box on your sheet. When you have finished, work with two classmates sitting near you and write some possible definitions of the word based on the context of the sentence or your experiences. Your predictions may be right or wrong—what's important is that you make predictions.

3. Give students a few minutes to share their ideas and to write possible definitions. Then have students share some of their ideas with the entire class. As ideas are shared, write predicted definitions on the chalkboard or an overhead transparency. Encourage students to look for commonalties among the definitions. It is possible that an actual definition might emerge from the discussion. It might also be necessary to look up the word in a dictionary or glossary. Through discussion and reference sources, help students arrive at the actual meaning of the word in that context. Students should write the definition in the appropriate box on their sheets. Be sure that students understand how the word is pronounced.

4. Ask students to complete the remaining two boxes by making connections to other content areas and to their lives. Then give students an opportunity to share their connections in small groups or with the entire class. Be sure you help make connections to other content areas when appropriate.

5. Have students add the completed sheet to their word study folder. Use the Predictions, Definitions, and Connections sheet from time to time with guidance. You can also provide blank copies of the sheet for students to complete independently while reading a text selection. Remember to provide time for students to discuss and share their work.

6. An example from social studies and a blank Predictions, Definitions, and Connections sheet follow.

Predictions, Definitions, and Connections

Unfamiliar Word

repudiated

Sentence Containing Unfamiliar Word

Congress repudiated the Alaska Statehood Bill several times during the period between 1916 and 1957.

Predicted Definitions Based on Sentence Context/Experiences

1. *refused*
2. *failed to act on*
3. *did not pass*

Actual Definition/Meaning

to reject or refuse to recognize

Connections to Content Areas

1. *In a novel one character repudiated another.*
2.

Personal Connections

Sometimes my parents repudiate my behavior.

Name _____ Date _____

Predictions, Definitions, and Connections

Unfamiliar Word

_____

Sentence Containing Unfamiliar Word

_____
_____
_____

Predicted Definitions Based on Sentence Context/Experiences

1. _____
2. _____
3. _____

Actual Definition/Meaning

_____
_____

Connections to Content Areas

1. _____
2. _____

Personal Connections

_____
_____

4.1 ▶ Contextual Redefinition

Contextual Redefinition (Readence, Bean, & Baldwin, 2001) is a strategy designed to assist students as they use context to determine the meanings of unknown words. Contextual Redefinition stresses the necessity for using syntax or word order in predicting word meanings and making informed decisions about an author's intent. When using this strategy, students have another method for developing independence in their reading.

Directions and Example

1. Identify several words in conjunction with a reading assignment. Select words that students must understand in order to adequately comprehend the text selection. Use an example from your content area or the following example. The following words have been selected from a world history text.

utopia	Huguenot
Reformation	theocracy
predestination	geocentric theory

2. Using the chalkboard or an overhead transparency, present the words in isolation, pronounce them, and ask students to provide a definition for each word.

3. As students present their definitions, they should try to provide a rationale for their thinking. Although trying to determine meaning without context seems to be counterproductive in teaching the strategy, this particular activity demonstrates the difficulty in determining the meanings of words presented in isolation. Record the definitions given by students. For example, one student might use the following definition.

   A utopia is like the perfect place to be. I read about a place that was supposed to be like that in *The Giver.*

4. After all of the definitions have been recorded, present the words in the sentences taken from the textbook or in the sentences you have constructed. Use the textbook sentences if they present the words in a manner that provides information for determining their meanings. Otherwise, create your own sentences. An example follows.

   Utopia was an imaginary perfect society.

   The *Reformation,* a religious crisis in the Roman Catholic Church, was started by Martin Luther.

   John Calvin's *predestination* doctrine stated that God has known since the beginning of time who will be saved.

   Calvin hoped for a *theocracy,* a government controlled by church leaders.

   Geocentric theory, or earth-centered theory, was defended by Aristotle.

5. Once again, ask students to provide definitions for the selected words. As students determine the words' meanings, they should use the context in which the words are presented. Students should provide a rationale for their definitions. A possible explanation follows.

    Predestination means that your path in life is set at the time you're born. That would fit Calvin's beliefs about everything being set since the beginning of time.

6. Have students use their dictionaries in order to confirm the definitions constructed using context clues. Students should share the dictionary meanings with the entire class and compare them with their own definitions. Point out to students that the quality of their definitions should increase from their initial encounter with the words in isolation to their use of context in determining their meanings.

Decoding and Meaning

Section

4.2

Goal To aid students in decoding words and using word parts to help construct meaning

BACKGROUND

Lewkowicz (2000) notes that the lack of decoding skills can be a serious handicap for older students and that teachers need to assume greater responsibility for identifying students who have decoding problems and providing help. Words are the catalysts that stimulate students' backgrounds so they can construct meaning from texts. The heavy vocabulary and concept load in the content areas means that teachers must devote special attention to the intentional and systematic learning of strategies that help students pronounce words and use word parts, when possible, to help them understand what the words mean. Johns and Lenski (2001) have provided a variety of foundational strategies to build essential phonics skills for readers who lack the most basic word skills. In this section, attention will be focused on promoting fluency and working with longer words. The intent is to help students acquire strategies for decoding longer words and using word parts (such as prefixes and suffixes) to help construct meaning. Attention is also given to some foreign words and phrases that appear in selected content area texts.

TEACHING STRATEGY 7

4.2 Repeated Readings

Repeated Readings is a strategy designed to help students develop fluency in word identification. Since its beginnings (Samuels, 1979), it has helped middle-grade students as well as second graders through college freshmen in regular, "remedial," and special education settings. Improvements in word accuracy, speed of word recognition, and comprehension have been documented, and the improvements appear to transfer from practiced passages to reading of new material (Dowhower, 1989). The version described here was initially developed for use with seventh- and eighth-grade students working in pairs (Ferroli, Beaver, Hagan, & Moriarty, 2000).

Directions and Example

1. Explain to students that they will be reading and rereading some portions of their books in a timed manner. This timed reading will help them increase their word accuracy, speed, and comprehension. (Note: While increasing rate is a by-product of word accuracy and not the primary goal of repeated readings, students, especially readers who struggle, enjoy the idea of speed reading.)

2. Explain the Repeated Readings Record Sheet (Ferroli, Beaver, Hagan, & Moriarty, 2000) to students. The numbered steps enable the students to independently complete the activities, after just a brief explanation and demonstration.

3. Show students that they will be timing one another in steps 2, 3, 5, 6, 8, and 9. The timing works well when the partner who is to read declares "ready," and the listening partner is taught to say "go" when the second hand of a wall clock or watch reaches the 12. Stopwatches, of course, make this step even easier.

4. Explain that in steps 4 and 7 listeners will write about what their partners have read. The explanation might go as follows.

    The sentences you write might be a simple summary of what you heard. This step helps you to follow your partner's story. On the other hand, you might want to express an opinion about or a personal reaction to your partner's passage. Tell what you like or don't like or what it makes you think of. Remember as you write that you are writing about the book or passage; you are not commenting on your partner's reading accuracy or rate.

5. Point out that in step 10 students read to themselves for the first time. No timer is used here. This final writing in step 10 is about their own passage. Some students are tempted to write step 10 without first doing the silent reading as they have read the passage three times already. Encourage students to enjoy the speed and ease of the fourth reading and to see completing the Repeated Readings Record Sheet as involving four readings and three writings.

6. Help students understand that the optional lines for vocabulary at the end of step 10 are intended to encourage readers to be alert for challenging words.

7. Assist students with text selections for the repeated readings activity. They should choose books of personal interest. The ideal selections are books they are reading for other purposes (e.g., the class novel, their own recreational reading, even content area texts). Choosing passages from those longer texts works nicely. It is important that partners do not read the same passages for repeated readings so that there is no direct comparison. Competing with another student rather than trying to increase one's own rate and accuracy misses the point of self-improvement.

8. Teach students to count passages of 200 to 250 words for step one. (Counting two words at a time helps.) The segments should begin and end with whole paragraphs. Students become adept at estimating 200 words after a few cycles through the Repeated Readings Record Sheet. This estimation procedure is acceptable so long as students understand that they can only compare themselves on a single passage and not across passages of different lengths. Four readings of passages of this length as one proceeds through the Repeated Readings Record Sheet will normally take about two-thirds of a 45-minute class period. The remaining time may be spent in a reading workshop or in voluntary reading.

Name _____ Date _____

Repeated Readings Record Sheet

Step 1 Both partners choose passages of about 200 words.

Step 2

Partner A	Partner B
Reads aloud—first reading	Times Partner A and listens.
Your time: _____	

Step 3

Partner A	Partner B
Times Partner B and listens.	Reads aloud—first reading
	Your time:_____

Step 4 Write one or two sentences about what your partner read.

_____

_____

_____

Step 5

Partner A	Partner B
Reads aloud—second reading	Times Partner A and listens.
Your time: _____	

Step 6

Partner A	Partner B
Times Partner B and listens.	Reads aloud—second reading
	Your time: _____

Based on Ferroli, L., Beaver, K., Hagan, R., & Moriarty, A. (2000, March). *Interventions for getting middle school readers caught up*. Presentation at the Illinois Reading Conference. Springfield, IL.

Step 7 Write one or two sentences about what your partner read.

_____

_____

_____

Step 8

Partner A   Partner B

Reads aloud—third reading   Times Partner A and listens.

Your time: _____

Step 9

Partner A   Partner B

Times Partner B and listens.   Reads aloud—third reading

                                                 Your time: _____

Step 10 Read your passage silently (fourth reading) and write two sentences about what you read.

_____

_____

_____

Write two challenging words from your reading.

1. _____   2. _____

Based on Ferroli, L., Beaver, K., Hagan, R., & Moriarty, A. (2000, March). _Interventions for getting middle school readers caught up_. Presentation at the Illinois Reading Conference. Springfield, IL.

4.2 ▸ Two Questions

Two Questions (Cunningham, 2000a) helps sensitize students to pronouncing words, spelling words, and seeing possible relationships between the key word in the lesson and other words in their listening vocabularies. Cunningham (2000a, p. 288) says that the two questions "could be used by any teacher in any subject area" from fourth grade through high school. The two basic questions follow.

Do I know any other words that look and sound like this word?
Are any of these look-alike/sound-alike words related to each other?

Directions and Example

1. Write the first question on the chalkboard or on an overhead transparency. Then write the key word that is being introduced. Use an example from your content area or the following example, adapted from Cunningham (2000a), from a mathematics text.

   equation

2. Direct students' attention to the word *equation* and use examples to build meaning for the concept. You might explain as follows.

   An equation is divided into two parts. One part is to the left of the equal sign. The other part is to the right of the equal sign. If the equation is correct, both sides are equal. A simple equation is 2+3=5. Give me some other examples of equations.

3. After students have provided several examples, have students pronounce *equation*. Then invite students to share any words they know that look and sound like *equation*. Write the words on the chalkboard or an overhead transparency as students share them. Be sure to underline the word parts that are the same. Have students pronounce the words, emphasizing the part that is pronounced the same as *equation*. Several examples are provided below.

<u>equa</u>te	addi<u>tion</u>
<u>equa</u>l	vaca<u>tion</u>
<u>equa</u>tor	multiplica<u>tion</u>
<u>equa</u>lize	subtrac<u>tion</u>
constitu<u>tion</u>	sensa<u>tion</u>
na<u>tion</u>	

4. Refer to the question on the chalkboard or the overhead transparency: Do I know any other words that look and sound like this word? Have a student read the question. Then help students understand that thinking of words that look and sound the same as a new word may aid in pronouncing and spelling the new word. Model as necessary, using appropriate words shared by students. Add additional words as needed. The *equa* and *tion* from the other known words are clues that can be used to help pronounce *equation*.

5. Direct students' attention to the second question: Are any of these look-alike/sound-alike words related to each other? Cunningham (2000a, p. 289) suggests taking sufficient time to help students understand that "words, like people, sometimes look and sound alike but are not related." Use examples from students (like hair color, eyes, and height) to help students understand that some people look alike but are not related. Other people look alike and are related. The analogy to people in families may be useful. In Cunningham's words (2000a, p. 289):

> Not all people who look alike are related but some are. This is how words work. Words are related if there is something about their meaning that is the same. After we find look-alike, sound-alike words that will help us spell and pronounce new words, we try to think of any way these words might be related in the same meaning family.

6. Guide students to understand that the words in the first column are related because of the meaning of *equa* in each of the words. You might explain in the following manner.

> *Equate* means to make equal. *Equator*, an imaginary line, divides our earth into two equal halves: the Northern Hemisphere and the Southern Hemisphere (demonstrate with a globe). *Equalize* means to make equal, like when we balance teams so there are the same number of players on each side. An *equation* is also balanced on each side of the equal sign. When words are related to each other, we get clues as to what they mean.

7. You might also present students with *sequel*. Explain that the word looks like it is related in meaning to the other words but it is not. If necessary, share the definition of *sequel* (something that follows; a continuation of an earlier movie or literary work). Note that recognizing *equal* in *sequel* is an answer to the first question and that realization can help with the pronunciation of *sequel*.

8. Post the two questions on a chart in the classroom, so students can use the questions to help them decode new words. Use the Two Questions strategy in an intentional manner to help students internalize the power of patterns and chunking to pronounce words and get possible clues to their meanings.

4.2 ▶ Compare-Contrast Procedure
TEACHING STRATEGY 9

Teachers of upper-grade readers necessarily concern themselves with helping students to improve vocabulary, comprehension, reading rate, literary appreciation, and study strategies. Some students, however, still need assistance in developing proficiency in word analysis—the ability to work out the pronunciation of longer words. The compare-contrast procedure provides students with a strategy for figuring out multisyllabic words by searching for letter patterns that are easily recognizable. It uses neither "rules" nor syllabication jargon; moreover, it is based on an understanding of what proficient readers really do when they encounter words that require some degree of word analysis. Originally used in a small group setting (Cunningham, 1978), this adaptation was developed for use with seventh and eighth graders in a whole class setting (Ferroli, Cooper, & Zimmerman, 2001).

Directions and Example

1. Select 8 to 12 longer words from reading material in your existing curriculum. The Compare-Contrast strategy requires no special materials or set of words.

2. Allocate about 10 minutes for a compare-contrast session. Students begin to adopt and apply the strategy when they receive regular instruction—about twice a week for four to six weeks. The lesson can be a prereading activity to prepare students for reading chapters of a class novel, selections from an anthology, or content area texts.

3. Explain to students that when they encounter longer words that are not immediately recognizable, they can employ the Compare-Contrast Procedure. They compare these new words to other words they know that have similar letter patterns. These are called "match" words.

4. Present a word to students without pronouncing it. Model the process by writing the word *quiddich* on the chalkboard or use a longer vocabulary word from your content area. You might think aloud in the following manner.

   If I can't immediately recognize this word, I make matches for each part. Looking at the first part, I make a match with *hid*. Looking at the second part I make a match with *itch*. I say the match words then the target word: *"hid . . . itch . . . quidditch."*

5. Encourage the students to refrain from pronouncing the target word until the matches have been made. This is important because, even if the target word is known, the activity causes them to search through their mental "word stores" for words that look like the target word. It can sometimes be more helpful to make matches for longer words that they already recognize than it is to make matches for words that are initially perplexing.

6. Provide additional examples, remembering to present each word in writing without pronouncing it. Two additional examples are shown below.

   mattress—Looking at the first part I make a match with *cat*. Looking at the second part I make a match with *less*. I say the match words and then the target word: *"cat . . . less . . . mattress."*

   suppose—Looking at the first part I make a match with *cup*. Looking at the second part I make a match with *nose*. I say the match words and then the target word: *"cup . . . nose . . . suppose."*

7. Continue to model more examples. Invite students to contribute and discuss their own matches. Remember that there are no certain matches that are the right ones. The only condition that must be met is that the match words must **look like** the target word. The words must share a spelling pattern.

8. Demonstrate, as opportunities arise, that partial matches occur and are resolved by remembering that the objective is to arrive at a close approximation of the target word so that it becomes recognizable. Presented with the target word *brilliant*, students might match it with *hill* and *giant*, resulting in something like *"brill – I – ant."* Having students say the resulting word a few times *"brill – I – ant," "brill – I – ant"* or even *"hill . . . giant . . . brill – I – ant"* often results in identification of the real word as the approximate pronunciation is close enough to trigger recognition of the actual word. Likewise, a word like *conjure* can be matched with *on* and *sure* and result in a pronunciation slightly removed from the actual target word. Again, saying the resulting approximate pronunciation a few times usually triggers recognition.

9. Demonstrate a similar solution for mismatches. Presented with *defrosting*, common matches are *he, most,* and *sing.* (Actually students often don't bother to make a match for a simple word ending like *ing*, choosing to add that part after other matches are made.) The mismatch of *most* for *frost* still might result in identifying the actual word, but even if it doesn't, the student should be praised for the match that is accurate in terms of its spelling pattern. The following chart shows how nine words might be matched with easy examples, partial matches, and mismatches.

Target Word	Easy matches	Partial matches	Mismatches
Quidditch	*hid . . . witch*		
mattress	*cat . . . less*		
accident	*tack . . . hid . . . went*		
conjure		*on . . . sure*	*won . . . pure*
Hagrid	*bag . . . hid; lag . . . bid*		
defrosting	*me . . . cost . . . ring*		*he . . . most . . . sing*
suppose	*cup . . . nose*		
brilliant		*will . . . ant*	*hill . . . giant*
bandages		*and . . . cages*	

10. Increase the amount of practice by having students make individual matches. For the target word *Hagrid*, students might write *bag . . . hid, sag . . . did, lag . . . bid,* or any combination. Have students pronounce the target word and discuss their match words. Emphasize that students can have different match words because readers have different words stored in their memories, or they simply retrieve different words from their memories.

11. Direct students to make written matches in a notebook. Writing increases the amount of individual practice, but it can slow down the activity. Students need only write match words, not the target word. One student's entries for the words *unimportant, chimpanzee, passenger, independent,* and *engagement* looked like this example.

unimportant	Sun, him or ant
chimpanzee	~~ant~~ him pan Me
passenger	pass end her
independent	in he pen Went
engagement	men age Went

12. Tell students that when they read on their own and they encounter words they do not immediately recognize, they should search for matches. Some students replace the idea of "sound it out" with "match it out."

4.2   TEACHING STRATEGY 10
Making Big Words

Cunningham (2000a) developed Making Big Words to help students learn how to create words by manipulating a series of letters. Each lesson begins with a strip of paper containing certain letters. The letters on the strip are cut or torn apart. These letters are then used by students to make words, as directed by the teacher. All lessons contain a big word or secret word that uses all the letters. As words are made, they are placed in a pocket chart. Later words are sorted into patterns of various types. The lessons help students learn about parts of words and how this knowledge can be used to make new words. Such knowledge can transfer to students' reading and spelling of new words. This strategy is easy for teachers to use because Cunningham and Hall (1994, 1997) have prepared books of lessons. The lessons follow the steps in the box below.

BASIC STEPS FOR MAKING BIG WORDS LESSONS (CUNNINGHAM, 2000a)

1. Give students strips of paper on which they write the letters that will be used for the Making Big Words lesson. Write the vowels first and then the consonants. Students should then cut or tear the strips so they can manipulate the individual letters. The teacher writes the same letters on large note cards and places them in a pocket chart or on the ledge of the chalkboard.

2. Know the order in which the words will be made. Tell students to make the first word and then have one student use the large letter cards to make the word. If necessary, use the word in a sentence. In addition, tell students when they should just change the order of the letters, add a letter, or remove a particular letter and add another letter.

3. Invite students to compare their words with the word made with the large letter cards. Students should correct any misspellings but maintain a brisk pace to the lesson. The student who makes the word with the large letter cards could begin shortly after other students in the class start making the word.

4. Every lesson has a secret word that uses all of the letters. After all words for the lesson have been made, invite students to make the secret word. If no one is able to figure out the secret word, say it and have students make the word.

5. Prepare large cards with all the words that were made. Then have students sort the words. Some patterns include the same prefix, root or base word, and ending. Students should spell a few words with the same part.

6. Sort the words into rhymes. Tell students that rhyming words can help them read and spell words. Write two new rhyming words on cards and have students "place these words under the rhyming words and use the rhymes to decode them. Finally, say two rhyming words and help them see how the rhyming words help them spell them. If possible, use some longer rhyming words" (Cunningham, 2000a, p. 287).

Directions and Example

1. Select the secret word (a word that can be made with all the letters) and other words that can be made using some of the letters. Choose some words that are easy to make, some that are harder, some that rhyme, and some that are morphologically (meaning) related. Prepare large index cards with each of the individual letters and words that will be used in the lesson. Place the large letter cards in the pocket chart or along the chalkboard ledge.

2. Give students strips of paper containing the letters arranged with vowels first. Arrange the consonants in alphabetical order. Have students cut or tear the letters from the strips of paper. Below are letters for a lesson (Cunningham, 2000a).

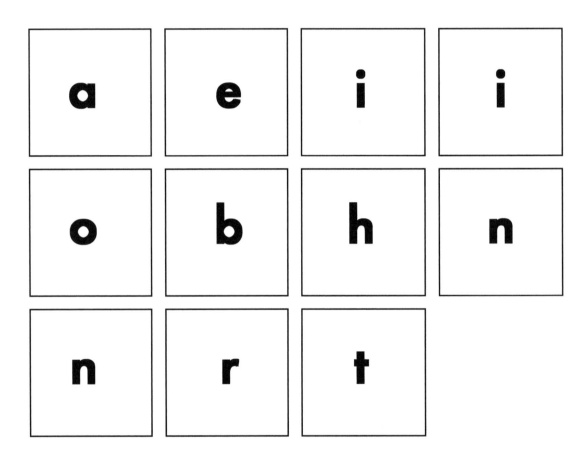

3. Begin the lesson by giving students directions for making words. As students make each word, have one student come to the pocket chart or chalkboard ledge and use the letters on large cards to make the word. Below are typical directions you can use for making words.

    Take three letters and make *hit*.
    The basketball player hit the final basket just as time expired.

    Take away a letter, add two letters, and make *hire*.
    I must hire someone to help me.

    Change the first letter in *hire* to make *tire*.
    The tire on the car is flat.

Let's spell another four-letter word you know—*neat.*
Your desk is very neat.

Now, just change the first letter and spell *beat.*

Using four letters, spell *hero.*
He was called a hero for saving the child.

Now, let's make some five-letter words. Spell *orbit.*
The planets orbit around the sun.

Take away the *i* and the *b* and then spell *other.*
She is my other sister.

Let's spell some six-letter words. Take six letters and spell *nation.*
Our nation is made up of 50 states.

Change just the first letter and *nation* becomes *ration.*
They had to ration water because of the drought.

Let's spell another six-letter word—*intern.*
The intern worked at the hospital.

Now, it's time for a seven-letter word—*inhabit.*
I watched the birds inhabit the dense bush.

Make this seven-letter word—*another.*
I have another chore to do.

I have only one word left on my list. See if you can figure out the secret word that can be spelled by using all of your letters. I am coming around to see if any of you have made the secret word *(hibernation).*

4. Once all the words are made, sort for various items (e.g., same prefix, root, ending, rhyming words, and -tion words). In this lesson, words can be sorted for -tion and rhyming words. Below are the words made in this lesson.

hit	neat	nation
hire	beat	ration
tire	hero	intern
	orbit	inhabit
	other	another
		hibernation

5. Engage students in a variety of sorting activities using all the words created. The words are placed in the pocket chart or along the ledge of the chalkboard. First, have students sort for patterns and related words. Two examples are shown below.

- Students may see that *other* and *another* are related. Use the word cards created prior to the lesson and place the words so that the relationship can be seen more easily. Help students see *other* in *another.* Then ask students how they might use *other* to spell *mother.*
- The words *ration, nation,* and *hibernation* are related because of the *tion.* Ask students how they would spell *motion, mention, conviction, contribution,* and *generation.*

6. Sort for rhyming words. As the rhyming words are sorted, help students see that rhyming words can help them read and spell words. Some examples are shown below.

   - *Hire* and *tire* rhyme. How would these words help you spell *fire* and *wire*? You can also place the new words on cards and place these words under the rhyming words and have students use the rhymes to decode them.
   - *Neat* and *beat* rhyme. How would these words help you spell *heat, retreat, wheat,* and *seat*?

7. Remember that books by Cunningham and Hall (1994, 1997) have many lessons that make this strategy easy to use. Some of the lessons focus on the following words and may be appropriate in various content areas. Below are the big words from Cunningham and Hall (1994) that might be incorporated in themes or units in the content areas. For example, the teacher of science, depending on the grade and the unit being taught, may be able to use words such as atmosphere, chimpanzee, circulation, computers, earthquakes, earthworms, experiments, and so on. A business teacher may use words such as advertisements, commercials, computers, headquarters, information, international, leadership, responsibility, and resourceful. In *Making More Big Words*, Cunningham and Hall (1997) assign the words to 13 themes or units to aid teachers in making curriculum connections.

advertisement	arguments	atmosphere
breakfast	championship	chimpanzee
circulation	commercials	communities
computers	conversation	constitution
construction	democratic	dictionary
disagreements	disappearance	earthquakes
earthworms	encyclopedia	entertainment
experiments	explosions	expressions
generations	grasshopper	headquarters
hospitals	hurricanes	imagination
information	instruments	intermission
international	introduction	investigator
jellyfish	languages	leadership
measurements	microphones	microscopes
mountains	operation	performances
personality	population	porcupines
president	rattlesnake	responsibility
resourceful	revolution	satellites
snowflakes	spaghetti	strawberries
submarines	subtraction	telephones
television	temperature	thermometers
thunderstorm	transportation	traveling
underground	unforgettable	vegetables
videotapes	Washington	weightlessness

4.2 ▶ 50 Essential Big Words

Cunningham (2000a, p. 290), with thorough and careful study, created a list of 50 essential words that contain "all the most useful prefixes, suffixes, and spelling changes" that can be used as transferable chunks for decoding, reading, and spelling many new words. The basic idea is to help students learn these words, their meanings, and how to spell the words. This knowledge can then be used to decode, read, and spell new words.

 Directions and Examples

1. The 50 words, along with their prefixes and suffixes or endings, can be found on pages 115–116. We have also assigned these words to some major curriculum areas in middle and high schools. This list is presented below and may be used as a beginning point for teaching the words and showing how they can be used to help decode or identify words in your content area.

Social Studies	Literature/General	Speech/Business
communities	beautiful	conversation
community	different	employee
continuous	encouragement	expensive
discovery	forgotten	illegal
dishonest	happiness	impossible
forecast	hopeless	impression
governor	impression	misunderstood
illegal	irresponsible	performance
impossible	midnight	rearrange
independence	misunderstand	replacement
international	prettier	richest
invasion	rearrange	semifinal
misunderstand	richest	signature
overpower	semifinal	supermarkets
prehistoric	signature	transportation
rearrange	supermarkets	unfinished
replacement	swimming	valuable
signature	unfinished	
submarine	unfriendly	
transportation	unpleasant	
unfriendly	valuable	

Science	Arts
antifreeze	beautiful
classify	composer
deodorize	discovery
discovery	musician
electricity	performance
forecast	unfinished
impossible	valuable
international	
misunderstood	
nonliving	
prehistoric	
rearrange	
swimming	
underweight	
valuable	

2. Choose one of the words for teaching. For example, *prehistoric* might be a part of a science or history unit. Print the word on the chalkboard or on an overhead transparency and have students say or chant the word several times. The word might also be placed on a Word Wall along with other big words from the list.

3. Talk about the word and the part or parts that could be applied to other words. If you use *prehistoric*, talk about the prefix *pre* and the root or base word *(history, historic)*. Cunningham suggests that students try to think of other words that look and sound like *prehistoric* and then decide if the *pre* parts of those words have anything to do with the notion of *before* or *prior to*. Have students suggest words that begin with *pre* and then categorize the words, perhaps along the lines shown in the example below.

Possibly means *before* or *prior to*	Probably doesn't mean *before* or *prior to*
preapprove	premier
prepay	preppy
predetermine	precision
precast	prefer
precancerous	premise
prefab	prepare
precook	predator
preheat	predict
preflight	present
precondition	president

4. Take time to have students realize that the *pre* may help with the meanings and pronunciations of the words in the first column. Equally important, however, is to help students realize that not all words that begin with *pre* will help with a word's meaning or pronunciation. Have students examine the words in the second column.

5. Guide students to the answers to questions like the following ones.

   - For which words might the *pre* be helpful in determining the pronunciation? (premier, precision, prefer)
   - What problems exist if you try to use *pre* in pronouncing *preppy* and *premise?*

50 Essential Big Words

Word	Prefix	Suffix or ending
antifreeze	anti	
beautiful		ful (y-i)
classify		ify
communities	com	es (y-i)
community	com	
composer	com	er
continuous	con	ous
conversation	con	tion
deodorize	de	ize
different		ent
discovery	dis	y
dishonest	dis	
electricity		ity
employee	em	ee
encouragement	en	ment
expensive	ex	ive
forecast	fore	
forgotten		en (double t)
governor		or
happiness		ness (y-i)
hopeless		less
illegal	il	
impossible	im	
impression	im	sion
independence	in	ence
international	inter	al
invasion	in	sion
irresponsible	ir	ible
midnight	mid	
misunderstand	mis	
musician		ian
nonliving	non	ing (drop e)
overpower	over	
performance	per	ance
prehistoric	pre	ic
prettier		er (y-i)
rearrange	re	
replacement	re	ment
richest		est

(continued)

50 Essential Big Words (continued)

Word	Prefix	Suffix or ending
semifinal	semi	
signature		ture
submarine	sub	
supermarkets	super	s
swimming		ing (double m)
transportation	trans	tion
underweight	under	
unfinished	un	ed
unfriendly	un	ly
unpleasant	un	ant
valuable		able (drop e)

From *Phonics They Use.* 3rd ed. by Patricia M. Cunningham. Copyright © 2000 by Addison-Wesley Educational Publishers, Inc. Reprinted by permission of Addison-Wesley Educational Publishers, Inc.

Take time to help students realize that it is important to be flexible in using word parts or chunks to arrive at the correct pronunciation of a word. The goal should be to try a particular chunk and, if it doesn't result in a word the student has heard before, to try other pronunciations. Sometimes the word will not be one the student has heard before, so it may be impossible for the student to know if it is pronounced correctly. In such cases, the dictionary or an expert source (e.g., another student or the teacher) is essential.

6. Help students learn how to spell and pronounce the 50 words over time and use patterns to help students see connections. For example, you might extend the lesson by using the following examples.

   - You know how to spell *prepare*. How would you spell *prejudge*? What about *predigest*?
   - Who knows the base or root word of *historic*? Yes, *history* is the base or root word and it often refers to events in the past. What do you think *historic* might refer to? (something that has importance, like an historic artifact from Egypt). Now, use what you know about the spelling of *historic* to spell *heroic*.

7. Help students understand that the suffixes or endings on the list of 50 words change how the word can be used in a sentence. Look for opportunities in daily lessons to help students use the 50 words to help them become more proficient in decoding words and using word chunks for assisting with meaning and spelling.

4.2 TEACHING STRATEGY 12
Foreign Words and Phrases

English contains a number of foreign words and phrases. Some words (for example, *essay* and *mesa*) may seem as though they have always been a part of our language. Other words (for example, *tête-à-tête* and *coup d'état*) contain accents and a form that suggest an etymology from another language. Many languages have influenced the words in the English language, and the resulting English word may have the same meaning as or a different meaning from the word in the original language. Students who learn the meanings of key words and phrases in your content area will better understand the material.

Directions and Example

1. Ask students if they are aware of any foreign words or phrases. List them on the chalkboard and have students predict their meanings. Then have students look up the words in their dictionaries to verify meanings. You could also suggest some words: *fiancé, fiancée, chic, passé, coup,* and *khaki.* Help students determine the origins of the words. Then tell students that some of the words in their text are foreign words and phrases that are important to know in order to understand the passages in which they occur. A list of foreign abbreviations, words, and phrases is presented at the end of this strategy for reference and possible use.

2. Survey your content area to identify key foreign words and phrases. Teach them in the context of the unit or passage in which they occur. The example below uses words from a social studies text: *coup d'état, faux pas,* and *laissez faire.*

3. Direct students to the passages in the text containing the words or phrases or print the sentences on the chalkboard or an overhead transparency.

   Several extreme groups in the country debated the government's *laissez faire* policy.

   Within a year, a *coup d'état* occurred.

   Historians agree that the major *faux pas* was the government's inability to reach a workable solution with the extremist groups.

4. Ask for a volunteer to read the first sentence. Have students identify the foreign phrase and invite students to use their experiences or the context as a possible clue to the meaning of the phrase. If necessary, use the glossary or a dictionary to help determine the meaning and pronunciation of the phrase. Then help students understand the meaning of the words or phrase in the context of the sentence. Stress that the meaning is more important than the pronunciation.

5. Proceed to the next two sentences and engage students in a similar manner as described in step 4. It might be helpful to have students keep a list of useful foreign words and phrases relevant to your content area. A sheet that can be used for that purpose follows.

6. Students could also be encouraged to bring to class any foreign words or phrases they encounter in their general reading for sharing and discussion. Be sure that attention is devoted to the meanings of the words or phrases.

TECHNOLOGY

Focus on Latin and Greek Elements of English

Students can experience the wonder of words by viewing the Latin and Greek elements of English by logging on to **Focusing on Words.**

www.wordfocus.com

Helpful Foreign Words and Phrases

Word/Phrase _____   Origin _____

Meaning _____

Sentence _____

_____

Word/Phrase _____   Origin _____

Meaning _____

Sentence _____

_____

Word/Phrase _____   Origin _____

Meaning _____

Sentence _____

_____

Word/Phrase _____   Origin _____

Meaning _____

Sentence _____

_____

FOREIGN ABBREVIATIONS, WORDS, AND PHRASES

A.D. (anno Domini)—in the year of our Lord

A.M. (ante meridiem)—before midday; the hours between midnight and noon

ad hoc—created for a particular purpose; frequently used to designate a committee

ad infinitum—indefinitely into the future

al fresco—painting on fresh plaster

alter ego—another self; a good friend

ancien régime—former regime

ante bellum—before the war; in the United States before the Civil War

a priori—a type of reasoning derived from self-evident propositions

aux armes—to arms, as in taking up weapons

avant-garde—leaders in new art forms

bas relief—sculpture in which the subject does not stand out far from the background

bon appétit—good appetite

bona fide—in good faith

bon mot—a clever expression

ca (circa)—about; approximately

carpe diem—take advantage of today; enjoy the day; seize the day

carte blanche—a blanket authorization

caveat emptor—let the buyer beware

c'est la vie—that's the way life is

coup d'état—unexpected overturning of the government; rapid political change

cul-de-sac—passage with only one outlet; dead end

cum laude—with praise; a phrase placed on diplomas indicating better than average scholarship

de facto—a matter of fact; actually

déjà vu—applied to a person imagining that certain scenes or events were seen previously

de jure—legal; rightfully

double entendre—an expression with two meanings

e.g. (exempli gratia)—for example

etc. (et cetera)—and so forth; and others

elite—upper class

en masse—in a crowd; together

e pluribus unum—one from many; motto on the great seal of the United States

esprit de corps—internal harmony and common purpose that motivates a group or an organization

et tu, Brute—and you, too Brutus. Last words spoken by Caesar in Shakespeare's play *Julius Caesar*

eureka!—I have found it! Exclamation of Archimedes whose experiment led to the discovery of the law of specific gravity

ex officio—by virtue of holding an office

ex post facto—after the deed is done

f. (forte)—loudly

f.v. (folio verso)—on the reverse side of the page

fait accompli—an action that cannot be undone

faux pas—a blunder, especially in the area of social conventions; mistakes

forte—loudly

genus homo—the human race

habeas corpus—when a prisoner posts bail and demands a hearing in court

homo sapiens—scientific name for human beings

hors d'oeuvres—bits of food served prior to a meal to stimulate the appetite

i.e. (id est)—namely; that is to say

in absentia—in absence

in loco—on the spot; in the place of

in toto—completely

joie de vivre—the joy of living

laissez faire—an economic policy; noninterference by government in business

magnum opus—masterpiece

mardi gras—literally, fat Tuesday, a day of fasting before the first day of Lent

mea culpa—through my fault

mezzo forte—moderately loud

n'est-ce pas?—is it not so

noblesse oblige—those who are nobly born must act nobly

nom de plume—pen name

non sequitur—it does not follow; an illogical inference

nouveau riche—one who has recently become rich

Objet d'art—a valuable piece of art

P.M. (post meridiem)—afternoon; from noon to midnight

P.S. (post-scriptum)—postscript

passé—out of date

per annum—by the year

per capita—for each person; share and share alike

per diem—by the day

per se—by, in, or of itself

persona non grata—person not accepted

pianissimo—very softly

piano—softly

por favor—please

pro rata—in proportion

quid pro quo—something for something; one thing for another

R.S.V.P.—please reply

raison d'être—reason for existing

résumé—summary

s.d. (sans date)—without the date

savoir faire—tact; cleverness; social know-how

s'il vous plaît—if you please

sine qua non—an absolutely indispensable condition

status quo—existing state of affairs; the way things are

sub rosa—confidentially; secret

tabula rasa—blank slate

tête-à-tête—confidential conversation

vice versa—reversing the relationship of forms; conversely

vis-à-vis—face to face; in relation to

wanderlust—passion for traveling

Section
4.3

Using Reference Sources

Goal To help students use various source materials to pronounce and understand words

BACKGROUND

Strategic readers learn and use various ways to decode words and determine their meanings. Some of those ways have already been described in earlier sections of this chapter. In this section, attention is focused on resources that may be available in the text and the dictionary. Within a text are footnotes, pronunciations of technical or unusual words, and definitions of words in a glossary. The dictionary is also a valuable tool that can be used for pronouncing words and determining meanings of words. The use of these resources can help students become more efficient and effective readers.

TEACHING STRATEGY 13

4.3   Right on the Page

Many content area texts have key words in bold or italic type, definitions in the text, and a pronunciation key in parentheses for the selected word. A precalculus book, for example, may have important words highlighted for emphasis and easy reference. It is important that you guide students in understanding how to use the particulars of your content area text or resource materials to help them pronounce and understand words.

 Directions and Examples

1. Invite students to share a page of their content area text that helps them pronounce words or understand what the words mean. Write their ideas on the chalkboard or an overhead transparency. Some key ideas follow.

    The especially important words are in bold type.
    The definition may be near the word in bold type.
    Sometimes there are pronunciation symbols in parentheses to aid in pronouncing the word.

2. Select a page from materials used in your content area that contains one or more features that may help students understand or pronounce a word. Then guide students through the particular items that relate to your text or materials, as shown in the following examples from different content areas.

3. For words highlighted with bold type, you might make the following comments.

> Take a look at page 2 in your precalculus book. How many words do you see that are in bold type? [Ask a student to answer the question.] Let's look at each of those six words in context. The first word is **real numbers**. It is in bold type. As I read the sentence, I see that real numbers describe quantities such as miles per gallon, age, and population. Then there are some examples of symbols to represent real numbers. I get 25.5 miles per gallon with my car, so that would be an example of a real number. Your age would also be another real number. Notice that the symbol for *pi* is also an example of a real number. What might be some other examples of real numbers? [Invite students to respond.] Note that the term **real numbers** was defined by using examples rather than an actual definition. Now let's look at the term **rational**. [Use a similar procedure and contrast *rational* with *irrational*.]

4. For words defined explicitly in the text, you might make the following remarks.

> On page 110 of your math text, there are two words in bold type: **perimeter** and **area**. Look where it says that the distance around a figure is called its perimeter. The word is defined right there. Then the next sentence says, "The amount of space a figure covers is called its **area**." Once again, the word is defined in the sentence. Sometimes words are defined directly in your text. Because they are also in bold type, they are likely to be important. In fact, you will probably need to know these words for a quiz.

5. When the pronunciation of a word is given in parentheses, you might print the following sentence on the chalkboard and then say what follows.

> A **scalene** (skay LEEN) triangle is a triangle in which no two sides have the same length.

> Read this sentence to yourself. You can see that the word is defined in the sentence. But how is the word pronounced? If you look inside the parentheses, you will be given an idea of how to pronounce the word. There are two syllables as indicated by the space between the two parts. The part in all capital letters means that the second syllable is given more stress or emphasis. I'd like someone who doesn't know how to pronounce the word to give it a try. Look at the actual word and refer to the information in parentheses. [Invite a few students to offer their pronunciations. Pronunciations may differ, but praise their efforts. Then have a student who knows the word pronounce it.] As you can see, your efforts using the pronunciation guide may or may not result in the correct pronunciation, and you may need to verify your attempt with someone who already knows how to pronounce the word.

6. Provide other examples of words and pronunciation hints. Invite students to share their ideas about how the words are pronounced. You may need to teach the sounds commonly associated with certain symbols (for example, ə). Emphasize that, in most cases, the meanings are more important than the pronunciations. Some examples of words to use for pronunciation from mathematics practice are presented below.

> pentagon (PEN tə gon)
> hexagon (HEK sə gon)

trapezoid (TRAP ə zoyd)
parallelogram (par ə LEL ə gram)
equilateral (ee qwə LAT ər əl)
quadrilateral (kwod rə LAT ər əl)

4.3 **Footnotes**   *TEACHING STRATEGY 14*

Footnotes may be used to assist with word meanings and pronunciations or to provide helpful information. Although students may frequently skip this in-text aid, a short lesson can help students realize the
value of footnotes.

Directions and Example

1. Select an example from your content text or use the following example about the Nile.

2. Tell students that footnotes may provide information and possibly help with the pronunciation
   and/or meaning of a word. Write the following sentence on the chalkboard or on an overhead
   transparency.

   We love you, O Nile![1]

3. Tell students that the raised numeral is a signal to look at the bottom of the page to find a
   footnote with the same numeral. Present the following information on an overhead transparency.

   [1] A river that runs through Egypt up to the Mediterranean Sea. The Nile is one
   of the world's longest rivers.

4. Have a student explain how the footnote helps with the word *Nile*. Clarify and expand the
   response if necessary. Then have students consider the following sentence.

   The flooding Nile nourished the orchards created by Ra.[2]

   Ask if anyone knows what the word *Ra* means. After students have made their predictions,
   refer them to the footnote on an overhead transparency.

   [2] Ra is the Egyptian god of the sun.

5. Provide other sentences and footnotes. Have students assess the degree to which the footnotes
   help with the pronunciations and/or meanings of the words. Several examples are provided
   below.

   Sentence: You are the greatest treasure of Seb.
   Footnote: Seb is the Egyptian name for Earth.

Sentence: The water flowed through the royal city.
Footnote: Cairo is the royal city being referred to.

Sentence: The gazelles roamed near the Nile.
Footnote: gazelles (g ZELZ): small antelopes

6. As students read their texts, have them share instances when footnotes helped them pronounce words or understand their meanings.

4.3   Glossary   *TEACHING STRATEGY 15*

A number of content area texts contain a glossary. A glossary might be thought of as a specific dictionary for the important words in that particular content area. It is also readily available for students to use. Generally, most glossaries will assist students with the meanings of words, and many of these words are in bold print in the text. Informal conversations with students in high school reveal that the glossary is a helpful resource, especially when key vocabulary is used in study guides, quizzes, and tests.

Directions and Example

1. Review your content area texts to determine whether a glossary is included. If so, introduce it early in the course of study. Adapt the following information, if appropriate, to the texts and materials used for instruction.

    Today I want to share an important part of your geometry text. Turn to page 705 where you will find a glossary. [Invite students to share information about a glossary.] Yes, that's correct—a glossary is like a dictionary because it contains meanings of many words. Let's look more closely at page 705 where the glossary begins.

2. Point out the features contained in the glossary. In the geometry book, there are definitions of words and a number of illustrations. A unique feature of the glossary is a page number in parentheses that refers to the location in the text where the word is found.

3. Choose one of the words in the glossary that students probably already know, discuss the word and definition, and relate the word to the text. You could make the following comments.

    Let's find the word *compass* on page 707 in the glossary. Follow along as I read. "A compass is an instrument used to draw circles and arcs of circles." You probably already understand this word. Here is a real compass. [Hold up a compass for students to see.] This compass is different from the one in a car you might use for directions. Now look at the end of the definition. You will see the number 25 in parentheses. That tells you where the word can be found in your text. Turn to page 25 and find *compass*.

4. When students have found the word, point out that the word is not in bold type. You might remark as follows.

> When you are reading this text, there will be times you come across an unknown word. You could check the glossary to see if the word is defined. Note that this word is not in bold type, but it is in the glossary. The word *straightedge,* on the same line as *compass,* is not in bold type. Check to see if *straightedge* is in the glossary. [Verify the definition and discuss it.]

5. Direct students to page 8 and have them locate the first word in bold type. Have them check for the word in the glossary. Lead students to the understanding that most words in bold type will be found in the glossary. Make the point that the glossary can be a useful resource.

6. Have students share their current understandings of a glossary and list them on the chalkboard or an overhead transparency. A chart could also be made and posted in the room for reference. Refer to the glossary when appropriate and encourage students to use this source to review important terms and clarify meanings of words.

4.3 ▶ Dictionary Orientation

TEACHING STRATEGY 16

A dictionary can be used to help students with both the pronunciation and meaning of a word. Being able to locate a word in an efficient manner by knowing the general organization of the dictionary and how to use guide words is critical. Johns and Lenski (2001) have developed foundational lessons to help students understand alphabetical order and how to use guide words. Refer to these lessons if needed. The following lesson serves as a general orientation to the dictionary.

 ## Directions and Example

1. Hold up a dictionary and invite students to share what they know about this reference source. Write their ideas on the chalkboard or on an overhead transparency. Tell students that most dictionaries contain over 50,000 words.

2. As students share, highlight or introduce the following items into the discussion. Use an example from your dictionary or make an overhead transparency from the master on page 127. Be sure to highlight the definition and the pronunciation symbols or respelling.

   - **Entry word**—This is the name given to each word, abbreviation, prefix, suffix, or group of words that a dictionary explains.
   - **Guide words**—These are two words printed in boldface type at the top of each dictionary page. The left guide word shows the first full entry word; the right guide word shows the last full entry word.
   - **Syllables**—The centered dots in the entry word show where the word is divided. Syllables can help you pronounce the word or show you where to divide a word when you cannot write it all on one line.

bit·tern[1] (bĭt´ərn) *n.* Any of several wading birds of the heron family having molted, brownish plumage and a deep, resonant call. [ME biture<OFr. butor]

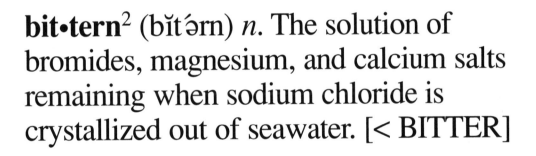

BITTERN

bit·tern[2] (bĭt´ərn) *n.* The solution of bromides, magnesium, and calcium salts remaining when sodium chloride is crystallized out of seawater. [< BITTER]

- **Pronunciation symbols** or **respelling**—The information appearing in parentheses following the entry word can help you pronounce the word.
- **Etymology**—The origin and history of the word are shown in brackets, using symbols and abbreviations. Some examples are shown below.

  > < means derived from
  > *OE* means Old English
  > *L* means Latin

- **Definitions**—Meanings of the entry word are listed together, according to their parts of speech. Parts of speech are usually abbreviated as follows: *n.* for noun, *adj.* for adjective, *v.* for verb, *interj.* for interjection, *prep.* for preposition, and so on.
- **Idioms**—An idiom is a group of words that has a meaning different from the meaning of the words by themselves. Idioms, if included, are at the end of the entry for the key word.
- **Illustrations**—Some entry words contain an illustration to exemplify or clarify the entry word.
- **Synonyms**—This is a word that means about the same as the entry word. Look for **syn.**
- **Example sentence**—Sometimes the entry word is used in a sentence to help clarify the meaning or to show how the word is used.

3. Have students use their dictionaries to look up some words you identify or conduct activities such as the following ones. Questions could also be asked about word origins and parts of speech.

- Compare and contrast the meaning of *plane* in your geometry text to the meanings in your dictionary.
- Is *bitumen* a food source people eat? (No, it's coal.)
  How is *bitumen* pronounced? (bi t͞oo mən)
- What color is *bisque*? (red-yellow)
- Where is a *bivalve* found? (on a mussel or clam)
- What is a *dobbin*? (horse)
- What is a common word for *calyx*? (leaves)
- What use might a *divining rod* have? (to help locate water below the surface)
- Could you put something on a *docket*? (yes)

4.3 ➤ Pronouncing Words

TEACHING STRATEGY 17

The pronunciation symbols found at the bottom of a dictionary page may be used to help pronounce unknown words. There are several points to keep in mind. First, most pronunciation symbols show how words are pronounced by those who speak General American. Some of the pronunciation symbols may not be appropriate for where you teach. Second, it is difficult for anyone who uses the pronunciation symbols to be sure that the word is pronounced correctly if it is not in the person's listening vocabulary. Often, however, someone who already knows how to say the word can verify its pronunciation. Third, the meaning of the word may be more important for students to understand than the pronunciation. Finally, this lesson represents an introduction to using pronunciation symbols. Remember to provide multiple opportunities for students to strengthen their use of pronunciation symbols.

Directions and Examples

1. If you have already used pronunciation symbols in the glossary of your content area text, make the connection from this source to the dictionary (or *vice versa*). Help students to also understand that they may know words similar to the words they are unable to pronounce, and they can use this knowledge to help decode or pronounce words. You may wish to refer to Teaching Strategies 8, 9, and 10 presented earlier in this chapter.

2. Have students locate the pronunciation symbols at the bottom of their dictionary pages. Keep in mind that not all dictionaries use exactly the same symbols or example words. Tell students that the pronunciation symbols at the bottom of the page can be related to the pronunciation symbols or respellings in parentheses beside each entry word.

3. Choose several entry words that most students can probably pronounce and have students establish the connection between selected symbols in words at the bottom of the page and the entry words. Some possible words to look up for this activity follow.

right	bittersweet	bison
coveralls	cower	crab
change	characteristic	collector
collarbone	erupt	modulate

4. From these and other examples, help students realize that no marks over a vowel indicate a "short" sound, and the macron (a "long" marking) indicates the "long" sound. You may also want to teach some of the other special marks that signify certain sounds. Several of these pronunciation symbols and examples are provided below. If you have a classroom set of dictionaries, be sure to verify that the pronunciation symbols are used in the same manner. Some dictionaries use a ˘ for the "short" sound (pat).

SOME PRONUNCIATION SYMBOLS

Symbol	Name	Example Word
ä	Two-dot a	Fär
ô	Circumflex o	tôrn
ũ	Tilde u	fũr
ə	Schwa	a in ago

---

5. Model how you would use the pronunciation symbols to pronounce an unknown word. Select a word of your choice or use the example below.

    Suppose I come across a word I can't pronounce, and I decide to look it up in a dictionary. Here are the pronunciation symbols for the word. [Write the following symbols on the chalkboard: mō-dăl´ ə-tē.]

6. Think aloud as you use the pronunciation symbols to try different pronunciations and link the symbols to specific sounds. For example, you might begin by making the following observation.

    I notice that the mark over the *o* represents the long sound like the *o* in *toe*.

7. Continue with the remaining sounds and then blend the sounds together to form an incorrect pronunciation of *modality*. Try another pronunciation and ultimately say the word correctly.

8. Invite students to use the pronunciation symbols and key words from their dictionaries to try to pronounce the following respellings to make real words. Consider using related words to help students become more familiar with the pronunciation symbols. The words should also be in students' listening vocabularies (i.e., words they are likely to have heard before). Be sure to remind students to try different pronunciations, especially for the vowels, until they say a word that they have heard before.

Pronunciation Symbols or Respellings*	Word
kwit	quit
rōd	road
rō´ stǝr	roaster
shôr´ sīd´	shoreside
skwûr´ǝl	squirrel
skwosh	squash
taz mā´nē ǝ	Tasmania
tō´gǝ	toga
un´kǝn fôr´mit ē	unconformity
ves´tǝ byōōl´	vestibule
wûrth´ lis	worthless

*From the unabridged version of *The Random House Dictionary of the English Language* (2nd ed.)

TECHNOLOGY

T I P

Online Dictionaries

Two sources for online dictionaries:

Merriam-Webster Online at:
www.m-w.com

Houghton Mifflin's American Heritage Dictionary of the English Language at:
www.bartleby.com/61

TEACHING STRATEGY 18
Choosing a Dictionary Meaning to Fit the Context

A dictionary or glossary can be a useful resource to help determine the meaning of an unknown word in the text. Context may also be used (see Teaching Strategy 4).

 ## Directions and Example

1. Begin with a word whose meaning in a sentence is likely to be unknown. Choose a sentence from your content area text or use the following example.

    A *bittern* was seen in the distance.

2. Invite students to share their thoughts about the word. Students might note that the word is likely to be a noun, because of its position in the sentence. Other students may make some predictions about the meaning of the word. Write students' ideas on the chalkboard. Then have students look up the word in their dictionaries or make an overhead transparency of page 127, which contains definitions of bittern. Have students read the definitions and choose the best definition for the word. Then have a student share why that particular definition was selected.

3. Ask students to name some words that have more than one definition. Write the words on the chalkboard and then select a few words to look up in the dictionary. Explore the various meanings of the words. You might also use a few words from your content area or choose from the following words.

case	base	compass	bisque
angle	bit	element	sum
colony	plain	mask	elevator

4. Then provide a sentence with a word that has more than one meaning (e.g., *element*). Have students look up the word and determine which meaning fits the context. Two possible sentences and brief definitions of *element* follow.

    The symbol Kr signifies an element.
    Setting is a story element.

    element
    1. a fundamental or essential part of something
    2. a number of a set
    3. a substance composed of atoms
    4. one of four substances (earth, air, fire, water) formerly regarded as a fundamental part of the universe

5. Think aloud for how you choose the definition that best fits the context of the first sentence. You might say the following.

> I'll read the definitions quickly to see if there is one that seems to make sense in the sentence. [Read the definitions aloud.] I think that the second definition is more related to math, so I will rule that out. The third definition seems like it might work, because I know that there are elements that are identified by symbols. The fourth definition seems like it doesn't fit this context, unless Kr stands for fire, water, earth, or air. I don't think Kr would stand for any of those elements. The first definition does not seem like it fits as well as the third definition, so I think the third definition works best.

6. Use examples and definitions for words with multiple meanings. Have students select the best meaning for the context and then share their thinking. Select both common words and more difficult words. Some possible words to use follow. Be sure to use them in sentences.

elevate	erupt	eradicate	flow
flock	grate	granule	hire
mobilize	mixture	pannier	powwow

Chapter 5
COMPREHENDING TEXTS

OVERVIEW

Reading comprehension involves making meaning while interacting with text. Comprehension of text is not just a mental process but also reflects who we are, how we relate to the world, and our accumulated store of background knowledge. However, some students may not be able to understand what they are reading in your class and content area. Consequently, they are not gaining the knowledge and experiences they need to be successful in your classroom. Although you may incorporate hands-on learning experiences, discussions, and technology into your teaching, your students still need to be able to read and understand various types of content-related materials such as textbooks, tradebooks, novels, online texts, newspapers, and magazines.

Effective readers are strategic readers who are able to apply various strategies while reading in order to enhance their comprehension. You need to provide students with the ability to approach texts strategically. Several authors (Readence, Bean, & Baldwin, 2001; Vacca & Vacca, 2002) have employed the term "content literacy" to describe the process of reading strategically. It has been defined as "the ability to use reading and writing to learn subject matter in a given discipline" (Vacca & Vacca, 2002, p. 15). A key component of reading strategically is to be metacognitively aware or to "systematically apply strategies and monitor comprehension" (Ruddell, 2002, p. 42). Strategic readers ask themselves questions while they are reading, and they consider whether what they are reading makes sense. They view reading as an active process that requires them to think, monitor their understanding, and apply strategies to "fix-up" their comprehension when they encounter comprehension problems.

Successful readers also know how texts are organized, and they use this information to enhance their comprehension. Novels and fictional stories, for example, are organized according to story grammars that include components such as setting, characters, goal, problem, and resolution. However, organizational patterns in textbooks can have different structures. If your students become aware of these structures, they will have a framework for approaching and comprehending texts more effectively.

Students also need to be able to interpret graphs, charts, and maps—all aspects of graphic literacy (Sejnost & Thiese, 2001). Visual aids function to summarize or condense and communicate the written information succinctly. They are designed to enhance or clarify concepts or ideas in texts and to facilitate students' understanding of content information.

"Teaching students to use comprehension strategies is sensible because self-regulated use of comprehension strategies is prominent in the reading of exceptionally skilled adult readers" (Pressley, 2000, p. 554). Additionally, through strategic reading, students are afforded the privileges, responsibilities, and advantages of skillful readers. To read actively and strategically means that students have the right to question the beliefs and statements of others rather than to passively submit to their ideas.

Learning does not end when your students have finished reading their texts. Understanding key ideas, reacting to what was read, and extending learning are important aspects of the reading process. By providing opportunities for students to discuss, write, and engage in projects after reading, you enable students to react to their reading by connecting it to personal responses. In addition, students can deepen their understanding of what they read by putting ideas into their own words, applying what they have learned, and by making judgments about ideas and concepts from their reading.

The strategies in this chapter promote comprehension and provide multiple opportunities for your students to apply these strategies in meaningful contexts so that they will begin to internalize and use them while reading independently. While it may not be easy for students to accomplish this goal, you will begin to notice improved comprehension as a result of teaching your students strategies for preparing to read, using text structure, monitoring understanding, extending meaning, and interpreting graphic aids.

Accessing Prior Knowledge

> **Goal** To help students use prior knowledge to comprehend texts

BACKGROUND

By accessing their background knowledge, or schema, students can create a framework for what they are about to read. They can also make connections between what they know and what they will be reading. Your students will find learning new information much easier if they can develop clear connections between new information and their background knowledge.

The schema theory of comprehension explains how prior knowledge helps students assimilate new information into what they already know about the topic (McNamara, Miller, & Bransford, 1991). Schema can be described as the abstract mental frameworks that organize knowledge into memory. As your students learn new information, they con-nect new ideas with their prior knowledge. In addition, they may reorganize their schema to incorporate new information into the framework. If students have prior knowledge about a specific topic, that information will allow them to approach the topic with confidence, make inferences as they read, and focus on the big ideas in the text rather than getting lost in the details (Brozo & Simpson, 1995). Students' background knowledge is an essential component in comprehension.

The strategies in this section are designed to help students access their prior knowledge and prepare for reading. By engaging students in these strategies, you will help lay the groundwork for their comprehension of texts.

5.1 Prereading Plan (PreP)

TEACHING STRATEGY 1

The Prereading Plan, called PreP for short, was developed by Langer (1981) to generate students' interest in content area reading and to access and determine the level of background knowledge that students bring to a reading assignment. PreP guides students to make associations with a topic, reflect on their associations, and reformulate their knowledge. You will probably find that students have differing levels of background knowledge about the topic to be studied. Based on this information about students' background knowledge, you can develop appropriate instruction to meet the needs of students, thus increasing the likelihood that students will comprehend the text they are asked to read.

Directions and Example

1. Select a section of text students will be reading. Examine the text for key words and concepts students will need to understand from the reading. Determine a central concept that will be the main focus of the strategy.

2. Once the central concept is identified, introduce PreP to students. Explain to students that the strategy will help them activate their background knowledge and better understand their reading. Model PreP by using an example from your content area or the following example from a biology text.

3. Identify the main topic of the reading selection. Tell students that they will be reading a new chapter from their textbook. Explain that before reading students should access their prior knowledge so that they will better understand the text. Tell students that they can access their prior knowledge before they read by thinking of words and phrases that they associate with the topic.

4. Divide the class into groups of three or four students. Have students list ideas and concepts about the central theme, focusing on any ideas that come to mind when they hear the key concept. Give students five minutes to list ideas; then have students share their initial lists with other members of the class.

5. As students share their ideas, write them on the chalkboard or an overhead transparency. Try to organize or group the ideas as students share them. Group ideas by making lists or by constructing a semantic map to show how ideas are connected. Consult the following example to see the types of responses students may generate at this stage of the strategy.

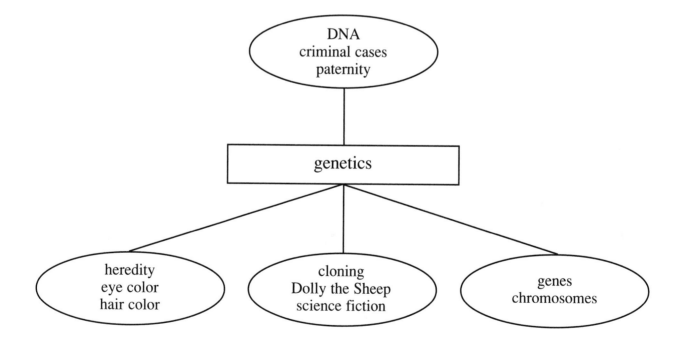

6. Assist students as they reflect on their initial associations with the topic. Ask students to explain their reasons for the associations they suggested for the semantic map. Explain to students that, by listening to ideas that other students share, they will develop an awareness of the networks of associations possible for the term. As students discuss the main concept, add new ideas to the semantic map. Encourage students to explain their thinking by asking them the following questions.

What made you think of _____?

How is _____ related to _____?

What do you know about _____ and _____?

7. Next, guide students to reformulate their knowledge about the topic. The following questions can be used at this stage of the strategy.

Based on our discussion about _____, what new ideas do you now have about _____?

Is there anything we need to delete or change from our earlier list of ideas about _____?

8. Add these ideas to what is already written. Because students have had a chance to access their background knowledge and to consider ideas shared by their classmates, responses during this stage of the PreP strategy often are more refined and detailed than earlier responses. During this stage, clarify any misinformation or gaps in ideas shared by students. If students have not shared ideas related to one or more of the key words and concepts, guide students by using questions such as those listed below.

What do you think of when you hear the term _____?

What do you know about _____?

9. Explain to students that when they use the PreP strategy they access their prior knowledge. Tell them to use the PreP activity to help them construct meaning as they read.

TECHNOLOGY TIP

Organizing Ideas

Storyspace is a hypertext program that facilitates outlining, mapping, and linking texts.

Eastgate Systems 800-562-1638

5.1 ▶ Text Preview

Students who preview a text before reading are in a strategic position to take control of their learning and comprehension. Using the text preview strategy before reading helps students consider what they already know about a topic they will be studying. By helping students activate their prior knowledge about the topic, the Text Preview prepares students to understand what they will be reading.

 ## Directions and Examples

1. Identify a section of text that may be challenging for students. This strategy works best for texts that contain organizational aids such as headings, subheadings, chapter introductions, summaries, chapter questions, pictures, diagrams, and other graphics. Begin modeling this strategy using a think-aloud procedure with the following example or create one from your content area.

   > Notice that our textbook contains many useful organizational aids. These organizational aids are helpful for preparing to read and while reading the textbook.

   > By using a prereading strategy called the Text Preview, you can figure out the kinds of information the text will contain and how it will be presented. In addition, the text preview will help you determine what is important to understand as you read.

2. Guide students through the organization of the chapter, focusing their attention on the important organizational aids in the chapter or section. For example, the textbook will probably contain a title, an introduction, headings, words in bold type, graphics, and chapter questions. Demonstrate this process by saying the following to students.

   > This section has a title, introduction, headings, words in bold type, graphics, and chapter questions. These organizational aids will be very helpful as you get ready to read the textbook. They indicate important information and let you know how key concepts are connected.

3. Direct students to look at the title and make predictions about the subject of the chapter. Provide time for students to share their predictions.

4. Tell students that this textbook also contains an introduction that will provide an overview of what the section will be about. Provide time for students to silently read the introduction. Ask them to list the major ideas that they think will be covered in the section. Provide time for students to share their ideas. Pose questions such as those listed below to help guide students through this step.

   > What seems to be the major focus of the chapter according to the introduction?
   > What are the key ideas mentioned in the introduction?
   > Based on the information in the introduction, what do you think you will learn in this section? Why do you think so?

5. Have students skim the section and look at the headings printed in large, bold type. Ask students to think about the kinds of information that will be contained under each of the headings and why. Guide them through the first section heading to model the process they should use when doing this activity. Use the example below or create one for your own content area.

> First, I will skim the section and look at the headings printed in large, bold type. I will think about what types of information will be contained in each of these sections.

> For example, if I turn to the heading **Population Growth**, I can ask myself questions such as the following ones.

>> What will this section be about and why?
>> What ideas do I already have about population growth?

> I think the section will be about how and why populations grow. I think it might also describe problems of overpopulation in an area. I know that population growth can be a problem for animals, like when too many deer survive the winter and there is not enough food for them in the spring. I also know that population growth can be a problem for humans when they need to expand the roads, increase food supply, and provide water for lots of people.

> I will also look through the paragraphs under this heading to see if there are any words in bold type. Under this heading, there are several words and phrases in bold type. They are **birthrate**, **death rate**, **standard of living**, **life expectancy**, and **population explosion**. I can ask myself the following questions.

>> Do I already know any of these words?
>> Do these words give me any clues about the subject of this part of the section?

6. Instruct students to continue this pattern of looking at headings and words in bold type until they have worked through the remaining headings in the section. Provide time for students to share their findings and ideas.

7. Direct students' attention to graphics in the section and provide time for them to discuss the types of information the graphics provide and why they might be included in the section. Model this process for them using the following example or create an example from your content area.

> On the next page, I see a photograph with a caption. What can I tell about the population of the area in the picture? I wonder why the textbook's authors included this picture in this section of the chapter.

> Figure 6-1 looks important. What types of information does this figure provide? Why might the authors include a figure about actual and projected world population growth in this section of the text? Does this figure give me any additional ideas about what this section might be about? Why?

Ask students to look at any remaining graphics in the section. Encourage students to ask themselves questions such as those that follow.

What types of information does the graphic provide?

Why did the authors include it in the section?

What does the graphic tell me about the types of information that will be in the section?

8. Inform students that the questions at the end of a section are very helpful when preparing to read. Tell students that these questions will help them understand what is important in the section and what they should understand when they finish reading the section. Model this stage of the strategy by using the following example or create an example from your content area.

> At the end of the section, I see the "Content Check" questions. I know these questions are important because we often discuss them in class. Sometimes similar questions are on a test. The first question asks me about some vocabulary words from the section. What important terms should I know and understand after reading this section? I should probably make a list of these words so I can pay attention to them when I read the section.

9. Ask students to look at the remaining questions and have them consider what they will be expected to know after reading the section. Remind students that the Text Preview strategy is an important prereading technique. Encourage them to think about the ideas from the Text Preview strategy as they read.

10. A Text Preview that you can use with students follows.

Text Preview

1. Chapter title _____

2. What do you think this chapter will be about? _____

_____

Introduction

3. What seems to be the major focus of the chapter according to the introduction?

_____

4. What are the key ideas mentioned in the introduction? _____

_____

5. Based on the information in the introduction, what do you think you will learn in this chapter? Why do you think so? _____

_____

Section Questions (to be completed for each section)

6. What will this section be about? Why do you think so? _____

_____

7. What ideas do you already have about the subject matter? _____

_____

Vocabulary in Bold Type

8. Do you already know any of these words?_____ If so, which ones?_____

_____

9. Do these words give you any clues about the subject of this part of the section?

_____

Graphics

10. What type of information do the graphics provide?_____

_____

11. Why did the authors include them in the section?_____

_____

12. What do the graphics tell you about the types of information that will be in the section?

_____

_____

Content Check

13. What important terms should you know and understand after reading this section?

_____

_____

5.1 ▶ Anticipation/Reaction Guide

An Anticipation/Reaction Guide (Herber, 1978) enhances students' comprehension by activating their background knowledge, focusing their attention on key concepts to be addressed in the text reading, and inviting them to react to ideas in the text. An Anticipation/Reaction Guide is composed of a series of statements that support students' opinions or challenge their beliefs about the topic of the text. The statements invite multiple responses based on students' experiences and opinions. Students mark whether they agree or disagree with a specific statement prior to reading about the topic. The real impact of this activity lies in the discussion that occurs after students have marked their responses. During this discussion, the teacher activates and agitates students' thoughts by asking open-ended questions such as "Why do you feel that way?" or "What ideas help to support your view?" Students then read the text to see if their responses change after reading or if their responses agree or disagree with the author's ideas. Another discussion occurs after reading to encourage students to discuss how and why their ideas and opinions changed after reading the text.

 ## Directions and Example

1. Analyze the text to be read. Determine the major ideas students will need to consider.

2. Write those ideas in short, declarative sentences. Try to focus the statements on experiences that relate to students' lives. Limit the number of statements from four to six so ample time can be devoted to thinking about and discussing each statement fully.

3. Arrange the statements in an order and format that will elicit predictions and invite students' participation.

4. Present the Anticipation Guide to students by providing a handout or by writing it on the chalkboard or an overhead transparency, or by using a computer with an LCD panel. Use the following example or create one from your content area.

Science Example

Anticipation/Reaction Guide

Directions: Before reading the section, read the following statements. Put a check mark in the "Before Reading" column next to each statement with which you agree. Be prepared to discuss your responses. After you read the section, put a check mark in the "After Reading" column next to each statement with which you agree. Be prepared to discuss your responses.

Before Reading		After Reading
_____	1. Water belongs to everyone.	_____
_____	2. There is plenty of water for people to use around the world.	_____
_____	3. Animals can migrate if there is not enough water.	_____
_____	4. Droughts mainly affect people and animals in desert climates.	_____
_____	5. The availability of water impacts the lifestyles of humans.	_____
_____	6. Pollution is the greatest threat to the availability of water.	_____

5. Give students a few minutes to respond to each of the statements and to consider how they will explain and support their responses.

6. Discuss each statement. Ask students to support their responses.

7. Explain to students that as they read the text they should consider their ideas from the Anticipation/Reaction Guide and whether their views have stayed the same or have changed after reading the text.

8. After students complete the reading, engage them in a follow-up discussion to determine whether their responses have changed and why.

5.1 Think Sheet

TEACHING STRATEGY 4

The Think Sheet strategy helps students compare and contrast their prereading ideas from the text (Clewell & Haidemenous, 1982). By examining their own background knowledge and questions about a topic to be studied, students will be better prepared to read. After reading, students compare and contrast their ideas and questions with information from the text to help them make connections between their prior knowledge and ideas in the text.

Directions and Example

1. Present the Think Sheet to students. Model the use of this strategy with the following example from a history text or create an example from your content area.

2. Select a text passage that students will be reading. Explain that content area reading often has a central issue. In this example, the central issue is the involvement of the United States in World War I. Write the central issue in the appropriate place on the Think Sheet.

3. Invite students to generate questions about the central issue and write them on the Think Sheet. Examples of questions follow.

> When and where did World War I start?
> Were things better for the United States after the war?
> How many casualties were there?
> How did the war affect the United States?
> Why did we get involved?
> What other countries were involved?

4. Tell students that the second column focuses on their ideas about the central issue.

Ask students to list their own ideas about the central issue on their Think Sheets. Model this stage of the strategy by using the following example or create one from your content area.

> The second column asks me to list ideas that I already know about the central issue. Let's see. I know that World War I started without the United States. I know that the United States only got involved later. I know that a ship sinking had something to do with the United States getting into the war, and I think the war was fought in Europe.

5. Explain to students that they should read to find answers to their questions and also to determine whether their ideas are supported or negated by the text. Ask students to record as they read important ideas from the text in the third column of the Think Sheet.

History Example

Central Issue: The involvement of the United States in World War I

My Questions	My Ideas	Text Ideas
When and where did World War I start?	World War I started without the United States.	
Were things better for the United States after the war?	The United States got involved later.	
How many casualties were there?	A ship being sunk had something to do with the war starting.	
How did the war affect the United States?	I think it was fought in Europe.	
Why did we get involved?		
What other countries were involved?		

6. After students have completed the text reading, ask them to share what they learned from the text. Guide students to make connections among their questions, their ideas, and the ideas in the text by posing questions such as the following ones.

> What did the text say about your questions?
> What questions were not answered in the text?
> What ideas from your Think Sheet did the text support?
> What ideas from your Think Sheet did the text negate?
> Were there some ideas that were only partially supported or negated?
> Explain.

7. A blank Think Sheet follows the example.

TECHNOLOGY
T I P

Literature Discussion Online

American Literature Survey Site provides students with an opportunity to discuss great works online.

www.cwrl.utexas.edu/~daniel/amlit

Name _____   Date _____

Think Sheet

Central Issue _____

_____

My Questions	My Ideas	Text Ideas

Section
5.2

Using Text Structure

Goal To help students use text structure to comprehend texts

BACKGROUND

Various types of texts are structured differently. Effective readers are aware of the structures of texts, and they can use this information to help them anticipate, monitor, and comprehend what they are reading (Taylor & Beach, 1984). Authors use a structure, or organization of ideas, to present their writing in a way that communicates with the reader (Ruddell, 2002). By helping your students develop an awareness of the common text organizational patterns, you will provide them with an important tool for comprehension. If your students understand and can identify text structures, they will be more likely to understand, remember, and apply the ideas they encounter in their reading (Weaver & Kintsch, 1991).

Fiction and nonfiction texts are structured differently. Fiction texts are organized around the concept of a story grammar that includes setting, characters, goal, problem, and resolution. Many of your students may already be familiar with the organization of fiction because, during the elementary school years, they received a great deal of instruction on reading fiction. They will need assistance, however, with developing a clear understanding of the more complex fictional stories and novels they

will be reading during their middle and high school years. In addition, more complex aspects of plot development, such as initiating events, internal responses, character motivation, and theme, may be new to middle and high school students.

Nonfiction texts are often more difficult for students to comprehend because they may not understand how these texts are organized. Nonfiction texts are generally organized around five common text patterns: description, sequence, compare-contrast, cause-effect, and problem-solution. Authors often use signal or flag words to help readers identify the text structure being used. For example, an author may use words such as *because, since, therefore, consequently,* and *as a result* to signal that the cause-effect text structure is being used (Vacca & Vacca, 2002). Most informational writing is complex, including content area textbooks, and several text structures may be used in a section of text. If you are aware of the text structures used in a specific text, you will be more able to help your students become aware of signal words and text structures. Helping your students to identify and understand common text structures will enhance their comprehension.

TECHNOLOGY
T I P

Learning to Read Literature

How to Read and Understand Drama CD-ROM: learn forms of drama and strategies to read plays.

How to Read and Understand Poetry CD-ROM: learn forms of poetry and techniques to understand the meaning of poems.

How to Read and Understand Short Fiction CD-ROM: see how a writer uses setting, tone, character, plot, and mood to convey themes in short stories.

UPDATA 800-882-2844

TEACHING STRATEGY 5

5.2 ▶ Graphic Organizers

Graphic Organizers are pictorial representations of how ideas in a text are connected and organized. They help students understand main ideas in what they read, how ideas are related, and how important details support main ideas. Graphic Organizers serve purposes similar to outlining, but they provide more flexibility and capitalize on students' interests and facility with visual representations (Vacca & Vacca, 1996).

TECHNOLOGY
T I P

Building Relationships Among Ideas

Learning Tool is a hypertext program that allows writers to build relationships among ideas.

Intellimation 800-346-8355

Directions and Example

1. Tell students that, when they understand the ways texts are organized, they will be able to organize the information and understand it better. Explain to students that by using Graphic Organizers they can organize information more readily.

2. Select a passage that you want students to read. Explain to students that you will be modeling the use of Graphic Organizers to help them understand how the information is organized, thus promoting better comprehension.

3. Explain that there are five main patterns for organizing content texts: description, sequence, compare-contrast, cause-effect, and problem-solution. Write these words on the chalkboard or an overhead transparency.

4. Model how to use a Graphic Organizer using examples from your content area or use the following example.

    We will be using a Graphic Organizer for a section of our social studies textbook. The section describes how the North and South felt about slavery. We will be using the Compare-Contrast Graphic Organizer for this activity.

5. Present the Compare-Contrast Graphic Organizer by displaying it on the chalkboard or an overhead transparency. Explain that one item being compared goes in each circle, and the overlapping area contains information that the concepts have in common as in the following example.

Compare-Contrast Graphic Organizer

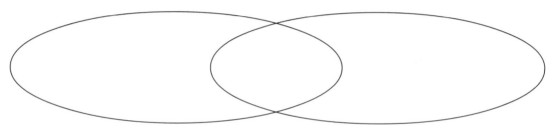

6. Model for students how to read the text and identify important information to include in the Compare-Contrast Graphic Organizer. Continue to use examples from your content area or use the following example.

    Compare-contrast pattern means that the text will present two different concepts and how they are alike and how they are different. Skim the section. Note that the text presents information about the North and the South. The introduction also states that the text will be comparing how the people in the North and the South felt about slavery during the Civil War. This information will be helpful as you start to fill in the Compare-Contrast Graphic Organizer. Fill in a title and label each of the circles to show what you are comparing and contrasting.

**Compare-Contrast Graphic Organizer for
North and South Positions on Slavery Issue**

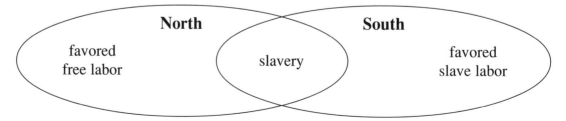

7. Read the first section aloud and demonstrate for students the thought processes you use to identify important information from the text. Continue to use examples from your content area or the following example.

> After reading the first part of the section, I learned that the North and the South had different opinions about the labor system. The North favored a free labor system, and the South favored a slave labor system. This is the main idea in this part of the section. I will add it to the compare-contrast chart.
>
> While that is an important difference, I also learned that when I compared the North and the South, they had something in common. They both needed a lot of labor to build their new and growing economies. I can add this to the compare section of the Graphic Organizer. I can continue to use the same strategy as I read the other parts of the text.

8. Ask students to read the remaining parts of the section and fill in important comparisons and contrasts between the North and the South on their Graphic Organizers. Then have students in small groups discuss their compare-contrast charts to clarify and expand on their comparisons. Students may also include some comparisons that are not important. Such comparisons should be deleted.

9. In future lessons, introduce other Graphic Organizers to help students learn how to use them for other text organizational patterns. (Several Graphic Organizers are provided on the following pages.) Provide modeling and practice so students can learn how to use Graphic Organizers to understand text organizational patterns and improve their comprehension of texts.

Graphic Organizer for Description

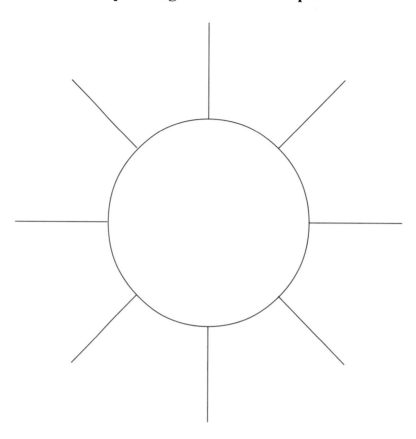

Graphic Organizer for Sequence

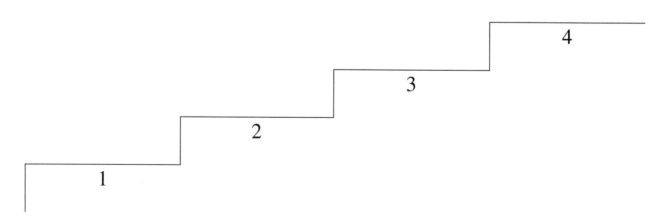

Graphic Organizer for Cause and Effect

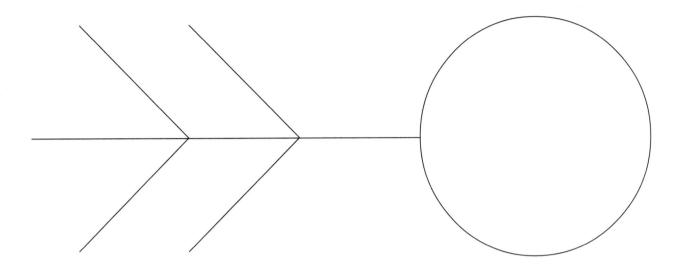

Graphic Organizer for Problem and Solution

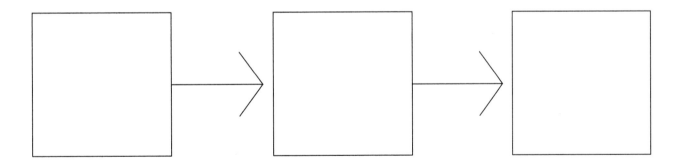

5.2 ▶ **Idea-Maps**

TEACHING STRATEGY 6

An Idea-Map is a strategy that helps readers see how information in an expository text is organized (Armbruster, 1986). The visual nature of the Idea-Map strategy helps students see and understand the organizational pattern of a text and how the various components fit together. Depending on the text to be studied, different forms of Idea-Maps can be used. For example, Idea-Maps can be designed for use with description, sequence, compare-contrast, cause-effect, and problem-solution patterns (Johns & Lenski, 2001).

 ## Directions and Examples

1. Select a passage that you want students to read and learn. Determine the organizational pattern of the text. Select the appropriate Idea-Map for the text. Several types of Idea-Maps are included at the end of these directions.

2. Tell students that you will be demonstrating how to use a strategy called Idea-Maps to help them understand how their content textbooks are organized.

3. Explain that there are five main patterns for organizing content texts: description, sequence, compare-contrast, cause-effect, and problem-solution. Write these words on the chalkboard or an overhead transparency.

4. Model the Idea-Map strategy using examples from your content area or use the following example from *Science Interactions* (1995). Tell students that the first step in using an Idea-Map is to identify the text's organizational pattern. Model how to determine the text's pattern as in the following example.

   > We will be reading section 11-2 from our science textbook. This section focuses on how the digestive system works. Skim through the section. You'll notice that there are a series of steps that occur in the digestive system. This is a good clue that the text is using the organizational pattern of sequence.

5. Present the Idea-Map for sequential text patterns by displaying it on the chalkboard or an overhead transparency.

Sequence Idea-Map

TOPIC:
↓
↓
↓
↓

6. Model for students how to read the text and identify the important information to include in the Idea-Map. Begin with the topic for the section. Continue to use examples from your content area or the following example.

> Sequencing ideas means that they need to be in order, just like the steps in a science experiment. As you read this section on digestion, look for the important steps. As you identify steps in the sequence, write them on the Idea-Map in the order they were presented.
>
> First, read the introduction of the section to clarify the topic of the section. The title of the section is "Digestion: A Disassembly Line." As you read the introduction, notice that the word **digestion** is in bold type and a definition is provided. The definition says "Digestion is the process that breaks down carbohydrates, fats, and proteins into smaller and simpler molecules used by the cells in your body" (p. 351).
>
> It seems like the topic of the section is digestion—a process that breaks down fats, carbohydrates, and proteins for use in the body. Fill that in on the topic section of the Idea-Map.

7. Continue to model the process for comprehending the passage by identifying details in order. Use examples from your content area or use the example provided below.

> Look at the next part of the section; it has a heading called **The Mouth**. As you read this part, notice that digestion begins in the mouth. The passage also states how the teeth, saliva, and enzymes begin to break down the food. This seems like an important first step in the digestion process, so add it to the Idea-Map.
>
> The next section of the passage has a heading **From Mouth to Stomach**. As you read this part, notice that the passage states that food travels from the mouth down the esophagus to the stomach. This is the next important step in digestion, so add it to the Idea-Map.
>
> Your Idea-Map should look something like the one that follows.

Sequence Idea-Map

TOPIC: Digestion is a process that breaks down carbohydrates, fats, and proteins for use in the body.
Digestion begins in the mouth with the teeth, saliva, and enzymes breaking down the food. ↓
Next, the food moves from the mouth down the esophagus to the stomach. This process is called peristalsis. ↓
↓
↓

8. Tell students that they can use the same techniques that you modeled to fill out the rest of the Idea-Map. Provide time for students to read the rest of the section and fill out the remainder of the Idea-Map.

9. Ask students to share and refine their Idea-Maps. Remind students that the Idea-Map is a helpful tool that uses text structure to improve their comprehension.

10. In future lessons, introduce other Idea-Maps that are appropriate for your texts. (Additional Idea-Maps can be found on the following pages.) Provide sufficient modeling and practice opportunities so students can learn how to use the Idea-Maps to improve their understanding of text structures and content texts.

Description Idea-Map

TOPIC:

Compare-Contrast Idea-Map

TOPIC:		TOPIC:
	=	
	=	
	=	
	=	
	=	
	=	

Problem-Solution Idea-Map

PROBLEM:

→

SOLUTION:

Cause-Effect Idea-Map

CAUSE:

→

EFFECT:

5.2 Story Maps

Story Maps are graphic organizers for fictional texts. Fictional texts have a different text structure than informational texts. Fictional texts are organized around the elements of fiction: setting, characters, theme, and events in the plot. Many middle and high school students are familiar with the elements of fiction because they have had many experiences reading stories and identifying the stories' elements. However, as middle and high school students read more sophisticated stories with subtle plots, they should be reminded to identify the structures of the stories to enhance their comprehension.

Directions and Example

1. Remind students that as they read they should identify the elements of fiction to help them understand the story.

2. Write the elements of fiction on the chalkboard or an overhead transparency. Include blank spaces after each term as listed below.

    Setting (time and place) _____

    Major characters _____

    Minor characters _____

    Problem _____

    Events _____

    Solution _____

    Theme (main point of story) _____

3. Review the elements of fiction using a story or book that students have read. Tell students that the setting is the time and place the story took place. If students are reading "The Ransom of Red Chief" by O. Henry, for example, tell them that the setting is in western Illinois during the westward expansion. Have students complete the blank next to the term *setting*. Then have students identify the major and minor characters in the story and write the names of the characters on the blanks. After that, have students identify the problem in the story, the events in sequence, and the solution. Finally, have students identify the theme of the story.

4. Tell students that they should use what they know about the way fiction is organized to help them understand the story. Invite students to explain how the Story Map can help them understand the story. Encourage students to use Story Maps to identify and record a story's elements during reading.

5. A blank copy of a Story Map follows.

Name _____ Date _____

Story Map

Title

Setting

Characters

Problem

Events

▼

▼

▼

Solution

From Susan Davis Lenski, Mary Ann Wham, and Jerry L. Johns, *Reading & Learning Strategies: Middle Grades through High School,* 2nd Edition. Copyright © 2003 by Kendall/Hunt Publishing Company (1-800-247-3458, ext. 4 or 5). May be reproduced for noncommercial educational purposes.

5.2

TEACHING STRATEGY 8

Signal Words

Signal Words help students identify text patterns and understand what they are reading. Teaching students common Signal Words and the signals they provide helps students become more skilled readers of content area texts. Tomlinson (1995) suggests teaching Signal Words through modeling and application activities. Teaching specific Signal Words helps students understand how text is organized and enhances their comprehension.

Directions and Example

1. Select a section of content text and identify its main organizational pattern. Develop a list of common Signal Words for this organizational pattern.

2. Make photocopies of the text section so students can write on the text.

3. Explain to students that authors use Signal Words to give readers clues about how the text is organized and what information is important. Use examples from your content area or use the following example to model this strategy for students.

    > Signal Words can help you understand our geography text. We will be reading a section called "Population Issues." This part of the text is mainly organized using a problem-solution pattern. We have a list of Signal Words that we will use to help you better understand how the text is organized and what ideas are important. A list of Signal Words follows.

    > because
    > since
    > therefore
    > consequently
    > as a result of
    > this led to
    > so that
    > nevertheless
    > accordingly
    > if . . . then
    > thus
    > subsequently

4. Model the process of identifying Signal Words and then annotating the text to focus on important ideas. Continue to use examples from your content area or use the example provided below.

    > As I begin to read the section, I am looking for Signal Words from the list. I see the word *therefore* in a sentence. It says, "One of the most basic needs threatened by overpopulation is food; therefore, many countries have programs for population control" (p. 119).

I will highlight the word *therefore*, and in the margin I will write a brief note called an annotation to remind myself of this important idea. I will write "overpopulation and limited food = problem; population control = solution." I can continue to use this same technique as I work through the text section.

5. Distribute the photocopies of the text section to students. Provide them with highlighter markers or colored pens to identify Signal Words and to write brief annotations in the margins.

6. Provide time for students to read the section and highlight and annotate the text.

7. Ask students to share the Signal Words they identified and the annotations they wrote. Discuss how this strategy is helpful when they are reading and studying.

8. In future lessons, introduce and model Signal Words for other text patterns. (See the box below for Signal Words.)

9. After multiple experiences with various text patterns and their common Signal Words, students will begin to identify text patterns and Signal Words on their own. A list of sample Signal Words is provided in the box.

Signal Words for Text Patterns

Description	Sequence	Compare-Contrast	Cause-Effect Problem-Solution
for instance	on (date)	however	because
to begin with	not long after	but	since
also	now	as well as	therefore
in fact	as	on the other hand	consequently
for example	before	not only . . . but also	as a result of
in addition	after	either . . . or	this led to
characteristics of	when	same as	so that
	first	in contrast	nevertheless
	second	while	accordingly
	next	although	if . . . then
	then	more than	thus
	last	less than	subsequently
	finally	unless	
		similarly	
		yet	
		likewise	
		on the contrary	

Monitoring Understanding

Goal To help students monitor their understanding while reading

BACKGROUND

Effective readers monitor their comprehension as they read. They consider whether what they are reading makes sense, the questions they have about the text, and what they expect to happen next. Effective readers are actively engaged in thinking while they are reading. They ask themselves questions such as "Do I understand what I'm reading?" and "What is the main idea of what I am reading?"

Metacognition is an important aspect of monitoring comprehension while reading. Metacognition refers to the awareness of one's own thinking processes, and it contains two major components: knowledge and regulation (Flavell, 1981). Knowledge includes self-knowledge, or how one thinks, and task knowledge, or the students' knowledge about skills, strategies, and resources needed to complete a task. The second component of metacognition is self-regulation, which involves the ability to monitor and regulate comprehension (Baker & Brown, 1984). Pressley (2000) suggests that students who ask themselves why each fact in the text makes sense remember much more of what is presented in the text.

Baker (1991) has identified six areas that will help students develop comprehension monitoring. Students should be on the lookout for the following items.

- Words they don't understand

- Information that doesn't connect with what they already know

- Ideas that don't fit together because they don't know who or what is being described

- Ideas that don't fit together because they don't know how the ideas are related

- Ideas that don't fit together because the ideas seem contradictory

- Information that is missing or not clearly explained

You can help your students become actively involved in their own reading by teaching them specific strategies to monitor and regulate their comprehension. In addition, you can encourage the use of comprehension-monitoring strategies by creating a classroom climate where you focus on helping students learn how to learn. By providing opportunities for students to reflect on and discuss their learning, you will help your students become more aware of how they read, comprehend, and learn.

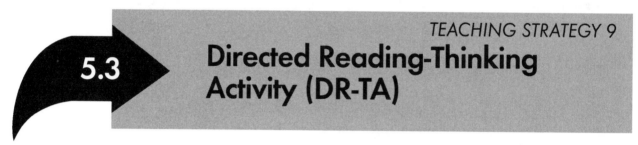

TECHNOLOGY

Teaching Comprehension

www.lessonplanspage.com

**T
I
P**

TEACHING STRATEGY 9

5.3 **Directed Reading-Thinking Activity (DR-TA)**

The Directed Reading-Thinking Activity (DR-TA) actively involves students in a prediction-reading-verification-prediction process (Stauffer, 1969). This strategy can be applied to fiction or content texts. The goal of the DR-TA is for students to integrate the prediction-reading-verification-prediction process into their independent reading. The teacher uses the following questions.

- What do you think is going to happen?
- Why do you think so?
- Can you prove it?

 Directions and Examples

1. Select a fictional text that students will be reading. Identify the key elements of the text such as setting, plot events, goal, problem, and solution. This information will help you determine appropriate stopping points for the DR-TA.

2. Use the following timeline to assist you with determining appropriate stopping points in the DR-TA. It is important to limit the number of stopping points so you do not interrupt students' comprehension or interest in the story. At the stopping points, ask students to make predictions about the story and then to support or explain their predictions. As you progress to the next stopping point, ask students to reconsider their earlier predictions in light of new information they have learned from reading the story. Also, invite students to make and support new predictions.

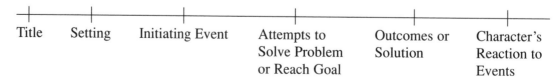

Title   Setting   Initiating Event   Attempts to Solve Problem or Reach Goal   Outcomes or Solution   Character's Reaction to Events

3. Model the DR-TA strategy for students using examples from your content area or use the following example from the story "Flowers for Algernon" by Daniel Keyes. Ask students to read the title and predict what the story will be about. Have students share their predictions with a classmate.

4. After students have predicted the contents of the story from the title, have them provide evidence for their predictions. Have them ask the following questions: Why do I think so? and What clues did I use to make my prediction? Model the questioning by providing an example similar to the following one.

> I predict that the story "Flowers for Algernon" will be about someone who receives flowers for a special reason. I know that you give someone flowers for special occasions or when someone is sick. I think Algernon must be the main character because his name is in the title. I think Algernon will get flowers for a certain reason, but I need more information to figure out this reason. When I read the first part of the story, I will pay careful attention to see if my predictions are right.

5. Next, ask students to read a portion of the text to a predetermined stopping point. Tell them that you will be discussing their initial predictions and asking them to make new predictions. Continue to use examples from your content area or use the following example.

> I will read from page 268 to the bottom of page 271. After I finish reading, I need to ask myself "Do my predictions about the title still make sense?" and "What do I think will happen next in the story?" Finally, I need to ask myself "What part of the story gave me a clue?"

6. Invite students to make and support their predictions about the story. Continue using this pattern for the remainder of the story. The questions in the box will be helpful as you engage students in the DR-TA strategy with fictional texts.

Questions for DR-TA with Fiction

- What do you think the story will be about?
- Why do you think so?
- What do you think will happen next?
- What part of the story gave you a clue?

---

7. Tell students that when they read content material they should use DR-TA questions that are adapted for expository reading. Using an example from your content area or the following example, model how readers use questioning while reading content area texts.

8. Select a content text that students will be reading. Determine appropriate stopping places based on the content and organization of the text. Suggested stopping places for content texts are listed below.

- Title, headings, and subheadings
- Introduction
- Discussion of key concepts or events
- Discussion of final concepts or events

9. Model the strategy for students using examples from your content area or the following example.

> I will be using the Directed Reading-Thinking Activity (DR-TA) to help me understand and monitor my reading from our science book.
>
> First, I will read the title, and then I will look at the headings and subheadings in the section. I can ask myself the question "What do I think this section will be about?" From the title, I know it will be about the insides and inner workings of living things.
>
> Next, I can ask myself what clues and information I used to make my predictions. From the headings and subheadings, I saw several mentions of cells. It seems that the section will teach me about how cells work. I also used what I know about science to help me make predictions.

10. Invite students to make and support predictions about what they think they will read about in the section.

11. Next, ask students to read a portion of the text to a predetermined stopping point. Tell students that you will be discussing their initial predictions and asking them to make new predictions. Continue to use examples from your content area or use the following example.

> After I finish reading, I need to ask myself "Do my predictions about the title, headings, and subheadings still make sense?" and "What other information do I think I will read about in this section?" Finally, I need to ask myself "Why do I think so?"

12. Invite students to make and support their predictions about the next section of text.

13. Continue using this pattern for the remainder of the text. The questions in the box will be helpful as you engage students in the DR-TA strategy with content texts.

Questions for DR-TA with Content Texts

- What do you think the section will be about?
- Why do you think so?
- What do you think you will read about in the next section?
- What clues did you use to make your predictions?

TEACHING STRATEGY 10

5.3 ▶ ReQuest

ReQuest (Manzo, 1969) enhances students' comprehension by teaching them to ask their own questions about what they are reading. When students ask themselves questions while reading, they have a greater likelihood of monitoring their understanding of the text and of having better comprehension. ReQuest was originally designed for use with individual students; however, it can easily be adapted for use with a group of students.

✛ Directions and Example

1. Select a content text your students will be reading. Choose a section that contains many new ideas that may be challenging to students.

2. Introduce the ReQuest strategy to students by modeling its use. Use examples from your content area or use the following example from a science text. Tell students that they will be using a strategy called ReQuest to help them read, monitor, and understand the textbook passage. Begin reading the first paragraph of the text aloud. Then ask and answer questions about the contents of the passage in the following manner.

Question:	What is heat?
Answer:	Heat is the transfer of energy from something with a higher temperature to something with a lower temperature. For example, if you touch a hot surface like a stove, you feel the heat on your hand.
Question:	What is temperature?
Answer:	Temperature is a measurement of how much heat or thermal energy there is in an object. Temperature is used to measure the weather, or how much heat there is outside. It is also used to measure the heat in a stove or the amount of heat in our bodies.
Question:	Are heat and temperature the same or different?
Answer:	Heat and temperature are related, but they are not the same. Heat is the amount of thermal energy in an object, and temperature is the way we measure heat.

3. Ask students to read the next section of text. Limit this section to no more than a paragraph or two. Tell students that they will be taking turns asking you questions about what they read, and you will answer their questions, just like you modeled for them.

4. Ask students to read the next section of text. Inform them that you will be asking them questions about the section and they will be answering your questions.

5. Continue to alternate between student-generated questions and teacher-generated questions until the entire passage has been read.

6. Remind students to ask themselves questions as they read, because such questions will help them monitor and understand what they are reading.

5.3 ➤ Expectation Outline

The Expectation Outline (Speigel, 1981) helps students ask questions about their text. The focus of this strategy is for students to predict what they think they will learn from reading an assigned text selection. Having students predict what they expect to learn from text helps them approach their assignment with a questioning, active stance. This stance will assist students as they monitor their comprehension of the material.

 ## Directions and Example

1. Select a text that students will be reading. Teach the use of the Expectation Outline strategy with an example from your content area or use the following example from a social studies text. The chapter in the example is titled "The Cultures of North Africa."

2. Tell students that as they prepare to read they should take a few minutes and preview the chapter by reading the title, headings, and subheadings. Some of the headings in this chapter are listed below.

   Culture in North Africa
   The Influence of Islam
   Five Pillars of Islam
   Cultural Change in North Africa

   Several subheadings follow.

   Preserving Muslim Culture
   The Diffusion of Culture
   Islam Unifies the People of North Africa

3. After students preview the text, have them ask themselves what they think the assignment will be about. Tell them to think of specific questions related to the text as they preview the headings and subheadings.

4. Invite students to share the questions they think the text will answer. Write their questions on the chalkboard or on an overhead transparency. For example, if they think the reading assignment will focus on the culture of North Africa, they might ask the following questions.

   What is culture?
   What are the cultures of North Africa?
   What is cultural diffusion?
   What is Islam?
   How does Islam influence the North African culture?
   What are the Five Pillars of Islam?
   Who are Muslims?

5. Ask students to explain how they decided on their questions. Encourage them to refer to specific clues in the text that helped them generate questions. For example, a student might say, "When I saw the title, The Influence of Islam, I wondered how Islam influenced the people who live there." Another student might suggest that the subheading Preserving Muslim Culture made her wonder about Muslims and ask the question, "Who are Muslims?"

6. On the chalkboard or an overhead transparency, group similar questions together and ask students to suggest labels for each group of questions as you write down their suggestions. From this example, students might have questions grouped and labeled in the following manner.

Culture
What is culture?
What are the cultures of North Africa?
What is cultural diffusion?

Islam
What is Islam?
Who are Muslims?
Who is Allah?
What are the Pillars of Islam?
How does Islam influence the North African culture?

7. Engage students in discussing the major areas that they expect to learn by reading the text. Explain that they may find gaps between their expectations and the text. For example, explain that they may find that some of their questions will not be answered and that other ideas may be included that were not on their Expectation Outlines.

8. Ask students to read the text keeping in mind the questions they generated.

9. After students have completed their reading, discuss the answers they found to their questions. Also, discuss other sources they can use to find answers to the questions that were not addressed in the text.

5.3 ➤ Think Aloud for Monitoring

TEACHING STRATEGY 12

The Think Aloud for Monitoring strategy is helpful for teaching students the types of thought processes they should be using as they monitor their reading. Often times, students do not fully understand the types of questions and prompts that good readers use as they read. Think Aloud for Monitoring helps students understand self-questioning techniques and strategies they can use to monitor and regulate their comprehension.

Directions and Example

1. Select a content passage that students will be reading. Look for a passage that contains difficult concepts, ambiguous information, and/or unknown words. Determine what strategy or strategies you will demonstrate during Think Aloud for Monitoring.

2. Implement Think Aloud for Monitoring by using examples from your content area or by using the following example.

> I am going to demonstrate how you can use strategies to monitor and regulate your comprehension while you read your textbook. I will be using the section "Radiation, Energy, and Atoms" in our chemistry textbook.
>
> As I read I see that food irradiation is being protested, but the book says it is safe. I think that all radiation comes from nuclear energy, but the book hasn't told me that yet. I wonder if that is the difference? Maybe food irradiation uses another kind of energy. I guess I will read on until the end of the page to see if the book clears up this problem.
>
> Now that I'm at the end of the page, I see that irradiation can be from nuclear energy, but it also can be from the sun. There is even microwave radiation that we use to cook our foods. Reading on to the end of the page really helped me understand what I was reading.

3. Encourage students to use Think Aloud for Monitoring regularly with various texts as they read independently. Suggestions for strategies to use with Think Aloud for Monitoring are provided below.

Think Aloud for Monitoring Strategies

- Making predictions
- Developing mental images
- Making analogies
- Connecting new information to background knowledge
- Self-questioning
- Using fix-up strategies to regulate comprehension

Extending Meaning

Goal > To help students reflect on and extend the meaning of texts

BACKGROUND

Reading does not end when students have finished a chapter or section in a text. In order to develop rich comprehension, readers need to reflect on and extend the meaning of the texts they have read. They need to clarify concepts and ideas from their reading, consider their personal responses, share ideas and insights with others, and apply the information they have read to new situations. If you provide opportunities for your students to engage in conversations, writing, and projects after reading, they will be able to extend and deepen their understanding of texts.

Reading is an interactive process and "first and foremost a conversation, a give-and-take exchange, between the reader and the text" (Vacca & Vacca, 2002, p. 28). All students will not interpret the same text in the same manner. Teaching strategies that encourage students to consider responses to open-ended questions will invite divergent thinking and extend and deepen students' understanding of what they have read. With this approach to comprehension instruction, emphasis is put on justifying and explaining responses rather than just producing simple factual information.

According to McKenna and Robinson (1990), content literacy involves a combination of general literacy skills, content-specific literacy skills such as reading maps and charts, and accessing prior knowledge related to the content being studied. One goal for students should be to achieve content area literacy. Content area literacy is strengthened when students interact with peers and teachers. Pearson and Fielding (1991) support a view of comprehension instruction that takes into account the social aspects of instruction and learning. During peer interactions, students tend to offer explanations rather than just right answers. This leads students to analyze, consider, and extend the meaning of the text. Students who are encouraged to work collaboratively with peers demonstrate increased productivity and achievement within the content areas (Readence, Bean, & Baldwin, 2001).

The teaching strategies in this section focus on helping students reflect on and extend the meaning of texts they have read. The emphasis is on providing opportunities for students to process text and to think deeply about what it means, to consider how the ideas relate to their lives, and to apply the ideas to new situations.

5.4   Biopoems

Biopoems (Gere, 1985) follow a pattern that allows students to creatively reflect on content material within a poetic format. Although generally used to incorporate biographic data, the Biopoem structure permits students to synthesize what they have learned about a person, place, thing, concept, or event. Additionally, constructing a Biopoem requires students to focus on the important aspects of a topic in order to synthesize the data into a concise format. An added positive aspect of using the Biopoem is that it naturally combines language arts with other content material.

Directions and Examples

1. Choose a section of content text that students have completed reading.

2. Tell students that you are going to show them how to incorporate aspects of their content material into a poetic format.

3. Begin by placing a copy of the basic structure of a Biopoem on an overhead transparency. Explain to students that this is the basic structure of the poem they will be writing. The basic structure of a Biopoem is printed at the end of the example.

4. For their first experience with a Biopoem, tell students that they are going to write a poem using themselves as the subjects.

5. Ask students to think for a minute about the personal traits that make them special and to compose a short list of these traits.

6. Using the formula for the Biopoem, write your own Biopoem on the overhead transparency as your students observe. It might look something like this.

>   **Subject:** Louise
>
>   **Four traits that describe subject:** busy, dedicated, happy, and organized
>
>   **Relative of:** Rich, Sally, and Heidi
>
>   **Lover of:** pizza, good novels, beaches, and Cubs baseball
>
>   **Who feels:** anxious, hungry, fortunate, and determined
>
>   **Who needs:** my family, my car, and my pets
>
>   **Who fears:** illness, terrorism, and tornadoes
>
>   **Who gives:** advice when asked, money to charity, and time to students
>
>   **Who would like to see:** world peace, an early spring, and George Clooney
>
>   **Resident of:** Iowa
>
>   **Last name:** Hunt

7. Give students time to write their personal Biopoems. After they have completed writing, suggest to students that they share their poems in small groups. After several minutes, ask for volunteers to share their work with the entire class.

8. Now tell students that they are going to apply the Biopoem format to an aspect of their content area. Students might choose to write their poems about a particular person from their social studies text or use the poem to describe their state or perhaps some scientific concept. In the example that follows, material from a science text that focuses on the human body and specifically on the skeletal structure is used.

Subject: Skeletal

Four traits that describe the subject: bones, white, porous, semirigid

Relative of: the muscular system

Lover of: calcium, blood, exercise

Who feels: pain, poor posture, and old mattresses

Who needs: muscles, ligaments, tendons, and nerves

Who fears: breaks, sprains, and excess weight

Who gives: shape, strength, movement

Who would like to see: healthy bodies, strong bones, balanced diets

Resident of: my body

Last name: System

9. Assign a content subject, such as social studies. Encourage students to select a specific person, place, or thing within the subject area and to begin writing a Biopoem using their texts and other materials as resources for ideas and words. Encourage them to discuss their ideas with a partner and to share their work if they choose to do so. You might want to develop a class notebook featuring their compositions.

10. A blank Biopoem follows.

Name _____ Date _____

Biopoem

Subject _____

Four traits that describe the subject:

_____   _____   _____   _____

Relative of: (list three things or people)

_____   _____   _____

Lover of: (list three things or people)

_____   _____   _____

Who feels: (list three items) _____   _____   _____

Who needs: (list three items) _____   _____   _____

Who fears: _____

Who gives: _____

Who would like to see: _____

Resident of: _____

Last name: _____

5.4 ► GIST

GIST (Cunningham, 1982) is a strategy designed to improve students' comprehension of text material and to enhance their ability to write a summary paragraph. The acronym **GIST** stands for **G**enerating **I**nteractions between **S**chemata and **T**ext. While practicing this strategy, students will have the added benefit of "honing their ability to analyze and synthesize content area readings" (Sejnost & Thiese, 2001, p. 160).

◄⊕► Directions and Example

1. Choose a three to five paragraph passage from your content area text. Reproduce it on an overhead transparency and display it on an overhead projector. You may use an example from your content area or use the following example from a history text about the emergence of capitalism during the Middle Ages.

2. Divide your students into small groups of four to six students per group. Show the students only the first paragraph of the passage.

    > The modern economic system of capitalism has its roots in the Middle Ages. Capitalism, also known as free enterprise, is defined as an economic system based on private ownership for the purpose of producing goods and services. Capitalism involves competition and profit.
    >
    > During the Middle Ages, as towns grew and manors declined, an economy based on land began to be replaced by an economy based on money. Thus the quantity and quality of goods and services being sold began to have an impact on prices.
    >
    > Because of the change in the economy, serfdom began to disappear. Although serfs were not slaves, they could not leave the land and were still obligated to a lord. By the end of the fourteenth century many serfs were paying rent. The serfs' obligations to their lords became a money payment as a reflection of the new capitalistic society.
    >
    > Adapted from *The pageant of world history*. (1994). Needham, MA: Prentice-Hall.

3. Ask students to read the first paragraph silently and to independently write a summary of the paragraph in 25 words or less. Tell students that it is important for them to use as many of their own words as possible.

4. After approximately 10 minutes, ask students to share their summary paragraphs with their groups. Direct them to pool their ideas and write one summary paragraph based on their group's ideas.

5. Using your students' suggestions as a basis for discussion, write a class summary of the first paragraph. It may look something like the following.

    > Capitalism had its beginning in the Middle Ages and is an economic system based on private ownership. It involves competition and profit.

6. Show students the second paragraph on the transparency and again have students independently write a summary of 25 words or less. This time, however, their summary paragraphs are to encompass the information from **both** paragraphs. Once again, ask students to share their paragraphs in their small groups and write one summary paragraph based on their group's ideas. Their paragraph may look something like the one that follows.

    > Capitalism is based on private ownership and involves competition and profit. It developed during the Middle Ages when towns grew and manors declined.

7. Continue this process until all three paragraphs are incorporated into a GIST summary. The final summary could look like the following.

    > Capitalism, based on competition and profit, developed during the Middle Ages. As manors declined, serfs were still obligated to their lords but started to pay rent.

8. As students become more proficient at generating GIST summaries, encourage them to practice the strategy on their own. This will help them learn to delete trivial information, focus on main ideas and use their own words to make generalizations.

TEACHING STRATEGY 15

5.4 ▶ Three Level Guides

Three Level Guides help students think about texts on the literal, interpretive, and applied levels. Three Level Guides facilitate students' comprehension by moving from lower to higher levels of comprehension (Herber, 1978).

 ## Directions and Examples

1. Select a text that students will be reading. Identify literal information that students should know after reading the text. This information should focus on explicit ideas that are clearly presented in the text.

2. Identify interpretive information you want students to understand after reading the text. Include inferences or other examples of "reading between the lines."

3. Identify applied level information that you want students to consider. These ideas go beyond what is written in the text and require students to use information, express opinions, and create new ideas.

4. Develop a Three Level Guide that presents three to six statements for each of the three levels: literal, interpretive, and applied. These statements should be written clearly and simply.

5. Present the Three Level Guide to students and model its use with examples from your content area or use the following example.

Social Studies Example

Three Level Guide for Southern Colonies

I. Literal Level
Check the items that specifically show what the author wrote in the chapter. Be prepared to support your choices.

_____ 1. Lord Baltimore founded the colony of Maryland to provide a place for Catholics to worship freely.

_____ 2. The Act of Toleration in 1649 provided religious freedom to all people.

_____ 3. The Carolinas had large estates that were worked by slaves.

II. Interpretive Level
Check the items that show what the author meant in the chapter. Be prepared to discuss supporting evidence from the chapter.

_____ 1. Wealthy tobacco planters controlled the best lands in Virginia because they arrived in the colony first.

_____ 2. Bacon's Rebellion was organized to show the colonists' lack of support for the Virginia governor.

_____ 3. Georgia was started as a place for freed debtors to get a fair, new start in life.

_____ 4. The colonies of North Carolina and South Carolina had more similarities than differences.

III. Applied Level
Check the items that you agree with and be ready to share examples from the text and your own knowledge to support your responses.

_____ 1. Religious freedom was the most important reason for starting the Southern colonies.

_____ 2. The settlers believed that they had the right to take land from the Native Americans.

_____ 3. The Southern farmers worked mainly for survival.

_____ 4. England wanted military men to lead colonies because they were good leaders.

6. Ask students to read the assigned text selection that will be addressed by the Three Level Guide.

7. Model the process of filling out a Three Level Guide using examples from your content area or use the example provided below.

> When I fill out a Three Level Guide, I need to first think about the literal information that I read. This means I need to know about the facts that are presented in the chapter. Statement 1 says "Lord Baltimore founded the colony of Maryland to provide a place for Catholics to worship freely." I think this is what I read in the text. I see that on page 109 of the text it says just this. I will check this statement and make a note of page 109 so I can support why I checked this statement.

8. Have students read and discuss the remaining statements in the literal level section of the Three Level Guide. Remind them to locate the places in the text that support their responses.

9. Model how to respond to the interpretive level statements by using examples from your content area or continue using the example provided below.

> I need to think about the interpretive level now. This means I need to think about what the author meant. I might need to make inferences, and I will need to put together pieces of information from different parts of the chapter to respond to these statements.
>
> The first statement in the interpretive level says "Wealthy tobacco planters controlled the best lands in Virginia because they arrived in the colony first." This sounds like it might be true, but I'm not sure. I need to go back to the chapter and look for support. I see that on page 110 it says that the wealthy tobacco planters controlled the best land near the coast. The chapter doesn't say that they got there first. It does say, however, that they were wealthy and powerful and that the government told other planters to take land from the Indians. I won't check this statement because the chapter implies that the reason the tobacco planters controlled the best lands was because they were wealthy people. I will make a few notes in the margin of the Three Level Guide to remind myself why I didn't mark this statement.

10. Have students read and discuss the remaining statements in the interpretive level section of the Three Level Guide. Remind them to make notes to support their responses.

11. Model how to respond to the applied level statements by using examples from your content area or continue using the example provided below.

> I need to think about the applied level now. This means I need to think about the statements with which I agree, and I need to be ready to share examples from the text and my own knowledge to support my responses.
>
> The first statement in the applied level says "Religious freedom was the most important reason for starting the Southern colonies." I know this was one of the important reasons, but I don't think it was always the most important reason. A lot of settlers wanted to make money, others wanted land, and still others wanted to create a buffer against Spanish Florida. I think each of these reasons was important to different groups of settlers, but I don't think that religious freedom was always the most important reason for starting the Southern colonies. I will make a few notes in the margin of the Three Level Guide so I will be ready to support my choice.

12. Help students read and discuss the remaining statements in the applied level section of the Three Level Guide. Remind them to make notes to support their responses.

13. Provide time for students to finish filling out the Three Level Guide. Engage students in discussion about the Three Level Guide. Be sure to ask them to provide support for their responses.

A Three Level Guide based on Robert Frost's poem "Mending Wall" follows.

Three Level Guide

I. Literal Level

Check the items that specifically show what the author wrote in the poem. Be prepared to support your choices.

_____ 1. During the winter, moisture in the ground freezes and causes the earth to swell under the wall.

_____ 2. Hunters damage the wall.

_____ 3. The speaker lets his neighbor know when it is time to repair the wall.

_____ 4. There is an area along the property line where a wall is not needed.

_____ 5. The neighbor believes that the wall is necessary for neighborly harmony.

II. Interpretive Level

Check the items that show what the author meant in the poem. Be prepared to discuss supporting evidence from the poem.

_____ 1. The author doesn't believe there is any practical need for the wall.

_____ 2. It is an easy task to replace the boulders in the wall.

_____ 3. The author is able to convince his neighbor that the wall is not necessary.

_____ 4. The wall was built a long time ago.

_____ 5. The author believes that good fences make good neighbors.

III. Applied Level

Check the items that you agree with and be ready to share examples from the text and your own knowledge to support your responses.

_____ 1. Hunters should be allowed to trespass onto private property during hunting season.

_____ 2. People should have fences enclosing their property because good fences make good neighbors.

_____ 3. In an ideal world, there would be no walls.

Based on "Mending Wall" by Robert Frost in _Literature & language._ (1994). Evanston, IL: McDougal, Littell.

5.4   Circle of Questions

Circle of Questions (Sampson, Sampson, & Linek, 1995) is a comprehension strategy that extends learning beyond the text. It engages students in brainstorming, predicting, generating questions, and categorizing. Because it is a small group activity, it provides students with the opportunity to learn from their peers as well as to clarify the meaning of the text material through discussion. The activities in this strategy are designed to be implemented over the course of several days.

Directions and Example

1. Select a section of text students will be reading and ask students to read it independently. Students should read without discussion in order to authenticate their individual interpretations of the text. For this example, the reading assignment focuses on the Industrial Revolution.

2. After the assigned reading is completed, divide the class into small groups of five or six students. Tell students that their group assignment is to generate as many questions as they can about the text selection on the Industrial Revolution. Allow 20 minutes for this activity.

3. While students are generating questions in their groups, draw a circle on the chalkboard or on an overhead transparency. Write the topic name (Industrial Revolution) in the center of the circle. The circle will represent the core around which students' questions will focus.

4. Next, solicit questions from each of the groups and write their questions around the perimeter of the circle. Some of the questions might include the following ones.

> What was the purpose of the Industrial Revolution?
> When did it start?
> How long did it last?
> Why was the Industrial Revolution important?
> Did it change the way Americans worked?
> Did women start to work outside of their homes?

5. After each group's questions have been written around the circle, invite students to assist you in categorizing the questions. Circle with colored chalk questions that belong in a specific category in order to facilitate categorizing. Categories for the above questions might look like this.

> What was the purpose of the Industrial Revolution?
> Why was it important?
>
> When did it start?
> How long did it last?
>
> Did it change the way Americans worked?
> Did women start to work outside of their homes?

6. After all of the questions have been categorized, assign one category of questions to each group. Explain to students that their group will become the experts of their category.

7. Have each group use their texts to locate answers to their category of questions. Tell students that, if their texts don't adequately answer their questions, they are free to use other resources, such as the Internet or additional reference materials.

8. Invite each group to report the information it has found. Encourage other students to ask questions of each group and to offer additional information about each category.

5.5

Achieving Graphic Literacy

Goal To help students interpret graphs, charts, and maps

BACKGROUND

In order to achieve content literacy, students need to be able to interpret and comprehend graphs, charts, and maps. These visual aids have a specific function, which is to summarize and condense written information into a visual form and to make it easier for readers to understand the meaning of the written material. In order for students to gain meaning from visual aids such as graphs, charts, and maps, they must be able to make connections between the graphic aid, the text, and their background knowledge (Sejnost & Thiese, 2001).

For many students, it is difficult to interpret and understand the graphics in their content area textbooks. The strategies in this section are designed to help students understand the information that is presented in a visual aid form within their texts. Many students will focus on the literal information found in the graphic aid. It is the responsibility of the teacher, however, to ask inferential and applied questions to help students make the link among the graphic elements, relevant parts of the text, and their background knowledge.

5.5 Bar Graphs

TEACHING STRATEGY 17

Graphs represent information visually so that readers can make comparisons between types of information. A bar graph is a drawing that shows a relationship between two sets of numbers. Graphs can take the forms of charts, maps, and diagrams. Graphic comprehension, or graphic literacy, refers to the ability to interpret charts, maps, and graphs that are frequently used to supplement textbooks and other nonfictional material.

Directions and Example

1. Many students skip over graphs and charts as they read their texts. However, these visual aids are intended to enhance and clarify comprehension. As you begin a lesson on reading graphs, have students open their texts to a graph. Briefly explain the purpose of the graph and show students how to read it.

2. Make a transparency of the graph on page 185 and make individual copies of the graph and questions for each of your students. You may choose to construct an example from your content area.

3. Put the transparency of the graph on an overhead projector and introduce the graph to your students. You might say, "This graph was constructed after a survey was given to students in a local high school." Ask students to look at the graph as you guide them through the following lesson.

4. Tell students to look at the title of the graph. Ask them the following questions.

    What is the subject of the graph? (Sports participation)

    What data are recorded on the graph? (Sports participation among girls and boys)

5. Direct your students' attention to the small boxes at the top of the graph. Ask, "How do we know which numbers on the graph represent girls and which numbers represent boys?" (Code indicates that the white bar is for girls and the black bar is for boys.)

6. Invite students to look at the sports categories on the left-hand side of the graph. Ask students how many categories of sports there are. (six) Ask for a volunteer to read the names of the sports. (golf, track, soccer, tennis, swimming, and volleyball)

7. Focus students' attention on the numbers at the top and at the bottom of the graph. Say something like, "These numbers represent the number of males and females who participated in each of the listed sports. You will notice that the numbers are displayed in increments of five. As an example, who can tell me how many boys participated in volleyball?" (10)

8. After a brief discussion of the graph, distribute copies of the graph and the related questions. Ask students to use the graph information to answer the questions.

9. After students have finished answering the questions, review the information as a class and suggest to students that they develop their own graphs. Students might enjoy polling class members for information regarding favorite TV shows, jobs held to earn money, or ways they spend leisure time.

Sports Participation Graph

1. How many girls participate in soccer? (40)   How many boys? (30)

2. How many girls play tennis? (25)   How many boys? (5)

3. In which three sports do girls outnumber boys? (soccer, tennis, and volleyball)

4. In which two sports do boys outnumber girls?   (track and swimming)

5. What is the total number of boys and girls who participate in volleyball? (35)

6. Which sport has the *most* female participants? (soccer)

7. Which sport has the *fewest* male participants? (tennis)

8. What is the total number of boys who participate in sports? (145)

9. What is the total number of girls who participate in sports? (165)

10. Which sport has the greatest overall participation? (soccer)

Sports Participation

Use the bar graph to answer these questions.

1. How many girls participate in soccer? _____   How many boys? _____

2. How many girls play tennis? _____   How many boys? _____

3. In which three sports do girls outnumber boys? _____, _____, and _____

4. In which two sports do boys outnumber girls? _____ and _____

5. What is the total number of boys and girls who participate in volleyball? _____

6. Which sport has the *most* female participants? _____

7. Which sport has the *fewest* male participants? _____

8. What is the total number of boys who participate in sports? _____

9. What is the total number of girls who participate in sports? _____

10. Which sport has the greatest overall participation? _____

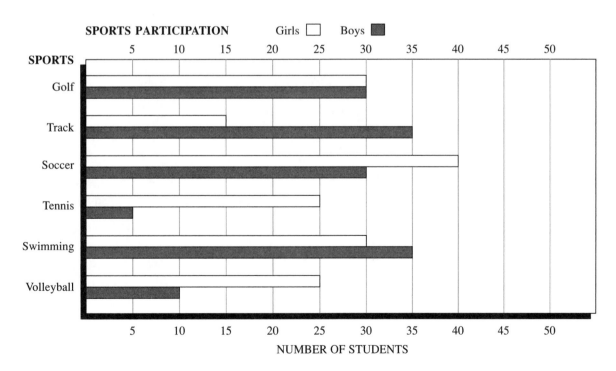

From Susan Davis Lenski, Mary Ann Wham, and Jerry L. Johns, *Reading & Learning Strategies: Middle Grades through High School,* 2nd Edition. Copyright © 2003 by Kendall/Hunt Publishing Company (1-800-247-3458, ext. 4 or 5). May be reproduced for noncommercial educational purposes.

5.5   Using an Atlas

An atlas is a book of maps that is used to obtain information about countries. It can be used to compare the size of countries as well as to gather information about other geographic features such as population and climate. Most map features, such as land boundaries, elevations, and bodies of water, are represented by the use of conventional symbols, lines, and patterns printed in appropriate colors.

Directions and Example

1. Explain to students that they can use an atlas to find out information about other countries. Tell them that many atlases contain information about geography, population, and climate and present historical and political maps. Apprise them of the facts that atlases are frequently used to map out travel routes and to find information about the earth's land and water features.

2. Divide your class into small groups of students and provide each group with a copy of a world atlas. Point out special features of the atlas such as the table of contents, the index, maps and legends, charts and graphs. Show students that by using the table of contents they can locate information about population sizes, climates, and even environmental concerns within countries.

3. Tell students that they are going to take an imaginary trip to France, which is the largest country in Western Europe. It is their job, with their group, to discover some factual information about France before embarking on their journey. Ask students to locate the map of France in their world atlas and point out some of the features of France such as its location, land size, and water access.

4. Write the following questions on an overhead transparency or on the chalkboard.

   What is the population of France?   (59,765,983)

   What is the capital of France?   (Paris)

   How large is the area of France?

   (80% the size of Texas or 211,208 square miles which is 547,030 square kilometers)

   What is the highest elevation in France?

   (Mont Blanc. It is 15,781 feet high.)

   Does France have any environmental concerns?

   (Yes, air pollution is a problem.)

   While you are in France, you may wish to visit some neighboring countries. What are some of France's neighboring countries?

   (Luxembourg, Belgium, and Germany)

When you look at the map of France, what bodies of water do you see touching its boundaries?

(The English Channel, Bay of Biscay, Gulf of Lion, and the Ligurian Sea)

5. Guide students through the first two questions by making the following remarks.

Some of these questions can be answered by looking at the map in your atlas. However, in order to find the population of France, I am going to look in the index. I see that the population information is located on pages 216 and 217 along with other interesting facts about France. By reading the paragraphs on France, I see that the population is 59,765,983. I also see that Paris is the capital of France and its currency is the Euro.

6. Ask each group to answer the remaining questions and to include any other interesting facts about France. The following website might be useful.

http://geography.about.com/library/maps/blfrance.htm#info

7. When your students have finished their atlas research, ask each group to share their information, including any additional interesting facts they have gleaned from their atlas research or from the website.

8. Your students may choose to investigate other countries using their world atlases as well as the following Internet website.

http://www.ricksteves.com/plan/tips/

5.5 Climographs

TEACHING STRATEGY 19

A graph is a drawing that shows a relationship between two or more variables. A Climograph is a type of graph that provides the average monthly temperature and precipitation data for a particular geographic location.

Directions and Example

1. Make an overhead transparency of the Climograph for Boston, Massachusetts, on page 189 and place it on the overhead projector.

2. Explain to students that the graph is called a Climograph and that it depicts the average monthly temperature and precipitation data for Boston, Massachusetts.

3. Tell students that the temperatures on the graph are given in degrees and the precipitation amounts are given in inches.

4. Show students how to read the graph by making the following statements.

    When I look at the month of December, I see that the average temperature in Boston is 34 degrees and the precipitation amount is 2.7 inches. I can probably conclude that the precipitation could be snow because of the cold temperature.

5. As students look at the Climograph, ask them the following questions.

    During which month is there the greatest precipitation? (July)

    What are the two warmest months in Boston? (July and August)

    Which month is the coldest? (January)

    Would you rather go camping in June or October? Why? (Answers may vary.)

    Should I plan on ice skating outside in September? Why?
    (No. The temperature in September is too warm for ice to form.)

    During which month is there the least precipitation? (November)

6. When you are comfortable with students' understanding of the Climograph, you might correlate their knowledge with a math activity such as writing story problems using the weather data. An additional activity might involve a study of the weather through a science lesson. Refer to the Technology Tip below for websites with additional weather information.

TECHNOLOGY

T I P

Weather Reports

Check on the weather before making plans! Visit

www.usatoday.com
or
www.weatherimages.org

for the latest outdoor conditions.

Climograph of Boston, Massachusetts

	Jan	Feb	Mar	April	May	June	July	Aug	Sept	Oct	Nov	Dec
Temperature	31	32	41	52	62	71	75	73	67	55	43	34
Precipitation	2.9	2.5	3.3	3.1	3.3	3.7	4.0	3.2	2.7	2.5	2.4	2.7

5.5 ▸ Timelines

TEACHING STRATEGY 20

A Timeline is a type of chart that shows events in chronological order, the order in which they happened. The bar of a Timeline is usually divided into sections of time, by days, months, years, decades, or centuries. Events are recorded at the selected dates placed on the Timeline.

Directions and Example

1. Tell students that a Timeline is a continuum that graphically delineates events that have occurred in succession from the past through the present and sometimes into the future. Make an overhead transparency of the Timeline labeled Historical Events on page 192 and place it on the overhead projector. Copies of Historical Events may also be made for students.

2. Tell students that this Timeline illustrates some historical events that occurred in the world between 1929 and 1942. Point out to students that the first event on the Timeline occurred in 1929 when the Stock Market crashed in the United States.

3. You might then say to students, "When I look at the year 1935, I see that the United States was experiencing a Dust Bowl in the Great Plains."

4. Point out the other events included on the Timeline up through 1941 when the United States entered World War II.

5. When you believe that students are able to read and understand the Timeline, ask them the following questions.

   How many years after the Stock Market crashed was Franklin Roosevelt elected president for the first time? (three years)

   According to this Timeline, how many times was Franklin Roosevelt elected president? (three times)

   When did Hitler become the leader of Germany? (1933)

   When did Germany invade Poland? (1939)

   When did the United States enter World War II? (1941)

6. Following a discussion about this Timeline, students might enjoy making their own Timeline depicting some of the events in their school lives starting with their kindergarten or preschool experiences. Invite students to tell the stories of their school experiences by writing one memory for each school year on the appropriate lines. You may choose to duplicate the Timeline on page 192 for students or have them develop their own Timeline on a sheet of paper.

7. Following completion of their personal Timelines, invite students to share their school histories in small groups.

8. As an additional activity, students might enjoy constructing a Timeline for events in a social studies or history text, or they might like to develop a Timeline for a biography or a literature selection. The following example is based on the book *Hatchet* by Gary Paulson.

Directions

Make a Timeline of Brian's adventure into the Canadian wilderness. You should be able to include at least one or two events from each chapter in the book. You may wish to include some illustrations on your Timeline.

Chapter 1	Brian leaves for Canada on a bush plane.
Chapter 2	Brian flies the plane.
Chapter 3	Brian crash lands into a lake and crawls to shore.
Chapter 4	Brian thinks about his mother and sleeps.
Chapter 5	Brian is hungry.
Chapter 6	Brian builds a shelter and eats some berries.
ETC.	
Chapter 19	Brian is rescued.

Historical Events

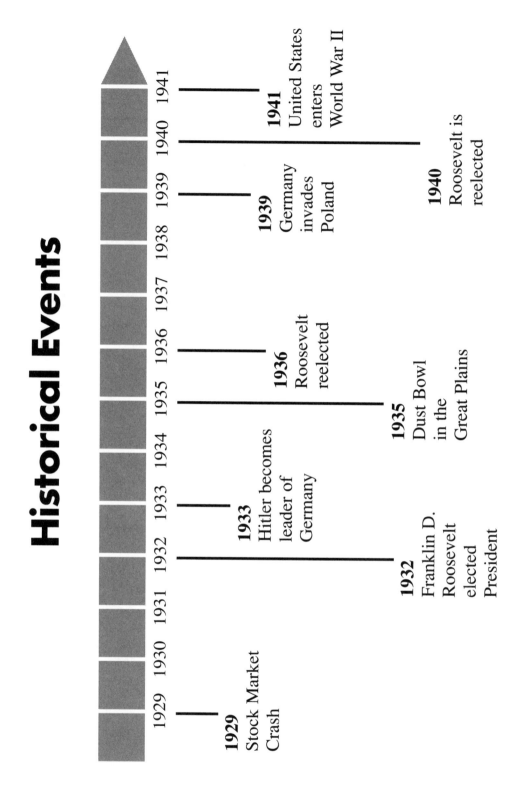

1929	Stock Market Crash
1932	Franklin D. Roosevelt elected President
1933	Hitler becomes leader of Germany
1935	Dust Bowl in the Great Plains
1936	Roosevelt reelected
1939	Germany invades Poland
1940	Roosevelt is reelected
1941	United States enters World War II

My School Memories

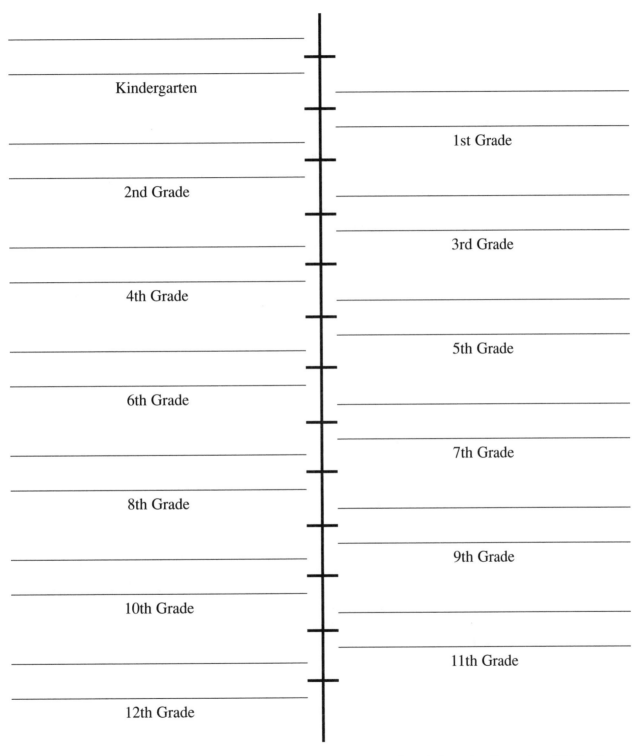

Kindergarten

1st Grade

2nd Grade

3rd Grade

4th Grade

5th Grade

6th Grade

7th Grade

8th Grade

9th Grade

10th Grade

11th Grade

12th Grade

Notes and Favorite Strategies

Chapter 6
CRITICAL READING/LITERACY

OVERVIEW

In order for students to develop an understanding of your subject, they must be able to construct meaning from the texts they read. Constructing meaning is more than merely understanding the message that print conveys; it's reading and thinking critically. Critical reading has traditionally been defined as unearthing authorial intention (Cervetti, Pardales, & Damico, 2001). That means asking students to look for assumptions, reasons, justifications, and implication in texts. Students also need to learn to interpret texts fairly. Critical reading is important for middle school and high school students, but many of them are not yet proficient at making reasoned judgments while reading. Scores from the National Assessment of Educational Progress (NAEP) during the last decade indicated that only

3% of all students read critically by eighth grade, and 6% read critically by high school (Donahue, Voelkl, Campbell, & Mazzeo, 1999).

In recent years, there has been a new focus on critical reading in schools. Instead of students merely trying to understand an author's message, teachers have encouraged students to question and comment on what they read. Teachers have asked students to move from constructing an initial understanding of text to thinking about text deeply and personally—taking a stand apart from a text and developing reasoned opinions. Teachers have required students to read text "in such a way as to question assumptions, explore perspectives, and critique underlying social and political values or stances" (International Reading Association &

National Council of Teachers of English, 1996, p. 71).

The theories underpinning critical reading, however, have begun to encompass new ways of thinking about literacy. Theorists are presently re-thinking critical reading so that it conforms to newer ideas taken from an educational movement called critical pedagogy (Siegel & Fernandez, 2000). Looking at critical reading from a critical pedagogy framework means that texts are understood from the contexts of social, historic, and power relations. The critical pedagogy movement has led to a revision of the term "critical reading" to "critical literacy."

Critical literacy is a step beyond critical reading. While it's important to teach students to evaluate and analyze text, as is emphasized in critical reading, there is more to critical literacy than interpretation. Critical literacy theories suggest that texts are products of social beings who have feelings, biases, and opinions (Wink, 2001). A critical reading of texts can uncover these biases, which, in turn, can lead to actions of social justice. A definition of critical literacy is "an active, challenging approach to literacy that encourages students to be aware of the way that texts are constructed and how such constructions position readers" (Fehring & Green, 2001, back cover). Readers recognize that texts are not neutral—texts influence and establish social identity and power relationships, and texts can reproduce or challenge cultural relationships (Luke, O'Brien, & Comber, 2001). When students read critically, they ask questions such as the following ones.

- How does the author represent social and cultural groups?
- Is underlying bias present?
- Which groups represent power?
- How are conflicts resolved and what does that say about humanity?
- What has the author left unsaid?
- What does this text reveal about our culture?

Critical reading/literacy is a topic that is currently evolving. Critical reading has moved from a set of skills, such as determining facts and opinions, to a more demanding set of mental processes, such as determining authors' credibility and perspectives, making intertextual links, considering alternative views, evaluating arguments, and forming judgments. In addition, critical literacy has come to mean using texts to understand the social realities of the world and to further social justice (Kempe, 2001). The strategies in this chapter are designed to promote both critical reading and critical literacy.

Determining Authors' Credibility and Perspectives

Goal To help students determine whether authors are credible sources and to evaluate the perspectives they bring to texts

BACKGROUND

The texts that you ask your students to read will vary in quality. Authors, who are fallible and have particular perspectives on issues, write texts. Therefore, some of the texts that your students read will be outdated; some will contain biased viewpoints; and others may treat issues superficially. One of the biggest legacies you can leave your students is to teach them to think about the authors of texts—to determine whether the authors are qualified and from what perspectives the authors are approaching the texts.

Writers make deliberate choices of the words, images, and information they use; they leave other information out of their texts. Critical readers become aware of the social context of writing by trying to understand something about the authors (Comber, 2001). Readers should "consider the source" by asking questions about the authors, the purpose of the text, and the conditions under which it was published. The answers to these questions can influence the judgments the reader makes when trying to determine what parts of the text to use to develop ideas and beliefs.

After students understand something about the authors' qualifications, the publication date, and the authors' word choices, they should think more deeply about the authors' perspectives. Texts are not neutral. Authors indicate or convey their perspectives in many subtle ways. As they analyze texts, critical readers try to understand from what perspectives the authors are writing.

6.1 ▶ Consider the Source

One of the first things students need to do as they think critically about a text is to make some determination about the credibility of the source. Although most of the texts you will ask your students to read probably have been sanctioned by you, a curriculum committee, or the school board, students still will need to think about the factors in the text that could influence text credibility. A strategy you can use to initiate critical questioning of the source by your students is called Consider the Source. This strategy is a list of questions with examples for you to model with your students in order to elicit questions about pertinent aspects of the text. You may want to use this activity several times during a school year with examples from your content area. Your goal, however, is for students to think independently about the credibility of sources before they read. Consider the Source can be used in various subject areas.

 ## Directions and Examples

1. Ask students to look at the source of the passage you have asked them to read. Ask them to look for the date of publication. Discuss the importance of the copyright date. Tell students that information with a copyright date of 2003 was probably written at least a year earlier and may be considerably older than that. Explain that, even when authors are discussing historical events, dates are important. New information can, at times, influence what is believed about an event. Books that are written in the near or distant past, however, are not necessarily incorrect. The date of the publication is one factor for establishing credibility, but newer is not necessarily better.

2. Use an example such as the following one to illustrate the importance of dates of publication. Discuss why the publication date is important in these examples.

   Today Germany is two separate countries. They are different from each other in a number of ways. One of the most important differences is the form of government. East Germany has a Communist government.

   Built in 1961, the Berlin Wall separates the city of Berlin into two sections—East Berlin, or the Communist section, and West Berlin.

   From *Exploring our world: Eastern hemisphere.* (1980). Chicago: Follett, p. 135.

3. Discuss the importance of the authors' qualifications. Many of the textbooks used in schools have a list of authors with their credentials stated at the front of the book. Look for the list of authors, read about their backgrounds, and discuss whether they appear qualified to write the book. You can use the following example for class discussion.

   In a middle school music class using a music text, students can look at the qualifications of the authors at the beginning of the book. Fourteen authors are listed: six middle school teachers of music, five university professors, one composer, and two choral directors.

   Discuss how the qualifications of a middle school teacher would be different from the qualifications of a composer. Discuss whether the balance among middle school teachers, university professors, and professional musicians is appropriate for the text.

4. Discuss what seems to be the authors' primary aim in writing the book. Some books are written primarily for information, some are written for instruction, and others are aimed at persuasion. Find examples of each type of text from your content field and discuss how readers can identify the purpose of the authors. The following is an example from a world literature class.

> In a world literature class reading a book on Celtic myths, scan the Contents looking for the topics that are included in the text. The Contents includes introductory chapters with titles such as "The Divine Race of Ireland" and chapters with categories of myths such as "Animals in Cult and Myth." Discuss whether the author's choice of words indicates a particular bias toward the subject.

> After reading portions of the text, discuss whether the writing was informational, instructional, or persuasive. The book on Celtic myths, for example, seems to be informational, but the author appears to have a heavy bias toward the subject. Discuss whether the author's bias might detract from the informational aspects of the book.

5. Once the type of text is determined, read several passages of the text with your students to determine whether the author relies on words that may indicate a bias. Use an example from your content area or the following examples to discuss how authors can subtly steer readers toward one way of thinking.

6. Make copies of the following passages taken from an American textbook and ask students to read the two passages. Discuss how phrases such as "the harsh new British policies" lead the reader toward the colonists' viewpoint.

> By the 1760s, however, the harsh new British policies spurred the growth of an American sense of community. A growing number of colonists now began to think of themselves as Americans drawn together by their hostility to British authorities. At the same time, colonial leaders began to take political action against what they felt was British suppression.

> The concluding paragraphs [of the Declaration of Independence] contain a statement of the colonists' determination to separate from Great Britain. These paragraphs explain that the colonists' efforts to reach a peaceful solution with England had failed, leaving them no choice but to declare their freedom.

> From *Government in the United States*. (1990). New York: Glencoe/McGraw-Hill, p. 162.

7. Make copies of the following passages taken from a British history book and ask students to read the two passages. Discuss how phrases such as "the thirteen rebellious states" express the British view of the war. Ask students to identify the differences between the authors' perspectives in the American and British texts.

> King George III was a pig-headed man rather than a tyrant—but from America the distinction was not clear to the naked eye.

> And the thirteen rebellious states were recognized as the United States of America.

> From *History of England*. (1974). London: Collins, p. 287.

8.   Finally, analyze several passages in the text to determine whether the author used any negative propaganda techniques. Propaganda is a one-sided statement that is used to sway the opinion of the reader. Discuss the most common types of propaganda techniques (see box below) and create examples of each that fit your content area.

PROPAGANDA TECHNIQUES

Appeal to bandwagon: Most people believe this and you should too if you want to be one of the crowd.
- Everyone in the school has a team jacket, so you should have one too.

Emotional language: Plays on connotations of words that evoke strong feelings.
- You'll be the one in power if you join the Student Council.

Appeal to prestige: Associating a product with someone important.
- Michael Jordan thinks hightop shoes are the best!

Plain-folks appeal: Typical people use this product, thereby invoking a sense of the common person.
- All of the members of the Pep Club have purchased our school shirts.

Testimonial: Use of a famous person to give credibility to a concept, idea, or product.
- Cindy Crawford studied acting here.

TEACHING STRATEGY 2

6.1 Perspective Guide

After students have considered the credibility of the author, they should think about the perspective the author may be taking. Many of the texts your students read will take a subtle perspective about a subject. Neutral texts would be bland beyond belief. It is important that students are able to identify the perspective the author is taking. A Perspective Guide presents quotations from two or more passages that have a similar theme but different perspectives. When students are able to identify an author's perspective, they are able to use what they know about the author's perspective along with the author's qualifications to make an informed decision about the topic.

 ## Directions and Example

1.   Choose two or more texts written around a central theme in which the authors have different perspectives about an issue. You can choose texts from the same medium, such as the two short stories in the example, or you can choose different types of texts. The texts, however, should have a similar theme.

2.   Choose four to eight quotations from each passage that relate to the central theme. Write the quotations in random order on the chalkboard or an overhead transparency. List the sources of the quotations at the bottom of the page.

3. Divide the class into groups of three or four students. Have students read and discuss the quotations, discussing ideas about the perspectives of the authors. Then have the students match the quotations with the sources as in the example below.

Literature Example

Perspective Guide

Directions: After reading the two stories "Aging in the Land of the Young" and "Woman Without Fear," match the following quotations with the stories and discuss the view of aging taken by each author. Use *a* for "Aging in the Land of the Young" and *b* for "Woman Without Fear."

1. _____ Aging paints every action gray, lies heavy on every movement, imprisons every thought.

2. _____ The world becomes narrower as friends and family die or move away.

3. _____ Although Grace was 64 years old, she was as active as a boy and worked with smooth dexterity.

4. _____ When she saw me, she hurriedly picked up the four-foot rattlesnake who had been sunning himself while his box was being cleaned and poured him into his cage.

5. _____ There is nothing to prepare you for the experience of growing old.

6. _____ I first heard of Grace Wiley when Dr. William Mann handed me a picture of a tiny woman with a gigantic king cobra draped over her shoulders like a garden hose.

7. _____ I am afraid to grow old—we're all afraid. In fact, the fear of growing old is so great that every aged person is an insult and a threat to the society.

8. _____ "Don't trip over an alligator," she added as I came forward. I noticed for the first time in the high grass a dozen or so alligators and crocodiles.

From Curtin, S. (1984). Aging in the land of the young. In *Literature* (pp. 389–391). Evanston, IL: McDougal, Littell. Mannix, D. (1984). Woman without fear. In *Literature* (pp. 325–333). Evanston, IL: McDougal, Littell.

4. After students complete the Perspective Guide, ask them to discuss their reasoning for their choices and guide them to identify the different perspectives of the authors. In this example, one of the authors discusses a woman's fear of aging while the other celebrates the life of a courageous older woman. Discuss reasons why perspectives about a topic may differ. Then discuss alternative perspectives on the topic. You might ask the students to write an essay or short story from a third perspective.

6.1 ▶ Ask the Author

Students who understand an author's perspective can gain a deeper understanding of the text by identifying with the author. Ask the Author is an adaptation of a Creative Reasoning Guide (Jacobson, 1998) that can be tailored to provide students with the opportunity to answer questions from the author's perspective. When students are able to put themselves in the place of the author, they develop a more thorough understanding of the author's perspective.

Directions and Examples

1. Identify an event that is not fully explained in the text. For example, your text includes Cicero's speeches for Archias. However, the text does not explain the reasons why Cicero would discuss literature with Archias.

2. Write the event as a scenario on the chalkboard or an overhead transparency. In the scenario, direct a question to the author for reasons that caused the event. See the following example for a sample scenario.

   > Earlier in this course you read stories from Pliny and Galleus and speeches from Cicero. This section contains several of Cicero's speeches for Archias, some dealing with the value of literature. With what you know about Roman culture and Cicero's character, what reasons would Cicero have to discuss literature with Archias? Give at least three reasons.

3. Divide the class into groups of three to five students. Give the students the Ask the Author scenario. Ask them to brainstorm at least three reasons that would answer the question. The reasons should be logical in light of past knowledge, but creativity should be encouraged. The following is a second example from a Latin class.

Latin Class Example

Ask the Author

Directions: After reading "The Value of Literature," in your Latin book, read the following scenario and think about answers to the question.

Scenario

In further passages, Cicero discusses his views on poets. Three of the speeches are titled "Poets are Sacred," "No Fame Without Poets," and "Poets Give Immortality." What reasons would Cicero have for revering poets to such an extent? Give at least three reasons.

4. In a whole group setting, ask the students to share the reasons listed during the brainstorming activity. List all of the reasons on the chalkboard or an overhead transparency. Discuss the ideas the students have generated and guide the discussion to identify characteristics and perspectives of the author.

Making Intertextual Links

Goal   To help students make intertextual links from current texts to past texts

BACKGROUND

When students read texts, they construct meaning using the texts they are reading, their prior experiences, and other texts. For example, middle school students learning about Impressionism may remember previous experiences with texts on the subject. One student may recall a trip to the Art Institute in Chicago. Another student may remember watching the movie *Pollack*. Yet another student may think about an Internet tour of the Louvre. A fourth student may remember reading Irving Stone's *Lust for Life* and discussing it with friends. A student's understanding of any passage, therefore, is shaped by prior experiences with texts and with life.

Students bring experiences with past texts to each reading event in your class. This process, called intertextuality, is a natural process. All of us are natural synthesizers. We learn new information by connecting it to what we already know, creating an evolving web of meaning. As readers construct meaning, they "transpose texts into other texts, absorb one text into another, and build a mosaic of intersecting texts" (Hartman, 1995, p. 526).

Texts that are stored in a reader's memory can be constructed from print or other visual or auditory

sources (International Reading Association & National Council of Teachers of English, 1996). Traditionally, text has been defined as communication in print, such as a textbook or a chapter in a book. A current view, however, suggests that the term *text* has a broader interpretation. Texts do not have to be print sources; they can be any source that communicates meaning. Texts, therefore, can be print sources such as stories, textbooks, novels, poems, and essays. Texts can also be nonprint sources such as music, drama, video, art, and gesture. All of these texts are stored in a reader's memory and are available for use in developing meaning from a current text.

In order to be critical readers, students need to make intertextual links. Although making intertextual links is natural, students need to be encouraged to integrate knowledge they have from outside school with school learning. When students are guided to make intertextual links, they generally do so. The strategies in this section were designed or adapted so that you can guide students, while they are critically reading new texts, to use texts they have already experienced.

6.2   Text Connect

Text Connect is a strategy that guides students consciously to use past texts to learn about a concept you are teaching. The steps in Text Connect parallel the thinking processes that people use as they solve problems. The processes used in problem solving generally include identifying a problem, dividing the problem into its main components, searching through memory for past knowledge to solve the problem, selecting pertinent past knowledge, relating past knowledge to the current problem, and solving the problem.

 ## Directions and Example

1. Model how people solve problems and answer questions using past texts and past experiences. Describe a time when you used past texts to solve a problem. The following description is the type of example that would exemplify using intertextual links to solve problems.

    I decided to refinish an old piano that had been sitting in my basement gathering dust. I had been given the piano by my mother who, in turn, had received it from my grandmother. I knew that the piano was an antique, but it had so many layers of varnish and paint that I didn't know whether the wood underneath would be worth refinishing. Before beginning the long task, I decided to find out what I could about refinishing this particular piece of furniture. To learn about the piano, I called my grandmother and mother and asked them what they had used to paint the piano when they had owned it. My grandmother told me where she had originally purchased the piano. I then called the piano factory to ask about what kind of wood was used on this particular model.

    To learn about refinishing, I talked to my father who had refinished many pieces of furniture. Then, I went to the library and checked out five books and one video on refinishing furniture. Finally, I discussed ways to refinish furniture with the local hardware store owner and was given four pamphlets on refinishing wood.

    I used the following texts to solve my problem.
    - interviews with my mother, grandmother, father, and hardware store owner
    - five books
    - one video
    - four pamphlets

2. Identify a topic from the text your students are reading that would have the potential for linking students to past texts. After you have identified a topic, develop a question that your students could answer using past texts that they have experienced. The following is an example from a social studies class.

    After students read about the Civil Rights movement, ask them the following question.

    In 1964, Congress passed Civil Rights laws to end segregation in public places. Why were these laws necessary?

3. Write the question on a chalkboard or an overhead transparency. Display the question for the students. Explain to the students that they will be using texts from their experiences to answer the question.

4. Explain that one way to solve a problem using past texts is to identify components of the problem. Ask students to use what they know about the topic to develop a list of selected terms that relate to the topic, as in the following example.

> Civil Rights laws
> segregation
> integration
> boycott
> Dr. Martin Luther King, Jr.
> NAACP
> nonviolent protest

5. Divide the class into mixed-ability groups. Ask the students to brainstorm past texts that relate to the listed terms. Provide students with a few examples from print and nonprint sources including movies, mathematical formulas, videos, personal experiences, music, art, fiction, and nonfiction. A list of selected fiction and nonfiction sources about Civil Rights follows.

SOURCES ABOUT CIVIL RIGHTS

Fiction and Nonfiction Books

King, C.S. (1983). *The words of Martin Luther King, Jr.* New York: Newsmaker.

Parks, R. (1996). *Dear Mrs. Parks.* New York: Lee & Low.

Parks, R., & Reed, G. (1994). *Quiet strength: The faith, the hope and the heart of a woman who changed a nation.* Michigan: Zondervon.

Thomas, J.L. (2001). *The blacker the berry.* New York: HarperCollins.

Nonprint Sources

Eyes on the prize. (1986). PBS. (videos)

www.stanford.edu/group/king
(Martin Luther King, Jr., biography)

http://www.newsavanna.com/Gravity/mlktribute/contents.html
("I Have A Dream" speech with hyperlinks to allusions in text)

6. Ask students to select past texts that would answer the question. Explain that not every text about a topic that students have experienced can be used to answer this particular question. Model how you would use selected texts in an answer using an example from your content area or use the following example.

Last year I read *Quiet Strength,* the biography of Rosa Parks (Parks & Reed, 1994) and saw *Eyes on the Prize,* the series of videos that document the Civil Rights movement. Since I knew we would be studying the Civil Rights movement in social studies, I also accessed two websites about Martin Luther King, Jr. All of this background information reinforced my belief that the Civil Rights laws were necessary in our country.

Although I was a teenager in the north during the 1960s, I did not fully realize how necessary the entire Civil Rights movement was to ensure equal rights for all people. Reading about Rosa Parks refusing to give her seat on the bus to a white person, however, reminded me how unfair life was for African Americans in the early part of the 1900s. Martin Luther King, Jr., said in his *I Have A Dream* speech that he hoped that one day his children would be judged by their character, not their color. I believe the Civil Rights laws were a necessary beginning step for that to occur.

6.2   Intra-Act
TEACHING STRATEGY 5

Intra-Act (Hoffman, 1979) is a strategy that can be adapted to encourage students to use intertextual links to reach a personal decision about a topic. The Intra-Act procedure has four phases. First, students construct meaning from a text selection. Second, they connect what they have learned about the topic with other texts. Third, students express their personal values and feelings about the topic. And fourth, they reflect on the values they have formed.

Directions and Example

1. Choose a topic or ask students to choose a topic that would be of special interest to them. The topic should be one about which students can form a personal opinion. Describe the differences between topics that lend themselves to opinions and topics that are explanatory. Provide a sample topic about which an opinion can be formed as in the following example.

    Read about the history and status of Puerto Rico. Think about whether Puerto Rico should remain a commonwealth, become the 51st state, or become an independent nation.

2. Use comprehension strategies to teach the reading selection.

3. Ask students to use contents of the text to write opinion statements that could be answered *yes* or *no.* Model examples of opinion statements that could be deduced from the text. Explain why a statement such as "Puerto Rico should become the 51st state" is an opinion and a statement such as "Puerto Rico primarily has an agricultural economy" is not an opinion.

4. List on a grid four or five of the most controversial statements students generated as in the following example. Distribute copies to students.

5. Divide the class into groups of four to six students. Students should be of mixed abilities. Assign one student from each group as the discussion leader. Then ask each student leader to conduct a discussion by summarizing the text selection. The members of each group can add details that clarify the leader's summary. Allow 7 to 10 minutes for discussion.

Social Studies Example

Puerto Rico at a Crossroads

Statements				
Since the people of Puerto Rico are already United States citizens, Puerto Rico should become the 51st state if its people vote for statehood.				
Operation Bootstrap is an illustration of the way the Puerto Ricans can maintain themselves as an independent nation.				
Because Puerto Rico primarily has an agricultural economy with limited natural resources, it cannot stand on its own as a nation and either should remain a commonwealth or become a state.				
Spanish is the basic language of Puerto Rico and, although many people speak English, the language barrier should prevent Puerto Rico from becoming a state.				

6. Ask the group leaders to brainstorm additional texts that supplement the summary of the text selection. You might list categories of texts so that students think of both print and nonprint texts. Encourage students to add categories as they think of other types of texts. List the remembered texts on a large piece of paper. An example of texts from the topic Puerto Rico follows.

MEDIA

Newspaper articles
Segment on National Public Radio discussing Puerto Rico and statehood
The *Cobblestone* issue on Puerto Rico

Stories and Poetry
"Roberto Clemente—Bittersweet Memory" by Jerry Izenberg
Poems of Jose Antonio Davila and Luis Llorens Torres

Websites
http://www.puertorico51.org (discusses statehood)
http://www.tld.net/user/lucast/Puerto%20Rico.html (discusses history)

7. After the members of each group have shared texts that relate to the topic, ask them to participate in the valuation phase of the discussion. Each group leader should distribute a paper with a set of four declarative statements based on the selection's content. These value statements should reflect opinions that could be inferred from the text.

8. Have students write the names of the group's members on the top line. Then ask students to agree or disagree with the statements independently. Direct them to write *yes* or *no* under their names for each statement. Finally, ask them to predict what they think other members of the group would answer by writing *yes* or *no* in the spaces under their classmates' names as shown in the following example.

Social Studies Example

Puerto Rico at a Crossroads

Statements	Shelly	Teresa	Juan	Aaron
Since the people of Puerto Rico are already United States citizens, Puerto Rico should become the 51st state if its people vote for statehood.	yes	yes	yes	yes
Operation Bootstrap is an illustration of the way the Puerto Ricans can maintain themselves as an independent nation.	no	yes	yes	no
Because Puerto Rico primarily has an agricultural economy with limited natural resources, it cannot stand on its own as a nation and either should remain a commonwealth or become a state.	yes	yes	no	yes
Spanish is the basic language of Puerto Rico and, although many people speak English, the language barrier should prevent Puerto Rico from becoming a state.	no	no	no	yes

9. Begin reflection by asking the members of each group to reveal how they each responded to the four statements. As students discuss their answers, others should check to see whether their predictions about their classmates' responses were correct.

10. Conduct a class discussion allowing students to discuss, challenge, support, and question one another's responses. Discuss how the roles of the central text and the texts from the students' memories influenced final opinions.

6.2 **Connections Graph**

TEACHING STRATEGY 6

As students read multiple texts, they make connections. At times, however, readers are unaware of the connections they are making unless the connections are brought to their conscious minds (Lenski, 2001). One strategy that helps students understand the connections they are implicitly making is the connections graph (Wooten, 2000). A connections graph provides students with a place to record the type of connections they make as they read multiple texts.

Directions and Example

1. Discuss with students the types of connections they make while reading fictional and informational texts by telling them about the types of connections you make as you read, such as in the following example.

   > Last night I was reading *Nickel and Dimed: On (Not) Getting by in America* by Barbara Ehrenreich (2001). It's about a journalist who worked minimum wage jobs to find out whether it was possible to pay for rent and food on that income. As I read the book, I thought about my Aunt Edie who was a single mom for many years and supported her family as a waitress. That was a connection to my family. I also remembered what it was like to work at a local bookstore for very little money while I was in college. That connection was to myself. Furthermore, I remembered an interview with Barbara Ehrenreich on National Public Radio that discussed the social implications of low-paying jobs. That connection was to media.

2. Have students record in a journal the connections they make for the books they are reading. Tell students that after they have read three or more books they will chart their connections on a connections graph.

3. Divide the class into groups of three or four students. Have students review their journal entries and discuss the types of connections they made during reading. Tell one student to record the categories of connections that have been mentioned (e.g., family).

4. After students have discussed the connections they made, invite them to share their lists of categories of connections with the entire class. Record a master list on the chalkboard or on a transparency with an overhead projector. Your list may include categories such as the following ones.

self	literature	media
family	characters	places
school	questions	society
activities	jobs	conflicts

5. Have students review the completed list. Invite them to suggest additional categories of connections that come to mind. Add these connections to the list.

6. Duplicate and distribute copies of the connections graph that follows. Have students select 10 categories from your class list to record in the spaces for categories. Remind students to leave several blank spaces so they can add more categories if needed.

7. Tell students to list, in the lower section of the graph, three or more books they have read. Have them include the approximate dates they read the books.

8. Using their journal entries, students should record on the connections graph the types of connections they made while reading. After they have finished, explain that readers subconsciously make many connections as they read and that comprehension increases if readers are able to consciously think about the connections.

9. An example of a connections graph using literature and a copy of a blank connections graph follow.

Literature Example

Categorizing Connections

Categories Generated

	Among the Hidden (Haddix, 2000)	*The Girls (Koss, 2000)*	*Stargirl (Spinelli, 2000)*						
family	X								
my friends	X	X	X						
school			X						
sports		X							
friendships	X	X	X						
Literature Read									

Name _____ Date _____

Categorizing Connections

Categories Generated

Literature Read								

Considering Alternative Views

Section

6.3

Goal To help students consider alternative views when reading

BACKGROUND

Critical readers who have determined the authors' qualifications and perspectives and have reached back into their memories for related past texts to connect with new knowledge can expand the meaning they construct by considering alternative views. One of the hallmarks of a thinking person is the ability to acknowledge new ideas and different points of view.

Students who are reading and learning in your content area need to keep their minds open as they read. Often, students who are learning about new concepts have already established ideas about those concepts. Sometimes those ideas are faulty. When students are exposed to counterintuitive concepts, or concepts that don't make inherent sense to them,

they tend to resist these new ideas, even after they are proved to them (Stahl, Hynd, Glynn, & Carr, 1996). For example, students often believe that a heavier object will fall faster than a lighter one even though one of the principles of physics is that all objects fall at the same accelerating rate. Because many students resist new information if it is in conflict with previously held beliefs, some textbooks directly refute misconceptions. An example of a refutational warning in an algebra class would be the note that "2 to the third power = 8 is not the same as $2 \times 3 = 6$." Because students bring misconceptions to reading situations, an important skill for critical readers is to take into account new ideas and to try to generate alternative views as they read.

6.3   Alternative Views in Your Subject

TEACHING STRATEGY 7

All of our content subjects have examples where there are two or more viewpoints. When we teach students to be critical thinkers and readers in our content areas, we need to point out the areas where students can consider alternative perspectives. Two content examples follow that you can use to model the teaching of alternative views. Finding and using examples from your discipline will reinforce students' understanding of ways to find many views in texts.

Directions and Example

1. Think of a situation that would be common to the lives of your students and would exemplify two or more viewpoints. An example of such a situation is the following one.

   > Currently, the legal age to obtain a driver's license in this state is 16. In some states, the legal age to drive is younger than 16. There is a movement to make the driving age consistent among the states and to raise that age to 18. What is your opinion about this matter?

2. Present the situation to the students and ask them to write down their points of view on index cards. After students have written what they think, collect the cards and write the viewpoints on a chalkboard or on an overhead transparency. Discuss the different views the students presented.

3. Tell students that one of the hallmarks of a critical reader is being able to identify and consider more than one point of view. Periodically, provide students with an application to reinforce their understanding that texts contain more than one perspective. Encourage them to identify and consider alternative views when they read.

6.3   Discussion Web

TEACHING STRATEGY 8

A Discussion Web (Alvermann, 1992) is an organizational tool for you to use to guide discussions that present an issue and opposing points of view. A Discussion Web is designed so that students can identify and discuss two viewpoints about the question, ponder the views, and come to a conclusion.

Directions and Examples

1. After the students have read a passage from your text, introduce a central question. The question should be one that lends itself to opposing viewpoints. Write the question on a chalkboard or an overhead transparency. For example, ask students the following question after they read "The Man Without a Country" by Edward Everett Hale.

   > Did Philip Nolan receive a just penalty?

2. Divide the class into groups of three or four students. Ask students to brainstorm at least three reasons for answering *yes* to the central question. Then have them generate at least three reasons for answering *no* to the central question. When students have written their reasons for answering the question in the affirmative and the negative, ask them to volunteer some of their ideas. Write the ideas in two separate columns as listed below.

Reasons why the penalty wasn't just	Reasons why the penalty was just
Nolan had a good background.	Nolan broke the law.
He was tricked by Aaron Burr.	He was a traitor to his country.
His words were impulsive.	He was aware of the consequences.
He was sorry.	He was part of a rebellion.

3. Discuss both sides of the question as objectively as possible. Then encourage students to take a position either for or against the issue. Some students will want to take both sides. Tell them that, although they understand both sides of the issue, they need to take one position.

4. Ask students to come to conclusions independently, defending the side they have chosen and using the alternative perspective as a counterargument. Have them write their conclusions on note cards. Collect the note cards when the students are finished and use them to learn which conclusions students have reached. An example follows.

Conclusion

Philip Nolan was a young, fiery man who was used by Aaron Burr. Although he deserved punishment for his wrongs, the punishment he received, banishment, was too severe for the crime.

---

5. An example of a completed Discussion Web and a blank copy follow.

Health Example

Discussion Web

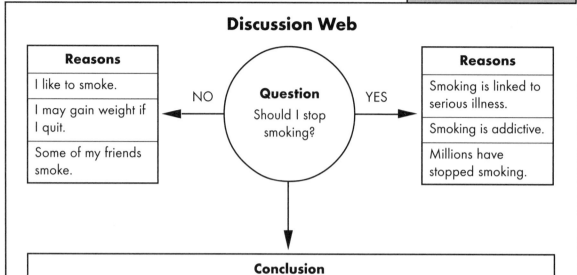

Reasons

I like to smoke.
I may gain weight if I quit.
Some of my friends smoke.

NO

Question

Should I stop smoking?

YES

Reasons

Smoking is linked to serious illness.
Smoking is addictive.
Millions have stopped smoking.

Conclusion

Although I like to smoke, I know it's not good for me. I need to find the best way to quit. I know I can stop smoking.

Based on Alvermann, D. (1992). The discussion web: A graphic aid for learning across the curriculum. *The Reading Teacher, 45,* 92–99.

Discussion Web

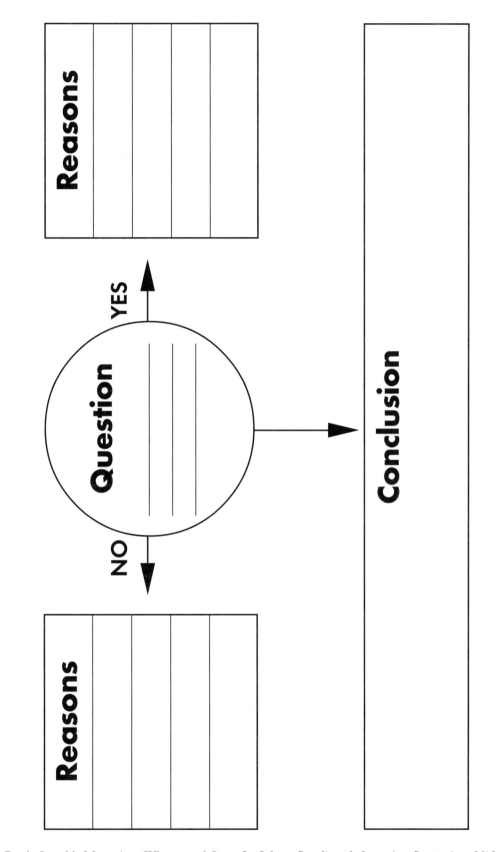

Reasons

YES

Question

NO

Reasons

Conclusion

Based on Alvermann, D. (1992). The discussion web: A graphic aid for learning across the curriculum. *The Reading Teacher, 45,* 92–99.

6.3   Discussion Continuum
TEACHING STRATEGY 9

A Discussion Continuum (Stephens & Brown, 1994) is a visual example of the range of views that are possible on a given topic. It provides students with the opportunity to express their viewpoints, listen to other students' ideas, and amend their own thinking. The ability to state and defend one's views and the capacity to appreciate the views of others is necessary when considering alternate views on a subject.

 ## Directions and Example

1. Give students opposite statements related to your content area that you think would elicit a range of responses such as these examples from a biology class.

    - The government should prohibit stem cell research.
    - The government should fund and promote stem cell research.

2. Write the statements on the chalkboard or on an overhead transparency on the opposite ends of a straight line.

3. Have students come up to the discussion continuum and write their initials at the points on the line that best represent their positions, as in the following example.

AF   WH   MC   RL   BB

The government should prohibit all stem cell research.   **The government should fund and promote stem cell research.**

4. After all of the students have had the opportunity to mark their positions on the continuum, have students discuss their positions in small groups using text material to support their views.

5. Invite students to share their beliefs with the entire class; then provide students with the chance to change their positions on the discussion continuum if they desire.

6.3   Options Guide
TEACHING STRATEGY 10

Students who are able to identify and consider alternative viewpoints in their reading should begin to think about the range of views that exist about any topic. An Options Guide (Bean, Sorter, Singer, & Frazee, 1986) is a type of study guide that helps students think of predictions and possibilities about an issue from their texts. Students read up to a critical point in the passage and then stop and consider possible options and the results of the different options.

TECHNOLOGY TIP

Computer Simulations

Computer simulations are ideal for an Options Guide. While the students are engaged in the simulation, ask them to stop, generate several options, and predict how the options will influence the results. A list of selected computer simulations that could be used to help students develop critical thinking follows.

Decisions, Decisions: The Environment (Tom Snyder Productions)
Students collect and analyze data as they choose actions that affect the environment.

Lunar Greenhouse (Minnesota Educational Computing Corporation)
Students control variables for plant growth.

Oregon Trail, Gold Rush, Wagon Train 1848 (Minnesota Educational Computing Corporation)
Students play the role of pioneers crossing the country who are met with dilemmas and challenges.

Directions and Examples

1. Identify a topic and a portion of a text that would be of interest to your students. Analyze the passage for major concepts that leave events in doubt. The following example illustrates an Options Guide for a parenting class.

2. Develop a brief scenario about the text. Write several questions and a list of options that could result from the scenario. Write the scenario on the chalkboard or an overhead transparency.

Parenting Example

Options Guide

Fifteen-year-old Nina was skipping school to spend the day with her older sister, Olivia, who was just recovering from the flu, and Olivia's month-old son, Hector. Just before noon, Nina and Olivia decided to drive to a nearby store to get some milk.

As they were getting into the car, Nina asked, "Where's Hector's car seat?"

"Oh, no," sighed Olivia. "I left it in the apartment. Well, it's only a few blocks. You just hold him. This won't take long."

Which option will Nina choose? Why do you think so? What could be the result of each option?

a. Nina will go along with Olivia and ride with the baby in her lap.
b. Nina will stay home with Hector.
c. Nina will drive to the store without a valid driver's license.
d. Nina will persuade Olivia to return to her apartment for the car seat.

3. Divide the class into groups of four or five students. Ask students to discuss the possible options and the results of each option. After students have discussed options in small groups, have them share their thinking with the entire group. If necessary, guide the discussion so that students understand the cause-effect relationship for each option.

4. An Options Guide from a science book follows.

Science Example

Options Guide

Directions: After reading a section about trees vs. people, read the scenario and answer the following questions.

Scenario

An old growth forest in the Pacific Northwest has been marked for clear cutting. The forest consists of some of the world's oldest and largest coniferous trees providing a habitat for over 600 species of wildlife. Environmentalists are arguing that this particular forest should be preserved. There is, however, a great demand for wood products in America. Timber workers want to provide lumber and save their jobs by cutting down the trees.

1. What are some of the options open to decision makers?

2. What are the possible results for each option?
    a. How successful would each option be?
    b. What would the loggers say?
    c. What would the environmentalists say?

6.3

TEACHING STRATEGY 11

Knowledge as Design

Students who have a solid understanding of the differing viewpoints that exist in texts and in their minds can further their understanding of the complexity of knowledge by using the strategy Knowledge as Design (Perkins, 1994). Knowledge as Design not only guides students to understand alternative viewpoints; it is also a strategy that promotes critical reading by identifying the relationship between the structure of a topic and its purpose and by identifying different perspectives on the issue at hand. Knowledge as Design is a way to organize a class discussion, or it can be used as a small group assignment. Whichever you choose, you will need to model the format for your students, and you may need to give input on the more complex sections.

Directions and Examples

1. Identify a topic that is interesting and relevant to your students. Select a topic about which students could have more than one opinion as in the following example.

    We have been reading about genetic engineering in our science text. Many of you have expressed an interest in this topic.

2. Identify the purposes of the topic. You may decide to identify one purpose as an example and ask students to identify others. If students are unable to think of purposes, direct them to the text. An example follows.

> Purpose for genetic engineering: To solve problems involving living things.

3. Share the structures, or organizing principles, of the topic. Since this is the foundation for the concept under discussion and also the most difficult part of the strategy, you may want to provide most of these answers.

> Structure: Genetic engineering is a type of biotechnology that transfers genes from one organism to another.

4. Ask students to think of examples of the topic. Have students generate examples that are written in the text as well as examples they think of themselves. If your students are unable to find all of the examples, you should provide them. List the examples on a chalkboard or an overhead transparency.

> Examples: Development of insulin
> Creation of new strains of plants

5. Explain that many issues have at least two different sides. Discuss the idea that when there is more than one side to an issue, one is not necessarily better than the other side. It may be a matter of opinion or personal preference. For the topic at hand, have students discuss arguments for the topic. Then ask them for arguments against the topic. List the arguments for and against the topic under the examples.

> In favor: Provides needed solutions for many problems
> Opposed: Fear of abuse

6. Discuss the importance of developing individual conclusions and of respecting conclusions peers have developed. Have students independently synthesize the information and develop their conclusions. Ask students to write their conclusions on index cards. After students have written their conclusions, have several of them volunteer and share their ideas. Reinforce the importance of respectful listening by asking the other class members to listen to the conclusions offered by other students. Remind students that some of their peers will have arrived at conclusions different from their own.

> Conclusion: Genetic engineering can provide needed solutions for many problems. However, as technology advances, further guidelines for genetic engineering may need to be established.

7. An example of a completed social studies Knowledge as Design and a blank copy follow.

Social Studies Example

Knowledge as Design

Topic

European Expansion and Colonization in Southeast Asia

Purposes

Find trade route to the Orient
Spread Christianity
Gain wealth
Protect natives from enemies

Specific Examples

Portuguese in India, Java, Spice Islands
Spanish in Philippines
Dutch in Java, Sumatra
British in India, Singapore, Burma,
   Malay Peninsula
French in Vietnam, Cambodia, Laos
Americans in Guam, Puerto Rico,
Philippines

Structure

Established as primary ruler
Formed government
Entered world trade market
Sent colonists

Pro

Improved transportation
Improved communications
Initiated public health projects
Implemented new farming methods
Established schools
Ended enslavement for debtors

Con

Ruled by foreign culture
Natives treated as inferior
Power in foreign language
Sent natural resources abroad
Small farmers became obsolete
Increased numbers of poor

Conclusions

The improvement of the infrastructure was not worth the cost to the natives.
Greed was the primary motivation of colonization.
Powerful countries should not take advantage of those with less power.

Based on Perkins, D.N. (1986). *Knowledge as design.* Hillsdale, NJ: Erlbaum.

Name _____ Date _____

Knowledge as Design

Topic

Purposes	Specific Examples

Structure

Pro	Con

Conclusions

Based on Perkins, D.N. (1986). *Knowledge as design.* Hillsdale, NJ: Erlbaum.

> ## 6.3

TEACHING STRATEGY 12
Questioning Editorial Perspectives

Students need to become aware that, unless they are critical readers, the way a writer presents information can sway them toward a particular opinion. By having students consider multiple viewpoints, rather than a single perspective, you are assisting them in reading critically (Paul, 1993). Newspapers provide an excellent tool for developing students' critical thinking skills and comparative analysis skills (Laffey & Laffey, 1986).

Most newspapers publish editorials written to express a stance on a particular issue. In addition to editorials, newspapers may report news events from their particular perspectives just as authors write textbooks from a variety of perspectives. The following strategy allows students to question a newspaper's editorial stance on a controversial issue.

 ## Directions and Example

1. Explain to students that, when they read newspapers, they need to be aware of the writer's perspectives. This is particularly true when reading editorials, as editorials provide a forum for newspaper writers to express their opinions on particular issues.

2. Discuss editorials that students may have read in the past. Ask students to share information about particular editorials they have read in which the writer presented an obvious opinion. Have copies of a variety of newspaper editorials available to facilitate the discussion.

3. Tell students that they need to ask themselves questions as they read an editorial. Write the following questions (Robinson, 1975) on the chalkboard or an overhead transparency.

   Questions for Reading Editorials
   - What is the title of the editorial?
   - What is the issue in this editorial?
   - What stance on the issue is represented here?
   - What specific evidence is given to support this side of the issue?
   - Is there any evidence apparent in this editorial to suggest another viewpoint?
   - Does the writer show a bias? Are there any particular words or patterns of writing used to accomplish this? If so, what are they?

4. Provide students with an editorial from a local newspaper or give students the *USA Today* (1998) example that follows. Ask students to read the editorial.

5. After students have read the editorial "Amendment Deprives Faithful of Protections" from *USA Today*, have them answer the Questions for Reading Editorials. Answers for the *USA Today* editorial follow.

   Questions for Reading Editorials
   Q: What is the title of the editorial?
   A: Amendment deprives faithful of protections.

Q: What is the issue in this editorial?
A: Religious freedom amendment

Q: What stance on the issue is represented here?
A: Editorial opposes amendment.

Q: What specific evidence is given to support this side of the issue?
A: Existing law has been misinterpreted and perfectly legal religious activity
     has been stopped.

Q: Is there any evidence apparent in this editorial to suggest another viewpoint?
A: Editorial presents samples of distortions used by amendment's supporters.

Q: How does the writer show a bias? Are there any particular words or patterns
     of writing used to accomplish this? If so, what are they?
A: Writer uses words such as *lies, attempt to portray,* and *religious tyranny.*

6.   Divide the class into groups of three or four students. Ask students to share their responses to
     the questions as they discuss the writer's viewpoint.

7.   Invite each group of students to write a counterargument to the published editorial. Share the
     students' editorials during a whole class discussion or as part of a class produced newspaper.

Today's debate: Religious freedom

Amendment deprives faithful of protections

OUR VIEW **Religious minorities would suffer; church groups could tap public funds.**

True or false:

- The Constitution bars children from carrying Bibles to school.
- The Supreme Court has banned kids from saying grace in school lunchrooms.
- Judges are distorting the law to drive the baby Jesus out of the town Christmas display.

All are false—just a sampling of the exaggerations, distortions and outright lies that have been used for years to mislead the public about religious rights, particularly in schools.

Today, they'll arrive on the floor of the House of Representatives, which is expected to vote on the grossly mislabeled "Religious Freedom Amendment" to the Constitution.

It's billed as a way of restoring prayer in schools. But far from protecting religious freedom, it could deprive religious minorities in any community of the protections written by the Founding Fathers. Further, it would open the public till to taxpayer subsidies for religious institutions.

In effect, the proposal would repeal the First Amendment ban on using the state to promote or finance a particular religion. It would authorize local authorities to use public events to proselytize for their own pet theologies. Those might include officially ordered sectarian devotions in schools or honored status for favored clergy. People of other religious beliefs would have little recourse.

Further, it would mandate taxpayer funding of some religious institutions, now largely prohibited under the Founders' doctrine that the state should stay out of church activities. They and their ancestors had experienced firsthand the tyranny of using the power of government to abuse religious minorities.

And all for little cause. Over the years, a few teachers, principals or other officials have misinterpreted the law and stopped perfectly legal personal religious activ-

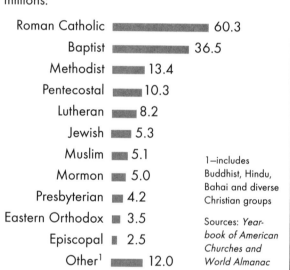

Many paths of faith
The USA comprises at least 150 denominations of 5,000 members or more, and many smaller groups. Estimated breakdown of major groups, in millions:

Roman Catholic 60.3
Baptist 36.5
Methodist 13.4
Pentecostal 10.3
Lutheran 8.2
Jewish 5.3
Muslim 5.1
Mormon 5.0
Presbyterian 4.2
Eastern Orthodox 3.5
Episcopal 2.5
Other[1] 12.0

1—includes Buddhist, Hindu, Bahai and diverse Christian groups

Sources: *Yearbook of American Churches* and *World Almanac*

ity. But almost all of those incidents have been resolved locally and the misunderstandings cleared up.

The fact that the amendment's promoters have to keep recycling the same handful of horror stories, some going back into the '80s, gives the lie to claims of widespread abuse.

They attempt to portray their opponents as hostile to religion. In fact, a broad coalition of religious and civil-rights groups stands opposed. They have a more responsible solution for incorporating religion in schools. It's a set of guidelines, *Religion in the Public Schools: A Joint Statement of Current Law*, that has been made available to every school district. President Clinton announced Saturday the Department of Education is issuing an updated version, based on recent legal developments. If followed, there would be few problems except for the folks who want to use the power of government for religious self-aggrandizement.

Down their path lies not religious freedom but religious tyranny.

Evaluating Arguments and Forming Judgments

Goal > To help students evaluate the argument, or logic, of a text and form judgments

BACKGROUND

Students are exposed to many different kinds of texts in school, from texts that are written by qualified authors with editorial review boards to texts that are written by someone with a biased viewpoint. For that reason, students need to be able to read texts in their content classes critically and to independently evaluate the logic of a passage and form a reasoned judgment.

Most of the writing that students read in our disciplines has a logical progression of ideas that leads to a conclusion. That conclusion is backed up by supporting claims. These claims can be about what the author thinks is true (knowledge claims), about what causes something (causal claims), about what is likely to happen (predictive claims), about what is good (evaluative claims), about what is right or wrong (moral claims), and about what ought to be done (policy claims). Some claims overlap into two or more categories and can be considered mixed claims (Unrau, 1997).

When students read texts, they need to be able to evaluate the worth of the author's conclusions and to evaluate whether the arguments the author makes support the conclusions without undue bias. Furthermore, students need to be able to examine the author's claims and to be able to determine what they believe about the topic. Merely challenging an author's point can lead to cynicism. Therefore, we want students to evaluate arguments in texts and come to independent conclusions about what they believe about the topic.

To assist your students in evaluating arguments and forming judgments, you can develop lessons that mirror the thinking process you do when you critically evaluate a text. This section provides four different strategies that help students begin to evaluate arguments and form judgments. As you use or adapt each of these strategies to your content area, remember that any activity that promotes the effective evaluation of an author's claims can assist students in becoming more critical readers of texts.

TECHNOLOGY

Online Service

An online service that offers examples of innovative questions and solutions and welcomes the contributions of inventive thinkers.

Registry for Better Ideas
cctr.umkc.edu/user/rbi/Foundation

**T
I
P**

6.4

TEACHING STRATEGY 13

State-Question-Read-Conclude (SQRC)

Critical readers draw conclusions as they read, but many students may need help learning how to come to reasoned judgments. State-Question-Read-Conclude (SQRC) (Sakta, 1998/1999) guides students through the thinking processes that occur during reading and helps them draw conclusions from their reading.

 ## Directions and Examples

1. Identify a text selection that is conducive for drawing conclusions as in a text on drilling for oil in the arctic. Teach unfamiliar vocabulary before the lesson so that students' comprehension is not hindered by lack of knowledge of text-specific words.

2. Duplicate and distribute copies of the SQRC sheet that follows.

3. Develop a question from the text that is controversial and write it on the chalkboard or on an overhead transparency. An example follows.

    Should drilling in the Arctic National Wildlife Refuge be permitted?

4. Tell students that people have a variety of opinions about this issue and that the text they will be reading will present one or more of these opinions. Before students read the text, have them write their own opinions on the first line of the SQRC sheets. Do not share your own opinion about the issue because it could influence some students' thinking.

5. Tell students to reframe their opinions in the form of a question. Explain that the question will guide their thinking as they read the text. Provide one or more examples of questions for students as in the following examples.

    Statement: Wildlife will be threatened.
    Question: Will wildlife be threatened by drilling?
    Statement: The world has enough oil without additional drilling.
    Question: Does the world have enough oil without drilling?

6. Have students read the text. Tell students to look for information to answer their questions as they read. If students find facts that support or refute their position statements during reading, have them write those facts on their SQRC sheets. Some students may not find facts that support or refute their statements in the text. These students might want to research the topic further.

7. After students have read the text and written facts that support or refute their position statements, have them reread their notes and write a brief conclusion in the final spaces of their sheets.

8. Have students share their position statements and conclusions. Tell students that people can reach different conclusions after reading the same material. If that occurs, discuss how students have applied different values or reasoning to the text to reach their conclusions.

9. An example of a SQRC sheet follows.

State-Question-Read-Conclude
SQRC

Statement _____

_____

Question _____

_____

Facts that support my position statement

_____

_____

_____

_____

Facts that refute my position statement

_____

_____

_____

_____

Conclusion

_____

_____

Based on Sakta, C.G. (1998/1999). SQRC: A strategy for guiding reading and higher level thinking. *Journal of Adolescent & Adult Literacy, 42,* 265–269.

6.4 ▸ Opinion-Proof

Students will read and be exposed to many opinions during their schooling. Opinions can be found in their textbooks, lectures, conversations with peers, and outside reading. By middle school, students should be able to identify an opinion. Evaluating opinions is much more complex. To help students learn how to evaluate the logic of an opinion, you can use the strategy Opinion-Proof (Santa, Dailey, & Nelson, 1985). Opinion-Proof is a strategy that helps students understand how to evaluate the arguments supporting an opinion and come to a conclusion about that opinion. It takes students through the steps of forming an opinion, supporting the opinion, looking for reasoning fallacies, and writing convincingly about the opinion. Below is a list of common reasoning fallacies that you may want to develop into a chart for classroom use.

REASONING FALLACIES

Appealing to authority: Invoking authority as the last word.

Appealing to emotion: Using emotion as proof.

Appealing to force: Using threats to establish the validity of a claim.

Appealing to the people: Justifying a claim based on its popularity.

Arguing from ignorance: Arguing that a claim is justified because its opposite cannot be proved.

Begging the question: Making a claim and producing arguments that do not support the claim.

Contradiction: Presenting information that contradicts a claim.

Evading the issue: Talking around the issue rather than addressing it.

False analogy: Comparing unmatched elements.

False cause: Crediting an effect to a cause without evidence.

Hasty generalization: Drawing a conclusion from too few examples.

Poisoning the well: Committing to one position and explaining everything in light of that position.

Directions and Example

1. Explain, if necessary, the characteristics of an opinion statement. Invite students to generate and share opinion statements.

2. Generate an opinion statement from one or more texts students have read. You may write the opinion statement or have students write one.

   After reading excerpts from Thoreau's book *Walden,* his essay "Civil Disobedience," and a section on Jeffersonian democracy, present the following opinion statement.

   Opinion statement: Thoreau believed in Jeffersonian democracy.

3. Explain that opinions need to have evidence to support them and that the weight of the evidence will assist the reader in forming a judgment. Discuss the sources from which students can find supporting evidence for the opinion statement. In this case, evidence can be found in their textbooks. Have students find and write supporting evidence for the opinion.

4. Ask students to share the evidence they found in their texts. Write the evidence on the chalkboard or an overhead transparency.

Evidence
- Jefferson believed that there are no limits to how much the human race can improve.
- Jefferson believed that free people should follow the dictates of reason.
- Jefferson believed in minimal government.
- Jefferson said that those who labor in the earth are the chosen people of God.
- Thoreau valued his freedom above all else.
- Thoreau said that people can elevate their lives.
- Thoreau believed that government should be restricted.
- Thoreau did not believe in governmental taxation.
- Thoreau said that government gets in the way of human accomplishments.
- Thoreau lived by himself for five years at Walden Pond, doing all of the manual labor.

5. Explain that not all evidence will support the opinion. Discuss which evidence supports the opinion and which does not.

Supporting Evidence
- Jefferson believed that there are no limits to how much the human race can improve.
- Jefferson believed that free people should follow the dictates of reason.
- Jefferson believed in minimal government.
- Thoreau valued his freedom above all else.
- Thoreau said that people can elevate their lives.
- Thoreau believed that government should be restricted.
- Thoreau did not believe in governmental taxation.
- Thoreau said that government gets in the way of human accomplishments.

Evidence that Does Not Support Topic
- Jefferson said that those who labor in the earth are the chosen people of God.
- Thoreau lived by himself for five years at Walden Pond, doing all of the manual labor.

6. Write an essay as a group or have students write independently using the opinion and the evidence the students have identified. In some instances, you might introduce some reasoning fallacies. For example, the following is a section from an essay.

The evidence from both Thoreau's *Walden* and his essay "Civil Disobedience" indicates that he was a strong believer in Jeffersonian democracy. Coming from the Age of Enlightenment, Jefferson believed that in a democracy people needed to use reason rather than government to rule themselves. Thoreau also espoused those beliefs. He did not believe that the government should tax people, for example. Instead, he thought that people should go about their own business and take care of themselves.

7. After students have written an essay, have them evaluate the persuasive power of the essay, looking for any reasoning fallacies. You might use or adapt the following rubric to evaluate the essays.

Name _____ Date _____

Essay Evaluation Rubric

1. Sophistication of Argument—Scope, Depth, and Clarity

   Shallow   Comprehensive
   1   2   3   4   5   6   7   8   9   10

2. Effectiveness of Supporting Claims

   Weak   Effective
   1   2   3   4   5   6   7   8   9   10

3. Effectiveness of Evidence

   Weak   Effective
   1   2   3   4   5   6   7   8   9   10

4. Effectiveness of Counterarguments

   Weak   Effective
   1   2   3   4   5   6   7   8   9   10

5. Coherence of Argument

   Disordered   Cohesive
   1   2   3   4   5   6   7   8   9   10

6. Organization

   Rudimentary   Clear
   1   2   3   4   5   6   7   8   9   10

Based on Unrau, N.J. (1997). *Thoughtful teachers, thoughtful learners: A guide to helping adolescents think critically.* Scarborough, Ontario: Pippin.

6.4 Socratic Questioning

Socratic questioning is the art of asking leading questions to stimulate the rational thinking that leads to conclusions. In Plato's dialogues, Socrates would pretend to be ignorant of a subject and would ask questions of his students and fellow citizens that probed their beliefs and assumptions in order to lead them through arguments to a conclusion. Socratic questioning is an appropriate strategy to use in schools to promote critical reading. This type of questioning helps students evaluate their own interpretations of texts by helping them think about their reasoning, by comparing their interpretations to those of others, by promoting relationships between ideas, and by forming reasoned judgments (Tanner & Casados, 1998).

 ## Directions and Example

1. Identify the underlying concepts from a text students have read. Think about the types of responses students would give to a question and the relationships between the responses. Ask students a question relating to the concepts. The following is an example of Socratic Questioning in a middle school literature class.

    > We have just finished the story "The Scribe" by Kristin Hunter and I believe you have a good understanding of the story. As you know, "The Scribe" is about a 13-year-old boy who lives above the Silver Dollar Check Cashing Service in an urban setting. He realizes that people who are illiterate are charged fees for having their checks cashed and their letters written or read. The boy set up a table in front of the business and told the customers that he would provide the same services free of charge. However, a town ordinance required that he purchase a business license. He then took the people in need of services to a bank and helped them with banking procedures.

    > Now I'd like to pose a question from the theme of the story for us to discuss. Is the ability to read important in our society?

2. After posing the question, allow approximately five minutes for students to think about their answers and have students write their ideas on paper. Then play the role of Socrates and have students try to convince you that their opinions are reasonable. As students offer ideas, guide them to reasonable conclusions. Some of the questions you might use to encourage discussion follow.

    - How are your ideas like those other students have offered?
    - How is your point of view different from others that have been discussed?
    - How did you reach this point of view?
    - Where do you think your idea takes us?
    - How does your idea help us form a conclusion?
    - What reasons do you have for your opinion?
    - What evidence can you offer to support your opinion?

3. Allow at least 30 minutes for discussion. After the class has discussed the question you presented, have students answer the question independently, either in writing or by an oral presentation.

6.4 **Generative Writing**

TEACHING STRATEGY 16

As students learn how to evaluate arguments and form opinions, they need to practice evaluating the arguments of their peers as well as the arguments of the texts read in school. Students are frequently exposed to (and engage in) faulty reasoning in conversations and in writing. Generative Writing (Ryder & Graves, 1998) is an activity that can help students evaluate written information from their peers. With Generative Writing, students identify a topic for which they would like to gather information from their peers, use e-mail as a tool to ask their peers about a topic, evaluate the information and arguments of their peers, and draw their own conclusions.

Directions and Example

1. Identify a task or a problem from your content area that involves critical thinking. You might choose a topic that you want your class to study, or you might ask students to suggest topics. Present the topic to your students. Have students revise the topic to fit their interests.

   We have been reading about air, water, and noise pollution. Do you think pollution is a problem?

2. Find several classes of students in various parts of the country or world who would be willing to engage in a dialogue about the topic. You might contact your professional organization (see Appendix A) for sources of classes that might be interested in a project of this type. Middle school students can pose the question to KIDCAFE.

TECHNOLOGY
TIP

E-Mail Discussions for Middle School Students

Any young adult between the ages of 10 and 15 can send a message to KIDCAFE. Moderators will check the message for appropriateness. The moderator sends all appropriate messages to a listserv, and the listserv distributes the messages to all e-mail addresses on the KIDCAFE list.

KIDCAFE: Youth dialogue
For information, send the message GET KIDCAFE GUIDE
to listserv@vm1.nodak.edu

KIDCAFE-SCHOOL: School-organized keypal exchange
Administrative address: listserv@vm1.nodak.edu
Participation address: kidcafe-school@ vm1.nodak.edu

3. Have students outline the problem and develop questions to elicit information from other students.

    - Where do you live? Describe your community.
    - Do you have a problem with air, noise, or water pollution?
    - How serious do you believe the problem is?
    - What health issues are involved with pollution in your community?
    - Do you have any solutions to suggest?

4. Have students discuss their own answers to the questions before soliciting information from other sources. Use the text to guide your discussion. After discussing the topic, have students write their own preliminary responses to the question, providing evidence and justifications. An example follows.

    We live in a rural community with no large city within 50 miles. Most of our parents are farmers or orchard owners. Since we live in the country, we don't have much noise pollution. The nearest airport is too far away to hear. We do, however, have air and water pollution from the pesticides the farmers use on their fields. We have a crop dusting company in our area that sprays crops several times a season. They spray from small airplanes. When they spray the crops, we have to go indoors and shut the windows. The air is filled with chemicals. These chemicals eventually run into our water supply. Since we have well water, we are very concerned that the ground water stays clean.

    We have a solution to propose. We have begun a petition asking the farmers to investigate alternative ways of growing crops that would not use pesticides. We are sorry if any change would diminish the amount of business the crop duster has, but we believe it is for the good of the community.

5. E-mail the outline, questions, and sample answer to other students around the country and the world. Ask that responses be returned within two weeks. After two weeks, collect the responses and duplicate them for the entire class. Divide the class into groups of four or five students to read the other students' papers and evaluate their logic.

6. Using input from all of the groups, come to a conclusion about the original topic. Write a short summary, as in the following example, and e-mail it to the participants in this project.

    Pollution seems to be a problem for students from many localities. Most of the students experience significant sources of pollution in their communities. The types of pollution vary although more students from urban areas find noise pollution to be a problem. Several solutions were suggested. Most of the solutions emphasized individual responsibility. All of the student groups felt powerless to change the biggest sources of pollution.

Promoting Critical Literacy

Section 6.5

Goal ▶ To help students acknowledge social and cultural factors present in texts

BACKGROUND

Critical literacy is an evolving set of beliefs about reading text that is based on Freire's idea that readers should read texts critically and then move beyond reading to become agents against oppression and for social justice. People learning words should also be engaged in a critical analysis of the social framework in which they exist (Freire, 1985). Social learning theorists have contributed to what we now call critical literacy (Green, 2001). Critical literacy cannot be easily explained and is not readily adaptable to teaching strategies such as those found in other sections of this book. Critical literacy is a way of approaching text with an understanding and knowledge of the influences texts have on readers: how texts can support or erode existing power bases and how texts influence culture. Critical literacy theories have also been applied to the viewing of media (Alvermann & Hagood, 2000).

TECHNOLOGY

T I P

Critical Literacy

This comprehensive site discusses critical literacy, its importance, questions asked of texts, what critical literacy looks like in the classroom, where to find more ideas to use with students, and much more.

www.discover.tased.edu.au/english/critlit.htm

6.5 A Lens on Language

Critical reading is "part of a real attempt to read the social: to make sense of the texts and signs of our culture" (Gilbert, 2001, p. 81). As students read, they can often detect gender bias in text by looking for ways in which males and females are portrayed—not merely by examining the use of personal pronouns such as *he/she*. By looking closely at the way language is used in text, students can become aware of power relationships and gender bias.

 ## Directions and Example

1. Locate a text from a book or the Internet that applies to your content area. Provide students with copies of the text.

2. Have students read the text looking for references to males and females. Prompt them by saying something like the following example.

    > In this article on polar expeditions, you'll find descriptions of the scientists and the crew at the polar outpost. Look for ways the authors have described different characters. For example, notice that they write about Bob's medical training, and they mention that Emily is petite. Pay attention to everything that refers to the people in the article.

3. Ask students to highlight the references to the different genders. Tell students that they are collecting facts and should not be looking for specific biases.

 4. Divide the class into groups of two or three students. Have students compile their highlighted lists so that they create group lists of gender references.

5. Collect the group lists and develop a class list. Write the list on the chalkboard or on an overhead transparency, as in the following example.

Bob	**Emily**
degree from Harvard	petite
wife and children at home	from the Midwest
former expeditions	only woman in group
athletic	personable

6. Have students read the completed lists and draw generalizations about the use of gender in the text. You might need to provide guidance using a think-aloud as in the example that follows.

    > As I read my lists, I noticed that the writers discussed Bob's degrees, while they said nothing about Emily's qualifications.

7. Remind students that gender stereotypes are often reinforced in subtle ways through language and that critical readers are aware of the influence language has on their views of cultural groups.

6.5 ➤ Problemitizing Texts

Students who read critically also need to explore the ways diverse cultures are represented in literature and problemitize texts as they read (Comber, 2001). Problemitizing texts means to look at what exists in the text, what isn't present, and what those authorial choices mean. Writers make choices during the writing process: they choose how to represent gender and cultural groups, what to say, and what not to say. If students read with attention to what is and is not in text, they problemitize the text.

Directions and Example

1. Select a picture book to read to students that presents an interesting story. For example, the book *Click, Clack, Moo: Cows that Type* (Cronin, 2000) is a picture book about farmyard animals that find a typewriter and make written demands on the farmer. The book illustrates the use of literacy in action.

2. Tell students that you want them to listen for more than the plot as you read aloud. Explain to students that you want them to problemitize the text.

3. Duplicate and distribute the list of Problemitizing Text Questions that follows. Explain that not all questions will apply to this particular story, but that the questions are representative of a different way of understanding text.

4. Read the book to students. Provide time during the reading for students to refer to the list of questions.

5. After reading, have students discuss the book in light of the Problemitizing Text Questions that follow.

6. A resource of ideas for picture books to use follows.

   Carr, K.S., Buchanan, D.L., Wentz, J.B., Weiss, M.L., & Brant, K.J. (2001). Not just for the primary grades: A bibliography of picture books for secondary content teachers. *Journal of Adolescent & Adult Literacy, 45,* 146–153.

   Teidt, I.M. (2000). *Teaching with picture books in the middle school.* Newark, DE: International Reading Association.

   Trelease, J. (2001). *The read-aloud handbook* (5th ed.). New York: Penguin.

PROBLEMITIZING TEXT QUESTIONS

- How does the author represent different groups in the text?

- How are meanings assigned to certain figures?

- How does the author try to convince readers to accept his or her premise?

- How are meanings assigned to a certain figure or events in the text?

- What is the purpose of the text?

- Whose interests are served by the dissemination of this text? Whose interests are not served?

- What view of the world is put forth by the ideas in this text? What views are not?

- What are other possible constructions of the world?

- What is included in this text?

- What is missing from this text?

- What does this text tell us about our culture?

6.5 ▶ Media Logs

TEACHING STRATEGY 19

The types of critical literacy activities that apply to print can also be applied to media (Paul, 2000). The media play a role in the lives of most students, both personally and academically. Students learn from television, music, drama, and the Internet as well as from content area textbooks and primary source materials. To promote a critical approach to media, Pailliotet, Semali, Rodenberg, Giles, & Macaul (2000) suggest that students use a media log. A media log is similar to any type of journal; the difference is that students will be recording their reactions to media rather than to written texts.

Directions and Example

1. Develop a list of television programs, videos, music, rap, commercials, and Internet sites that apply to your content area. To develop the list, you might ask for students to provide input, as in the example below.

   We're going to be looking at the ways the media influence and are influenced by our class content. To do that I'm going to prepare a list of the media that apply to our class. I'll list a few examples, and I'd like you to add other examples that you know.

2. Develop class rules about the media that should and should not be on the list. For example, you might have a rule against media that portray excessive violence.

3. Once you have a list of the media, have class members select an example from each of the categories of the media (e.g., videos). Have students watch or view each medium and respond using a media log.

4. Duplicate and distribute the Media Log Prompts that follow. Tell students that a media log is similar to keeping a journal but has different purposes and prompts. Have them respond in their media logs to the media they view or hear.

5. After students have written several responses in their media logs for a week or so, divide the class into groups of three or four students and have them discuss their entries.

6. Discuss the media log entries with the entire class. Encourage students to respond critically to the media and guide students toward discussions that further critical media literacy.

MEDIA LOG PROMPTS

- What message is conveyed by the media?
- Who is the central audience of the media?
- How is this message presented?
- Do you personally agree or disagree with the media's message? Why?
- How is language used to present the message?
- How could you resist the message if you wanted to do so?
- What sorts of movement and space are used?
- What social knowledge is assumed?
- What is implied by the media?
- What is missing from the presentation?
- How is the text situated culturally and historically?
- How does this text position me as a viewer or listener?

6.5 Taking Social Action
TEACHING STRATEGY 20

The primary aim of critical literacy is to promote social justice by taking social action. Literacy can be used as a tool for furthering this aim. One example of taking social action is when students in Kentucky used reading, writing, speaking, and listening skills to influence those in power to responsibly mine the highest peak in the state (Powell, Cantrell, & Adams, 2001). Looking for ways to promote social action is the most effective type of strategy you can use as you promote critical literacy.

Directions and Example

1. Encourage students to become aware of local social issues that apply to your subject area, such as the need to clean up vacant yards, the underfunding of schools, and so on. Post newspaper and Internet site listings about these issues in a prominent place in your classroom.

2. After you've collected a number of postings about issues, have students generate a list of the issues that are represented by these texts.

3. Duplicate and distribute the list of issues to students. Ask students to prioritize the list starting with number one and continuing until all issues are included.

4. Collect the prioritized lists and determine which issue is of most interest to the class as a whole. Announce the number one issue.

5. Have students collect print and nonprint information related to the issue. For example, if the social issue that the class wants to study is a city zoning law that limits the number of persons to six individuals who could live in a single-family, three-bedroom house, have students collect the following types of information about the subject.

   - Newspaper clippings
   - Radio broadcasts
   - Editorials
   - Internet sites
   - Interviews with zoning commissioners
   - Interviews with the mayor and city council members
   - Interviews with residents of subdivisions
   - Interviews with residents from another town
   - Interviews with zoning commissioners from other areas

6. Have students bring to class their information and discuss the social implications of the zoning restriction. You might ask the following questions.

   - Is a specific cultural group the focus of the restriction?
   - Is the restriction a safety concern?
   - Are the members of the zoning board a specific cultural group?
   - Does the language from the texts indicate biases?
   - Do the texts about the issue have underlying prejudices?
   - Are the media's messages balanced and neutral?
   - Is anyone being disenfranchised by this restriction?

7. Tell students that taking social action means acting responsibly—not making false accusations, but presenting a reasoned, thoughtful account of the facts. Have students use the facts they have collected to develop a "white paper" about the topic to present to the people in power—in this case, the zoning commission.

8 Explain to students that their social action may or may not bring results, but, as members of a democracy, they should continue to use critical literacy skills to further social action whenever possible.

Chapter 7
STUDYING

OVERVIEW

Studying is a unique skill, different from the reading strategies presented in other chapters of this book. When students read, they focus attention on the text; then they use their ability to process print to construct meaning. While reading, students rely on textbook features and use their ability to reason in order to fulfill their reading purposes. Studying is different. When students study, they read, understand, learn, and remember information from texts for a specific task (Anderson & Armbruster, 1984).

To illustrate the difference between reading and studying, think about textbook passages you assign students to read in preparation for class discussion. You expect them to read, understand, and remember information that they can apply to a general discussion about the topic. You expect students

to know some of the content information. When you assign students studying tasks, your expectations are often different. You expect students to identify the important ideas in the text, to learn and remember those ideas, to be able to understand the relationship between the information they studied and past material, and to retrieve that material in certain ways for a test or a performance.

Studying has two basic components: knowing what to study and knowing how to study. Students need to be aware of the learning task. If studying is to accomplish a specific task, students must understand the task. Generally, you will be the one who determines the studying task. For example, you might ask students to study material for a test, a performance, or a presentation. Your role is to make sure that students understand the nature of the task. Then students need to identify the subsets of the task and set study goals to accomplish each one. As students decide what to study, they may survey the materials and use flexible reading strategies to determine what information to learn and remember. They may set goals, manage their study time, and monitor their studying effectiveness. Once students have determined what they should study, they need to use study strategies to learn and remember the material for the specific study task.

Knowing what to study is not enough; students also need to know how to study. When students study to read and remember, they need to focus attention on the material, encode that information, and learn the material in such a way that they can retrieve it for the task. Students need to read the text information and form it into their own words, so that it makes sense and they are able to repeat that information in any one of a variety of forms for a test. To do this, students need to learn how to use study strategies. The following strategies are generally considered useful for most students who are studying (see Block & Pressley, 2002).

- Preview text
- Predict
- Skim or scan text
- Read slowly and carefully
- Reread difficult sections
- Paraphrase
- Relate new information to existing knowledge
- Create mental images
- Develop questions
- Highlight, underline, or take notes
- Outline
- Create a diagram
- Summarize

Because studying is task directed and people learn in different ways, study plans and methods tend to be idiosyncratic. For example, students who are studying a history text could be faced with five new vocabulary words, eight pages to read, three charts, two graphs, and five pictures. Some students prefer to read the text in sequential order, taking detailed notes using the Cornell notetaking method. Other students prefer scanning the chapter and using the REAP strategy, taking annotative notes. Still others may use the REST strategy and take notes along with writing their own comments and questions. Because there isn't one correct way to study, you should present students with a variety of study strategies and let them choose those strategies that work for them (Simpson & Nist, 2002).

Studying in schools is often assigned so that students learn material for a culminating activity such as a test or a performance. Students should know, however, that studying is a useful life skill. Even though students are not formally graded in their everyday life in the same way they are in schools, they still have many opportunities to study: to read and learn to perform a specific task. For example, students who are learning to drive will read the driver's manual, learn driving skills from an adult, and practice driving. Students are actually studying; they are reading and learning in order to perform a specific task. Therefore, as you teach students how to study for your class, also tell them that they can use the skills they are learning for many important activities in which they will engage as adolescents and adults.

Learning to Study

Goal > To help students learn how to study

BACKGROUND

Studying is generally a self-directed activity. You can teach students a variety of study strategies, but they have to assume the responsibility for their own studying. You can assist students in learning how to take that responsibility by helping them create study plans, manage their study time, and monitor their study habits.

Helping adolescents learn how to accept the responsibility for the outcome of studying is a challenge. One of the hallmarks of adolescent thinking is the difficulty in accepting reality. Most adolescents employ "magical thinking" at times. They believe that simply because they want something to happen it will, and they don't have to work to cause it to happen. For example, many times a student who is receiving a poor grade in a class will say, "I'll raise my grade next quarter." The next grading period comes and the student has earned the same grade. When confronted with the situation, the student is disbelieving. The grade was supposed to be higher simply because of wishful thinking. Adolescents frequently confuse wanting something to happen with making it happen. For that reason, you should help students learn that studying takes time and attention. Students will need to make study plans, set study goals, and use study strategies to accomplish their goals.

Even though studying is generally an individual endeavor, students should study with friends at times. Middle and high school students are social beings. Therefore, students should be encouraged to study in groups for part of their study time. Certainly, there are times when solo studying is best, but many adolescents learn better when they can share ideas with their peers. Consequently, you should encourage students to learn how to plan, manage, and monitor their individual studying, but you should also encourage students to spend some of their study time learning from each other.

TECHNOLOGY

T
I
P

ITools

Online dictionary (Webster's), rhyming dictionary, thesaurus, maps, phone directories, and more.

www.itools.com

TEACHING STRATEGY 1

7.1

Preplan-List-Activate-Evaluate (PLAE)

Research indicates that students who construct and implement an effective plan of study do better on tests than students who do not have a study plan (Nist & Simpson, 1989). For that reason Nist and Simpson (1989) created PLAE, a study strategy to help students create goals and plan what to do during study time. PLAE incorporates the following methods necessary for strategy control and regulation: goal setting, understanding of a variety of strategies, the ability to select appropriate study strategies, the ability to activate and monitor a plan of action, and the ability to evaluate a study plan. When students employ PLAE, they **P**replan or define their tasks and goals, **L**ist or select the strategies they will use, **A**ctivate or implement the study plan, and **E**valuate the plan's effectiveness after they receive feedback.

Directions and Example

1. Tell students that you will be demonstrating a study strategy that they can use in all subject areas to improve their learning of content material. Use examples from your content area or use the following example.

2. Write PLAE on the chalkboard or an overhead transparency. Tell students that PLAE is an acronym for **P**replan, **L**ist, **A**ctivate, and **E**valuate.

3. Identify a study goal that students will need to accomplish in the near future. Tell students that you will be using the following example to demonstrate the **P**replan stage of PLAE.

Study Goal

For French class you will be asked to learn vocabulary and language structures associated with various foods and grocery shopping. We will have a mock grocery store with food to sell. To demonstrate your knowledge, you will be evaluated on your ability to conduct a conversation in French. Students in the fourth-year French class will play the role of the shopkeepers.

4. Divide the class into groups of three or four students. Have students create a list of tasks designed to accomplish the study goal. After students have developed lists, have them discuss their ideas with the whole group. A sample list follows.

Study Tasks

- Scan your French book, looking for the chapter that discusses the vocabulary of grocery shopping.
- Create note cards or write notes with the terms to learn.
- Memorize the vocabulary.
- Practice the new vocabulary with classmates in conversations about grocery shopping.

5. Tell students that the next step in PLAE is to list their prior knowledge of successful study strategies. Have students discuss the strategies they could use to accomplish their study tasks.

6. Have groups of students discuss possible study options. Then have students brainstorm strategies that they could use to accomplish each task. Students should individually decide which study strategy to use. Ask students to write their study plans on index cards. An example of a study plan follows.

Study Plan

Skim section 1 from chapter 6.
Identify words to learn.
Memorize new words.
Practice new words in dialogue with classmates.

7. Have students activate their study plans. Each day ask students whether they were able to accomplish their study goals.

8. After students have completed their study plans and have demonstrated their learning, have them evaluate their study plans. For students to evaluate their study plans, they need to identify the outcome of the culminating event. For example, if students were being graded on their ability to use French in a grocery shopping scenario, have them list the grades they received. Then ask students to determine whether their grades were higher or lower than they expected. If the grades were lower, have students reread their study plans, think about whether they implemented the plans, and write reasons why their grades were not as high as they expected. Students should evaluate not only their final grades but also the effectiveness of their studying. If they identify a weak point, students should revise future study plans.

9. Duplicate and distribute the following description of PLAE for students to use as they study.

PLAE STUDY PLAN

Preplan—Preplan or define study tasks and goals.

List—List or select strategies to accomplish study tasks and meet study goals.

Activate—Activate or implement the study plan using appropriate strategies.

Evaluate—Evaluate the effectiveness of the study plan.

From Nist, S.L., & Simpson, M.L. (1989). PLAE, a validated study strategy. *Journal of Reading*, *33*, 182–186.

7.1 Managing Studying

TEACHING STRATEGY 2

Teaching students all of the strategies in the world will not necessarily help them learn content information. Students also need to learn how to manage their study time. Middle and high school students often have full schedules. However, they need to make time to study and manage their study time so that they can learn the necessary material from your content area. Middle and high school students need to assume the responsibility for managing their own study time, but you can help them understand the factors involved in using time wisely.

 Directions

1. Tell students that you will be discussing effective techniques for managing studying. Explain that even though many of them know how to study, unless they manage their study time they will not use their study time effectively.

2. Write the following list of Tips for Managing Study Time on the chalkboard or an overhead transparency. Discuss each of the items on this list with the students. Tell students that if they follow these suggestions they will have more productive study sessions.

TIPS FOR MANAGING STUDY TIME

- Study in a comfortable environment with good lighting and minimal distractions.

- Set study goals for each study time. List the goals and estimate the amount of time each study goal will take.

- Determine whether short periods or long periods of study time are best.

- Schedule study time at your best time for learning (e.g., early morning).

- Keep a pencil or pen available when studying to summarize, underline, or write down key notes or ideas.

- Keep a positive attitude during study time. Do not try to rush through studying. Become engaged in learning.

- Use study questions or create self-questions while studying. Keep your mind focused.

- Actively read and study. Monitor your attention to the task.

- Relate what you are studying to your life.

- Compliment yourself for productive study periods.

Based on Risko, V.J., Fairbanks, M.M., & Alvarez, M.C. (1991). Internal factors that influence study. In R.F. Flippo & D.C. Caverly (Eds.), *Teaching reading & study strategies at the college level* (pp. 237–293). Newark, DE: International Reading Association.

7.1 Monitoring Study Habits

TEACHING STRATEGY 3

As students study, they need to constantly monitor the effectiveness of their study time. You can teach them how to manage their study sessions, but students need to independently monitor their use of those management techniques as they study. Students may not be aware of the need to monitor studying. Therefore, you can teach them ways to become aware of their progress.

Directions

1. Tell students that they should become aware of the study strategies they use and should make changes so that studying is more productive. Tell students that one way to increase self-awareness is to complete a survey about study habits.

2. Duplicate and distribute the following survey. Have students answer the questions by circling the number that best describes their study habits. After students have completed the survey, have them reflect on their strengths and weaknesses and make a plan to change any habits that interfere with learning. Have students take the survey periodically so they can monitor changes in their study habits.

STUDY SKILLS SELF-ASSESSMENT

	Always		Sometimes		Never
1. I read material more than once if I don't understand it the first time.	5	4	3	2	1
2. I try to identify the most important points as I read.	5	4	3	2	1
3. I preview reading assignments before reading.	5	4	3	2	1
4. I concentrate when I study.	5	4	3	2	1
5. I study with a friend when I think it will help.	5	4	3	2	1
6. I try to "overlearn" material as I study.	5	4	3	2	1
7. I take notes that help me when I study.	5	4	3	2	1
8. I study in an environment that is conducive to learning.	5	4	3	2	1
9. I set goals for each study time.	5	4	3	2	1
10. I underline or take notes as I study.	5	4	3	2	1

Based on Davis, S. J. (1990). Applying content study skills in co-listed reading classrooms. *Journal of Reading, 33,* 277–281.

7.1 Project Journals

TEACHING STRATEGY 4

Many secondary school students have large projects to accomplish, either individually or in groups. One of the biggest difficulties with projects is managing the work. "A project journal is a device used by students to plan, organize, develop, and implement their ideas" (Stephens & Brown, 2000, p. 156). It can also be used to help them plan how to study large amounts of material.

Directions and Example

1. Tell students that they will be keeping a project journal with their assignment and that the entire class will decide upon the format for the project journal.

2. Duplicate and distribute the project journal sheet that follows. Explain to students that the format you're showing them is only one way to use a project journal and that project journals need to reflect the task assignment and goals.

3. Discuss the assignment you have given to students, explaining each of the components of the students' responsibilities. You might say something like the following example.

>   Your assignment is to work in groups to learn and understand each of the constitutional amendments in the Bill of Rights. Then you will choose one amendment and provide a historical background that explains how that amendment was conceived. This assignment will consist of two parts. First, you will be given a quiz on the Bill of Rights. Your individual grade will be the average of the grades for the group's members. Second, you will need to develop a pamphlet, cartoon, or newspaper article explaining one amendment. You will have two weeks to finish the assignment and will have two class periods to work on it.

4. Ask students if they understand the assignment. Then divide the class into groups and have them discuss what tasks they will need to accomplish as in the example that follows.

    - Identify each of the amendments in the Bill of Rights.
    - Write them on index cards.
    - Memorize the amendments and quiz each group member.
    - Select one amendment.
    - Use source material to determine the amendment's historical background.
    - Develop a pamphlet, cartoon, or newspaper article.

5. Discuss additional sections of the project journal such as a timeline, individual group members' tasks, and group assessment of progress.

6. Use students' ideas to develop a project journal that can be used with the entire class. Once students have become accustomed to using this strategy, allow groups to develop their own unique project journals.

Name _____ Date _____

Project Journal

Class_____ **Period** _____

Students' Names _____
_____
_____
_____

Assignment _____
_____
_____
_____

Tasks to accomplish   **Person in charge**
_____   _____
_____   _____
_____   _____
_____   _____
_____   _____

Tasks accomplished   **Date**
_____   _____
_____   _____
_____   _____
_____   _____
_____   _____

Comments on progress
_____   _____
_____
_____
_____
_____
_____
_____

Understanding Textbook Features

Goal > To help students understand the features of textbooks

BACKGROUND

Many students have difficulty studying because they don't understand how to read textbooks. They approach studying like they do reading novels—begin at the first paragraph and lightly read until the end. Textbooks, however, are not meant to be read like novels; they have features such as headings, subheadings, and indexes to help readers gain information.

Some texts have features that make them "friendly" for students (Armbruster, 1984). "Unfriendly" texts do not have these features or have other attributes that cause readers to work especially hard to comprehend the text. These attributes include an organization that is hard to decipher, a writing style that is too difficult, passages that are too long, and/or graphics that are difficult to read (Olson & Gee, 1991; Smith, 1992). When students are required to read a text that is "unfriendly," many students decide that the effort they must expend to read the text is not worth it.

Teaching students strategies that help them understand textbook features helps some students study more effectively. Once students know how to approach a textbook, they are able to learn and remember as they study.

7.2 > **Book Tour**

TEACHING STRATEGY 5

A book tour is a strategy that helps students become familiar with text features. Many students are unfamiliar with the features of content area texts that assist the reader with comprehension. Book tours "front-load" or guide readers through features that warrant special attention and can help students as they learn from textbooks (Buehl, 2001).

Directions and Example

1. Tell students that a book tour is like a guided tour through a museum, a historical mansion, or an art gallery; it helps readers pick out certain features of the text. Ask students whether they've experienced a guided tour. Have them share their experiences.

2. If none of the students has experienced guided tours, create an example of taking a visitor on a guided tour through your school as in the following example.

    > As you enter the building, you'll notice the signs to the administrative offices. Here you'll need to sign in and take a visitor's badge. Now we'll move down the hall toward the gymnasium. In the display cases to your right, you'll see the trophies students have won for participating in sporting events. Of special note is the first place trophy for girls' basketball. Last year they won the state tournament.

3. Explain to students that you're going to take them through a tour of their textbook and that it will be similar to other guided tours.

4. Open your textbook and point out the features that are important to your content area subject. The following list includes some of the features that you might emphasize.

    Authors
    Table of contents
    Titles and subtitles
    Graphs and charts
    Pictures
    Primary sources
    Cartoons
    Margin notes
    Bolded vocabulary words
    Chapter outlines
    Chapter questions
    Index
    List of references
    Appendices
    Footnotes
    Glossary

5. After you've given students a book tour, have them create their own book tour for students in other classes by developing a survey using the book features they have learned. Have students exchange papers and tour the book again to become even more familiar with the text.

7.2 ➤ Textbook Survey

TEACHING STRATEGY 6

Students who know textbook features study more efficiently. Textbook surveys can help students internalize their knowledge about textbooks, which helps them learn from texts.

Directions and Example

1. Tell students that knowing textbook features helps them read and study from their textbooks. Describe the features of the textbook using book tours (Teaching Strategy 7-5).

2. Then tell students that you're going to give them a textbook survey so that they can think more deeply about text features.

3. Duplicate and distribute the textbook survey that follows. Ask students to complete the survey independently.

4. After students have finished the textbook survey, facilitate a classroom discussion about each of the items on the survey. In this way, you'll be using the survey as a teaching tool rather than as an assessment device.

5. Encourage students to elaborate on their answers to the survey. Acknowledge instances where students need further instruction about textbook features and use those times to teach students more about their textbook.

Name _____ Date _____

Textbook Survey

1. Can you name some of the parts of a textbook that can help you as a reader?

   _____

2. Can you tell me how you would use the index? _____

   _____

3. Can you show me the table of contents and explain what is listed there?

   _____

4. If you wanted to look up a word you didn't know, where would you look?

   _____

5. When you look at the chapters in this book, are there any features contained in the chapters
   that make reading easier? _____

   _____

6. Do the chapters contain graphs and charts? How are they used? _____

   _____

7. Do the chapters have headings and subtitles? What purpose do these features have?

   _____

8. Before reading a chapter in the book, what could you do to make the chapter easier to
   understand? _____

   _____

9. Do you think this book is friendly or unfriendly? Why?

   _____

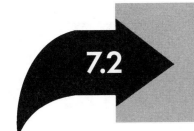

TEACHING STRATEGY 7
7.2 Friendliness, Language, Interest, and Prior Knowledge (FLIP)

Texts can be friendly or unfriendly, based on how difficult they are to read. Good readers monitor how difficult a text is and adjust their reading accordingly. To help students determine text difficulty, Schumm and Mangrum (1991) developed the FLIP strategy. FLIP stands for **F**riendliness, **L**anguage, **I**nterest, and **P**rior Knowledge—four of the aspects that influence text difficulty. FLIP can be used as a teaching tool, as a student strategy, and to assess students' comprehension (Sadler, 2001).

Directions and Example

1. Write the letters FLIP on the chalkboard or on an overhead transparency. Explain that these letters are an acronym for ways to determine text difficulty.

2. Next to the F, write the word "Friendliness." Explain to students that texts that are friendly are easy to read. Elaborate on friendliness of texts as in the example that follows.

    Some texts are easier to read than others. Texts that are friendly have titles and subtitles that divide sections of text. They also have a reasonable number of difficult or new vocabulary words. Friendly texts also have print that is easy to read and may have margin notes or embedded questions to help the reader focus attention on the content of the text.

3. Next to the L, write the word "Language." Explain to students that some language is difficult to read while other language is easy. Read an example of difficult language such as can be found in a college textbook. Then read a section from the textbook you're discussing. Ask students to determine whether the language in the textbook is appropriate for their age and reading level.

4. Write "Interest" next to the I. Tell students that texts will vary in interest based on the topic of certain sections. Read a chapter subheading and discuss ways students can find this section interesting.

5. After the P, write the words "Prior Knowledge." Remind students that prior knowledge is necessary for comprehension of text. Also tell students that they need to access prior knowledge about the text before they read.

6. Tell students that the FLIP strategy is a textbook monitoring strategy that they should use as they encounter new textbooks. Remind students that when they are given a textbook assignment they should evaluate the text's friendliness based on FLIP.

7. Explain to students that they may find many textbooks that are unfriendly, have difficult language, are not interesting, and about which students have little prior knowledge. Tell students that when that is the case FLIP can help them determine what reading strategies to use as they read and study. For example, if a text is unfriendly, they will have to read with more attention than if a text is friendly. If a text has difficult language, students will have to use reference tools to find the meanings of unknown words; if a text is uninteresting, students need to generate their own interest; and if a text requires additional prior knowledge, students may need to read from other sources to learn about the topic.

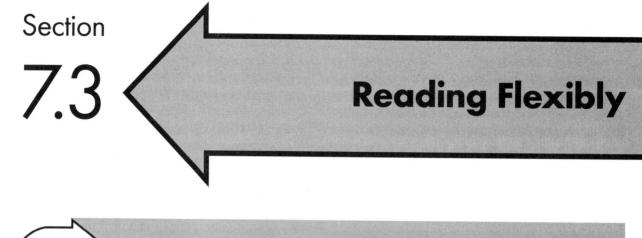

7.3

Reading Flexibly

Goal To help students develop the ability to read flexibly

BACKGROUND

Reading flexibly is a necessary skill when studying. Flexible readers modify their reading rates and their choice of strategies to fit different kinds of texts for different purposes. Flexibility can be viewed as an aspect of metacognition (i.e., thinking about thinking). Good readers are metacognitively aware. They know when comprehension is failing and when it is time to apply fix-up strategies, including an adjustment of reading rate. The rate at which students read material is influenced by at least four factors: 1) the speaking-listening rate to which they have become accustomed; 2) prior knowledge or familiarity with the material; 3) the rate at which they can receive and think about incoming information; and 4) their purpose for reading the material (Manzo & Manzo, 1990a). Additionally, reading rate is affected by the organization of the text and the author's writing style.

According to many authors, including Crawley and Mountain (1995), there are three types of reading behaviors: skimming, scanning, and precise reading. Skimming is used to gain an overview or a general idea of text. This level of reading is appropriate for previewing a chapter in a textbook or deciding whether to choose a particular library book by skimming the book jacket. Scanning is used to locate specific information or to answer a question. For example, when looking up a phone number in the directory, we scan the page until we get close to the name we are seeking. At that time, we probably begin to do precise reading. Precise reading requires analyzing words or an author's ideas in a purposeful and deliberate manner. This type of reading is used when we read textbooks for the purpose of learning and retaining information, or when we read websites. Internet reading requires students to incorporate the three traditional levels of reading (skimming, scanning, and precise reading) and incorporates one more: scrolling. When students read websites, they use scrolling, scanning, skimming, and precise reading recursively. The following strategies can provide opportunities for your students to increase their reading flexibility while maintaining adequate comprehension.

7.3 ▶ Skim-Away

Skimming involves reading quickly over material in order to gain a general impression of its content. When readers skim, they preview material and start to forge links with their background knowledge as they gain a general impression of the text. According to Fry (1978), skimming is usually done at rates of about 800 to 1,000 words per minute. The following strategy is designed to develop students' ability to skim a text selection.

 ## Directions and Example

1. Tell students that this reading strategy is one they can use to get an overall idea about the contents of the chapter or text. Explain that when readers skim they are reading text quickly to get a main idea. To demonstrate skimming, use an example from your content area or the following example.

2. Ask students to open their history text and turn to the chapter on Ancient Greece. Tell students that they are going to skim the first section of the chapter in order to get a sense of the chapter's contents and to begin to think about the main idea of the chapter. Tell students that, as they do this, they are activating their background knowledge about the chapter's subject. Allow about three minutes to complete this activity. Tell them that, as they skim, they should do the following things.

   - Read the chapter title and glance over the headings and subheadings included in the chapter as they slowly turn the pages.
   - Think about the focus of the chapter as they skim over the maps, charts, and illustrations.
   - Quickly read the section review.

3. After students have completed skimming the first section of the chapter, ask them to close their books and write a paragraph that includes everything they can recall from this first section. Invite students to share their paragraphs and talk about the techniques they used as they skimmed. An example of a student's paragraph follows.

   This section is sort of a preview about the battle between the Persians and the Athenians for the city of Athens. It looks like the chapter will focus on the geographic setting of Greece and include lots of information about the Bronze Age, the Dark Ages, and the Greek Gods. There are several photographs of Greek art works, a map of Greece during the Bronze Age, and a great photograph of the Acropolis. The section review includes some vocabulary words and questions about the contents.

4. Discuss with students the value of skimming before they read a chapter. Tell students that now that they have skimmed the first section, they have the gist, or the general idea, of the chapter and are prepared to scan it more carefully for precise information.

7.3 On Your Marks, Get Set, SCAN!

TEACHING STRATEGY 9

Scanning is used by readers to locate specific information. Readers use scanning when they look up a number in the phone book or a word in the dictionary. In scanning, readers know what information they are seeking and work at a speed of about 1,500 words per minute. This speed usually results in 100% accuracy of obtained information (Crawley & Mountain, 1995). The following strategy uses scanning as a way for students to experience finding specific information within a selection of text.

Directions and Example

1. Tell students that this reading strategy involves scanning their texts as they look for specific information. Explain that when readers scan they move their eyes quickly down the page until they locate the information they are seeking. Tell them that it is important that they read quickly and try to skip words or descriptions that do not seem pertinent to the information for which they are looking.

2. Ask students to open their history text and turn to the chapter on Ancient Greece or use an example from your content area.

3. Look over the chapter and pick out facts that students can locate as they scan. Try to pick out facts that are important to the contents. Write 5 to 10 questions, based on text information, on the chalkboard or an overhead transparency. Allow five minutes for the completion of this activity. Tell students that they are going to scan the first section of the chapter in order to find answers to the following questions.

   - How did geography shape Greek civilization?
   - How much of Greece is covered with mountains?
   - Describe briefly the life of the Minoans.
   - What was the main business of the Bronze Age kings?
   - When did the Olympic Games begin?
   - What are myths?

4. Ask students to work as quickly as possible to locate the answers to the questions. Tell them to write down the answers but not to worry about spelling at this time. Remind them that it is not necessary to read every word in the text in order to obtain the information they need to complete the activity. Say to students, "On your marks, get set, scan!" as they begin the activity.

5. After students have completed the scanning activity, invite them to share their answers and to discuss the techniques they used as they located information. Encourage them to practice using scanning with other textbook assignments in order to increase their reading efficiency.

7.3 ➤ SCROL

TEACHING STRATEGY 10

SCROL (Grant, 1993) provides students with an opportunity to use skimming, scanning, and precise reading as they study a chapter of text. Students will scan the table of contents to locate the appropriate chapter, skim the headings of the chapter as they preview it, and carefully read the chapter in order to construct an outline of its contents. Grant (1993) has identified four advantages to using SCROL:

1. Students increase comprehension by activating their background knowledge prior to reading,
2. Students are guided in understanding the relationships among ideas in the text,
3. Students use content structure as a method for remembering text information, and
4. Students' motivation for reading text is increased.

 ## Directions and Example

1. Tell students that good readers use three levels of reading: skimming, scanning, and precise reading. Explain that all of these levels are incorporated into a strategy called SCROL.

2. Explain to students that when they scan they are looking for specific information and they should read quickly down a page. When they locate information they want to read, they may want to skim it to determine if it is information they are seeking. Then they begin to do precise reading. Model the SCROL strategy for students using examples from your content area or use the example provided below.

   Scan the table of contents in your text on careers and look for the page number for chapter 10, "How to Get Jobs and Work Experience." When you find it, open your books to the appropriate page.

3. Tell students that SCROL stands for **S**urvey, **C**onnect, **R**ead, and **O**utline. As you direct students' attention to chapter 10 in their texts, model how to use SCROL.

4. Ask students to skim the chapter and **S**urvey the headings. As they skim, they should look at the headings, subheadings and illustrations in order to get the main idea of the chapter. Tell them to consider what they already know about the topic, "How to Get Jobs and Work Experience." Tell students that when they see the heading "newspaper advertisements" they probably already know that newspaper advertisements are a good place to look for jobs. As they survey the chapter, they are skimming it for general information.

5. After students have surveyed the chapter, ask them to share some of their ideas about the chapter's contents as you write their ideas on the chalkboard or an overhead transparency. For example, one student might say, "This chapter is going to tell us about work permits. I think work permits are necessary if we want to get a job and we're under 15 or 16. I'm not sure which." Another student might say, "There's a section called Distributing a Flier. This sounds interesting. Maybe it's going to tell us how to make up our own fliers when we're looking for a job."

6. Invite students to **C**onnect the headings to one another. Ask them to look for key words in the headings to help them make the connections. As they do this, tell them that they are using scanning because they are looking for specific information.

7. Ask students to continue to scan the headings and to offer suggestions about the chapter's contents. For example, one student might say, "There are also sections about entrepreneurship and private jobs so the chapter must have some information about working on your own." At this point, students have used skimming in order to preview the text and scanning to find text topics.

8. Now ask students to **R**ead the text, looking for words and phrases that explain the headings. As they do this, explain that they are employing precise reading or reading in a purposeful manner.

9. After students have finished reading the chapter, explain that they should **O**utline the chapter by listing the headings and writing under the headings the details that they remember from their reading. An example follows.

Newspaper Advertisements

- Classified advertising by employers
- Help-wanted section
- Read carefully before responding
- Place an ad for a job in situation wanted

10. Direct students to look back at the text to determine the accuracy of their outlines. As they do, point out to them that, once again, they are scanning the chapter to look for specific information. If they have written down incorrect information or wish to add additional information, they should revise their outlines.

Newspaper Advertisements

- Classified advertising lists available jobs.
- Help-wanted advertisements are for full-time jobs or adult skills.
- Some ads are for teenagers over the age of sixteen.
- Situation wanted ads should be brief but include essential information.

11. To conclude this strategy, review with students the different types of reading (skimming, scanning, and precise reading). Point out to them that they used all three types as they employed the SCROL strategy.

7.3 TEACHING STRATEGY 11
Reading Flexibly on the Internet

Media literacy, defined as "the understanding and production of messages through physical devices," incorporates six components: the ability to access, analyze, synthesize, interpret, evaluate, and communicate messages (Flood & Lapp, 1995, p. 3). Successful integration of these components requires adequate comprehension and emphasizes the necessity for flexible reading. Students must be able to vary their reading rates as they navigate information sources on the Internet in order to successfully determine the quality and relevancy of the information. This means that, as they scroll down the screen, sometimes they skim or scan, and often they use careful reading in order to analyze ideas and words.

 ## Directions and Example

1. Model the use of flexible reading on the Internet for students by using the following example or an example related to your content area. Use an LCD panel to project the following Internet activity for the entire class or, if an LCD panel is unavailable, print a copy of a web page or several web pages for each student.

2. Tell students that they need to use various strategies when reading on the Internet. They will use scrolling, skimming, scanning, and precise reading as they locate and evaluate information and determine its relevancy to their search.

3. Type the following address onto your Internet address bar.

   http://library.advanced.org/11163/gather/cgi-bin/wookie.cgi/

   This will open up a website titled *You Are What You Eat*. Tell students that you are researching nutrition and would like to find some information about how exercise relates to good health.

4. Show students that the website has several sections or choices for them to skim as they scroll down the screen and look for information about the relationship between nutrition and exercise. As they skim, they read quickly and look over the topics. They will see the following choices: Introduction, Food Database, Applications, Nutrients, and Contribute. These topics give them a general idea about the information that is available through this website. Although they have several choices of web pages, none appears to relate directly to exercise. A logical choice, at this point, will probably be the site labeled Introduction. Click on this site.

5. Tell students to scan this site in order to locate information about exercise. As they do, they will see that exercise is listed under the web link Applications. Point out to students that the type of reading they did on this page was slower and more precise as they were trying to locate a specific piece of information—the location of information about exercise.

6. Click on the word Exercise under Applications. This will take you to a page titled Exercise, with two paragraphs about the relationship between nutrition and exercise. Ask students to answer the following questions as they read this web page.

- What effect does exercise have on your metabolic rate?
- What are some benefits of exercise?
- What type of information is available on the following link?

7. Point out to students that, in order to answer these questions, they need to scan the paragraphs. However, if they wish to take notes on the material or analyze some of the information, they will need to employ precise reading or study reading. This is described as slow, careful reading for the purpose of learning or studying.

8. Guide students in conducting their own Internet research project. They should use flexible reading rates as they encounter web pages.

Taking Notes

Goal > To help students learn how to take notes from textbooks

BACKGROUND

Taking notes facilitates learning in at least two ways: by the process of taking notes and by the product, or the notes themselves (McKenna & Robinson, 1997). When students take notes, they use many cognitive processes that aid learning. First, students select what information to take down as notes. Then, they condense the information into words, phrases, or sentences. Finally, they write the notes in some type of organized form. These processes are ways to learn content material.

The notes that students write are the product of the activity. These organized, selected phrases from the text help students as they review in order to learn. The product of taking notes is important, but the mental processes involved in taking notes produces the learning (Herrell & Jordan, 2002).

Students will not automatically know how to take notes. If you do not teach students note-taking strategies, they may not select the most important information to write, and they may not write notes in an organized manner (Stahl, King, & Henk, 1991). It's important, therefore, that you teach students how to take notes.

There are many types of note-taking strategies, some using paper and pencil and some electronic. Taking notes is an activity that is individualistic; different students prefer different types of notes. Therefore, you should teach several types of note-taking strategies and encourage students to use the ones that are most helpful to them.

TECHNOLOGY

Computer Software that Creates Note Cards

T
I
P

Learning Tool is a hypertext program that allows writers to make note cards and build relationships among concepts.

Intellimation 800-346-8355

7.4 Note Cue Cards

Note Cue Cards (Manzo & Manzo, 1990b) have two instructional purposes: they help students identify important information in texts, and they facilitate discussion of key terms and concepts after reading. Note Cue Cards contain questions, answers, and comments written on note cards by the teacher about the ideas presented in a passage. When you use Note Cue Cards, you are able to guide students' attention to ideas and information as they read. After students read the text, Note Cue Cards focus the discussion on important ideas and information. Note Cue Cards scaffold learning for struggling readers by identifying key terms in the text and modeling the thinking-questioning process readers use as they learn from text.

Directions and Examples

1. Choose a passage that is important for students to read and learn. Prepare enough prereading Note Cue Cards so that each class member has at least one card. Some cards should have questions, some cards should have answers to the questions, and some cards should have comments about the topic. For example, say:

    > Today we're going to read a section about human rights in our civics textbook. This section is important because it describes the basis for our rights in the United States.

    Question: What are some of the limits on the rights of the American people?

    Answer: The government can establish laws to restrict certain rights to protect the health, safety, security, and moral standards of a community.

    Comment: The restriction of rights must be reasonable and must apply to everyone equally.

2. Explain that you will be using Note Cue Cards to help students identify the important information in the text and to facilitate discussion and learning. Distribute the cards to students. Ask students to preview the identified passage of the text, read the cards, and think about how their cards apply to the text.

3. Ask a student to read a question card. After a student has read a question, ask students to read a card that would answer the question, and then ask for a comment card.

4. Have students read the passage of the text. After students have read the text, distribute more Note Cue Cards. You may decide to give students blank cards, so they can write their own questions, answers, and comments. For example, here are some student-generated Note Cue Cards.

    Question: How are an individual's rights limited for the common good?

    Answer: The rights of any individual may be limited to prevent interfering with the rights of others.

    Comment: Americans do not have unlimited rights.

5. Continue class discussion using Note Cue Cards. Explain that using Note Cue Cards helps students know what information to look for as they read. Discuss the ways the cards are used (i.e., questions, answers, and comments). Explain that, as they read independently, students should create self-questions similar to the questions written on the Note Cue Cards. They should ask themselves questions about the contents of texts, they should try to answer those questions, and they should make comments as they read.

6. Later, students could be invited to prepare Note Cue Cards on another section or chapter in the text.

TEACHING STRATEGY 13

7.4 Record-Edit-Synthesize-Think (REST)

Record-**E**dit-**S**ynthesize-**T**hink (REST) (Morgan, Meeks, Schollaert, & Paul, 1986) is a notetaking strategy that takes into account the integration of textbook readings, lectures, and class discussions. When students use REST, they record what they have read in the text or heard in class, edit those notes by condensing them and deleting irrelevant material, synthesize notes by recording information stressed both in class and the textbook, and think about the notes while studying and learning the content information. REST can be used when teachers assign textbook reading before class discussion, or it can be used when class discussion precedes textbook reading.

Directions and Examples

1. Tell students that you will be demonstrating a study and note-taking strategy that they can use to learn content material. Use an example from your content area or the following examples.

2. Identify a concept that will be the topic of a class discussion and will be assigned to students to read. Have students read the passage independently or in groups.

3. Have students record notes from the reading on the left half of a sheet of paper in a manner similar to the following example.

Science Example

REST

Notes from text (pp. 17–19)	Notes from class
• St. Paul's Island in the Bering Sea near Alaska • 41 sq. miles • 1911—25 reindeer introduced • no predators • 1937—reindeer population increased to 2,000 • by 1950 no more reindeer	

Summary

4. After students have recorded notes from their reading, present a lecture or conduct a class discussion about the topic. Tell students to write notes from the lecture or class discussion on the right half of the paper as in the following example.

Science Example

REST

Notes from text (pp. 17–19)	Notes from class
• St. Paul's Island in the Bering Sea near Alaska • 41 sq. miles • 1911—25 reindeer introduced • no predators • 1937—reindeer population increased to 2,000 • by 1950 no more reindeer	• food capacity of island limited • interdependence involves limiting factors • no data on reindeer population in 1941–1942 • carrying capacity—maximum population of a particular species that the habitat can support

Summary

5. Tell students that lectures and class discussions may repeat information that students have read in their text and written in their notes. Some of the contents of lectures and class discussions, however, will be different. Tell students that both types of notes are important to study. After students have recorded notes from the class lectures or discussions, have them edit their notes and delete information that is redundant or irrelevant.

6. Explain that the next step in REST is to synthesize the information from textbook reading and class discussions. Tell students to read both columns of their notes carefully, looking for a synthesis of the information from both sources. Have students write the synthesis of the notes at the bottom of the sheet as in the following example. After students have synthesized their notes, they should think about their summary and study the content information.

Science Example

REST

Notes from text (pp. 17–19)	Notes from class
• St. Paul's Island in the Bering Sea near Alaska	• food capacity of island limited
• 41 sq. miles	
• 1911—25 reindeer introduced	• interdependence involves limiting factors
• no predators	• no data on reindeer population in 1941–1942
• 1937—reindeer population increased to 2,000	
• by 1950 no more reindeer	• carrying capacity—maximum population of a particular species that the habitat can support

Summary

Reindeer were introduced to St. Paul's Island, a small island in the Bering Sea, in 1911. The reindeer population increased for 26 years but then exceeded the carrying capacity of the habitat. Reindeer were extinct by 1950 due to a lack of food.

7. REST can also be used as a notetaking strategy when students first hear a lecture or a class discussion. Students using REST to take notes from a class discussion should record notes on the right half of the sheet of paper. When they edit their notes, they should add questions and notes on the left half of the paper to direct their reading. After reading the textbook passage, students should synthesize both of the sources by writing a summary at the bottom of the page. The following example shows notes taken from a lecture and class discussion on the right side of the paper and notes and questions about a future reading assignment on the left side.

REST

Topic and notes to yourself	Notes from lecture and class discussion
Check textbook for examples.	The subject of a verb is in the nominative case.
Check notes for pronouns in nominative case.	A predicate nominative is in the nominative case.
That doesn't sound right. I guess I'm used to the sentence "It's me."	An objective form of a pronoun is often used in the sentence, "It's me." Although that is now acceptable in speech, when writing you should use, "It is I."
I need to review indirect objects.	The direct object and the indirect object of a verb are in the objective case.
I'm glad I learned the prepositions last year.	The object of a preposition is in the objective case.

Summary and main ideas

Standard English has rules that are often ignored in speech. In this lesson, I learned when to use different cases of pronouns. Pronouns used as subjects and as predicate nominatives are in the nominative case. Pronouns used as objects are in the objective case.

TEACHING STRATEGY 14

7.4 Cornell Note-taking

Cornell note-taking (Pauk, 1974) is similar to the REST strategy (see Teaching Strategy 7-13) in that it is a two-column note-taking strategy. With Cornell note-taking, however, notes from textbook reading or class discussions are written on the right side of the page, and key words that organize the notes are written on the left. Cornell notetaking is an excellent strategy for topics that can be organized with main ideas and details as opposed to cause-effect and problem-solution structures.

Directions and Example

1. Tell students that you will be demonstrating a note-taking strategy that can help them study and learn content information. Use an example from your content area or use the following example to model Cornell note-taking.

2. Identify a topic that would be organized with the structure of main idea-details. Be sure students understand this type of text structure. Conduct a class discussion or have students read a passage from a textbook about the topic.

3. Distribute sheets of paper that have a vertical line drawn approximately three inches from the left side of the paper. Tell students that they should take detailed notes about the topic of the reading assignment or class discussion by writing their notes on the right side of the sheet of paper as in the following example.

Literature Example

Cornell Note-taking

Key Words	Notes from reading or class discussion
	• literature in early 20th century
	• depicts life as it is: brutal, difficult
	• expansion of West, after Civil War
	• growth of industry
	• books increased
	• Stephen Crane (1871–1900)
	• "An Episode of War" "The Open Boat" *The Red Badge of Courage*

4. Divide the class into groups of three or four students. Have students share the notes they wrote on the right half of the paper. Then ask students to generate ideas for key words to write on the left side of the paper.

5. Tell students to independently decide which key terms would be appropriate to write on the left side of their notes, as the following example illustrates.

Cornell Note-taking

Key Words	Notes from reading or class discussion
Realism in literature	• literature in early 20th century
	• depicts life as it is: brutal, difficult
Historical factors	• expansion of West, after Civil War
	• growth of industry
	• books increased
Crane's works	• Stephen Crane (1871–1900)
	• "An Episode of War" "The Open Boat" *The Red Badge of Courage*

Summarizing Content Information

Goal   To help students learn content information by summarizing

BACKGROUND

The goal of studying is to learn content information. All of the reading strategies and skills in this book can have a positive impact on learning; however, students can go through the motions of preparing a study plan, reading flexibly, and taking notes without learning the material. To learn content material, students need to be able to translate ideas into their own words and retrieve that material to accomplish a task. When students use their background knowledge to make predictions, take notes, and summarize content material, they have a better chance of really learning (Caverly, Mandeville, & Nicholson, 1995).

When students study to learn content material, they need to encode the ideas in the text. One of the best ways to encode text, or paraphrase the ideas, is to write summaries of the material. Summary writing involves identifying important information, then organizing and recasting the ideas into the gist of the larger text. Summarizing is beneficial be-

cause it gives students the opportunity to rethink the content material and process that material deeply.

You can teach students to write summaries of content material and to summarize independently as they study. Teaching students to write microthemes and to use GRASP facilitates learning the skill of summarizing. Your goal, however, is to have students automatically summarize as they read. Students reading about the particles in matter in their science text, for example, first read an introduction that reviews ideas presented earlier in the text. Then the text presents a short experiment, and finally it explains a diagram of particles in solids, liquids, and gases. When students read these two pages, they should summarize each section before reading the next section. Summarizing during reading is one of the most effective strategies students can use as they learn content information.

TECHNOLOGY TIP

Computer Software that Creates Prediction Maps

Inspiration: graphically maps words, creates flow charts, and develops outlines.

Inspiration Software Inc. www.inspiration.com

TEACHING STRATEGY 15

7.5 Read-Encode-Annotate-Ponder (REAP)

One way to take notes is to make annotations on note cards, in a learning log, or on the computer. Annotative notes are at the heart of the REAP strategy (Eanet & Manzo, 1976). When students employ REAP, they **R**ead text passages, **E**ncode the message by translating the passage into their own words, **A**nnotate or write their messages in their notes, and **P**onder the messages they have written. Annotations can take various forms. Students can write a summary annotation that condenses the main ideas of a passage into one or two concise statements. A second type of annotation is a thesis annotation that states the main point the author has tried to relate. A third type of annotation is a critical annotation. A critical annotation answers the question "So what?" Students' critical annotations first state the author's thesis and then state an opinion about that thesis. A final type of annotation is a question annotation. For this type of annotation, students write a question about a significant aspect of the passage.

TECHNOLOGY TIP

REAP Chat Corner

The Reader Exchange is an Internet chat corner that uses the REAP strategy.

cctr.umkc.edu/user/rbi/Foundation

Directions and Example

1. Tell students that you will be demonstrating a study strategy that they can use as they read textbook material and learn content information. To demonstrate the REAP strategy, use an example from your content area or the following example.

2. Identify a passage that you want students to read. Tell them to read the passage independently. After they have read the passage, tell students to identify the main points and restate them in their own words. The following is an example of a textbook passage and an encoded message based on that passage. Write the passage and message on the chalkboard or an overhead transparency.

Investing in Savings Accounts

When you invest your money in savings accounts, the money is essentially risk-free; it has the greatest safety of any investments you might choose. Even though banks might fail, as long as your investment in a bank is insured by either the Federal Deposit Insurance Corporation (FDIC) or the Federal Savings and Loan Insurance Corporation (FSLIC), your savings are risk-free. Even if the bank fails, your money is insured. Bank savings accounts are virtually risk-free investments; however, money invested in banks does not return a high rate of interest.

Encoded Message

This paragraph is about investing in savings accounts. When you invest in savings accounts your money will not accrue much interest, but it will be safe.

3. Distribute note cards to students. After students have practiced encoding, or restating, the main points of the passage, have them write their restatements on the cards. Tell students that there could be many different ways to write a summary and that one type of message is not superior to any other type.

4. Divide the class into groups of three or four students. Have students share their statements with each other. Then have them ponder, or think about, the different types of messages represented by the group.

5. Tell students that there are four main types of annotations: summary annotations, thesis annotations, critical annotations, and question annotations. Write an example of each type of annotation on the chalkboard or an overhead transparency. Use examples from your content area or the examples that follow. Have the students identify the types of annotations they have written. Then remind students to use the REAP strategy as they study content information.

REAP Annotations

Summary Annotation

Money invested in banks is insured, so it is virtually risk-free.

Thesis Annotation

Investing money in banks has low risks and low returns.

Critical Annotation

Investing money in banks has low risks and low returns. I don't think money that is not needed to pay bills should be invested in banks. The low risks don't compensate for the low returns.

Question Annotation

I thought that there was a ceiling on the amount of money that is insured by the banks. Are all savings entirely insured?

TEACHING STRATEGY 16

7.5   Summary Microtheme

In order to learn content information, students need to process that information deeply. One way to process information is to create a short summary of a passage in a textbook or a section of notes. A summary microtheme (Brozo & Simpson, 1995) is a type of summary that can be used in content area classes to help students process and learn material. A microtheme can be used in a number of ways. Teachers can assign microthemes to get a general picture about how well students understand main concepts; teachers can use microthemes to hold students accountable for learning a concept; and students can use microthemes to process information as they study.

Directions and Examples

1. Explain to students that a microtheme is a way for them to summarize a passage or concept in order to learn the material.

2. Tell students that you will be modeling an example of a microtheme. To demonstrate how to write a microtheme, use an example from your content area or use the examples that follow.

3. Identify a concept that you want students to understand. Locate a passage of text that explains the concept. Distribute copies of the passage to students. The following example is a passage about the chemical reaction that takes place when hair is curled or straightened.

The curliness of your hair depends on how disulfide bonds are joined between parallel protein chains. When a person gets a permanent, curls are created or removed in three steps. Here's the chemical recipe. First, break the disulfide links between protein chains. Next, use a form (curlers, rollers, etc.) to curl or uncurl the hair. Third, rejoin the disulfide links between protein chains in their new orientation.

4. Distribute note cards to each student. Ask students to read the passage and write a microtheme, or a short summary about the passage. After students have written a microtheme, write your own summary on the chalkboard or an overhead transparency. Explain how you arrived at your summaries by thinking aloud. Then have students compare their summary to yours. Many different summaries should be considered correct. An example of a summary microtheme about the preceding passage follows.

   A chemical reaction of breaking and reforming disulfide bonds is necessary to permanently change the curliness of hair.

5. Tell students that as they study they should stop occasionally and write a summary microtheme about the text. Tell students that by processing material they will remember it better.

6. An example of a summary microtheme based on a literature example follows.

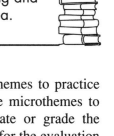

Literature Example

Summary Microtheme

Daedalus was exiled from Athens, so he sailed to Crete where he was befriended by King Minos. King Minos would not allow Daedalus to leave Crete, so Daedalus married and had a son, Icarus. Since Daedalus was homesick for Athens, he built wings for himself and Icarus. As they flew toward Athens, Icarus ignored his father's warning and soared too close to the sun. The heat melted his wings, and Icarus fell into the sea.

7. Microthemes can be used in a number of ways. Students can use microthemes to practice identifying and summarizing information they have learned. You can use microthemes to assist students in processing information, or you may decide to evaluate or grade the microthemes that students write. A rubric is an appropriate assessment tool for the evaluation of summary microthemes. A six-point rubric that you can use or adapt to score summary microthemes follows.

Summary Microtheme Evaluation Rubric

6   A summary that is scored a "6" meets all of the criteria for accuracy, comprehensiveness, and clear sentence structure. The main points in the text should appear correctly in the summary with all main points developed. The summary should be as comprehensive as possible and should read smoothly from beginning to end with appropriate transitions between ideas. The sentence structure should be clear and varied, without vagueness or ambiguity, and without more than one grammatical error.

5   A summary that is scored a "5" should be accurate and comprehensive, but it may lack perfect sentence structure. The summary may be clearly written but be somewhat unbalanced or less thorough than a "6" paper. It may show that the student has a minor misunderstanding of the material. A "5" summary should have no more than two grammatical errors.

4   A summary that is scored a "4" is one that is good but not excellent. It reveals a generally accurate reading of the passage with a clear sense of the main points of the material, but it will be noticeably weaker than a summary that is scored a "5" or a "6." The paper may be weak in its content, organization, or conventions but not all three.

3   A summary that is scored a "3" is strong in at least one area of competence, and it portrays a fairly clear and accurate view of the material being summarized. A "3" paper is either unbalanced or lacks the clarity and precision of a top-ranked summary. The sentence structure of a "3" paper frequently prevents the inclusion of sufficient ideas for good comprehensiveness.

2   A summary that is scored a "2" is weak in all areas of competence, either because it is so poorly written that the reader cannot understand the content or because the content is inaccurate or disorganized.

1   A summary that is scored a "1" fails to meet any of the areas of competence.

7.5

Guided Reading And Summarizing Procedure (GRASP)

Summarizing text passages is a complex skill that takes guidance and practice. All too often, students are asked to summarize complex text without really understanding what a summary is or how to compress many ideas into a brief synopsis. Students can practice summarizing passages by using microthemes (see Teaching Strategy 7-6), or you can teach students how to summarize using the **G**uided **R**eading **A**nd **S**ummarizing **P**rocedure (GRASP) (Hayes, 1989). The goal of teaching GRASP is to enable students to summarize independently when they try to understand texts and when they study to learn text material.

Directions and Example

1. Provide students with a short passage of text that they can read easily. Explain that they will be writing a summary of the passage. You can use an example from your content area or the following example about Texas independence.

   > In the 1820s, Americans began migrating into Mexican territory. Stephen Austin received permission from the Mexican government to found a colony of about 300 settlers in what is now east Texas. Austin led the first group of American settlers into the territory in 1822. By 1824, over 2,000 settlers lived in the area.

   > Soon other agents arranged contracts for Americans to settle in Texas. By 1830 over 7,000 Americans lived in the area, more than twice the number of Mexicans in the territory. Worried that it was losing Texas through immigration, Mexico passed a law in 1830 prohibiting settling there.

   > The Americans continued to move into the territory. As their numbers increased, the Americans demanded more political freedom. They declared independence for the Republic of Texas in 1836. Under the leadership of William Travis, the Americans began to fight for freedom. At the battle of the Alamo, the Mexicans routed the Americans. At a later battle, however, Sam Houston led the Americans to victory. Texans elected Sam Houston as their first president late in 1836.

2. Ask students to read the passage independently with the purpose of remembering all that they can. After all students have finished reading, ask them to tell you what they remembered. List the items they volunteer on the chalkboard or an overhead transparency. The following examples are taken from the preceding passage.

Students' first recollections

Americans moved into Mexican territory.
Austin was the leader of the settlers.
Mexico began to discourage settlers.
Americans continued to move into the area.
Americans declared independence.
Mexico won at the Alamo.
The Americans won the next fight.

3. Have students reread the passage with the purpose of making additions and deletions to the list. Revise the list as needed.

Students' first recollections	Additions/corrections
Americans moved into Mexican territory.	During the 1820s, Americans moved into Mexican territory.
Austin was the leader of the settlers.	There were over 2,000 settlers by 1824.
Mexico began to discourage settlers.	Mexico passed a law prohibiting more settlers.
Americans continued to move into the area.	Americans continued to move into the area.
Americans declared independence.	In 1836 Americans declared independence.
Mexico won at the Alamo.	Mexico won at the Alamo.
The Americans won the next fight.	Under the leadership of Sam Houston, the Americans beat the Mexicans.

4. Ask students to organize the remembered information. Suggest categories for the list they generated. List the categories and ask students to divide the items on the list into categories. The following example is based on the preceding passage.

Category: Settling Mexican Territory

During the 1820s, Americans moved into Mexican territory.
There were over 2,000 settlers by 1824.
Mexico passed a law prohibiting more settlers.
Americans continued to move into the area.

Category: War for Independence

In 1836 Americans declared independence.
Mexico won at the Alamo.
Under the leadership of Sam Houston, the Americans beat the Mexicans.
In 1836 Texas elected its first president, Sam Houston.

5. Using the outline generated by categorizing the information, write a summary of the material. You might suggest that students begin with a main idea statement for the first main heading with the details as subheadings. Show students an example of a summary paragraph as in the following example.

Summary

During the 1820s Americans began settling Mexican territory, which is now east Texas. By 1824 there were over 2,000 settlers. Americans kept moving into the territory. Then Mexico passed a law prohibiting more settlers. Americans, however, continued to move into the area. By the 1830s the Americans began to want independence from Mexican authority. In 1836 the Americans declared independence. Mexico and the Americans went to war. Mexico won the famous battle of the Alamo, but the Americans won the war.

Notes and Favorite Strategies

Chapter 8

PREPARING FOR ASSESSMENTS

OVERVIEW

We can all remember taking tests. For some of us, it's a distant memory—perhaps the comprehensive examination that was part of our master's program. For others, test taking happens when we get a notice from the Secretary of State that tells us a written test will be required to renew our driver's license. Still others think about the anxiety that frequently accompanies the thought of taking the *Graduate Record Examination, Miller Analogies Test*, or some other test as part of the application process for graduate study.

Test taking is an ongoing occurrence for students because teachers use tests to assess students' progress. Think about the types of tests you give to students. Perhaps you use mostly true-false, multiple-choice, and essay tests. A colleague may use

mostly matching and fill-in-the-blank tests. By the time students leave high school, they have probably also taken a driver's license test and several standardized tests.

Students take many tests during their school experience. Because students take so many tests, they can profit from the acquisition of general and specific test-preparation strategies and test-wiseness training. Such strategies and training can be useful for the tests you give to students as well as for the standardized tests students are required to take. Preparing for tests can lead to enhanced performance and higher scores.

In this chapter you will find a number of strategies that are helpful to students as they prepare for tests. First, you can help students learn or review some general test-preparation strategies by showing students how to find out about tests they will be asked to take. A six-day test-preparation plan is presented. Second, a number of tips and strategies for taking the four major types of objective tests (true-false, multiple-choice, fill-in-the-blank, and completion) are presented. Helping *all* students learn and use these strategies should increase test validity. Third, we focus on essay tests and begin with a general plan to assist students in taking them. Students will learn to estimate how much they should write and how to identify the topic and task when answering essay questions. Fourth, a section is devoted to helping students understand scores from your tests as well as from standardized tests. You are encouraged to use examples of scores from tests you are using as you facilitate students' understanding.

Finally, we have included some tips for using portfolios in your classroom since you may wish to consider exploring alternatives to content area tests and standardized tests. Standardized tests, in particular, provide limited information about the progress of individual students (Wilkinson & Silliman, 1997). One authentic alternative approach to regular testing is the use of portfolios. Portfolios serve as an authentic assessment device and provide a portrait of students' work, rather than just a snapshot. This chapter will provide several tips for using portfolios effectively in your classroom.

The strategies and ideas presented in this chapter should help students develop an overall study plan and learn valuable test-taking tips. You may also choose to assist your students in developing portfolios to showcase their work in your content area. Through your careful, reflective instruction, students will be better able to demonstrate their understanding of the content taught.

Planning for Tests

Section

8.1

Goal To help students develop and use a plan for general test preparation

BACKGROUND

Effective strategies for reading, learning, and studying provide the basis for good performance on tests. Previous chapters in this book have provided useful information and numerous strategies. In this section, we offer ideas to help students develop a plan for test preparation. As with most plans, there will probably need to be adaptations to fit your modes of assessment. Ideally, the information in this section would be presented early in your course so students can use the strategies throughout the semester or year.

TEACHING STRATEGY 1

8.1 Finding Out About the Test

Preparing for a test is easier when numerous specifications are available to students. In this strategy, students will learn more about some of these specifications and how to ask questions to acquire helpful information about a test.

1. Ask students to write down any questions they may have about the upcoming test.

2. Have students share their questions with partners or in small groups. Then engage in whole class sharing where the questions are written on the chalkboard or on an overhead transparency. Accept all ideas, even those that are offered for a comic effect (e.g., What are the answers?).

3. Give students time to assign the various questions to logical categories. The questions might be categorized into areas such as general information (e.g., day, time, what can be used), types of test items, point values, general areas covered, and specific tips. Prioritize the questions within each category through discussion and sharing. Categories and questions will vary; nevertheless, you may want to ensure that the following questions are included.

- When is the test (exact day)?
- How much time do we have for the test?
- What must we have for the test (pencil, calculator, etc.)?
- What can we use while taking the test (notes, calculator)?
- What kind of test is it (essay, true-false, matching, etc.)?
- Are different types of items included on the test?
- If there are different types of items, how many of each type are there?
- What are the point values of the various items?
- Will a choice of questions be offered?
- What specific chapters are covered on the test?
- What information is especially important to know from our reading and/or notes that might be on the test?
- What important vocabulary words or concepts should we know?
- What study strategies might be especially useful?
- Will you give us some sample items like those on the test?
- What study tips do you have so we can do well on the test?

4. Encourage students to take responsibility and ask you questions from the list a week or so before a test is given. Consistent use of this list should help students begin to internalize the types of questions that will give them useful information for tests.

5. Consider compiling and distributing tips from the foregoing discussion that are especially useful to your students. Students can also be invited to use these or similar tips in their other classes where tests are used. A reproducible of "Finding Out About the Test" follows.

Name _____ Date _____

Finding Out About the Test

1. When is the test (exact day)? _____

2. How much time do we have for the test? _____

3. What must we have for the test (pencil, calculator, etc.)? _____

_____

4. What can we use while taking the test (notes, calculator)? _____

_____

5. What kind of test is it (essay, true-false, matching, etc.)? _____

6. Are different types of items included on the test? _____

7. If there are different types of items, how many of each type are there? _____

_____

8. What are the point values of the various items? _____

9. Will a choice of questions be offered? _____

10. What specific chapters are covered on the test? _____

_____

11. What information is especially important to know from our reading and/or notes that might be on the test? _____

_____

_____

_____

_____

12. What important vocabulary words or concepts should we know?

_____

_____

_____

_____

_____

_____

_____

13. What study strategies might be especially useful?_____

_____

_____

_____

14. Will you give us some sample items like those on the test?_____

15. What study tips do you have so we can do well on the test?

_____

_____

_____

_____

_____

_____

8.1   A Test-Preparation Plan

Students who perform well on tests consciously or unconsciously have developed a plan for study and test preparation. Other students may be uncertain or confused about what they can do to enhance their chances of doing well on a test. Although individual differences exist among students' test-preparation strategies or the lack of them, the following general plan is offered as a foundation upon which to build. The plan begins at least six days before the test is given.

Countdown: 6 Days Before the Test

1. Remind students that many of the questions in "Finding Out About the Test" (see Teaching Strategy 8-1) are useful for developing a test-preparation plan.

2. Discuss and review the important areas in which to gather information.

    - areas that will be included on the test
    - the type of test items and point values
    - general and specific tips for the test

3. Stress that students need to begin studying for the test at least six days in advance. Help students develop a study schedule with specific times for studying set aside. Tell students that the types of items on the test will influence their test preparation and, if necessary, help students make the connection between studying and types of test questions. (See Sections 8.2 and 8.3 for specific strategies for taking objective and essay tests. Teach these strategies as appropriate.)

Read, Review, Study, and Plan: 5, 4, 3, and 2 Days Before the Test

1. Have students note the assigned readings that will be included on the test. Any reading not already completed should be done.

2. Tell students that they can begin reviewing immediately. Have students share ideas about what to review. Examples follow.

    - text
    - text notes
    - class notes
    - important vocabulary

Encourage students to raise questions in class so you can explain information that is unclear or unknown.

3. Help students refine their plans for study and review. (See Chapter 7 for a number of ideas related to studying.) Stress the need for regular study periods distributed over time. Tell students to begin learning and putting into memory main ideas, important concepts, and supporting details and to review this information several times a day over a period of several days.

4. Encourage students to review their texts and class notes. One way to review is to rewrite the information in briefer form. To be most effective, review should be both thoughtful and intentional. You should model this process for students.

5. Tell students to devote time to predicting questions that might be on the test and have students practice answering these questions. At first, students can refer to their texts and/or notes, but later the answers should be written from memory. You may want to model the process of predicting questions by writing them on the chalkboard or on an overhead transparency.

> A science teacher, for example, might say the following: "We have been studying different types of root systems. I want to predict possible questions that might be asked about root systems. I am able to ask four different types of questions about root systems. For the test, it may be a good idea to learn the two types of root systems, be able to recall and describe them, and to know at least one example of each." Then invite students to react to the questions and share additional questions.

> True-false: There are two basic types of root systems. (T)

> Completion: The two basic types of root systems are _____ and _____. (fibrous, taproot)

> Matching: Match the two root systems with the correct characteristics or examples.

> | | | |
> |---|---|---|
> | 1. fibrous | __2__ | carrot |
> | | __1__ | many branching roots |
> | 2. taproot | __1__ | corn |
> | | __2__ | dandelions |
> | | __2__ | go deep into the soil |

> Essay: Describe the two basic root systems and give an example of each.

6. Remind students that the night before the test is a time for final preparations. In addition to study and review, a good night's sleep is helpful, and such sleep is likely to occur if an intentional study plan has been initiated and executed. Students should also be reminded to gather materials needed for the test (e.g., pencils, pens, calculator, paper) before going to bed.

The Day of the Test

1. Before leaving for school, students should eat a breakfast that will give them the energy they need. They should also be sure they have the necessary supplies for the test.

2. If time exists before the test, students should review their course materials and notes.

3. When the test is given, students may find the following suggestions useful.

    ● Take two or three deep breaths to help you relax.
    ● Survey the entire test to get a general idea of what you will need to do.
    ● Read the directions carefully and underline any key words.
    ● Make sure you answer the questions asked.
    ● Answer the easy questions first.
    ● Look over your test when you have finished; double-check your answers to be sure you did not omit any questions.

8.1 ► *TEACHING STRATEGY 3*
Questioning the Answers

Rarely are students given the opportunity to improve their performance on norm-referenced tests or to see which of their answers were correct and which were incorrect. Taylor and Walton (2002) have developed a strategy called Questioning the Answers that is designed to improve students' approaches to taking standardized tests.

1. Begin by administering a practice test to your students that is difficult enough for them to make some mistakes but not so difficult as to frustrate them. Tell students that you'll work together the next day in order to determine the best answers for each of the questions.

2. Do not correct the tests for correct responses, but rather tally the students' responses in the following way. For each question, note how many students chose each possible response. A question and tally sheet might look like the following example.

    To which country are the majority of Canada's exports sent?

a.	Ireland	3 students
b.	United States	5 students
c.	Mexico	14 students
d.	England	9 students

    Your purpose in tallying the responses is not to determine how many students selected the correct response, but rather to examine trends and patterns that exist within your students' choices.

3. Select three or four of the questions for which you have prepared tallies. Write each question on an overhead transparency followed by the distribution of responses as in the example above.

4. The next day tell students that you are going to discuss several of the questions. Put one of the transparencies on the overhead projector with the tallies covered. Invite a student to read the question out loud.

5. Reveal the tally for the first possible answer showing that three students selected "Ireland" as the correct response. Invite students to discuss why someone might choose this response to the question. Emphasize that you are not asking if it's the correct response, but that you want to know what they think would lead a student to choose "Ireland" as the correct answer.

6. Proceed in this manner until each of the answers has been revealed with the tally of responses. Discuss the words used in each question and help students figure out clues that might lead them to the correct response. Words such as *never, always*, and *most likely* should be examined. With your guidance, students will discover the clues that will help them improve their test-taking strategies.

8.1 Fake Pop Quiz (FPQ)

TEACHING STRATEGY 4

Readence, Bean, and Baldwin (2001) designed the Fake Pop Quiz (FPQ) strategy to prepare students for a testing experience through a simulated pop quiz. The purpose of the FPQ is to stimulate interest and review material rather than to test knowledge. According to the authors, "Tests are really a lot of fun once the anxiety over being externally evaluated has been neutralized" (p. 285). FPQs can be interjected into daily lessons and can become a routine occurrence, thus helping students overcome test anxiety.

1. Develop a quiz based on current textbook material. For ease in grading, include 10 questions on the quiz with a value of 10 points per question. Place the quiz questions on the chalkboard or on an overhead transparency or prepare individual handouts.

2. Tell students that they are going to take a Fake Pop Quiz as a way to review for an upcoming unit test. Assure students that their scores on the quiz will not impact their grades, but will give them a good idea about their level of knowledge of the subject matter. You might choose to say something like the following.

> Today we are going to have a Fake Pop Quiz over the events of the Civil War. The scores you receive on the quiz will not impact your grades but will give you an idea about how well you understand the information in our textbook. The FPQ will serve as a warm-up for the real test, which will be given in class on Friday.

3. After students have completed the quiz, invite them to score their own papers by locating the correct answers in their textbooks. Tell them to give themselves 10 points for each correct response and to multiply that number by the number of correct responses.

4. When students have completed grading their FPQs, conduct a class discussion using the questions on the quiz as the basis for further review of the material.

Taking Objective Tests

Goal To help students learn strategies for taking objective tests

BACKGROUND

This section considers true-false, multiple-choice, matching, and fill-in-the-blank or completion tests. For each type of objective test, a series of tips and some ways to put the tips into practice are provided.

Ritter and Idol-Maestas (1986) have suggested the use of SCORER, a general memory device to help students take tests.

S = Schedule your time while taking the test.
C = Use clue words to help answer questions.
O = Omit difficult questions at first.
R = Read questions carefully.
E = Estimate your time.
R = Review your responses.

Share and discuss SCORER with your students. Budgeting time, reading carefully, noting key words, and reviewing thoughtfully are general test-taking strategies that can be developed within the context of your content area. Help students learn strategies for the specific types of objective tests you use. Whenever possible, the following ideas should be integrated into your content area to increase meaning and relevance. Also, remind students that, even though there are some strategies for successfully completing objective tests, learning the content is key.

TECHNOLOGY TIP

Creating Tests with Software Programs

There are a number of software programs that you can use to create tests. The programs have format flexibility and may help you save significant amounts of time.

Quiz Writer Plus: a test generator that also has databases of questions in popular subject areas. Midwest Agribusiness Services, Inc. (800-523-3475).

Test Designer Supreme: used by teachers and students to create and modify tests and assignments. Super School Software (800-248-7099).

Test Quest: supports multiple-choice, true-false, completion, matching, and essay test formats. Snowflake Software (914-876-3328).

Test Quick: helps create tests in multiple-choice, true-false, question-response, and fill-in-the-blank formats. Jackson Software (800-850-1777).

TEACHING STRATEGY 5

8.2 True-False Tests

True-false tests are used in many content area classrooms. To help ensure that you are actually assessing content knowledge, you can share tips for taking true-false tests. The usefulness of the various tips to taking true-false tests will be made more powerful by using examples from your content area.

1.   Begin by sharing and discussing the following tips for taking true-false tests.

- Read each statement carefully. Statements that contain *never, always, all, more, impossible,* or *nothing* are usually false. Words such as *usually, generally, sometimes,* and *seldom* indicate that the statement is probably true. As a general guideline, help students understand that absolute statements (e.g., *all, none*) are usually false, while qualified statements (e.g., *usually, seldom*) are usually true.
- Assume that long statements are more likely to be true than short statements.
- Watch for negatives such as "not" or the prefix "in," because a negative can completely change the meaning of a statement.
- Simplify a statement that contains a double negative by eliminating both negatives.
- Look for statements that are partially true. If a statement is not completely true, the statement is probably false. All parts of a statement should be correct before it is marked as true.
- Assume that a statement is true unless it can be proved false.

- Never leave a true-false statement unanswered unless there is a penalty for guessing. Make a calculated guess if the answer is unknown, because there is a 50% chance of getting the answer correct.
- Assume that the statements are straightforward; do not read too much into them.
- Write T and F neatly or be sure you mark the correct space on the answer sheet.

2. Model (think aloud) how you would put these tips into practice with several questions based on materials you have been using for instruction. The following items are based on the reading passage "Frozen in Time." The thought process is what you and students can model with specific items from your content area as in the following example.

Item 1. Pliny wrote about the destruction of Pompeii.

Thought process for answer: I remember someone wrote about Pompeii being destroyed, but I can't remember the name. I remember he was a young boy and his writing wasn't read for many years. Pliny could be his name, but I really don't know. I won't lose anything by trying, but if I leave it blank, I'll get it wrong for sure. I know there is no penalty for guessing so I'll mark this answer true.

Item 2. Volcanoes always erupt so quickly that people in their paths can't escape.

Thought process for answer: I think that's what happened to Pompeii, but I'm not sure it always is that way with volcanoes. I think I heard Mt. St. Helens in Washington erupted, and the people were warned in time to get off of the mountain. I don't think volcanoes always erupt that quickly, and I know that I should be cautious about answering true for a question that has the word always. I think the answer is false.

Item 3. Pompeii was destroyed by a hurricane 2,000 years ago.

Thought process for answer: I know Pompeii was destroyed, and I remember that it was about 2,000 years ago. The reason I remember the date is because my house address is 2000. We saw pictures of Pompeii after it was discovered again, and I remember a mountain in the background. Pompeii was also by the sea, but I'm sure it wasn't destroyed by a hurricane. That means the answer is false because the part about the hurricane is false.

Item 4. Pompeii was discovered when some workmen were digging a tunnel and found an ancient wall.

Thought process for answer: This question has a great deal of specific information and is longer than most of the questions. I remember that Pompeii was discovered by some local people, and I think the answer is true.

Item 5. The people of Pompeii were frozen in time when they were covered by the volcanic eruption of Mt. Vesuvius.

Thought process for answer: There's part of the question that I know for sure, and that is that Pompeii was covered by the volcanic eruption of Mt. Vesuvius. I'm not sure, however, what "frozen in time" means. That might mean something about a glacier or an ice flow, but I don't see how that could have happened. Maybe it means that all of their clocks stopped. That doesn't make sense. They didn't have clocks back then. Perhaps "frozen in time" doesn't mean anything special, just that people were stopped at what they were doing. That would be the simplest answer, and I know we're not supposed to read a lot into the test question. I think I'll just answer true.

▶ Adapted from Johns, J.L., & Lenski, S.D. (2001). *Improving reading: Strategies and resources* (3rd ed.). Dubuque, IA: Kendall/Hunt.

3. Assign groups of students to prepare true-false items on different sections of text materials or information shared in class. Information from laboratory experiences may also be used. Then mix the groups so the statements can be shared, answered, discussed, and verified. Refer, when appropriate, to the tips for answering true-false statements. You may also wish to duplicate and share a list of tips with students so they can use them in developing their questions and refer to them later when studying for a test.

8.2 Multiple-Choice Tests

TEACHING STRATEGY 6

1. Tell students that multiple choice tests are made up of a stem and choices. Stress that students need to read the stem *before* reading the choices and should try to predict a correct response. If necessary, clarify the meaning of the term *stem*. Also, tell students to read all the choices carefully before making a final choice. Sometimes a response may be partly correct, but it is not the best choice. Make a sample question based on the material being taught and model the process by "thinking aloud" as exemplified in the section on the true-false tests. The following tips are designed to be used when students do not know the correct answer.

2. Remind students to note any negatives because they can choose the wrong answer by skipping an important word in the question. An example of a negative follows.

   Which of the following was not a cause of World War I?

   In this example, students could eliminate causes and then select the choice that is not a cause.

3. Explain to students that they should also look for clues in the tests. Tell them that if a choice is much longer and more detailed than the others, it is usually the correct answer. If a word in a choice also appears in the statement, it is probably the correct choice. Stress that these clues are tips, and they should be applied with careful thought.

4. Encourage students to try to eliminate incorrect choices. Stress that if they eliminate an unreasonable answer, they have a greater chance of choosing a correct answer. You might model this type of thinking in a manner similar to the following example.

   The speed of sound through air is

   A. 3,700 feet per second.
   B. 1,085 feet per second.
   C. 2 feet per second.
   D. 186 miles per second.

Thought process for answer: My chance of selecting the correct response increases if I can eliminate one or more possible answers. If there are four choices, my chance of selecting correctly by guessing is 25%. If I can eliminate two of the choices, my chance of selecting correctly is 50%. I'm really not sure about the speed of sound. Let me see. I know it's really fast. Looking at the answers, I can tell that one answer is definitely false. There's no way C could be correct because I know sound travels more than two feet per second. I'm ruling out C, and I'm not thinking about it again.

5. Explain that when two choices are similar, they are both probably incorrect. Again, modeling the thinking behind this tip might be helpful.

   The universal donor is

   A. O.
   B. H_2O.
   C. AB.
   D. water.

   Thought process for answer: I think I know which type of blood is the universal donor, but I'm not sure. The answers that have two types of blood, are A and C. The other two answers are the same. H_2O (answer B) is the same thing as water (answer D). I can choose only one correct answer, and neither B nor D could be correct because they both say the same thing and water is not a blood type.

6. Explain that when two of the choices are opposites, one of them is always wrong and the other is usually correct. Refer to A and B in the following example.

   A molecule is

   A. the largest part of something.
   B. the smallest part of something.
   C. always solid.
   D. invisible.

7. Remind students that the answer must be grammatically correct. If students find answer choices that do not fit grammatically with the question, they are probably incorrect. An example follows.

   The largest land animal is an

   A. whale.
   B. elephant.
   C. horse.
   D. hippopotamus.

8. Tell students that a viable choice that includes one or more of the others is likely to be correct. Use an example from material being taught and share your thought processes with students.

9. Remind students that there may be clues in the stems of other items that could be helpful in resolving a question with which they are experiencing difficulty. Then ask students to explain how these clues might be discerned. It is possible that students could remember and share a specific example from a past test.

10. Tell students to skip a difficult question and go to the next question. They should make a mark beside the skipped question so they can return to it later. This strategy has four advantages: 1) it does not waste time; 2) the correct answer may come to students while they are thinking of something else; 3) helpful clues may occur in the stems of other questions; and 4) students will not become overly frustrated about any single item.

11. Additional clues that may be useful to students are offered by Antes (1989, p. 20).

   - If the word *none* or *all* is used in a response, it is usually incorrect.
   - If *some* or *often* is used in a response, it is likely to be correct.
   - If *all of the above* is a response, determine whether at least two of the responses seem appropriate before selecting all of the above.
   - If one response is more precise or technical, it is more likely to be correct than a general response. If you are unsure about a response and the correct response for many items on the test tends to be longer, select the longer response.

12. Assign groups of students to prepare multiple-choice questions on different sections of material being used in class. The questions can be written on the chalkboard or overhead transparencies and discussed with the entire class. Have students share the tips they use to select their answers. To enhance learning opportunities, individual students can also be invited to share their thought processes by thinking aloud.

13. Duplicate and share the following tips for taking multiple-choice tests so they can be referred to by students when studying for tests.

20 Tips for Taking Multiple-Choice Tests

1. Read the stem *before* reading the choices and try to predict the answer.

2. Read all the choices carefully before making a final choice.

3. A response that is only partly correct is *probably* not the best choice.

4. Note any negatives (e.g., no, not) and be sure your choice fits the stem.

5. If a choice is much longer and more detailed than the others, it *may* be the correct answer.

6. If a word in a choice also appears in the statement, it *may* be the correct answer.

7. Improve your chances by eliminating one or more unreasonable choices.

8. When two of the choices are similar, they are both *probably* incorrect.

9. When two of the choices are opposites, one of them is always wrong, and the other choice is *usually* correct.

10. If answer choices do not fit grammatically with the question stem, they are *probably* incorrect.

11. A choice that includes one or more of the other choices is *likely* to be correct.

12. If *none* or *all* is used in a choice, it is *usually* incorrect.

13. If *some* or *often* is used in a choice, it is *likely* to be correct.

14. If *all of the above* is a choice, determine whether at least two of the other choices seem appropriate before selecting *all of the above*.

15. If one choice is more precise or technical, it is more likely to be correct than a more general choice.

16. If you are unsure about a response and the correct choice for many items on the test tends to be longer, select the longer choice.

17. For a difficult question, put a mark beside it and go to the next question. Come back to the question at the end of the test or at any time when other questions give you a helpful clue to the answer to the difficult question.

18. Be alert to clues in the stems of other questions that may be helpful with a difficult question.

19. Mark your answers or your answer sheet carefully.

20. Make a calculated guess if you are not sure of the right answer, unless there is a penalty for guessing.

From Susan Davis Lenski, Mary Ann Wham, and Jerry L. Johns, *Reading & Learning Strategies: Middle Grades through High School,* 2nd Edition. Copyright © 2003 by Kendall/Hunt Publishing Company (1-800-247-3458, ext. 4 or 5). May be reproduced for noncommercial educational purposes.

8.2   Matching Tests

1. Explain to students that in a matching test items from one column are matched with those in another. If needed, provide a simple matching test related to your classroom, such as the following one.

_____ on the wall	A.	chart
_____ near the chalkboard	B.	clock
_____ in the front of the room	C.	books
_____ on the shelf	D.	desk

    Spend a few minutes and demonstrate or model how you would take the test, using the process of elimination.

2. Share and discuss the following tips for taking matching tests.

    - Carefully read all of the items in both columns before answering.
    - Begin by making the easiest matches.
    - Cross out items in both columns as they are used.
    - Make all the correct matches possible before guessing at any of the other matches.
    - Make the best guesses possible for the remaining items.

3. Provide an example of a matching test from your content area and model the reasoning used to select the various answers. Try to incorporate the tips listed above. A sample is shown below (Johns & Lenski, 2001).

__C__ an animal with a backbone	A.	butterfly
__D__ an amphibian	B.	starfish
__B__ a spiny-skinned animal	C.	snake
__A__ an animal without a backbone	D.	alligator

4. Share the rationale for the above choices by saying something like the following. After reading all of the items, it seems that a spiny-skinned animal is the starfish. An amphibian can live in and out of the water. Only an alligator can do that; I know that a butterfly and starfish can't. I also know a snake and an alligator have backbones, but if I use alligator as an amphibian, that would leave snake as the animal with a backbone. I think the butterfly is the animal without a backbone. Even though I don't know if the starfish has a backbone, it is the only spiny-skinned animal.

5. Have students develop matching tests from materials used in your content area. Students can share their tests with others. Use discussion and invite students to think aloud to enhance their ability to perform well on matching tests.

TEACHING STRATEGY 8

8.2 ➤ Completion or Fill-in-the-Blank Tests

1. Begin by sharing the tips for completion tests listed below.

   - Read the entire sentence or paragraph containing the blank line.
   - Use the length of the blank line as a clue unless all of the blank lines are similar in length.
   - Decide on the word or phrase that best fits.
   - The word or phrase must fit the blank grammatically.
   - Reread the entire sentence including your word to determine if it fits and sounds correct.
   - When a blank begins the sentence, be sure to capitalize the first word.

   Invite students to share additional ideas from their experiences.

2. Remind students that fill-in-the-blank tests are different from other types of objective tests because information for the answer must be recalled from memory. Because many true-false and multiple-choice items tap recognition, guessing is usually much easier with such items.

3. Encourage students to learn key vocabulary and important details that may be possible test items. One way to help such acquisition is to provide sentences with blanks that cover specific and key parts of a chapter. For example, the following items are based on a chapter dealing with plant support and transport.

   - Herbaceous stems are usually _____ and _____ in color.
   - Bundles of xylem and phloem in herbaceous stems are arranged _____.
   - Some examples of herbaceous stems are _____, _____, and _____.
   - The tissue that stores food in plants is known as _____.

4. Take time to discuss answers for the blanks and stress the importance of knowing the information so it can be recalled on a test. Help students realize that "knowing the information" means that it is memorized.

5. Share some memorization techniques for recalling information that may be used for objective and essay tests. Mnemonic devices represent memory strategies that can help students retain and recall bits of information. Whenever possible, have students make a personal connection to the material. Examples of mnemonic devices that can be taught to students follow.

   - *Rhyme*
     Create a rhyme or a song that includes the points you have to learn.

     Thirty days hath September . . .

- *Acronyms*
  Form words by using the first letter from each of the words to be recalled.

  HOMES (Names of the Great Lakes: Huron, Ontario, Michigan, Erie, Superior).

- *Pegwood*
  Memorize a short rhyme and then create the images that link the nouns in the rhyme with the items to be remembered.

- *Method of Loci*
  Select a spatial layout, such as your home. Mentally place the items to be recalled in each room.

- *Clustering*
  Memorize the material in categories and learn them as a pattern.

- *Silly Sentences*
  Make up a silly sentence from the first letter of each word to be remembered. Even After Dinner, Giraffes Bend Easily (guitar strings E, A, D, G, B, E).

- *Numbering*
  When you are memorizing a group of words, remember how many items there are to avoid missing any when you need to recall them.

6. Provide opportunities for students to develop fill-in-the-blank items based on their readings and/or class notes. These items can be exchanged, answered, and discussed.

Taking Essay Tests

Section

8.3

Goal > To help students learn strategies for taking essay tests

BACKGROUND

Broadly defined, essay items may be answered in a sentence, a paragraph, or a composition. In this section, the focus is on written responses, a paragraph or longer, that are completed in class.

Essay questions may be one of the best ways to assess how well students can evaluate, analyze, and synthesize course content. In addition to these higher-order thinking skills, essays also test memory. Galica (1991, p. 8) has offered seven keys to help students prepare for and write good essay examinations. We have adapted them as follows.

1. Be prepared: know your material.
2. Try to anticipate the questions and practice answering them.
3. Tell the answer to each question; show that you know the material (support or explain your answer); then end.

4. Think of your response more as an intelligent conversation; avoid the perfect draft syndrome.
5. Plan your response to fit the allocated amount of time.
6. Use simple, clear, and direct writing.
7. Integrate good information (e.g., facts, examples) with the big picture (e.g., intelligent generalizations, conclusions).

To help students achieve in these seven areas, you can first teach a broad plan to assist students with essay tests. Then teach students how to use PORPE (Simpson, 1986) to prepare for essay tests. Next, teach students how to react to the test itself. Finally, teach students strategies for organizing and writing the essay.

TEACHING STRATEGY 9

8.3 Taking Essay Tests: An Action Plan

When students receive an essay test, they need an overall plan. Although the action plan we present takes several pages to describe, it only requires a few minutes of students' time in an actual test situation. Here are the five parts of the action plan (Galica, 1991).

1. Look over the test.
2. Estimate length of responses.
3. Read the questions.
4. Choose your question (if there is a choice).
5. Decide on the order for answering.

You may wish to develop a chart that contains the five steps of the action plan. It can be used for teaching each of the five steps, and it can be posted in the classroom as a reference for students when they take essay tests.

We recommend that you model the steps below using one of your tests, highlighting specific, helpful elements. Modeling the entire process should be especially helpful to students. Do your best to use examples from previous tests or guide students in areas that are particularly useful for your tests. Spending ample time to teach students to use the steps will enhance their performance on your essay tests.

Look over the test

1. Tell students that their first task is to look over the test quickly and determine how many questions need to be answered. They should also read the directions. If there are several sections, students should read the directions for each one.

2. You might model using the following directions. Below are four essay questions. Choose two of the questions and answer them. Each question is worth 50 points. You have the entire period for the test.

3. Think aloud by saying something like the following paragraph.

    As I read the directions, I see that I must answer two questions so I'll circle the two. I also have a choice of questions. Because each question is worth the same number of points, I'll need to spend about the same amount of time on each. The class period is 50 minutes long, and there are now about 40 minutes left. That means I can spend about 20 minutes on each question. I'll write 20 minutes beside each question so I can remember.

4. Invite students to explain what you did. Then share some different directions and ask a student to think aloud, sharing his or her plan.

5. For those questions worth more points than others, be sure students understand that the time spent on each one should probably be proportionate to the value of the question. In addition, students should write down the estimated time to devote to each question.

6. Invite a student to summarize the important points, and write them on the chalkboard or an overhead transparency, as in the following example.

- Read directions.
- Determine the number of questions that must be answered (circle or note the number).
- Decide how much time to spend on each one (note the amount of time beside each question).

7. Have students make up directions for an essay test, exchange them with another student, and then think aloud with the partner. Invite whole class sharing and discussion.

Estimate length of responses

The following activity will help students realize how much they can write in a specific amount of time. This understanding should help students visualize the amount they can write in five-minute intervals.

1. Invite students to take out a sheet of paper and write on every line at a swift pace until you say stop. Students should write legibly. The content can be whatever passes through their minds. The same sentence could also be written repeatedly. After exactly five minutes, tell students to stop.

2. Ask students to count the number of words they have written. According to Galica (1991), most people will write approximately 125 words in five minutes.

3. Have students share the number of words they wrote. If you wish, determine the class average. Then have students compare their papers. Students whose handwriting is extraordinarily large will appear to have written more; those with extraordinarily small handwriting will appear to have written less. After comparisons, have students look at the area of the page they covered. This coverage is what can be expected in five minutes of writing if the paper on the exam is similar to the paper used for this activity.

4. Help students see that if they were going to devote 10 minutes to an essay question, they could estimate writing twice as much as their samples.

5. Remind students that the amount they write on the actual test will probably be somewhat less because of the time needed for thinking, organizing, and composing. The important point is to help students see what might be a realistic estimate of length for a 10-minute essay, a 15-minute essay, and so on.

Read the questions

1. Tell students that an essay question will always specify the two Ts: a topic and a task (Galica, 1991). The topic identifies the material students have to demonstrate they know. The task is what students have to prove they can do. Often, the task will appear as a direction (discuss, compare, contrast, summarize, etc.).

2. Use a question from your content area and demonstrate how students can identify the topic (underline it) and task (circle it). A mathematics teacher might share the following example.

    Define the term relation.

    In this example, the topic is the term relation and the task is to define it.

3. Note that the above question has only one topic and one task. Help students realize that, while other essay questions may be longer and more complex, they can be marked up (circles and underlines) in a manner similar to the one-topic, one-task example.

4. Present more complex examples on the chalkboard or an overhead transparency and invite students to circle the task and underline the topic. Assist students as necessary. Although examples from your content area or other classes students are taking will be the most relevant and helpful, several questions from the science area are provided below.

(Compare) the two common kinds of wetlands and give an example of each.

(Identify) and (describe) the five layers of woody stems.

(Compare) and (contrast) bacterial cells and human cells.

Choose your questions

1. Remind students that sometimes they may be able to choose among several questions. Invite students to share their ideas for how they will choose the questions they want to answer and those they want to omit.

2. Write students' ideas on the chalkboard under the categories Reasons to Choose and Reasons to Omit. Discuss their responses.

3. Invite students to share how they could choose among questions they are not sure about. Fuse their ideas with the questions and tips listed below.

   - Do I know enough about the topic to develop a suitable answer? (You could jot down any information that seems relevant.)
   - Is the question broad or narrow? (Decide if you're a "big-picture person" or a "detail person.")
   - How do the details fit into the big picture? (You could connect the main ideas by creating a concept map.)
   - Which question may be more like others I have answered in the past? (You may have answered compare and contrast questions in the past and may feel comfortable with the basic way to respond. Or you may be able to take a position and support it.)

4. Tell students that once they have made their decisions they should circle the numeral beside their selected questions.

Decide on the order for answering

1. Invite students to share their ideas for the order in which to answer questions. Because of individual differences, it is likely that students will have different response patterns.

2. Honor their patterns of responding, but suggest the following tips.

   - Begin with the short-answer questions. They may be the types of questions that help you activate other bits of knowledge and information that can be used in longer questions. Also, you won't get bogged down initially in a longer essay question.
   - For the longer essay questions, begin with the question you feel most prepared to answer.
   - Do not begin with a question just to get it out of the way.
   - Remember that in the process of answering questions you may recall some information that would apply to a question you have not yet answered. Jot down a word or phrase next to that question to help you recall the information when needed.

8.3

TEACHING STRATEGY 10
Preparing for Essay Tests: PORPE

To help students become adept at taking essay tests and learning important course concepts, a metacognitive strategy called PORPE (Simpson, 1986) can be taught. PORPE stands for **P**redict, **O**rganize, **R**ehearse, **P**ractice, and **E**valuate. The keys to teaching PORPE successfully are to share the specific steps, provide extensive modeling, give repeated practice in concrete and realistic contexts, and tell students why these five areas are important to their learning (Simpson, 1986). You can readily see that teaching this strategy will take some time, but the result will be that students "learn how to behave as effective and mature readers" (Simpson, 1986, p. 408).

An overview of PORPE is given in the box below; it may be shared with students or developed into a chart to be placed in the classroom.

PREPARING FOR ESSAY TESTS
PORPE STRATEGY

1. **P**redict possible essay questions from your reading.
2. **O**rganize the information to answer the questions.
3. **R**ehearse and memorize the information so it can be recalled from long-term memory.
4. **P**ractice recalling the answers to the questions by writing the answers.
5. **E**valuate the quality of your practice essay answer.

Predict

1. Introduce the language used for writing essay tests by sharing and discussing a list such as the following one.

Key Word	Meaning
enumerate	to name one at a time
illustrate	to explain with examples
trace	to tell the history or development
compare	to point out similarities and differences
contrast	to discuss the differences
summarize	to give a brief description of important points
evaluate	to discuss the merits of
justify	to give reasons for
critique	to summarize and evaluate
apply	to put into action
analyze	to separate into parts or basic principles
criticize	to judge the merits or faults of
explain	to make plain; expound

2. Model the procedures you use to predict possible essay questions from a chapter of your text or a particular unit of instruction. Write the questions on the chalkboard or an overhead transparency. Then discuss how and why they were selected. Help students realize that important aspects of the chapter or unit are the basis for most essay questions.

3. Continue to model the process of formulating questions. Then gradually guide students to provide the stems for potential essay questions relating to a specific topic. For example, if part of a text chapter discussed bacterial cells and human cells, you could have students begin their predicted questions with the words *compare* and *contrast* or possibly *explain the difference between*.

4. When you believe students are getting the knack of formulating questions, have them develop their own questions for a specific chapter or unit. Often, boldface headings and chapter summaries provide possible topics for essay questions and reduce the common tendency for students to focus on details instead of key ideas.

5. Have students share their questions with partners or in small groups. Then use whole group discussion and sharing to arrive at the most plausible questions for the essay test.

Organize

1. Organize means to summarize and synthesize the key ideas from the chapter, unit, or area of study. Students are asked to organize their answers to one of the plausible essay questions using a graphic map, chart, outline, or other suitable scheme.

2. Model this process for students from your own map, chart, or outline. Show students how this aid can be used to rehearse and practice for the essay test.

 3. Have students work in small groups to brainstorm possible questions and organize possible answers. Invite a student from each group to share the predicted questions and organizational structure (probably a map, chart, or outline).

4. Discuss the work of various groups and possibly have students develop their own map or outline for a different essay question. Provide written or oral feedback to the students. Feedback can focus on the areas shown in the following chart, or you can adapt the chart to fit your particular situation.

Unit/Chapter _____ Name _____			
Areas for Evaluation	**Improve**	**OK**	**Good**
Accuracy of information			
Completeness of information			
Organization of information			
Examples (if appropriate)			

Rehearse

1. Stress that the goal of rehearsal is to help students place the organization, key ideas, examples, etc. of the chapter or unit into their long-term memory so they can be recalled during the essay test. Remind students that to rehearse means to perfect by repetition.

2. Help students recognize that recall is different from recognition, a skill often used in multiple-choice tests. Recall demands memorization and is best accomplished over several days of study.

3. Share the following guide with students to help them with their rehearsal and memorization. Remind students that the rehearsal time necessary to memorize information will vary. Stress, however, the need to rehearse the material over several days.

4. Have students work with a partner or in a group to talk-through (Simpson, 1993) their map, chart, or outline. After a specified amount of time, have students discuss and evaluate each talk-through. If desired, a chart similar to that provided under "organize" may be used.

Practice

1. In this step, students practice writing, from memory, the answers to their predicted essay questions. Prior to actual practice, it is helpful to provide numerous examples of essay answers of varying quality. A clear and focused discussion of the strengths and weaknesses of the answers should help students acquire more knowledge about what makes a good essay.

2. Model the process of answering an essay question through the use of a talk-through. Specific tips are contained in An Action Plan (see Teaching Strategy 8-9) and Writing an Essay (see Teaching Strategy 8-11).

Evaluate

1. In this step, students evaluate the quality of the practice essays they have written for their self-predicted questions.

2. Share an evaluation sheet similar to the one on the next page and have students evaluate their answers.

3. Distribute other sample essay answers and have small groups of students use the checklist to rank the various essays. Be sure to spend time discussing reasons for the rankings. After sufficient practice, students can complete similar tasks in pairs to evaluate each other's practice essays. Ultimately, each student should acquire the critical stance necessary to evaluate his or her practice questions in an objective manner so necessary review and rehearsal will be the natural outcome.

Name _____ Date _____

Tips for Rehearsal and Memorization

What You Can Do	Check ( ) Times Practiced								
1. Recite aloud the overall structure of your map, chart, or outline.									
2. Test yourself by repeating the structure orally or by writing it.									
3. Add key ideas and examples one section at a time. Test yourself as in 2.									
4. Add other sections and test yourself as in 2.									
5. Test yourself several times over a few days to ensure the information is in your memory. Go back to previous steps as needed.									

Based on Simpson, M.L. (1986). PORPE: A writing strategy for studying and learning in the content areas. *Journal of Reading, 29,* 407–414.

Name _____ Date _____

Evaluating Practice Essay Answers

	Below Average	Average	Above Average
1. I directly answered the question that was asked.	1	2	3
2. I had an introductory sentence that restated the essay topic.	1	2	3
3. I organized the essay answer with key ideas or points that were obvious.	1	2	3
4. I included in the answer relevant details or examples to prove and clarify each idea.	1	2	3
5. I used transitions in the answer to cue the reader (e.g., first, finally).	1	2	3
6. My answer made sense and demonstrated a knowledge of the content.	1	2	3

Adapted from Brozo, W.G., & Simpson, M.L. (1999). *Readers, teachers, learners: Expanding literacy across content areas* (3rd ed.). Columbus, OH: Merrill.

8.3 Writing an Essay

Every essay answer has three parts: an introduction or beginning, a middle or body, and a conclusion or end. These three parts of an essay answer are the foundation upon which responses are developed, although there are some special challenges for various types of essay questions. Galica (1991) has identified four types of essay questions.

1. single-topic questions
2. explicit multiple-part questions
3. implicit multiple-part questions
4. multiple-topic questions (such as compare-contrast)

Decide which type of questions you use and then model the appropriate strategies shown below. Whenever possible, use questions from your content area.

Single-Topic Questions

1. Provide a sample question. For example, describe the environments in which the three types of archaebacteria exist.

2. Help students to see that in a question of this type they will probably use a straight-line pattern. In other words, they will discuss a number of points one after another.

   - hot environments
   - high salt concentrations
   - lack of free oxygen

3. Show students, by writing on the chalkboard or using an overhead transparency, how they might compose their answers. An example follows.

   There are three types of environments where archaebacteria can exist. One type of archaebacteria lives in hot environments that are acidic. An example of an environment would be hot sulfur springs.

   Another environment requires a high concentration of salt in order for the archaebacteria to exist. They can be found in salty areas along ocean borders and in places like the Great Salt Lake.

   The third place where archaebacteria exist is in areas where there is no free oxygen. They can be found in sewage treatment plants and even in the digestive tracts of some animals—including us!

   In summary, archaebacteria can live in environments that are hot and acidic, that contain lots of salt, and where there is no free oxygen.

4. Invite students to evaluate the quality of the answer. Show how the straight-line pattern was used to answer the question.

Explicit Multiple-Part Questions/ Implicit Multiple-Part Questions

1. Write the words *explicit* and *implicit* on the chalkboard. Ask students to share their knowledge of the two words.

2. Develop the idea that *explicit* means that something is clearly defined or carefully spelled out. *Implicit*, on the other hand, means not directly expressed or readily apparent.

3. Relate these two words to answering essay questions. Develop the understanding that explicit questions divide the question into component parts in a fairly straightforward manner. The task is stated quite directly. Implicit questions have more than one part, but the parts are not as clear. Students need to break the question into smaller questions or tasks in order to answer it fully.

4. Show students a sample of an explicit question with several parts and model how an answer would be formulated. The following example can be used.

    1) What major causes led to the <u>beginning</u> of World War II? 2) What were several of the significant results of the war?

    After reading the question, make the following remarks. I can see that this essay has two major parts so I'll number them 1 and 2. For the first part, I need to list the major causes of the beginning of the war. I'll list causes, and then I'll write about them. Then I can do the same for the results of the war.

Causes	**Results**
1. the treaty of World War I	1. massive destruction
2. economic problems	2. new power struggles
3. rise of dictatorships	3. many displaced persons
	4. fear of powerful weapons
	5. birth of the United Nations

    Now I'll use these lists to answer the questions with two mini-essays. One mini-essay will contain a list and discussion of the three causes; the other mini-essay will focus on the five results.

5. Explain to students that this same basic strategy can be used with implicit multiple-part questions. However, there is a major difference: students will need to identify the parts of the question. Write the following question on the chalkboard and invite students to come up with ideas for breaking the question into parts.

    Think about the beginning and end of World War II and discuss important causes and significant outcomes of the war.

6. Guide students to realize that the approach to this question would be very similar to the explicit question presented earlier. Then ask a student to think aloud how he or she would rephrase the question into other questions. Be sure students come to understand that these rephrased questions (e.g., What are important causes of the war? What are significant outcomes of the war?) make the question more manageable and create a plan for writing the essay.

7. Provide several essay questions related to your content area (both explicit and implicit) and have students identify whether they are explicit or implicit. For implicit questions, direct students to rephrase questions to clarify the writing task. Students should also circle the task and underline the topic.

Multiple-Topic Questions (especially compare-contrast)

1. Write compare-contrast on the chalkboard and tell students that such words are a common part of essay tests. Share the meanings of the words with students.

    compare—to examine in order to note similarities or differences
    contrast—to discuss the differences

2. Suggest topics from daily life that students could compare and contrast and have students brainstorm ideas. Possible topics could include the following ones.

    - your class with another class
    - a school day and a Saturday
    - surfing the Internet and playing video games
    - watching TV and reading a book

3. Write the students' ideas on the chalkboard or an overhead transparency. For example, if the example is comparing your class (e.g., English) with another class (e.g., science), a list may look like the following one.

English	**Science**
read novels and short stories	read textbook
discuss readings	do experiments
class lasts 43 minutes	class lasts 43 minutes
take three tests each grading period	take six tests each grading period
meets on first floor	meets on second floor
male teacher	female teacher

4. Help students organize a response to the essay question "Compare and contrast your English class with your science class." Students might be asked to place the material into a Venn diagram to help with organization and visualization. Responses to compare-contrast questions usually follow one of the patterns listed on the following page (Galica, 1991).

Pattern 1: Straight-Line (subject-by-subject)	**Pattern 2: Zigzag** (point-by-point)

Subject A
    Point 1
    Point 2, etc.
Subject B
    Point 1
    Point 2, etc.
Comparison Comments
    Similarity or Difference 1
    Similarity or Difference 2
	Point 1
	    Subject A
	    Subject B
	    A and B Compared
	
	Point 2
	    Subject A
	    Subject B
	    A and B Compared
	    (and so on)

A chart containing the two patterns may be developed for the lesson or future reference.

5. Invite students to think about which pattern may work best for the questions about the two classes. Encourage discussion and help students see that the zigzag pattern works best when the topics can be matched exactly. The straight-line pattern is easier to control and may more closely match the way students have studied. In the case of the two courses, the zigzag pattern may be the best to use because the topics match up very well.

6. Using the chalkboard or an overhead transparency, model how to answer the questions for one of the points (perhaps the types of readings done). Then invite students to write the next part of the answer. Have them share their responses. Continue this process until the answer is completed.

7. Transfer learning to your content area in two ways. First, point out to students how certain topics being studied may lend themselves to compare-contrast essay questions. Second, provide sample questions to students, guide them through the writing process, and provide additional opportunities for practice. By your carefully teaching and practicing the above strategies within the context of your content area, students will improve their ability to answer compare-contrast essay questions and demonstrate the knowledge they have gained.

Notes and Favorite Strategies

Understanding Test Scores

Goal To help students understand test scores

BACKGROUND

There are two major classifications of tests: teacher-made and standardized. The scores on most teacher-made tests are often reported in raw scores and percentages. These scores can also be converted into grades using a grading scale. Standardized tests have numerous scores (e.g., percentiles and stanines) that can be derived from the raw score. In addition, most of these tests use the concept of score bands or standard error of measurement (SEM).

As you consider the teaching strategies in this section, adapt the ideas to your specific classes using examples that are a regular component of your assessment procedures. For the information on standardized tests, if possible, use examples of scores from standardized tests students take (e.g., a state test, a group standardized achievement test). Additional easy-to-understand information on test scores can be found in Lyman (1997).

TEACHING STRATEGY 12

8.4 **Understanding Teacher-Made Test Scores**

1. Reflect on the types of scores used for your classroom tests. Review your grading scale. Use actual examples from your classroom so they are meaningful to students. This example will use raw scores and percentages.

2. Tell students that the raw score refers to the number correct in relationship to the total number of possible questions or items. Perhaps it is getting 8 out of 10 correct on a math quiz or 18 out of 20 on a social studies test. The raw scores are 8 and 18.

3. Show students how these same scores can be converted into percentages. A score of 8 out of 10 would be the same as 80%. Percentages are figured by dividing the number correct (8) by the total number of questions (10) and then multiplying by 100. If appropriate, model the process for students.

4. Relate the scores to your grading scale. Two common types of grading scales are those based on total points or percentages. Share your grading scale. For example, 90% or greater may indicate a grade of A, 80% to 89% may be a B, etc. If you use points, share how your points relate to grades. Be sure students also understand how grades are determined for the grading period, semester, and course.

5. Consider sharing a grade record sheet so students can keep an ongoing record of their performances in your class.

8.4 Understanding Standardized Test Scores

TEACHING STRATEGY 13

1. Identify a standardized test taken by students. Explain to students that their raw scores on such a test are compared to other students throughout the nation using a norm or comparison group.

2. Tell students that two types of scores commonly derived from raw scores are percentiles and stanines.

3. Explain that both percentiles and stanines show how a student's score compares to the norm group. A percentile rank of 50 is considered an average score. If a student achieves a percentile rank of 58, it means that the student scored better than or equal to 58% of the norming group. This score is slightly above average. Be sure that students do not confuse percentiles with percentages, although percentiles are based on the idea of percent.

4. Tell students that stanines are derived scores that divide all possible scores into a "standard nine" scale. Scores in stanines 1, 2, and 3 are classified as below average; stanines 4, 5, and 6 are average; and stanines 7, 8, and 9 are considered above average. Stanines are very broad scores. Because of these broad categories, scores can be misleading. An example may help students understand this idea.

   Let's say Samantha has a percentile rank of 23 and Brad has a percentile rank of 22. Samantha's score could be a stanine of 4, which is considered in the average range of stanines. Brad's score could be a stanine of 3, which falls into the below-average range of stanine scores. There is only 1 percentile rank difference between Samantha and Brad. But, as these scores are converted to stanines, Samantha may be ranked as an average student, while Brad may be seen as below average. Stanines, therefore, give a very broad picture of achievement.

8.4 Standard Error of Measurement

1. Tell students that test scores often give an incorrect impression of exactness. Invite students to share some of the variables that may have influenced their performances on tests taken over the years.

2. Write their ideas on the chalkboard or an overhead transparency and discuss them. Some variables students might offer are listed below.

   stayed up late
   lost my notes and couldn't study
   didn't feel well

   family emergency
   overslept and had to rush
   didn't study

3. Tell students that test publishers calculate a standard error of measurement (SEM) for each test. The SEM helps guard against putting too much importance on a single score. The SEM is used to create a score band or confidence interval. For example, suppose the publishers of an achievement test have calculated the SEM on the science subtest to be 4. If a student's percentile rank were 71, it would be reported as a score band of 67 to 75. That means that the test publishers have added to and subtracted from the student's score the SEM of 4 to take error into account.

4. Show students how this score band might look in printed form.

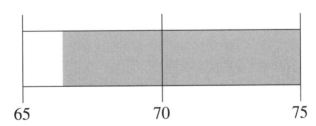

65   70   75

Relate the concept of score bands to meaningful differences in test results. Tell students that when scoring bands for two or more tests overlap, there are no meaningful differences between these scores. If two scoring bands do not overlap, there is a meaningful (significant) difference between the two scores.

Section
8.5

Establishing Portfolio Assessment

Goal To help students develop portfolios for assessment

BACKGROUND

Portfolios are an authentic assessment measure that is student centered and personal. Unlike standardized measures of assessment, portfolios reflect students' motivation and personal growth (Guthrie & Wigfield, 2000). Portfolios serve as a vehicle for assembling evidence of students' learning, because they include a selection of students' work produced over a period of time. In essence, portfolios provide a framework for ongoing assessment and represent what students have learned and are learning in your content area. "Portfolios also represent a collaborative approach to assessment and the means to link assessment to teaching and learning" (Readence, Bean, & Baldwin, 2001, p. 93). Students and teachers work together to determine the selection of artifacts for inclusion in a portfolio. Although portfolios are relatively new to the field of content area literacy, they are gaining credibility as an assessment measure because they reflect the current understanding that learning is a process and not merely a product (Brozo & Simpson, 1999). The strategies in this section will help you develop guidelines for initiating portfolio assessment in your classroom.

TEACHING STRATEGY 15
8.5 Implementing Classroom Portfolios

Implementing portfolio assessment in your classroom will provide students with a sense of empowerment that is not provided through a strict regime of repeated testing. Being able to document students' progress through a display of artifacts provides teachers with a naturalistic assessment measure that can effectively be used to enhance traditional testing routines. To implement portfolio assessment, consider the following recommendations.

1. Talk with students about the idea of portfolios and establish the types of artifacts to be gathered. Portfolios can include a wide variety of items such as projects, research papers, chapter or unit tests, homework samples, and extra credit papers. It is essential that you consider which contributions are appropriate for your content area. For example, in math class students might be asked to include all of their end-of-chapter tests, in English class you might require the drafts and final copy of an essay, and in social studies students may be asked to include a timeline depicting the events of World War II.

2. Set a time frame for collecting portfolio items. Establish due dates for placing items in portfolios and determine the process for dealing with late assignments.

3. Determine the specific number of items to be included in portfolios. As the content area teacher, you will probably wish to require a specific number and type of assignments. However, students may wish to include some "free choice" items as well.

4. Create a rubric for grading the contents of the portfolios. After you have established the general requirements for the portfolios, identify which of the selections will be graded and determine the point value for particular items. Apprise students of the scale you will use for grading their portfolios. (Strategy 8-16 provides directions for developing a portfolio rubric.)

5. Conference with students throughout the semester regarding the selection processes for their portfolio items. Discuss with them how to select items for inclusion in their portfolios. Students may wish to choose items that show their progress in a particular area. Also, they may wish to include a paper written earlier in the semester and one produced later in the semester in order to substantiate their improvement. Help students reflect on their choices as they establish an accurate portrait of their learning throughout the semester. (Teaching Strategy 8-17 explains how to implement the student self-reflection process.)

TEACHING STRATEGY 16
8.5 ▶ Developing a Portfolio Rubric

It is essential to establish evaluation criteria for assessing students' portfolios. Brozo and Simpson (1999) recommend that students' portfolios be individually evaluated on the basis of personal growth in academic achievement rather than on the basis of comparison with other students' work. It is important for teachers to keep this in mind as they apply a rubric to a portfolio. The following strategy delineates the process of developing a rubric for use in portfolio evaluation.

1. Discuss with students the characteristics of an exemplary portfolio. Engage them in thinking of appropriate words to describe it.

2. Compile a list of their words and phrases and write it on the chalkboard or on an overhead transparency. Student suggestions most likely will include descriptors such as *neat, well-organized, creative, complete, grammatically correct,* and *contains the required elements.*

3. Tell students that you will use these words, indicative of a top level of academic endeavor, as you evaluate the contents of their portfolios. Elements within their portfolios that meet these exemplars will receive a point value of 4.

4. Now ask students to describe a portfolio that completely lacks the appropriate elements they have established for a point value of 4. They will probably offer descriptors such as *poorly organized, uninteresting, has missing elements, confusing.* Write these descriptors on the chalkboard or on an overhead transparency.

5. Tell students that elements in a portfolio that can be described with these suggested words will receive a point value of 1.

6. If time allows, you may wish to discuss descriptive words for a "middle group" of portfolio elements, those worthy of receiving point values of 2 or 3.

7. The following rubric was designed to evaluate portfolios in a high school English class. For their portfolios, students were required to:

   - design a cover,
   - write an introductory letter introducing the contents of their portfolios,
   - include one completely revised essay and several personal choice items, and
   - write a letter reflecting on their growth throughout the semester.

8.5 ▶ Students' Personal Reflections

TEACHING STRATEGY 17

Students' portfolios should contain personal reflections as well as work samples. These reflective records serve as documentation of self-reflection and self-evaluation and are essential elements of the portfolio process (Brozo & Simpson, 1999). It is important to provide opportunities for students to examine their portfolios at various times throughout the semester in order for them to personally evaluate their progress. Guide students through the reflective process by having them ask themselves questions such as those that follow as they examine their portfolios' contents.

1. Initiate a class discussion about the questions students consider important to ask themselves as they examine their portfolios' contents. An example of a question might be: *Why did I select this piece of work?*

2. List students' questions on the chalkboard or on an overhead transparency. You may also choose to make copies of the questions for inclusion in their portfolios. These questions will provide an opportunity for students to reflect on their portfolios' contents at other times.

3. Student questions may include the following ones.

   - Why did I select this piece of work?
   - How does this selection demonstrate my progress in this class?
   - What have I learned about (math, science, writing, etc.) from producing this paper?
   - If I revise this paper, what will I do?
   - How does this selection show evidence of careful thought?
   - What was most important to me during my completion of this piece of work?

4. After students have offered their suggestions for reflective questions, allow them 15 to 20 minutes of class time in order to examine the contents of their portfolios, using the questions as a guide. Encourage them to write brief responses to the reflective questions and to include any other comments they consider appropriate. Suggest that they place their reflective question guide and their responses inside their portfolios for future reference. A reflective question guide follows.

Name _____ Date _____

Portfolio Rubric for an English Class

Scale: 4 = A; 3 = B; 2 = C; 1 = D

Criteria	4	3	2	1
Cover: Title is appropriate for contents.	Clearly delineates contents	Related to contents but somewhat vague	Student struggles to relate title to contents.	Totally unrelated to contents
Introductory letter: Introduces contents and reflects on each choice	Letter is well written, grammatically correct, and contains reflections on each portfolio piece.	Letter contains 1–2 errors, and the majority of pieces are accompanied by a reflection.	Letter contains 3–5 errors, and the majority of pieces are not accompanied by reflections.	Letter contains more than 5 errors and does not contain reflections.
Essay: includes revisions and drafts	Includes all drafts and revised pieces show improved content/style and grammar	Some drafts are missing, but revised pieces are present and show improved elements.	Most drafts are missing, and some pieces are not revised.	Contains no drafts or evidence of revisions
Personal choice: Items selected from semester's work to demonstrate growth in writing skills	Contains 3 or more items personally chosen to demonstrate growth in writing	Contains 2 items personally chosen to demonstrate growth in writing	Contains 1 item personally chosen to demonstrate growth in writing	Contains no items demonstrating growth in writing
Reflective letter: Describes skills and growth as a writer throughout the semester	Letter is well written and thoughtful, demonstrating the ability to honestly reflect on strengths and weaknesses in writing.	Letter contains 1–2 errors but is thoughtful and reflective in most areas of writing development.	Letter contains 3–5 errors and shows minor thoughtful reflection on writing progress.	Letter contains more than 5 errors and is not reflective or thoughtful.

Name _____ Date _____

A Reflective Question Guide for Portfolio Work Samples

1. Why did I select this piece of work? _____

   _____

2. How does this selection demonstrate my progress in this class?

   _____

3. What have I learned about (math, science, writing, etc.) from producing this paper?

   _____

   _____

4. If I revise this paper, what will I do? _____

   _____

5. How does this selection show evidence of careful thought? _____

   _____

6. What was most important to me during my completion of this piece of work?

   _____

   _____

7. Additional comments _____

   _____

Notes and Favorite Strategies

Chapter 9
CONDUCTING RESEARCH

OVERVIEW

Conducting research is not merely a school activity; it is an integral part of life. All of us respond to our natural curiosity by asking questions, forming hypotheses, gathering data, and drawing conclusions. We conduct research in many areas of our lives. One of the reasons we research is to learn about new situations. For example, when we are planning a trip to a new place, many of us investigate the options available to us. We look into travel arrangements, places to stay, restaurants, and things to do once we are there. We research by gathering information, weighing the various options, and making decisions. Another type of research we conduct is to solve problems. When we encounter a problem such as deciding what make of car to buy, we learn about the different cars, decide which car

we want, and make a decision. These practical types of research are part of our everyday lives.

Middle and high school students also conduct research regularly. They may investigate career and college options; they may find out about sports teams and players; or they may learn about musicians and movie stars. All of these activities that students do on a regular basis are research activities. Researching is a natural part of life for middle and high school students, just as it is for adults.

Although researching is an activity in which all of us participate from time to time, there are skills and strategies that make researching more efficient and productive. Researching is usually comprised of the following strategies: generating a research question; locating and evaluating information;

selecting, organizing, and synthesizing information; and conveying the findings to the appropriate audience. The steps in researching are individual, just as the steps in the writing process are individual. Students may go through the steps in the research process in a linear manner, they may spiral back through the research stages, or they may move through the research stages recursively (Lenski & Johns, 1997). Each researching situation is different, and the context of the research and students' preferences influence the manner in which students proceed through the stages of research.

There are two main purposes for having students conduct research in middle and high schools. First, learning how to research is an important life skill. Because students will be conducting informal research during their lives, it is important for you to help them learn the strategies that will allow them to ask and answer pertinent questions. Even though students naturally draw on multiple knowledge sources to learn, guiding them in the research process is an important function of schooling. Learning how to research and practicing research in a school setting can help students develop skills that will be an important part of their lives (Rogovin, 2001).

A second reason for having students research is so they can personalize their learning by conducting research about content area topics. For example, students who are learning about space in science class will learn more deeply about one aspect of the subject if they conduct research. Some students may be interested in learning about individual planets; others may want to learn about the stars; and others may be more interested in space flight. Allowing students to research topics from your content area provides them with the opportunity to learn about topics that interest them.

Our society thrives on information; we are glutted with it. In order to make sense of our world, we need to know when we need more information; we need to be able to ask the right questions; we need to have the ability to sift through abundant sources of material; we need to have the ability to evaluate what we find; and we need to have the ability to organize data so that a reasonable conclusion can be drawn or a decision can be reached. These steps in the research process can be taught in your content area classes (McLaughlin, 2000). As you teach students to conduct research, they will derive dual benefits: students will learn more about topics in your content area, and they will be able to obtain and evaluate information for work and for leisure.

Generating Research Questions

Goal > To help students generate questions to research

BACKGROUND

Generating a question to research is the first step in the research process. Students may have a vague idea of a topic that they want to research, but refining their questions so that they can actually find answers is a difficult task for novice researchers. Many times students generate research questions that are either so broad that they find too many sources or so narrow that they find too few sources. Students need guidance in order to generate research questions that can actually be answered.

You can help students pose research questions by assisting them in accessing their background knowledge. When students remember what they already know about a topic, they can identify what they want to learn through researching. While students are accessing their prior knowledge, they should read general source texts such as encyclopedias. As students remember what they know about the topic, they should also build their background knowledge so that they can ask a research question that will be sufficiently narrow and not overly broad. Students need practice in generating a question that would be appropriate for school research.

Many of the research assignments you give your students will be linked to your content area. Since students learn from researching, giving them opportunities to research in your discipline will help them become more interested in your subject and will help them learn about topics that you believe are important. These research assignments are valid and useful for students. You may also decide to give students authentic research assignments, or research assignments that provide information for real-life situations. When students research a problem that is authentic, they become more highly motivated to answer the research question. For that reason, you might consider incorporating Problem-Centered Research into your curriculum. Giving students practice generating research questions that stem from your content area and assisting them in identifying questions for real problems are both important ways to help students learn to conduct research.

TECHNOLOGY TIP

References on CD-ROM

Multimedia reference texts are now available on CD-ROM. Selected references available on CD-ROM from DK Publishing (888-342-5357) are listed below.

Eyewitness Encyclopedia of Science 2.0
Eyewitness History of the World 2.0
The Ultimate Human Body 2.0
Earth Quest

9.1   Factstorming

TEACHING STRATEGY 1

When students begin to think about the topic they want to research, they first need to identify what they know about the subject. Factstorming, a strategy adapted from the cooperative learning activity Fact Storm (Klemp, Hon, & Short, 1993), encourages students to access their background knowledge so that they can begin to identify topics that would be appropriate for researching. Factstorming is similar to brainstorming but with an important difference. When students participate in Factstorming, they think about facts and associations that are pertinent to the topic. When they brainstorm, they generate ideas to solve a problem or answer a question. Factstorming is an excellent strategy to generate ideas that will eventually form a research question.

Directions and Example

1. Explain that before students research they need to access their background knowledge and identify what they know about the topic. Tell students that Factstorming allows them to call up facts and associations about a topic.

2. Divide the class into groups of three or four students of mixed abilities and interests. When students Factstorm with others who have different backgrounds and interests, they are able to generate more ideas.

3. Tell students that they will be researching a topic related to what they are learning in class. Have them Factstorm what they know about the topic by writing all of their ideas in a list. An example follows.

> We have been reading about cardiovascular fitness. Your next assignment will be to write a research paper on ways you can participate in a cardiovascular fitness program to improve your fitness level. List as many types of cardiovascular fitness activities as you can. If other related issues come to mind, such as experiences, add them to the list.

4. Give students 10 minutes to complete the Factstorming activity. After 10 minutes, have students share their ideas with the entire group. Write the ideas on the chalkboard or an overhead transparency. Encourage students to share other ideas that come to mind during this time. Some examples follow.

aerobic dancing	speed swimming	karate	bicycling
in-line skating	baseball	horseback riding	racquetball
rowing	skiing	tennis	hiking
soccer	ballet	basketball	walking

5. Have students think about the entire list of ideas. Then have them individually choose two or three ideas that appeal to them for further thought. Explain that when researchers select a topic about which to write research questions, they process many initial ideas. Tell students that they are generating ideas from which their research questions can be developed.

6. Encourage students to use a similar process when they identify or generate topics for research.

9.1   Quick Writes

TEACHING STRATEGY 2

Students who are thinking about the topic they want to research need to briefly explore several topics before deciding which topic is of interest to them. Quick Writes are short writing assignments that help students access their background knowledge about a topic and clarify their interest in the topic. During Quick Writes, students write about a topic for five minutes. Their writing should be a conscious stream of ideas rather than an organized essay. As students write, they should not be concerned about spelling or punctuation; rather, they should write as much about the topic as they can in the time allotted. Students should then use their Quick Writes to decide which topic is of most interest to them as they generate research questions.

Directions and Example

1. Explain that when researchers generate a topic they probably have several ideas from which to choose. Tell students that as researchers ponder their topics they think about the information they know about each topic. As they access their background knowledge, researchers decide which topic is of most interest at that time.

2. Have students reread the list of topics that they produced during the Factstorming activity. As students read the list, have them think about what they know about each topic. Give students several minutes to think about each topic.

3. Explain that when researchers choose a topic they make a choice among several possible options. Tell students that they need to make a preliminary decision about their topic of research. Even though several topics may be appealing, students must limit their choice to one topic for the present assignment. Explain that there probably will be opportunities to research other topics of interest in the future.

4. After students have chosen their topics, divide the class into groups of two or three students. Have students discuss their topics with the group. Give the class 10 minutes to talk about their topics.

5. Explain that ideas are often clarified through discussion and through writing. Tell students that they will be writing about their topics as a basis for generating a research question using the strategy Quick Write. Explain that they should write anything that comes to mind about the topics and that they should not worry about writing in an organized fashion. Give students five minutes to write about their topics. Encourage students to write about what they have learned from their textbook, in class, and from other sources (e.g., background knowledge).

6. During the next class meeting, have students reread their Quick Writes. Tell students that they can add to their writing if they choose, or they can choose other topics about which to write. Give students five minutes to write more about their topics or to choose other topics.

9.1   RAFT

TEACHING STRATEGY 3

RAFT is a writing strategy that can be used for developing research questions and supporting inquiry (Shearer, 2000). RAFT is an acronym for Role, Audience, Format, and Topic, all of the major components of research.

Directions and Example

1. Tell students that they will be writing research using the RAFT technique. Explain that RAFT stands for Role, Audience, Format, and Topic.

2. Explain to students that when generating research questions they need to consider all of the components in RAFT.

3. Provide an example of RAFT using your content subject or use the following examples from Shearer (2000).

Role	Audience	Format	Topic
Newspaper reporter	Readers in the 1870s	Obituary	General Ulysses S. Grant
Chemist	Chemical company	Instructions	Combinations to avoid
Plant	Sun	Thank you note	Sun's role in plant's growth
Repeating decimal	Set of rational numbers	Petition	Prove you belong to this set

4. Explain how RAFT applies to research in your content area such as in the following example.

   In chemistry we've discussed how some chemicals interact with others. Develop a research question such as: What types of chemicals produce unfavorable reactions? Research that question using your textbook, the Internet, and other resources. The product of your research will be a set of instructions from a chemist to a chemical company about the types of combinations to avoid.

5. Remind students that as they develop their research questions they need to consider the RAFT components of research.

9.1 ➤ *TEACHING STRATEGY 4*
Problem-Centered Research

When students conduct research using Problem-Centered Research, they generate a research question based on a real-life problem. Problem-Centered Research is the type of research that is most often used by people to solve everyday problems or to find out about important issues. For example, consider the following problem. You have moved to a new house that does not have a fenced-in yard. You have two dogs that will wander off if left to themselves. You have a "problem." How should you keep the dogs in the yard? Of course, there are many solutions to that problem. You can build a fence; you can put in an invisible fence; or you can put the dogs on tethers. To solve the problem, you would need to conduct research to determine your options, collect facts about each option, consider the advantages and disadvantages of each option, and come to an informed conclusion. Usually real problems have many solutions, not one correct answer. Using Problem-Centered Research in the classroom is an excellent way for your students to understand how research is used to solve problems that exist in real life.

✛ Directions and Examples

1. Identify a real problem that exists in your school, in your community, or in the lives of your students. To decide what problem to research, ask students to think about issues that are important to them.

2. Divide the class into groups of three or four students. Have students generate a list of ideas that could be used for a Problem-Centered Research project. Tell them the criteria for a Problem-Centered Research question are listed below.

   - Solutions to the problem exist.
   - There are many solutions.
   - There is not one correct solution.
   - The research could be done in the allotted time.
   - There is an authentic audience for the solution to the problem.

3. Ask members of the groups to share their ideas. As students volunteer ideas, write their ideas on the chalkboard or an overhead transparency. Help students frame the ideas as real problems, as in the following example.

One of the problems generated by the class is that there aren't enough parking spaces for students. Many students have to park their cars on the side streets which are quite narrow. Last year 12 cars were sideswiped. The problem expressed is the lack of student parking.

4. Using the entire list of ideas, discuss which problems are possible to research and solve given time and money constraints. For example, you may make the following comments.

   Parking is one of the biggest problems students report on their yearly survey. The parking issue is currently being discussed by the Board of Education. Perhaps we should wait for them to make recommendations before we act on that particular problem.

   Another problem that was raised was that our town has no Sister City. Of course, the lack of a Sister City is more of a situation than a problem, but it does meet our criteria: the situation has a solution; there is more than one possible solution; there is not one correct solution; the research could be done in the allotted time; and there is an authentic audience for the solution to the problem.

5. Create a modified list of problems that the class could actually research and solve. Have the class vote on a problem to be solved.

6. Have students conduct research to solve the problem or adapt the example that follows.

Cross-Curricular Example

Problem-Centered Research

Problem

A group of students petitioned the Student Council for their school to sponsor a trip to Mexico to study Spanish. The Student Council President discussed the request at a faculty meeting. The faculty members decided that the request for foreign travel would be an excellent topic for research.

Research Question

Should the school sponsor trips to foreign countries?

Procedures

1. In class, have students brainstorm different subtopics for research. For example, the following might be subtopics for this research question.

Insurance	Opinions of parents
Faculty interest in sponsoring	Connection to school curriculum
Funding	Student interest
Destinations	Existing travel programs
Safety	Red tape (passports, visas)

2. Tell students that each subtopic will be the task of an expert group. Have students apply to these groups for membership.

3. After expert groups have been formed, have groups develop mission statements, goals, and timelines. This material should be shared with the entire class.

4. Guide students toward information and resources that will accomplish their goals. Students may need to develop and distribute surveys, conduct an Internet search, interview people, telephone or write to a country's embassy, read books, or find information in other ways.

5. Have students decide on a way to disseminate their information to the entire class. Then have students share the information they found.

6. Invite students to use information from all of the groups to develop an answer to the research problem. Discuss different forms this final report could take.

7. Have students present their findings to the audience for which it was intended. In this case, the findings would be presented to the faculty of the school.

Section

9.2

Locating and Evaluating Sources

> **Goal** To help students locate and evaluate sources that answer their research questions

BACKGROUND

Finding enough information to answer a research question is rarely a problem anymore. Quick clips of information frequently bombard us. When we watch television, 10-second commercials try to persuade us to buy a product. When we log onto the Internet, advertisements clutter the websites. At the websites, we can link to a wide variety of additional sources. When we access a CD-ROM reference, we have the option of accessing links, photos, and video clips. We are truly living in the information age.

Students who are conducting research need different types of skills than were needed only a few years ago. Because of the abundance of information that is readily available, students now need help in learning how to make decisions about which infor-

mation to access. Locating information has taken on a new meaning. Although we do need to teach students how to use search tools and conduct Boolean searches, we also need to teach students how to decide which information they should locate at different points in their research process. Students need to decide whether to locate sources through the library, the Internet, or on CD-ROMs. They need to decide whether to use primary or secondary sources. They also need to learn when to use general information and when to use specific information. These decisions for locating sources can be taught through Self-Questioning (see Teaching Strategy 9-5). These srategies can help students as they research.

TECHNOLOGY

T I P

Online Reader

The Online Reader provides full-text magazine articles that are assigned a reading level. The Online Reader also provides teaching suggestions and student activities for the articles.

EBSCO Curriculum Materials 800-633-8623

9.2 Self-Questioning

Researching is a recursive process. Even though students have generated research questions and subtopics, they need to continue to revise their questions as they interact with sources. As students locate sources that they believe will provide information to answer their research questions, they need to ask themselves questions about the sources and about their research questions. There are several types of questions students should ask themselves as they research. First, students need to ask themselves when to use the library, CD-ROMs, and the Internet. Many different types of resources are available to students. Most students have library print sources available. Many students also have nonprint sources at their disposal, such as reference texts on CD-ROMs and the Internet. Even though the Internet is new and appealing for most students, conducting a search on the Internet may not be the most efficient way to locate sources.

A second question students should ask as they research is whether they need primary or secondary sources. The Internet has provided easy access to many primary sources that were difficult for students to locate in the past. At times, primary sources are the most appropriate choice for research. At other times, however, secondary sources provide better information. Students have to ask themselves which kinds of sources they need at different points in the research process. Finally, students need to ask themselves whether the information they are reading is of interest to them. Researchers need to balance the time they can devote to the research project with their interest in the topic. Students need to continually monitor their levels of interest in their research topics and revise their research to sustain their interest. Teaching students how to use Self-Questioning can help them make informed decisions about which sources to use, locate sources efficiently, and monitor their interest in their topics.

TECHNOLOGY TIP

Selected Internet Sites of Primary Sources

Newslink: over 2,000 newspapers, broadcasts, and web resources.
www.newslink.org

FedWorld: United States government resources including government reports.
www.fedworld.gov

Index of History
kuhttp.cc.ukans.edu/history

Internet Public Library
ipl.sils.umich.edu

Library of Congress
lcweb.loc.gov

Directions and Examples

1. Tell students that even though they have decided on preliminary research questions they need to continue to revise their questions as they locate and evaluate sources. Write the following questions on the chalkboard or an overhead transparency. Tell students that the following questions are typical questions researchers ask themselves as they locate source texts.

   - What is my research question? Do I need to revise the question?
   - What do I know about my topic? How does that influence the sources I am locating?
   - How interested am I in my topic? Can I sustain my interest for the length of this project? If not, how can I revise my question to promote interest?
   - Where is the best place to search for sources: the Internet, CD-ROMs, or the library?
   - Do I need primary sources, secondary sources, or both?
   - Are the sources I have located appropriate for my purposes? Is the information too broad, too specific, or just right?
   - Is the text too difficult for me to read with good understanding?

2. Ask students to generate other questions that they think will be useful as they locate and evaluate sources for researching. Compile and duplicate a complete list of questions to distribute to students to use as they research.

3. Model how researchers answer questions about sources. Use a research topic from your content area or use the following example. The following is an example of Self-Questioning to determine a research question from a high school literature class.

   - What is my research question? Do I need to revise the question?

     I want to know what the members of the Bloomsbury Group thought about the challenges women writers faced during the early 20th century. I think the question is fine for now.

   - What do I know about my topic? How does that knowledge influence the sources I am locating?

     From my reading of the text about Virginia Woolf, I learned that Virginia Woolf was one of the founding members of the Bloomsbury Group. I know that Virginia Woolf wrote the book *A Room of One's Own*, which deals with the topic of obstacles women writers faced.

   - How interested am I in my topic? Can I sustain my interest for the length of this project? If not, how can I revise my question to promote interest?

     I am mildly interested in the topic. I think I really want to learn more about Virginia Woolf's views. I was really intrigued by the portion of her book *A Room of One's Own* in which she discussed a hypothetical sister of Shakespeare who was as talented a writer as he was. I never thought how difficult it would be for a girl who was as talented as a boy to be brought up in the same house but with different treatment. I think if I changed my research question to learning about Woolf's views rather than the views of all of the members of the Bloomsbury Group, I would enjoy my research more.

- Where is the best place to search for sources: the Internet, CD-ROMs, or the library?

  I have a *Grolier's Encyclopedia* on CD-ROM at home. I think I'll start with that source. After I read the encyclopedia entry under Virginia Woolf, I'll go to the library to find books written about Woolf's life. After I find books in the library, I'll log onto the Internet to see what else is available.

- Do I need primary sources, secondary sources, or both?

  I need to start with secondary sources. I need to learn more about Virginia Woolf before I try to read primary sources such as her letters.

- Are the sources I have located appropriate for my purposes? Is the information too broad, too specific, or just right?

  The encyclopedia entry told about Woolf's life. It seemed as if she was influenced by her father, Sir Leslie Stephen, and his friends. I wonder if she really wished she were a man, so that she could have had the same opportunities her father and his friends had. This information gave me some valuable insights into Woolf's views about women. The information was general, but I needed general information at the time. I think I'll read at least one more general source before I try to read anything specific.

- Is the text too difficult for me to read with good understanding?

  The encyclopedia was easy to read. It was a synthesis of Woolf's life and was written in language that I could understand. I think when I read some of the primary sources, however, I will have difficulty with the texts. Some of the writing from that time period is hard for me to understand.

4. Ask students to discuss other issues that may arise when they research. After the discussion, have students begin to locate and evaluate their sources using Self-Questioning. As students research, ask them to write down any other issues, questions, or decisions they face as they research. Use the students' questions to revise your list of Self-Questions.

5. The following page is a list of Self-Questions that can be duplicated and distributed to students.

Self-Questions During Researching

Directions: Answer the following questions as you are locating sources to use to answer your research question.

1. What is my research question? Do I need to revise the question?

   _____

   _____

2. What do I know about my topic? How does that influence the sources I am locating?

   _____

   _____

3. How interested am I in my topic? Can I sustain my interest for the length of this project? If not, how can I revise my question to promote interest?

   _____

   _____

4. Where is the best place to search for sources: the Internet, CD-ROMs, or the library?

   _____

   _____

5. Do I need primary sources, secondary sources, or both?

   _____

   _____

6. Are the sources I have located appropriate for my purposes? Is the information too broad, too specific, or just right?

   _____

   _____

7. Is the text too difficult for me to read with good understanding?

   _____

   _____

TEACHING STRATEGY 6

9.2 Search Plan:
Do, Ask, Watch, Read

Students now have access to a variety of different sources, so research has currently become more than a search through encyclopedias. Teachers are becoming more aware of the different resources for research including those that have students do, ask, watch, and read (Zorfass, 1998). In order for students to organize these various modalities, however, they need to develop a search plan.

Directions and Examples

1. Tell students that they will be conducting research but that they will be using a variety of resources to find materials.

2. Develop a list of possible resources with students by asking them to volunteer ideas. List the ideas on the chalkboard or on an overhead transparency. Some ideas are suggested below.

interviews	experiments
fiction	pamphlets
television programs	trips
newspapers	questions
Internet	videos
surveys	slides
databases	magazines
CD-ROMs	textbooks

3. Explain to students that researchers have to develop a search plan to organize their resources and that this search plan can be divided into four categories: what researchers do, what they ask, what they watch, and what they read.

4. Have students categorize the list of resources under the headings of Do, Ask, Watch, and Read such as in the following example.

   Do: experiments, trips

   Ask: interviews, questions, surveys

   Watch: television programs, videos, slides

   Read: fiction, pamphlets, newspapers, Internet, databases, magazines

5. Have students develop their own research plans using the ideas from the list of resources and their own ideas. Duplicate and distribute the form that follows to help keep students organized.

Name _____ Date _____

Research Plan

Research Topic: _____

What I plan to do: _____

_____

_____

_____

What I plan to ask: _____

_____

_____

_____

What I plan to watch: _____

_____

_____

_____

What I plan to read: _____

_____

_____

_____

9.2 ▶ **Website Evaluator**

TEACHING STRATEGY 7

After students have located websites to read and before they decide whether their sources are appropriate for research, students should evaluate their websites. Even websites that have been published by authorities in their fields need to be evaluated to determine how appropriate they are for a particular research project. The Internet is a different type of publishing system. Typically, publishers claim responsibility for the materials they publish. No one, however, is responsible for the resources found on the Internet. Because many websites have not been subject to review boards or external editors, they may be inaccurate, unreliable, misleading, or false. Students, therefore, need to evaluate websites before they use them as a source for research.

TECHNOLOGY

**T
I
P**

Internet Evaluation Guides

www.library.webster.edu

Directions and Example

1. Explain that the Internet is a huge network of computers from which a great deal of information can be accessed. Tell students that the sponsoring agency or individual for each website is responsible for the contents of its site. Explain that some sources have a vested interest in presenting information that is incomplete or not wholly accurate. Tell students that the texts they read on the Internet need to be evaluated before being used and that they need to become skilled consumers of information on the Internet.

2. Duplicate and distribute copies of the Website Evaluation Questionnaire that follows. Explain that students should fill out the Questionnaire for each of the sites they decide to read for their research.

3. Model how to evaluate a website by choosing a site that applies to your discipline and by answering the questions posed by the Website Evaluation Questionnaire, or use the example that follows for the website GlobaLearn at http://www.globalearn.org/.

4. Make a transparency of the Questionnaire, display it on an overhead projector, and discuss each of the sections with your students or duplicate the Questionnaire and distribute it to your students. Explain that there are five categories of questions students must consider as they evaluate websites: the authority of the author, the accuracy of the contents, the objectivity of the sponsoring organization or individual, the recency of the material, and the coverage of the contents.

5. Explain that researchers must determine whether the authors of the site are credible. To determine credibility, students should find out the authors of the website, the authors' qualifications, and the authors' reasons for producing the site. Listed below are questions and answers about the authority of the author.

Authority

- Who is the author or producer of the page?

  I accessed the section of the web page that described the organization. GlobaLearn is a nonprofit company founded in 1993 by Murat Armbruster. The page is sponsored by the company.

- What are the author's qualifications for the information written on the site?

  The author of the site is unknown, but the staff and Board of Directors of GlobaLearn are listed. Several of the staff members are associated with Yale University.

- If the website is sponsored by an organization or business, is the sponsoring organization clearly stated? Who is the sponsor?

  Yes, the sponsoring agent is listed and described. GlobaLearn is a company that sponsors live expeditions around the world. Students can become involved by interacting with the explorers through the Internet.

- Can the legitimacy of the organization be verified? If so, how? If not, why not?

  The existence of GlobaLearn can be verified by looking at an index for nonprofit companies.

- What is the purpose of the website?

  The purpose of the website is to educate people about the company.

6. Explain that it is also important to determine whether the contents of the site are accurate. In general, information should not be taken at face value unless it can be verified by at least one other qualified source. Since information on the Internet usually is not verified by an editor, researchers should use information on websites cautiously unless other informed sources verify the contents of the site. Tell students that traditional print information is read by several reviewers and at least one editor who prepares the manuscript for publication by reading it for grammatical errors. When reading a website, students should evaluate the accuracy of the language. If the site has numerous errors, students can conclude that the authors of the site either do not have an adequate command of the language or that the site was hastily written. In either case, a site that has many grammatical errors may also have errors in its contents and should be read with that in mind. Listed below are questions and answers about the accuracy of a website.

Accuracy

- Can information on the site be verified by another source? If so, how?

  After one becomes involved in GlobaLearn, the site can be verified by other participants.

- Is the page relatively free of grammatical errors? If not, what conclusions can you draw?

  Yes, it is well written.

- Who has the responsibility for the accuracy of the contents of the site?

  It doesn't say.

7. Explain that all authors take a personal interest in their subjects. At times, however, authors can distort information, thereby making it biased. Tell students that they must be especially aware that the materials they read on the Internet are objective. Although students may not be able to determine whether an author of a website is completely honest, several questions can make students aware of blatant subjectivity. Listed below are questions and answers about the objectivity of a website.

Objectivity

- Is any sort of bias evident? If so, what seems to be the author's bias?
  No bias seems to be evident.

- Is the author's motivation for writing the website clear? What do you think it was?
  I think the author wants more students to learn about this project.

- If there is advertising on the page, is it clearly differentiated from the contents?
  There is no advertising on the site.

8. Information on websites may be more current than print sources, but that is not always true. Some websites may be several years old and contain information that is just as dated as a print source. To guard against the thinking that all electronic information is current, tell students that they need to determine when the website was developed. One of the benefits of electronic publishing is that it is easier to update information on the Internet than it is for print sources. Tell students also to look for a note saying whether the site has been revised. When websites are updated, links that were once operational may no longer work. Explain that when students evaluate websites, they also need to check whether the links are working. Listed below are questions and answers about the recency of a website.

Recency

- When was the website produced?
  The site was copyrighted originally in 1997.

- Has the website been updated? If so, when? If not, are the contents out of date?
  Yes, it was revised this year.

- Are the links in operation? Are the links accurate? If not, which links are not in operation or are inaccurate?

  There were several links, all of them in operation.

9. Tell students that websites are frequently on the Internet while they are being constructed. A web source title may sound perfect for research, but that site may be under construction. As students evaluate websites, have them look for parts of websites that are unfinished. Also have students survey the entire website before deciding whether it will be a good source for their research projects. Explain that they need to know what contents are covered on the site and that they should survey the site just as they would scan a table of contents in a textbook. Listed below are questions and answers about the coverage of a website.

Coverage

- Has the website been completed, or is it under construction? If it is under construction, is there an indication of when it will be finished?

  The site is complete.

- Are the topics of the website clearly stated? If not, what is unclear?

  Yes, the topics are clear.

- Does the page address the topics stated? If not, what is missing?

  Yes, all of the topics are addressed.

10. Have students independently evaluate the websites on their research lists using the Website Evaluation Questionnaire.

11. Divide the class into groups of three or four students. Ask students to share what they have learned about their website evaluations. Have students discuss which sites are appropriate for their research projects and which are not. Encourage students to discuss the reasons the sites they deemed inappropriate do not apply to their research.

TECHNOLOGY
T I P

Evaluating Web Resources

Provides a variety of forms that student can use to evaluate websites.

www2.widener.edu/Wolfgram-Memorial-Library

Name _____ Date _____

Website Evaluation Questionnaire

Website name and location _____
_____

1. Who is the author of the site? _____
_____
_____

2. What are the author's qualifications? _____
_____
_____

3. What are the purposes of the site? _____
_____
_____

4. What other sources can verify the information on this site? _____
_____
_____

5. What author bias is present? _____
_____
_____

6. What date was the site produced and updated? _____

7. How valid do you think this site is? _____
_____
_____

Section
9.3

Selecting and Organizing Information

Goal To help students select and organize information that answers their research questions

BACKGROUND

Once students have located and evaluated source texts, they are ready to begin reading the texts and looking for information that will answer their research questions. As students read, they need to select information to write down as notes, and then they need to organize that information. While reading, students make complex cognitive decisions about what to select for their notes and what not to select. Readers of source texts look for the organizational patterns of the texts they are reading, select what parts to read and remember, and connect that information to their background knowledge (Spivey, 1997). Students use many strategies to accomplish this difficult task. They need to identify the structure of the text they are reading. Then they need to decide whether to skim the selection, scan for information, or read the passage carefully. Finally, students need to connect what they have read to the information they already know about the topic. Finally, students need to write their findings as notes. Selecting information

to answer research questions involves the use of many reading strategies.

As students select information, they need to monitor all of the strategies they are using. Questioning the Author (QtA) is one strategy that helps students monitor their reading. QtA is a useful strategy for students who are selecting information from texts while researching.

Students can take notes as they select information, but then they need to organize their notes for easy access. Two popular ways to organize information are using databases and using I-Charts. When students have a great deal of discrete data, databases are an ideal organizational tool. If the information that students have selected is conceptual, I-Charts are a good choice. Selecting and organizing information that answers research questions is possibly the most difficult of the steps in the research process. Students will need much practice and guidance as they decide what information to select and how the material should be organized.

TECHNOLOGY
T I P

Computer Software to Organize Information

The Research Helper: stores and sorts information, writes bibliographic entries.

Harcourt Brace 800-237-2665

9.3 — TEACHING STRATEGY 8
Questioning the Author (QtA)

After students have located sources for their research and evaluated the appropriateness of those sources, they need to read the texts for information that will answer their research questions. The selection process entails making determinations about which information would be helpful in accomplishing the students' goals and which information is not useful. To facilitate the thought processes necessary in selecting information, the strategy Questioning the Author (QtA) (Beck, McKeown, Hamilton, & Kucan, 1997) can be used. QtA is a comprehension strategy designed to increase students' active understanding of texts. When using the QtA strategy, students step back from the text and ask pertinent questions to help them understand what the authors are expressing. As they make decisions about what the authors are saying, students can also take an additional step and ask questions about whether that information answers their research questions.

Directions and Example

1. Tell students that they will be reading their source texts using a strategy that is different from the usual strategies they use as they read. Explain that as they read to select information they need to think that authors are real people who may or may not have been successful in communicating their ideas. Help students realize that they need to actively discern what the authors are trying to communicate and how texts answer students' research questions.

2. Tell students that you will be demonstrating a strategy that promotes active thinking about texts during reading and that guides them in ways to select information that answers a research question. Begin modeling the QtA strategy by choosing a text from your content area or by using the following example.

   We have been reading about fungi in biology class and are answering the following research question: In what ways do we encounter fungi in everyday life? To begin researching, we decided that it would be appropriate to read the section from our biology book to develop general knowledge before reading more specific sources. Therefore, I will use the QtA strategy using material from Chapter 20 in our biology text.

3. Explain that before they begin reading their source texts students should remind themselves of their research questions. Rereading their research questions will help students focus on the pertinent information from the text. Then as they begin reading, they should ask the following questions.

> What are the authors trying to say?
> What are the authors' messages?
> How do the authors' messages answer my research question?

4. Choose a passage of text from your content area or use the following example to demonstrate how a reader would Question the Author. To use the example, make a transparency of the text and display it on an overhead projector.

> Fungi are important in many ways. For example, mushrooms are a type of fungus, and breadmaking requires another type of fungus. Yeasts are used to make bread rise. Molds that spoil food are fungi. Mushrooms are part of the recycling of nutrients of decaying matter that is released back into the ecosystem. A few fungi cause diseases in plants and animals. Other fungi are used for food, to make medicine, and to give flavor to cheese. Fungi are essential organisms.

5. Demonstrate questions you could ask about the meaning of the text. An example follows.

> What do the authors mean when they write "fungi are important?" Does that mean they are an important part of everyday life? What does the term "important" imply? Are fungi so important they are essential, or do fungi exist to accomplish many purposes. Later, the author states that "fungi are essential organisms," but I'm not sure whether they are essential for food and medicine, or whether they are essential for life. I need to find out more about how and why fungi are important.

6. Demonstrate questions you could ask that help students select information from the text, as in the following example.

> My research topic is about ways fungi are used in everyday life. This paragraph has many different ideas that would fit my research topic. The paragraph mentions several different ways fungi are important: mushrooms are fungi, fungi are used to make bread rise, they cause food to spoil and wood to rot, and they are used in food, medicine, and cheese. I think I will concentrate on a few of these items. I can't research them all. I think I'll focus on the ways fungi help humans. Therefore, I will only select the facts that fit this idea. I will write that fungi are used in making bread, cheese, and medicine.

7. Tell students that each time they select information their decisions influence which information they will select in the future. Demonstrate how researchers make decisions about future selections. Use your own content area example or use the following example.

> Since I have decided that I will only select information about the uses of fungi for humans, I will need to read the portions of text that discuss mushrooms, yeast, cheese, and medicine. While I read, I will also look for other ways fungi are useful to people. When I see sections of text that discuss the ways fungi help the ecosystem, I will skim over those parts. Although that topic is of interest to me, I will not be using it for this project, so I will not read those sections carefully.

8. Provide students with a list of QtA questions to use as a prompt as they read sources and select information. Copy the following page and distribute it to your students.

Questioning the Author (QtA)

Directions: Ask the following questions as you read source texts and select information to write as notes. If you think of additional questions that would be useful to you, write them on the blank lines.

1. What are the authors trying to say here?

2. What are the authors' messages?

3. What are the authors talking about?

4. Did the authors explain this clearly?

5. Is this passage consistent with other passages?

6. How does this passage connect with previous passages?

7. Do the authors adequately explain things?

8. Why are the authors telling us this now?

9. Are the authors giving me information that will answer my research question?

10. Does what the authors say change my research question? If so, how?

11. _____

12. _____

13. _____

14. _____

Adapted from Beck, I.L., McKeown, M.G., Hamilton, R.L., & Kucan, L. (1997). *Questioning the author: An approach for enhancing student engagement with text.* Newark, DE: International Reading Association.

9.3

TEACHING STRATEGY 9

Organizing with Databases

Using a database is an excellent way to organize information when researching information that was collected from multiple sources. A database is a collection of information that can be organized for searching and retrieving information in a variety of ways. According to Braun, Fernlund, and White (1998), a telephone book is a type of database. Of course, it is difficult to organize or reorganize data using a print source such as a telephone book. An electronic database, on the other hand, allows data to be sorted according to a variety of categories. Students can design and build their own databases to access and manipulate the data they have gathered for researching. As part of a curriculum unit on weather, for example, a group of students collected data daily from the school's rooftop weather station. Then they pooled the information into a common database accessible to all networked students through Local Area Networks (LANs). Students from other schools then added information about the weather in their community to the database. Eventually, the students had a large data set of recorded weather that was used for a variety of research projects.

TECHNOLOGY
T I P

Software to Build Databases

Students can build databases using programs such as ClarisWorks (Apple), FoxPro (Microsoft), and FilMaker Pro (Claris).

Directions and Example

1. Tell students that, even though they have collected a great deal of information from reading their sources, they need to organize it before they can write a report. Explain that data can be organized in many ways and that students need to decide how they want their data organized.

2. Model how a researcher would read data and decide on categories for inputting the data in a database. Use an example from your content area or use the example that follows.

   One of the research questions we have been considering, based on our textbook, is careers in health occupations. Several sources, both print and nonprint, were used to find the information. A partial list of the information is contained in the following chart.

Health Careers

Medical Practitioners	Medical Records Personnel	Rehabilitation Occupations
Treat patients	Keep records	Work with patients
Diagnose illness	Office jobs	Hands-on work
Work in offices or hospitals	Work in offices or hospitals	Work in hospitals or homes
Need M.D.	Various positions	Need special training

3. Discuss ways these data could be organized into a database. In this example, one of the categories could be the education needed for a career. Another might be the location of the job.

4. Tell students that data in a database can be accessed in many different ways. Have students read their data, thinking of ways their data could be categorized. Then have the students input their data into a database.

5. Explain that the way data are retrieved from a database depends on the research question that is asked. Have students think about their research questions and manipulate their data so that their questions can be answered.

TEACHING STRATEGY 10

9.3 Information Charts

An Information Chart (I-Chart) is a strategy developed by Hoffman (1992) that has been adapted by Randall (1996) to help students select and organize relevant information from multiple sources as they conduct research. An I-Chart has three components: the preparation of the charts, research and note-taking using the charts, and the completion of a final product using the information organized within the charts. Teachers can use I-Charts as an instructional tool to explicitly teach the processes students need to use during research. As students become proficient researchers, teachers should guide students to use I-Charts independently.

Directions and Examples

1. Guide students in choosing topics and developing general research questions. After students have chosen topics, have them develop lists of sources from which they can find information.

2. Explain that once researchers have identified general research questions they need to develop additional questions that are more specific. These additional questions will be subtopics of their general research questions.

3. Divide the class into groups of three or four students. Have students read their research questions to the group. Then have students discuss subtopics of the questions that they intend to research. Model an example for the students before they begin by writing your research question and subtopics on the chalkboard or an overhead transparency. See the following example.

We have been learning about the Harlem Renaissance. Several of you have developed research questions that center around the African American artists and musicians who were popular during the 1920s. The following is a general research question about that topic.

Who were the driving forces behind the Harlem Renaissance?

From the general research question, we can think of specific questions that we need to answer before we can answer the general question. The following are some subtopics of our general research question.

- Who were some of the popular African American writers of the 1920s?
- Who were some of the popular African American artists of the 1920s?
- Who were some of the popular African American musicians and performing artists of the 1920s?
- Why were these people so influential?

4. Make a transparency of a blank I-Chart to display on an overhead projector. Write one of the subtopics of the research question in the blank as in the following example.

> Subtopic: Who were some of the popular African American musicians and performing artists of the 1920s?

5. Distribute several copies of blank I-Charts to all students. Have them write each of their subtopics on a different chart.

6. Explain that students have a great deal of background knowledge about each of their subtopics but that reading other sources will provide them with more information. Tell students that part of researching is to identify what the researcher knows about the topic. Then have students write on the next line a brief statement about what they know about the subtopic.

> What I already know: I know that Louis Armstrong (Satchmo) was a cornet player who was well-known for his jazz playing. I also know that Duke Ellington was a composer and conductor. I think he is known for the song *Mood Indigo*.

7. Have students write what they know about each subtopic on their charts under the section "What I already know."

8. Ask students to begin reading their source texts. Tell them that as they read their first source they should write the name on the line next to Source #1. If the source has information that answers the subtopic question, they should record that information on the Source #1 line. An example follows.

> Source # 1 *Microsoft Encarta Encyclopedia* (CD-ROM)

> Rose McClendon was one of the most popular American actresses early in the 1900s. McClendon acted in the play *Deep River* and later in *Porgy*, a play about African American life in South Carolina. McClendon was one of the founders of the Negro People's Theater in Harlem.

9. After students have taken notes from several sources and written the notes on the I-Charts, invite them to write in the blank labeled "Interesting related facts" that information that does not answer their research question. Tell them that, even though this information will not be used for their current research, it is additional knowledge that they have gained by researching.

10. Explain that if students read any words that are new to them, they should note those words under the section "Key words." Finally, explain that as students read they should be considering additional research questions. Tell students that when they have new questions they should write them in the section "New questions to research."

11. A blank copy of an I-Chart follows.

Information Chart

Name _____ Topic _____

Subtopic _____

What I already know_____

_____

Source # 1 _____

_____

_____

_____

_____

Source # 2 _____

_____

_____

_____

_____

Interesting related facts _____

_____

_____

Key words _____

New questions to research _____

_____

_____

Adapted from Randall, S. N. (1996). Information charts: A strategy for organizing student research. *Journal of Adolescent & Adult Literacy*, 39, 536–542.

9.3 Dialectical Journals

Another method of recording information is to use a dialectical journal. A dialectical journal is a type of two-column journal where information from texts is written on the left side of the page and personal responses are written on the right. Poorman and Wright (2000) recommend dialectical journals for students who are taking notes for a research project.

Directions and Examples

1. Tell students that research papers include two types of writing: information from various sources and personal responses. Students may not realize that they can include their own personal opinions in research papers.

2. Ask students how they currently take notes for their research papers. Some students may have learned how to take notes on index cards, others may type notes on a computer, and still others may have learned different note-taking methods.

3. Tell students that you will be introducing a method of note-taking, called dialectical journals. Explain that dialectical journals are a two-column type of note-taking where the writer copies short excerpts from a source on the left side of the sheet and records a personal response on the right.

4. Explain to students that when they are recording information from sources, they might record summaries, quotations, interesting words or phrases, key information, or questions. These notes should be written on the left side of the page.

5. Tell students that they can record their personal responses on the right, such as comments, thoughts, connections, reflections, and answers to questions. An example of the types of things to write follows.

Dialectical Journals

Text on left	Response on right
Summaries	Your comments
Quotations	Your thoughts
Interesting words or phrases	Connections
Key information	Reflections
Questions	Answers to questions

6. Provide an example from your content area to illustrate the use of a dialectical journal or use the following example.

I was researching tornadoes when I came across a story of a tornado that circled back and hit a town a second time. I wondered whether that was a common occurrence. In my notes, I wrote the question on the left. I wrote a comment about the question. Then as I continued to research, I found that a tornado changing directions so that it hit a place more than once is exceedingly rare.

Question	**Response**
Do tornadoes typically change directions so that they hit a place more than once?	It must be horrible to think you are safe and have a tornado come back again. Fortunately, this is a rare occurrence.

7. Duplicate and distribute copies of the Dialectical Journal that follows for students to use in their research.

Name _____ Date _____

Dialectical Journal

Source of Information	Response

Section
9.4

Synthesizing and Writing Information

Goal To help students synthesize and write information gathered from research

BACKGROUND

When students conduct research, they find information from multiple sources that answers their research questions. This information is carefully selected and organized. Then students need to synthesize into a logical progression of thought the information they have selected. As they synthesize their material, they need to transform their texts into their own thoughts and words.

Synthesizing information from multiple sources is a complex undertaking. As researchers synthesize information from texts, they look for patterns in their material and weave together their knowledge to form new patterns of thought. This integration of information into something new is what makes researching different from paraphrasing or summarizing. Researchers take thoughts and ideas from outside sources and state them in new ways, thereby transforming ideas from many sources into their own words.

The paper or presentation that results from student research should be an integration of what the student knew about the topic before researching, what the student has learned from reading multiple sources, and how the student has transformed the material into new knowledge. Student research should be original in the sense that the products of research projects should indicate that students have learned from their research. Student research does not have to present ideas that no one else has thought of before, but the product of student research should be new learning.

TECHNOLOGY

T
I
P

Writing Assistance Website

The Paradigm Online Writing Assistance is an interactive, menu-driven, online writers' guide distributed over the web. The main menu offers advice on the ways to organize writing.

Paradigm Online Writing Assistance
www.idbsu.edu/english/cguilfor/courses.htm

TEACHING STRATEGY 12

9.4   Writing Frames

Once students have generated a research question, gathered information, and organized that information, they need to synthesize the information into a coherent whole. Students may present their information in a number of ways: they may decide to write a report; they may give an oral presentation; or they may present the material visually. No matter how students choose to present their research, the research needs to be organized so that an audience can follow the relationships among the ideas. To promote a logical flow of ideas, Ryder (1994) suggests using Writing Frames to organize ideas gathered from multiple sources. Writing Frames are grids with categories to organize material into patterns. The patterns that are most commonly used are descriptive, goal, and problem-solution. Teaching students to organize their thoughts into Writing Frames can help them synthesize and write their research findings.

Directions and Examples

1. Tell students that they need to look for relationships among their thoughts, ideas, and information and that they need to organize that information into a logical progression of thought. Explain that when students read or hear ideas that are clearly related, they can more easily understand what the author is saying. Tell students that there are three types of organizational patterns that are commonly used in writing: descriptive, goal, and problem-solution. Have students read their research questions and their notes and decide which type of pattern best fits their purposes. Model how a researcher would make those decisions. Use an example from your content area or use the following example.

    We have been reading about desert regions in our text *States and Regions* (1997) and have asked the following research question: How should the water in the Colorado River be allocated?

Some of the information we found is that the Colorado River is the main source of water for much of Arizona, California, and Nevada. Over 30 years ago, representatives from the three states agreed on the amount of water each state would use. As these states became more inhabited, however, they began to need greater amounts of water. California needed additional water first. That wasn't a problem because there was plenty of water available, and Arizona and Nevada weren't using their shares. Now Arizona and Nevada need their shares of the water.

To solve the problem, some people in California think that less water should be kept in Lake Mead. A group from Nevada thinks a commission should be created to determine how the water should be used. People in Arizona want to keep their supply of water in a water bank to be used as needed. So far the three groups do not agree on ways the water should be allocated.

2. Explain that once students have decided on an organizational pattern they should write their main points on the appropriate Writing Frame. Tell students that Descriptive Frames should be used to present information that has the following relationships: compare-contrast, cause-effect, forms-functions, and advantages-disadvantages. Goal Frames should be used to display organizational structures of material such as goal-plan-action. Problem-Solution Frames should be used when problems and solutions are identified. Use your content area example or the following example to model how to list ideas in a Writing Frame.

Problems	Solutions
The states disagree on water allocation of Colorado River.	Allocate water to three states using former agreement.
Nevada anticipates growing water needs.	Create a commission to make allocation decisions.
California needs more water now.	Store less water in Lake Mead.

3. Have students use their Writing Frame as an organizational structure for their writing or presentation. Blank copies of Writing Frames follow.

Writing Frames

Cause-Effect Writing Frame

Causes	Effects	Locations

Goal-Action Writing Frame

Goals	Actions	Outcomes

Problem-Solution Writing Frame

Problems	Solutions

Based on Ryder, R.J. (1994). Using frames to promote critical writing. *Journal of Reading*, 38, 210–218.

9.4 ▸ Thinking Over-Thinking Through

When students synthesize information they have collected from their research, they need to transform it so that the ideas and words are theirs. Transforming text is the highest level of writing. When students transform text, they integrate new knowledge into their own knowledge base. Thinking Over-Thinking Through (Moffett, 1989) is a strategy that facilitates the complex cognitive act of transforming related information into a writer's own thoughts and words.

 ## Directions and Example

1. Explain to students that, as they synthesize the information they have gathered, they will need to incorporate that information into what they already know about the topic and then transform that knowledge into new thoughts and ideas. When students restate what other authors have said, they are not making a contribution to knowledge about the research topic.

2. Tell students that they can transform texts by using the strategy Thinking Over-Thinking Through. Demonstrate the use of the strategy by employing a content area example or by using the example that follows. Begin by modeling how researchers rehearse their background knowledge and their research question. To model this, make the following comments.

    > I have been researching 20th century Chinese history. My question for this research is: How did The Long March impact the Communist China movement?

    > I know that the Communist Party of China was founded in 1921 and that it became popular early in the 1930s under the leadership of Mao Zedong (formerly Mao Tse-tung). I know that the Nationalist government attacked the Communists who escaped in a 6,000 mile journey, which is now called The Long March.

3. Explain that after they rehearse background knowledge researchers should "Think Over" what they have learned from their research. As students "Think Over" their material, they should read it, reread it, and look for answers to their research questions. Model how to use the "Think Over" strategy, as in the following example.

    > As I read about The Long March, I found that the Communists marched and fought their way from south central China to northwest China. The journey took over a year. They crossed 18 mountain ranges and 62 rivers. As they journeyed, they fought an average of one skirmish a day. As they moved through the countryside, the Communists publicized their cause in meetings and performances. They also redistributed land from the landlords to the peasants. Today The Long March is told and retold in stories and songs.

4. Tell students that after they have reread their notes they need to "Think Through" the topic by thinking about their background knowledge, remembering their research questions, and answering their research questions from the information they have learned. Tell students that in order to transform text they need to answer their research questions, not state facts. Demonstrate how to answer a research question using information. Use an example from your content area or say the following.

My research question is: How did The Long March impact the Communist China movement? I found out about The Long March, and now I need to answer my question. The Communist movement was being overshadowed by the Nationalist government before the journey. After the journey, several things happened. First, the high visibility of The Long March may have turned popular opinion toward Communism. Second, the March happened right before the Chinese had a long war with Japan. The war increased discontent with the Nationalist government. Therefore, the Communists looked like heroes. Finally, the March became one of the important cultural tales of China. That also indicates that it was influential in the Communist movement in China. In summary, The Long March was one of the influential factors in the Communist takeover of China. Taken with the other historical events, it may have been the impetus for the Communists' swift takeover of China.

5. Have students synthesize their information and write their reports using the Thinking Over-Thinking Through strategy. Remember that transforming text is a complex process that students learn over a long period of time and that they will need many opportunities to practice this skill before they are proficient at it.

9.4 ▶ **I-Search**

TEACHING STRATEGY 14

An I-Search paper is an alternative to a traditional research paper. The I-Search paper was devised by Macrorie (1984) to make writing research papers more meaningful to his students. When writing an I-Search paper, students write about their search process as they refine their research questions, locate and evaluate sources, select and organize information, and synthesize their findings. In essence, students tell the story of their research in a narrative paper. Since I-Search papers describe students' research processes as well as answers to research questions, these types of papers are useful tools when planning instruction for future research projects.

Directions and Example

1. Assign a research project that students can complete independently or in groups. (See Section 9.1 for ways to generate research questions.) As students think about their research questions, have them reflect on their process by writing in a journal or on the computer. Demonstrate how you could reflect on the process of generating a research question. Create a question that applies to your content area or use the following example.

I have been watching the National Basketball Association (NBA) playoffs, and I decided that I could make better decisions than some of the coaches make. I have been watching basketball for my entire life, and I know most of the important statistics for players in the entire NBA. I want to use my interest and my knowledge for this research project. I know there are many directions I could take. I think what I want to do most is to create my own all-star basketball team using information I know or can find out about the players.

2. Tell students that as they gather information that answers their research questions they should write both the information they located and how they found it. Model the process of narrating the search for information with an example from your content area or use the example that follows.

> To create my all-star basketball team, I accessed the NBA website at www.nba.com. From that site, I found all sorts of statistics on the players I thought were stars. As I read that information, I decided that I would also ask others for their recommendations for my all-star team. I created a short survey with the names of 20 top players and e-mailed it to other basketball fans I know through the middle school newsgroup k12.ed.chat.junior. When my friends e-mailed me back, I added their ideas to a database that I created. Then I used the Microsoft *Explorapedia—The World of People* CD-ROM to find out additional information about my favorite players. Finally, I went to the library to find books written by and about the players on my top 20 list. I listed most of my information on I-Charts. Finally, I created my all-star team and e-mailed it to the Commissioner of the NBA for consideration. He had an assistant reply by e-mail. The assistant thanked me for my careful work.

3. Explain that, even though students are writing a narrative research paper, their work can be assessed in a manner similar to traditional research papers. Tell students that together you will be creating a rubric to assess their research papers. Divide the class into groups of three or four students. Have students generate components for assessing their research papers or use the following Research Paper Rubric Components list.

4. Use the ideas generated by the students and your own ideas to create a rubric for scoring the I-Search papers. Then use that rubric to assess the research papers. You may also want the students to assess their own papers.

Research Paper Rubric Components

Topic Selection	No				Yes
• Topic is compelling.	1	2	3	4	5
• Topic is realistic.	1	2	3	4	5
• Topic is important.	1	2	3	4	5
• Topic is not overly broad or too narrow.	1	2	3	4	5

Research Question					
• Question has a clear focus.	1	2	3	4	5
• Question addresses an important issue.	1	2	3	4	5
• Question is meaningful.	1	2	3	4	5
• Question is compelling.	1	2	3	4	5

Information Selection					
• Sources are appropriate.	1	2	3	4	5
• Sources are varied.	1	2	3	4	5
• Sources chosen evidence a broad search.	1	2	3	4	5
• Sources were evaluated before use.	1	2	3	4	5

Information Organization					
• Organization is apparent.	1	2	3	4	5
• Organization follows recognizable relationships.	1	2	3	4	5
• Organizational choice is appropriate.	1	2	3	4	5

Synthesizing Information					
• Information answers research question.	1	2	3	4	5
• Information is in student's own words.	1	2	3	4	5
• Information is synthesized in a compelling manner.	1	2	3	4	5

Based on Harvey, S. (1998). *Nonfiction matters: Reading, writing, and research.* York, ME: Stenhouse.

9.4

Multigenre Research Paper

The product of research in schools is often a formal paper. Some educators such as Allen (2001) have suggested that, instead of a formal paper, students write multigenre research papers. A multigenre research paper uses different types of genres in the paper, such as diary entries, bumper stickers, letters, essays, and stories. Allen defines multigenre research papers like this: "The best way I can describe a multigenre paper is to say that each piece in the paper utilizes a different genre, reveals one facet of the topic, and makes its own point" (Allen, 2001, p. 3). Multigenre papers are not organized like traditional papers but are like a collage, which is an artistic expression of thought and meaning.

 ## Directions and Example

1. Tell students that they will be writing a different type of research paper, a multigenre research paper. Review the term genre, if necessary, by explaining that a genre is a type or pattern of writing that is consistent. Give an example such as the following one.

   > You've all read advertisements in magazines. An advertisement is a type of written genre. When you see an advertisement, you know what to expect: you'll see a picture or a name of a product and images or text that try to persuade you to purchase the product. An advertisement is different from, say, a bumper sticker. A bumper sticker is a different type of genre with different text characteristics.

2. Provide students with a list of genres that they could use for their research papers. List several types of genres on the chalkboard or on an overhead transparency such as the ones that follow.

List of Genres

Advice column	Love note
Announcement	Motto
Bedtime story	Mystery
Biographical sketch	Myth
Bumper sticker	Novel
Catalog description	Persuasive speech
Diary	Picture book
Diet	Poem
Epilogue	Poster
Fairy tale	Prescription
Fortune	Realistic fiction
Horoscope	Report
Interview	Short story
Journal entry	Speech
Jump rope rhyme	TV commercial
Legend	Warranty
Letter	Yearbook inscription
List	Yellow pages ad

3. Ask students to add other types of genres to the list. Post the completed list in a visible place in the classroom or duplicate copies for all students.

4. Tell students to use four or more types of genres as part of their research papers. You might also want to require that every student write at least two or three pages of a traditional report as well as using the other types of genres.

Notes and Favorite Strategies

Chapter 10

SUPPORTING READERS WHO STRUGGLE

OVERVIEW

Many students in middle grades through high school have difficulty reading content area textbooks and, as a result, are unable to learn through reading print texts. It is possible to teach content subjects without using print materials, and teachers who have readers who struggle try a variety of methods. They have students learn by listening, through group discussions, by experiences, and by interacting with visual information. Reading, however, is still an important skill in today's society. From reading labels on soup cans to reading signs in an airport, we rely on accessing information from print. Therefore, it is important that you support your students' reading in order to help them learn content by reading.

There are two groups of students who need additional guidance in reading content materials. The first group is comprised of students who do not read well enough to be able to understand difficult text. There are various reasons why students have difficulty reading textbooks: some may not have the cognitive ability to read complicated text; others may have processing difficulties; and still others may have social or emotional difficulties (Fisher, Schumaker, & Deshler, 2002). Some students who struggle with reading may have limited background knowledge in content subjects, or they may have difficulty using their knowledge. Students who struggle may also have difficulty decoding unfamiliar words, or they may have limited vocabularies.

Whatever the reason for their students' problems with reading, teachers need to address these concerns with instructional interventions in authentic contexts (Purcell-Gates, 2001). Students who have had difficulties with reading throughout their schooling tend to view reading as a "dreaded chore" and see themselves as hopeless (Mueller, 2001). While content teachers can't change the past experiences of their students, Ohanian (2001) believes that teachers can change their teaching so that students who struggle with reading have positive experiences with texts and learn that reading can be an enjoyable pursuit. Further, teachers of readers who struggle need to circumspectly address strategy instruction. The number of strategies that you teach in your classroom may overwhelm students who have difficulty with reading. For struggling readers, you should select a small number of strategies to teach and then repeat and review them throughout the year (Sinatra, Brown, & Reynolds, 2002).

A second group of students who need a modified approach when learning from textbooks is comprised of students whose native language is not English. Estimates by the United States Census Bureau (1998) indicate that people of color made up 28% of the nation's population in 2000, and the Bureau predicts that that number will rise to 38% by 2020. The first two decades of the 21st century will also see an increase in the number of students in schools, so demographers predict that by 2020 students of color will make up 46% of the school-age population (Banks & Banks, 2001). More students in content area classes than ever before are unable to speak or read English.

Culturally responsive teaching entails applying two principles to instruction. First, we need to recognize that teaching is a cultural activity (Gay, 2000). American education has relied heavily on traditional white middle class culture. When we recognize that schooling is based on culture, we can develop strategies that empower students to link their home cultures to content knowledge (Au, 2001). The second principle that is crucial to culturally responsive teaching is understanding how to scaffold instruction so that students become successful in the mainstream culture. Delpit (1995) convincingly argues that when teachers do not teach nonmajority students the skills necessary for today's society, they withhold the opportunity for those students to become part of the power structure of the country. Therefore, content area teachers need to support student learning so that students who have difficulty reading English learn the content knowledge in their classes.

TECHNOLOGY

T I P

Internet TESL Journal

On-line journal that offers articles, teaching techniques, lesson plans, and links to issues of interest to Teachers of English Language Learners.

iteslj.org

Linking Experiences to Text

Section

10.1

Goal To help students use their cultural experiences to understand text information

BACKGROUND

All your students, whether they have lived in your community for their entire lives or whether they are new to the area, have different background experiences. Each of us brings our own background to every learning situation. Those backgrounds shape our view of the world, our behavior, and how we interpret events. Each of us also brings assumptions about the reading process, and we bring our individual values about reading to every learning situation. Our experiences influence who we are and how we approach school learning.

Experiences and cultures vary. Some of the experiences, beliefs, and values students have will be similar to yours; others will seem to be in contrast to what you believe. To be a culturally responsive teacher, it is important to honor each student's background, even if it is very different from your own. In an essay entitled *"Buscando Su Voz en Dos Culturas*—Finding Your Voice in Two Cultures," Cline (1998), a teacher, presents a compelling argu-

ment from a parent in her school. The parent believed that keeping her daughter home from school would teach the values of the family's culture: to raise daughters to be good homemakers. This essay sensitively describes the need to honor the parent's wishes and yet provide the daughter with the opportunities that schooling can bring. We need to listen to and honor cultures that may not value schooling, while at the same time scaffolding learning for students in our classes.

As a culturally responsive teacher, you can structure opportunities for students to link their own background knowledge and cultures to the information you are teaching. Teaching school concepts does not invalidate home cultures. By asking students to discuss their cultural experiences and by connecting them to instruction, you can scaffold instruction for students who have cultural backgrounds different from your own.

10.1 ▶ PhOLKS

Students who come from cultures that are not mainstream often have rich funds of knowledge to bring to content area learning (Moll, Amanti, Neff, & Gonzales, 1992). To capitalize on what students know about a topic, Allen, et al. (2002) suggest using the strategy PhOLKS (Photographs of Local Knowledge Sources). This strategy can help students merge their own lives with learning content area material.

Directions and Example

1. Tell students that you value the knowledge they have about your subject area and that you are aware that all students have knowledge about subjects outside of school.

2. Explain to students that what they know about life outside of school can be integrated with the topics you will be studying in class. For example, you might say the following.

   > This week we will be studying environmental pollution. Our textbook does a wonderful job of describing different pollutants, and it also gives ideas for cleaning up the environment. However, much of the discussion in the book focuses on communities that are different from our own. I'd like you to connect where you live with what we're learning in our class.

3. Tell students that you would like them to take photographs of their families, neighborhoods, or communities that relate to the topic, in this case environmental pollution. (If students do not have access to a camera, you can ask them to find photographs in newspapers or magazines.) Give students several days to take the photographs or to find the pictures.

4. During the time students are engaged in taking photographs, have them read the textbook about the topic, using reading and learning strategies that were presented in earlier chapters of this book.

5. Have students bring in their photographs and ask them to write captions of the photos based on the knowledge that they've gained by reading and learning from the textbook. For example, if a student brought in a picture of a neighbor burning garbage, the caption might read: Smoke from fires such as this one contributes to air pollution.

6. Post the photographs and captions on a bulletin board and encourage students to make connections between their lives outside of school and content area learning.

10.1   Oral Histories

English Language Learners (ELL) who have difficulty reading and writing benefit from expressing themselves through oral language. One way to encourage oral language is through oral histories (Power & Hubbard, 2002). Oral histories provide students with experiences using language to discuss something that is familiar to them—their families. However, some ELLs came to this country when they were relatively young and may not know much about their native countries. When discussing oral histories it will be important to reassure students that whatever they know will be a valued aspect of the history, but that they aren't expected to know everything about their countries of origin.

Directions and Example

1. Tell students that you are interested in finding out about their families' backgrounds. Explain that oral histories and memoirs are ways to use oral or written language to describe families.

2. Reassure students that the information you obtain from the oral histories will not be given to other governmental organizations. If a student is concerned that a family member has entered the country without permission, explain that you will not use the oral history to harm his or her family's members.

3. Read an example of a memoir so students understand that you're interested in learning about their lives, their families, their thoughts, and their cultures. Examples of memoirs follow.

    Bunting, E. (1996). *Going home*. New York: Harper Trophy.
    Byars, B. (1996). *The moon and I*. New York: Beach Tree.
    Cisneros, S. (1994). *The house on Mango Street*. New York: Knopf.
    Garza, C.L. (1996). *In my family: En mi Familia*. San Francisco: Children's Book Press.
    Nolen, J. (2001). *In my momma's kitchen*. New York: Harper Trophy.
    Polacco, P. (1995). *Babushka's doll*. New York: Aladdin.
    Wong, J.S. (1996). *A suitcase of seaweed*. New York: Margaret K. McElderry.

4. Pair English Language Learners with students who write and speak both English and the students' native languages. If you don't have any students who can speak the native languages, invite an adult to participate in the oral history project as a translator.

5. Duplicate and distribute the oral history interview questions that follow. Instruct the interviewer to ask all questions in a natural manner, to ask follow-up questions when needed, and to encourage the students to talk freely. An example of a conversation follows.

    Marta: I understand that you came from El Salvador. Why did your family leave their home?

    José: My family left El Salvador because my grandfather and father could not find work.

    Marta: What kind of work did they do in El Salvador?

José: My grandfather is an engineer and my father is a dentist, but someone in the bureaucracy didn't like them, so they couldn't get jobs. They could only work on the plantations picking coffee beans.

Marta: Did they find jobs in the United States?

José: They have to qualify here, and they are working on their qualifications.

6. After students have completed the interviews, have the paired students write a memoir from the oral history. The student more proficient in English should do much of the writing, and the English Language Learner should participate where possible.

7. Use the information in the oral histories and memoirs to guide your teaching, both in teaching language and in teaching content area subjects. For example, you can relate the teaching of government to the students' experiences with government in El Salvador. Make connections between students' experiences and your content area subject whenever possible.

Name _____   Date _____

Oral History Questions

Name of interviewer_____

Name of student being interviewed _____

1. Describe your ethnic background.

2. When did your people first come to this place where we live?

3. Who were the first family members to come here?

4. Where did they come from?

5. Why did they leave their former home?

6. Why did they come to this place?

7. What types of jobs did they get when they arrived?

8. What jobs did they have before?

9. In which wars or struggles did any of your relatives play a role?

10. What are your best memories of your native country?

Adapted from Zemelman, S., Bearden, P., Simmons, Y., & Leki, P. (1999). *History comes home*. Portland, ME: Stenhouse.

10.1 Interactive Journals

Students who struggle with English and reading and who are also English Language Learners face increased difficulty learning in content areas. One way to promote reading and learning for these students is for them to engage in interactive journals in their native languages (Ruiz, Vargas, & Betrán, 2002). An interactive journal is a journal discussion where students write or draw pictures of their ideas and feelings and a teacher or peer responds in the students' native languages.

 Directions and Example

1. Explain to students that they will be writing what they think or feel in their native languages about their lives in relation to their content area. For example, if you teach art, you might say the following.

    I'd like you to write about your experiences with artistic expressions. Perhaps your grandmother weaves cloth or your father makes wood carvings. They may consider these artistic expressions part of their everyday life, especially if the cloth is used to make clothing and the carvings are for your father's boat. However, weavings and carvings can also be considered an art form. Write or draw a picture about the kinds of art that you experience in your lives.

2. Provide students with journals and pens to write. Give them several minutes to think about the topic before they write. Have students who cannot write in either English or their native languages draw a picture and label the picture with words in either language. A sample journal entry follows.

    My mother and older sister spend hours each morning making tortillas. The tortillas they make feed our entire family for the day. Each tortilla is a perfect circle and the stacks are placed in tortilla baskets. The baskets are made from dried grasses near our home. My four sisters make most of the baskets. When the baskets are finished, they embroider designs with brightly colored yarn. We keep baskets in the kitchen for the tortillas, and my sisters sell the rest of the baskets to a shop in a nearby town.

    Making tortillas is an art form. Each one needs to be formed with love and care so that it can nourish the family. The baskets are lovely and when we look at them, we are reminded that we can have beauty anywhere.

3. Read the journal entries and respond to them by scaffolding students' knowledge of your content area. (If you cannot read the students' native language, have another student or a parent read it for you and provide a translation.) For example, consider the following journal response.

    You're right in thinking that a well-made tortilla is an art form. Later in the class we'll talk about still life pictures and look at some famous ones. Perhaps you can set up a still life picture of the tortillas your mother and sister make.

The tortilla baskets sound beautiful! I have seen several basket weaving designs and would like to see the baskets your sisters made. Let's compare your family's baskets to some of the baskets in the basket collection in the town's museum.

4. As you read the students' journal entries, you'll begin to learn more about the cultures of your students. Wherever possible, weave your knowledge of the students' cultures into the curriculum that you teach.

10.1 ➤ Stretch-to-Sketch

TEACHING STRATEGY 4

The Stretch-to-Sketch (Short, Harste, & Burke, 1996) strategy invites students to respond to text through visual representation rather than language. This strategy is useful for students who struggle with reading or who have difficulty writing English. Students do not draw pictures of the passage; rather, they "show what a story means to them by sketching lines, colors, shapes, symbols, or pictures. This visual response is not to be confused with drawing a 'favorite part'" (Whitin, 2002, p. 444).

Directions and Example

1. Tell students that they will be responding to the content of your lesson or a passage they have read through a visual representation. Explain to students that they do not need to draw a picture, but that they can write or draw what they feel.

2. Read a passage from your text or give a lecture about a concept. The first time you have students participate in Stretch-to-Sketch, guide them through the strategy as in the following example.

   Teacher: I just read a passage on electricity. What image do you think of when I say the word *electricity*?

   Student: I think of sparks flying.

   Teacher: What colors are the sparks?

   Student: They're yellow and gold.

   Teacher: What do you feel when you think of this image?

   Student: Energetic and powerful.

   Teacher: What image comes to mind with these feelings?

   Student: I'm picturing waves crashing on the shore.

   Teacher: Draw the images that you've thought of that relate to the word *electricity*.

3. Have students represent their responses with a drawing or sketch. After they are finished, have them share their sketches with the class and describe what they were thinking and feeling as they drew.

4. Use the sketches to help students connect their thoughts, feelings, and visualizations to content area learning. For example, you could use students' images of electricity to further your instruction on the principles of electricity and ways to harness electrical power.

Increasing Fluency in Content Areas

Goal To provide students with language experiences in content areas that increase fluency in and knowledge of the subject

BACKGROUND

Students for whom reading is difficult need many opportunities to experience the thoughts, vocabularies, and ideas of your content area. Because content knowledge is learned through rich, meaningful language, students do not need to be proficient in English to take advantage of learning content material (Au, 2001). Struggling readers can learn from picture books, audiobooks, and easy-to-read texts. These texts scaffold instruction by making information in your content area accessible and by building background knowledge necessary for understanding new concepts.

Some of the experiences that you organize for students who cannot read the book assigned to your content area should be different from those you provide for the rest of your class. In the case of English Language Learners (ELL), these experiences are even more important. Although English Language Learners are able to master conversational English in approximately two years, it takes five or six years for students to be able to learn academic subjects in English (Cummins, 1994). As a result, many immigrants in the past have been unable to take advantage of educational opportunities until the second or third generation has attended school in the new country (Rothstein, 1998). The increasing numbers of ELL and students who cannot read texts that are used at their grade level have caused a demand for different types of content materials. The materials described in this section can assist you in helping students build fluency in your content subject and in supporting students who struggle with reading.

TECHNOLOGY

T I P

Barahona Center for the Study of Books in Spanish for Children and Adolescents

Contains a searchable database of more than 6,000 Spanish books. Headings and descriptions are bilingual.

www.csusm.edu/csb

10.2   TEACHING STRATEGY 5

Using Picture Books

Picture books can support content learning by providing a catalyst for conversations in content areas (Albright, 2002). Picture books are books whose stories can be understood through their illustrations rather than through the text. While picture books often have words or a simple story in text, readers rely on the illustrations to tell the story. Content area teachers can use picture books to facilitate discussions about specific topics. Picture books can draw students into discussions with the language of the content area, which, in turn, develops concepts that form the groundwork for academic understanding and learning.

Directions and Example

1. Identify a topic or a concept that is central to your content area. Choose a picture book that relates to the topic. Present the picture book to the class by reading the title and asking students to form predictions about the contents of the book. You may choose to model a prediction of your own. Guide the students into a discussion about the topic you have identified, as in the following example.

    A central concept in mathematics is that math is used in many life situations, not just in math class. Jon Scieszka's book *Math Curse* (1995) gives examples of math that are found in everyday life. Think about mathematical situations that you have experienced. Here's an example.

    When I drove to school this morning, I had a teachers' meeting at 7:45 a.m. but wanted to stop at a convenience store for coffee before the meeting. I had to estimate whether I would have enough time to leave at my usual time of 7:00 a.m. or whether I would have to leave earlier. It usually takes me 45 minutes to drive to school, park, and get into the building. I estimated that it would take me an additional 10 minutes to stop for coffee. The mathematical formula I used in my head to figure out what time I had to leave was:

X (time to leave) + 55 (minutes driving) = 7:45 a.m. (time to arrive)

I decided I would have to leave the house at 6:50 a.m.

What mathematical situations have you experienced in your lives?

2. Read or show the book to the class, sharing the illustrations. Several times during reading ask students to summarize the story and predict what will come next.

3. After reading, have students retell the story or create their own stories using the text illustrations. Encourage discussion about the central topic of the book. Use as many relevant vocabulary terms from your content area as possible.

4. Selected picture books for several content areas are listed below. Of course, the picture books you select should relate to the specific topic you are teaching.

CONTENT AREA PICTURE BOOKS

Agard, J., & Nichols, G. (1994). *A Caribbean dozen: Poems from Caribbean poets.* Cambridge, MA: Candlewick.

Bridges, R. (1999). *Through my eyes.* New York: Scholastic.

Bunting, E. (1990). *The wall.* New York: Clarion.

Cech, J. (1991). *My grandmother's journey.* New York: Bradbury.

Cherry, L. (1993). *The great Kapok tree.* San Diego: Harcourt Brace.

Cherry, L., & Plotkin, M.J. (1998). *The shaman's apprentice: A tale of the Amazon Rain Forest.* San Diego, CA: Gulliver.

Cordova, A. (1997). *Abuelita's heart.* New York: Simon & Schuster.

Goble, P. (1992). *Love flute.* New York: Bradbury.

Grimes, N. (1999). *My man Blue.* New York: Scholastic.

Hart, T. (1994). *Antarctic diary.* New York: Macmillan/McGraw-Hill.

Hoffman, M. (1991). *Amazing Grace.* New York: Dial.

Jordan, M., & Jordan, T. (1995). *Angel Falls: A South American journey.* New York: Kingfisher.

Keller, L. (2000). *Open wide, tooth school inside.* New York: Henry Holt.

Martin, J. (1998). *Snowflake Bentley.* Boston: Houghton Mifflin.

Tarbescu, E. (1998). *Annushka's voyage.* New York: Clarion.

Williams, S.A. (1992). *Working cotton.* San Diego: Harcourt Brace.

10.2 ▶ Choral Reading

TEACHING STRATEGY 6

Choral Reading is a strategy to help students develop fluency. Choral reading is simply having students read aloud short passages, poems, or plays together. Scala (2001) recommends choral reading for struggling readers and English Language Learners in all subjects, including content area subjects. Scala believes that choral reading helps students learn to enjoy the material they are learning, builds community, and is an outlet for creative expression.

Directions and Examples

1. Tell students that they will be reading a passage aloud together in a strategy called choral reading. Explain that choral reading is much like singing in a chorus except the group will read together rather than sing together.

2. Identify a short passage, poem, or play that contains important concepts for your subject area. If you have students who speak Spanish and English, you might select a poem from one of the anthologies that print both the Spanish and the English versions of the poem such as the books that follow. Or if students speak only Spanish, consider using only the Spanish texts (Schon, 2002).

   > Alarcon, F.X. (1997). *Laughing tomatoes and other spring poems*. San Francisco: Children's Book Press.
   >
   > Herrera, J.F. (1995). *Calling the doves*. San Francisco: Children's Book Press.
   >
   > Medina, J. (1999). *My name is Jorge: On both sides of the river*. Honesdale, PA: Boyds Mills Press.

3. Read the passage or poem for the students, clarifying pronunciation of words and explaining new vocabulary terms.

4. Have students read the passage or poem with you at least once.

5. Divide the class into groups of three or four students. Ask students to read the passage or poem together aiming for a fluent rendition of the piece. Explain that they should decide which words to emphasize and that this emphasis can alter the meaning of the text.

6. After giving students time to practice, have each group read or recite the piece for the class. When all of the groups have performed, discuss the meaning of the passage or poem with the entire group, helping students make connections to the concepts you are teaching.

7. The books you might use for choral reading would also be appropriate to read aloud to the class. A list of books appropriate for choral reading and/or reading aloud follows.

Asch, F. (1998). *Cactus poems*. Orlando, FL: Harcourt Brace.

Baylor, B. (1986). *I'm in charge of celebrations*. New York: Aladdin.

Bouchard, D. (1995). *If you're not from the prairie*. New York: Aladdin.

Buchholz, Q. (1999). *The collector of moments*. New York: Farrar, Straus & Giroux.

Cherry, L. (1992). *A river ran wild*. Orlando, FL: Harcourt Brace.

DeFina, A.A. (1997). *When a city leans against the sky*. Honesdale, PA: Boyds Mills Press.

George, K.O. (1998). *Old elm speaks: Tree poems*. New York: HarperCollins.

Heard, G. (1997). *Creatures of earth, sea, and sky*. Honesdale, PA: Boyds Mills Press.

Hendershot, J. (1992). *In coal country*. New York: Knopf.

Hopkins, L.B. (1993). *Extra innings*. Orlando, FL: Harcourt Brace.

Livingston, M.C. (1986). *Earth songs*. New York: Scholastic.

London, J. (1998). *Hurricane!* New York: Lothrop, Lee & Shepard.

MacLachlan, P. (1983). *Through grandpa's eyes*. New York: Harper Trophy.

Mann, E. (2000). *Machu Picchu: The story of the amazing Incas and their city in the clouds*. New York: Mikaya.

Polacco, P. (2001). *The keeping quilt*. New York: Aladdin.

Van Allsburg, C. (1990). *Just a dream*. Boston: Houghton Mifflin.

Xiong, L. (1996). *The gift: The Hmong New Year*. Los Angeles: Pacific Asia Press.

Yolan, J. (1987). *Owl moon*. New York: Philomel.

TECHNOLOGY TIP

Orbis Pictus Award for Outstanding Nonfiction for Children

Lists award winners of books suitable for reading aloud or choral reading.

www.ncte.org

TEACHING STRATEGY 7

Using Adapted and Easy-to-Read Texts

One of the goals of your teaching is to help struggling readers learn content material. Although it is preferable that students read the texts that are commonly used at your grade level, there are many instances when students cannot read such texts. Some books are too complex, have language that is too complicated, or are too conceptually dense for students. You can choose other ways to teach content material. However, students need to be able to learn from reading books in your content area. Using adapted or easy-to-read texts is a strategy that takes into account the reading abilities of students and still provides them with the opportunity to read content area material.

Adapted or easy-to-read texts are books that are of interest to middle or high school students; however, they are written at a lower reading level. (See Appendix B for information on readability formulas.) Many of the texts you use for regular classroom instruction have a readability that would approximate your grade level. For example, if you teach eighth grade, many of the textbooks in your grade level would be texts that are written at or near the eighth-grade reading level. Because some students will have difficulty reading books written at this level, consider using materials written at a lower grade level. Books written at a lower grade level usually present the type of concepts you want to teach but are written with language that is easier to read. Students who are unable to read texts assigned to your grade level can learn information in your content area from adapted or easy-to-read texts. Reading these books can increase background knowledge, fluency, and content knowledge.

Directions and Example

1. Identify topics or concepts in your subject area that form the foundation of a unit of study. Choose books in that area that are adapted or written at a lower reading level. If possible, compare samples from the two texts, the original version and an adapted or easy-to-read version. Examples of passages from an original text and an adapted version follow.

"The Purloined Letter"
Original first paragraph

At Paris, just after dark one gusty evening in the autumn of 18—, I was enjoying the twofold luxury of meditation and a meerschaum, in company with my friend C. August Dupin, in his little back library, or book-closet, *au troisième,* No. 33, *Rue Dunot, Faubourg St. Germain.* For one hour at least we had maintained a profound silence; while each, to any casual observer might have seemed intently and exclusively occupied with the curling eddies of smoke that oppressed the atmosphere of the chamber. For myself, however, I was mentally discussing certain topics which had formed matter for conversation between us at an earlier period of the evening; I mean the affair of the Rue Morgue, and the mystery attending the murder of Marie Roget. I looked upon it, therefore, as something of a coincidence, when the door of our apartment was thrown open and admitted our old acquaintance, Monsieur G—, the Prefect of the Parisian police.

▶ From Poe, E.A. (1974). The purloined letter. In *The American tradition in literature* (pp. 844–860). New York: Grosset & Dunlap.

"The Purloined Letter"
Adapted version

In Paris, just after dark one gusty evening in the fall, I was enjoying a smoke with my friend, August Dupin. We were sitting silent in his little back library, busy with thought, watching the curling smoke waves.

I was thinking of that affair of the Rue Morgue, which Dupin had solved for the police. In fact, I was thinking of the Prefect of Police when the door of our apartment opened and he walked in.

▶ From Poe, E.A. (1979). The purloined letter. In *An Edgar Allan Poe reader: Adapted classic tales* (pp. 45–56). New York: Globe.

2. After reading a passage from the original version and comparing it with the sample from the adapted or easy-to-read version, determine whether the easier version would be appropriate for your instructional purposes. Some questions that might guide your decision follow.

   - Is the original version too difficult for the students to read?
   - Does the vocabulary in the original version preclude easy reading?
   - Would the language in the original version make reading difficult?
   - Are the sentences in the original version long and difficult?
   - Would students be able to read the adapted version, or is it too difficult?
   - Does the adapted version accurately represent the contents of the original version?
   - Would the adapted version accomplish my teaching goals?

3. Use comprehension strategies to teach the adapted or easy-to-read texts. After students have read the selection, to supplement your teaching, you might choose to read passages from the book assigned to your subject and grade level. When students build background knowledge in a subject, they are sometimes able to read more difficult text. See the following box for sources of adapted and easy-to-read texts.

Sources for Adapted and Easy-to-Read Texts

Cobblestone
800-821-0115
Easy-to-read science and social studies materials, reading levels 4–9.

EMC Paradigm
800-328-1452
Adapted classics, reading levels 4–8.

Jamestown Publishers
800-621-1918
Easy-to-read and adapted short stories, science, and social studies materials, reading levels 2–6.

Kids In Between
800-481-2799
Easy-to-read science, math, history, life skills, and reading materials, reading levels 3–8.

Phoenix Learning Resources
800-221-1274
Easy-to-read science, math, language, reading, and social studies materials, reading levels K–6.

Rosen Publishing
800-237-9932
Easy-to-read science, life skills, and career materials, reading levels 3–8.

Steck-Vaughn
800-531-5015
Easy-to-read science, literature, social studies, math, and health materials, reading levels 3–9.

Wieser Educational
800-880-4433
Adapted classics, reading levels 3–8.

10.2   Using Audiobooks

TEACHING STRATEGY 8

Certain types of literature are more easily understood by listening to audiobooks than by reading (Baskin & Harris, 1995). Audiobooks, or books on tape, are another way to encourage fluency in content areas. When students are unable to read difficult texts, they can benefit from listening to portions of them. For example, Mark Twain's writing is entertaining and has themes that are usually of interest to middle and high school students. Twain's writing, however, is difficult to read because of his heavy use of dialect. Students who have difficulty reading the book can listen to it, learning the content in a different way. Audiobooks are especially useful for texts that have complex or archaic language, texts that are written in a dialect different from the one students speak, and texts with complicated plots. As students listen to audiobooks, they learn about the genre that you are teaching, increase their background knowledge in the subject, and increase their knowledge of the vocabulary of your content area. Students from cultures that value storytelling are likely to derive special benefit from using audiobooks.

Directions

1.   Choose an audiobook that supports learning in your content area. Many publishers now produce their texts on audiotapes, videodisks, or CD-ROMs.

2.   Tell students that they will be hearing a book rather than reading it. Explain that listening is an alternative means of experiencing text and will help them learn the content material.

3.   Use appropriate prereading strategies that link the students' backgrounds to the text.

4.   Play sections or chapters of the audiobook. After 10 to 15 minutes of listening, stop the tape and have students discuss what they have heard. You may continue playing the entire audiobook, or you may choose to play only a few segments. After you have finished playing the audio selection, extend comprehension by using strategies found in Section 10.3

Sources for Audiobooks		
Audio Bookshelf 207-845-2100	Listening Library 800-243-4504	Recorded Books 800-638-1304

Making Texts Comprehensible

Goal — To help struggling readers and English Language Learners construct meaning from textbook passages

BACKGROUND

For many of the concepts that you teach, there will be no picture books, easy-to-read texts, or audiobooks available. For those situations, you will need to use your textbook as a basis for instruction. Books can be important learning tools for your students, even if the books are difficult for students to read. One of the ways to support students who cannot read textbooks easily is to modify the texts through the use of reading strategies. As you teach strategies that help make texts comprehensible, remember that students who struggle with reading need to have strategies demonstrated explicitly (Duffy, 2002), and students who are not proficient in English need to have concepts taught clearly and concisely (García, 2000).

10.3 Group Frame

TEACHING STRATEGY 9

A Group Frame (Brechtel, 1992) is an excellent strategy to modify content area texts in English or in students' home languages. Students who have difficulty reading selections in English may have a rich knowledge about a subject that you are teaching. A Group Frame allows students to access their background knowledge about a topic and to express that knowledge in English or in their home languages. After students have created their own passages, teachers are able to scaffold that knowledge by adding information from the content area textbook. The roles of the teacher in a Group Frame are to help students clarify their initial understandings of concepts before reading and to provide an English translation if necessary. The text is then comprehensible for students, who now should be able to read portions of the age-appropriate textbook.

Directions and Example

1. Choose a topic from a textbook about which students have some background knowledge or preliminary thoughts. Develop a question about the main topic. Explain that you will be asking a question about a chapter the students will eventually be reading. An example follows.

    Before teaching students about the properties of a circle in a geometry text, ask the following question:

    What is a circle?

2. Divide the class into groups of three or four students. If you have students who share a home language, group those students together. Have students read the question and write several sentences about the topic. Tell students that they can write the sentences in English or in their home languages.

3. After the students have finished, ask them to share their sentences. Write the sentences on a chalkboard or an overhead transparency as in the following example.

Dictation from Students (English)	Dictation from Students (Spanish)
A circle is one of the shapes.	Un círculo es una de la figuras.
A circle consists of points around another point.	Un círculo consiste en puntos alrededor de otro punto.
The middle is a point with a name.	El centro consiste de un punto nombrado.
A point from the middle to the edge is a radius.	Un punto del medio hasta el filo se conoce como un radio.

4. Explain that these initial sentences represent the knowledge that students bring to the topic. Tell students that their background knowledge is necessary for learning new information. Explain that you will revise the sentences to closer represent school learning about the subject. Revise the sentences in English or in the students' home languages as in the following example.

Revised sentences (English)	Revised sentences (Spanish)
A circle is a geometric shape.	Un círculo es una figura geométrica.
A circle is the set of all points in a plane at a given distance from a given point in the plane.	Un círculo es el grupo de todos los puntos en un plano que estan a una cierta distancia de un punto dado en el plano.
The given point is the center of the circle. The circle is named by its point.	El punto dado es el centro del círculo. El círculo es nombrado por su punto.
A segment from a point on the circle to the circle's center is called the radius.	Un segmento de un punto en el círculo hasta el centro del círculo es llamado el radio.

5. Have students read the revised sentences and use these sentences to learn the content information. After students have fluently read the sentences they have created, ask them to find the passage from which the ideas were taken. Read the passage aloud to the students, pointing to the areas of similarities and differences between the student-generated ideas and the ideas from the text. Note specific examples where the students' knowledge exceeded the information presented in the textbook.

6. Ask students, in partners or independently, to read selected portions of the textbook. Explain that they already know much of the material from reading the sentences they have created but that they should practice reading textbooks commonly used in class. Encourage students to read the text selection several times.

TEACHING STRATEGY 10
10.3 Zooming In and Zooming Out

Struggling readers often need strategies to help them read text more closely and to learn new concepts. One strategy that helps all readers, especially struggling readers, read more closely yet learn how concepts fit in a larger context is a strategy called Zooming In and Zooming Out (Harmon & Hedrick, 2001). Zooming In and Zooming Out is a map that guides students into thinking about concepts they are reading about in content area texts.

 Directions and Example

1. Identify a passage or chapter that contains a concept that is crucial to learning a larger topic.

2. Make a transparency of the example of Zooming In and Zooming Out or create one of your own.

3. Tell students that they will be learning a strategy that helps them comprehend texts more deeply. Explain to students that they will need to think about the meanings of a new term as it relates to their reading but also as it relates to a larger topic.

4. Divide the class into groups of three or four students. Duplicate and distribute a blank copy of the strategy to each group.

5. Have students write down the term in the center of the map. In this case, the term is *plate tectonics*.

6. Have students read the passage and find three or more important facts about the term and two or more facts of lesser importance. Explain to students that as they are searching for facts they are "zooming in" on the term.

7. Discuss with the entire class the facts that were generated by the groups. As students begin to understand the term, ask them what they would not expect from plate tectonics. Have students list these ideas on the right side of the map.

8. Then tell the class that they need to think about plate tectonics in a larger sense: that they need to "zoom out." Have groups of students generate what plate tectonics are similar to and have them list other related ideas and concepts. These items should be listed in the zooming out portion of the map.

9. Tell students that they should now have a good understanding of plate tectonics and that they should understand how the concept fits the topic of the earth's crust. Then have students develop a summary statement in their groups and write that statement at the bottom of the map.

10. Provide continued support with the Zooming In and Zooming Out strategy until students feel comfortable working independently. Use the strategy occasionally when students need to focus in on a new concept or term.

Zooming In

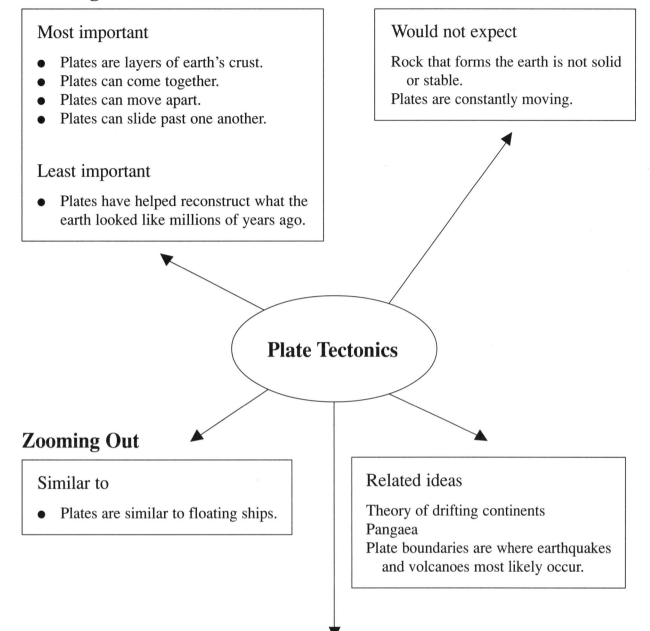

Most important

- Plates are layers of earth's crust.
- Plates can come together.
- Plates can move apart.
- Plates can slide past one another.

Least important

- Plates have helped reconstruct what the earth looked like millions of years ago.

Would not expect

Rock that forms the earth is not solid or stable.
Plates are constantly moving.

Plate Tectonics

Zooming Out

Similar to

- Plates are similar to floating ships.

Related ideas

Theory of drifting continents
Pangaea
Plate boundaries are where earthquakes and volcanoes most likely occur.

Summary Statement

Plate tectonics refer to layers of rock that move slowly. There are seven major plates in the world. Plates continue to move. The plate's movements help explain the history of earth and predict its shape.

Zooming In and Zooming Out

Zooming In

Most important Least important	Would not expect

Zooming Out

Similar to	Related ideas

Summary Statement

10.3 ► THIEVES

THIEVES (Manz, 2002) is a strategy for previewing textbooks that encourages students to "sneak into the chapter and 'steal' information ahead of time" (p. 434). Students who use THIEVES are guided to identify the elements of the passage that should be considered before reading. Struggling readers who use this strategy have accessed their background knowledge and have begun to prepare their minds for learning new information.

Direction and Example

1. Tell students that you are going to describe a strategy that they should use before reading textbook material. Emphasize that they will be following the steps of THIEVES before reading.

2. Write the steps for THIEVES on a chalkboard or on an overhead transparency. Tell students that you will be guiding them through the steps for the first few times they use the strategy. For some groups of students, you might introduce one or two steps during a single class period. The steps for THIEVES follow.

   T = Title
   H = Headings
   I   = Introduction
   E = Every first sentence in a paragraph
   V = Visuals and vocabulary
   E = End-of-chapter questions
   S = Summary

3. To begin THIEVES, tell students that they will be reading the title of the book, chapter, or passage. Remind students that they have been taught to read the title before beginning to read the text but that many readers omit this important step. Then guide students by asking the following questions.

   - What is the title?
   - What do I already know about this topic?
   - How does this topic relate to the preceding chapter?
   - Does this title express a point of view?
   - What do I think I will be reading about?

4. After students have read and thought about the title, have them read the headings in the chapter. Explain to students that headings are the skeleton of the chapter, the organization of the material. As students think about headings, ask the following questions.

   - How do the headings shape my thinking about the topic?
   - What are the topics of the passages under the headings?
   - How can I turn this heading into a question?

5. The introduction of a chapter usually provides a preview of the content that will be covered. If goals or objectives are placed in the introduction, tell students to preface each one with the words, "I will. . . ." For example, "I will learn about the causes of the Gulf War." In addition, help students think about the content of the introduction by asking the following questions.

- Is there an opening, perhaps italicized?
- Does the first paragraph introduce the chapter?
- What does the introduction let me know about the topic?
- Do I know anything about this topic already?

6. After students have read the introduction, direct them to read every first sentence in the paragraphs of the chapter. If the chapter is lengthy, have them read every first sentence in the paragraphs under the main headings.

7. Often students skip over the visuals (photographs, maps, charts, and so on) and vocabulary. Explain to students that they can glean much important information from reading the graphic aids and paying close attention to new vocabulary terms. As students preview the chapter, ask the following questions.

- Are there photographs, drawings, maps, charts, and/or graphs?
- What can I learn from these visual depictions?
- How do the captions help me understand the topic?
- Is there a list of key vocabulary terms?
- Are vocabulary terms highlighted in bold type or any other manner?
- Do I know the meanings of the key terms?
- Can I figure out the meanings of the terms from the sentences?

8. Many books include questions at the end of every chapter. If that is the case, have students skim through questions that end the chapter. Tell students that by reading the questions at the chapter's end they can sharpen their focus during reading. As students read end-of-chapter questions, ask students the following questions.

- What do the questions ask?
- What information do they earmark as important?
- What information do I learn from the questions?
- How can I remember these questions as I read?

9. Some chapters also include summaries at the end of the chapters. Tell students that they should read the summary before reading the entire chapter. Also explain to students that summaries do not include all of the details of the chapters so they shouldn't be substituted for reading the entire chapters.

10. As students become familiar with THIEVES, ask fewer of the probing questions and encourage students to ask the questions themselves. Another alternative is to have students work in groups as they follow the steps for THIEVES and to discuss their ideas with their peers.

11. Remind students to use THIEVES before each reading assignment and provide students with time to complete the strategy before reading.

TEACHING STRATEGY 12

Noting, Interacting, Prioritizing, Summarizing (NIPS)

10.3

NIPS (Herrell & Jordan, 2002) is a small group strategy that helps struggling readers comprehend informational text by combining several important reading and study strategies into one. Although NIPS is a valuable strategy for all students, it's especially useful for readers who have a difficult time understanding how the reading process works in its entirety.

Directions and Example

1. Tell students that you will be introducing a strategy that combines four strategies. Explain to students that while reading they need to make use of multiple strategies and that NIPS combines strategies that are useful when reading content area texts.

2. Write NIPS in a vertical line on the chalkboard or on an overhead transparency as is shown below.

   N = Note-taking
   I = Interacting
   P = Prioritizing
   S = Summarizing

3. Provide students with a passage from a common text such as a content area textbook. Have them read the passage silently and take notes as they read.

4. After students have taken notes, divide the class into groups of three or four students and have them share the notes they have taken. As students interact, encourage them to add to their notes as meaning of the passage becomes clearer.

5. After all of the group members have shared their notes, distribute copies of the NIPS sheet that follows.

6. Explain to students that they need to prioritize the information that they learned. Tell students that prioritizing means to place information in order of importance. Encourage students to make decisions as a group.

7. The final step in NIPS is to summarize the text. Tell students that summarization means to provide a short synopsis of what they have learned. Then have students develop a group summarization on the NIPS sheet.

8. Invite groups of students to share their lists of priorities and summarizations with the entire class. As students share their ideas, encourage them to listen to each other and to modify or adapt their own understandings when appropriate.

NIPS

N = Note-taking
I = Interacting
P = Prioritizing
S = Summarizing

List of Priorities

1. _____

2. _____

3. _____

4. _____

5. _____

6. _____

7. _____

8. _____

Summarization _____
_____
_____
_____
_____
_____
_____

APPENDIX A

PROFESSIONAL ORGANIZATIONS

Note: The information below is subject to change, especially telephone numbers.

Art

National Art Education Association (NAEA)
1916 Association Dr.
Reston, VA 20191-1590
Phone: (703) 860-8000
FAX: (703) 860-2960
E-mail: naea@dgs.dgsys.com
Website: http://www.naea-reston.org
Publications: *Art Education, Studies in Art Education*

Business

National Business Education Association (NBEA)
1914 Association Dr.
Reston, VA 20191-1596
Phone: (703) 860-8300
FAX: (703) 620-4483
E-mail: nbea@nbea.org
Website: http://www.nbea.org
Publication: *Business Education Forum*

English

National Council of Teachers of English (NCTE)
1111 West Kenyon Rd.
Urbana, IL 61801-1096
Phone: (217) 328-3870
    (800) 369-6283

FAX: (217) 328-0977
Website: http://www.ncte.org
Publications: *English Leadership Quarterly, English Publication, NOTES Plus, Research in the Teaching of English, Language Arts, English Journal*

International Reading Association (IRA)
800 Barksdale Rd.
P.O. Box 8139
Newark, DE 19714-8139
Phone: (302) 731-1600
(800) 336-READ
FAX: (302) 731-1057
E-mail: 74673.3646@compuserve.com
Website: http://www.reading.org
Publications: *Reading Research Quarterly, Reading Today, Journal of Reading, The Reading Teacher, Lectura y vida* (Spanish), *Thinking Classroom*

Foreign Languages

American Association of Teachers of French (AATF)
Mail Code 4510
Southern Illinois University
Carbondale, IL 62901-4510
Phone: (618) 536-5571
FAX: (618) 453-3253
E-mail: @uiuc.edu
Website: http://www.frenchteachers.org/
Publications: *AATF National Bulletin, French Review*

American Association of Teachers of German
   (AATG)
112 Haddontowne Ct. #104
Cherry Hill, NJ 08034
Phone: (609) 795-5553
FAX: (609) 795-9398
E-mail: AATG@compuserve.com
Website: http://www.aatg.org
Publications: *American Association of Teachers of German Newsletter, Die Unterrichtspraxis: For the Teaching of German*

American Association for the Teachers of Spanish
   and Portuguese (AATSP)
c/o Dr. Lynn A. Sandstedt, Executive Director
University of Northern Colorado
210 Butler Hancock
Greeley, CO 80639
Phone: (970) 351-1090
FAX: (970) 351-1095
E-mail: lsandste@bentley.UnivNorthCo.edu
Website: http://www.aatsp.org
Publication: *Hispania*

The American Classical League (ACL)
Miami University
Oxford, OH 45056
Phone: (513) 529-7741
FAX: (513) 529-7742
E-mail: American Classical League@muohio.edu
Website: http://www.umich.edu/~acleague
Publication: *Classical Outlook*

American Council on the Teaching of Foreign
   Languages (ACTFL)
6 Executive Plaza
Yonkers, NY 10701
Phone: (914) 963-8830
FAX: (914) 963-1275
E-mail: actflhg@aol.com
Website: http://www.actfl.org
Publications: *Foreign Language Annals, ACTFL Newsletter*

Teachers of English to Speakers of Other
   Languages (TESOL)
1600 Cameron St., Suite 300
Alexandria, VA 22314-2751
Phone: (703) 836-0774
FAX: (703) 836-6447 or (703) 836-7864
E-mail: tesol@tesol.org
Website: http://www.tesol.org
Publications: *TESOL Journal, TESOL Quarterly*

Mathematics

National Council of Teachers of Mathematics
   (NCTM)
1906 Association Dr.
Reston, VA 20191-1593
Phone: (703) 620-9840
(800) 235-7566
FAX: (703) 476-2970
Website: http://www.nctm.org
Publications: *Mathematics Teacher, MCTN News Bulletin, Mathematics Teaching in the Middle School, Teaching Children Mathematics, Journal for Research in Mathematics*

Music

Music Educators National Conference (MENC)
1806 Robert Fulton Dr.
Reston, VA 20191
Phone: (703) 860-4000
(800) 336-3768
FAX: (888) 275-6362
E-mail: mbmenc@aol.com
Website: http://www.menc.org
Publications: *Music Educators' Journal, Journal of Music Teacher Education, Journal of Research in Music Education, Teaching Music, General Music Today*

Music Teachers National Association (MTNA)
441 Vine St., Suite 505
Cincinnati, OH 45202-2814
Phone: (513) 421-1420
FAX: (513) 421-2503
E-mail: MTNadmin@aol.com
Website: http://www.mtna.org
Publication: *American Music Teacher*

Physical Education

American Alliance for Health, Physical Education,
   Recreation and Dance (AAHPERD)
1900 Association Dr.
Reston, VA 20191
Phone: (703) 476-3400
(800) 213-7193
FAX: (703) 476-9527
E-mail: evp@aahperd.org
Website: http://www.aahperd.org

Publications: *AAHPERD Update, Health Educator, Journal of Physical Education, Recreation and Dance, Journal of Health Education*

Science

National Science Teachers Association (NSTA)
1840 Wilson Blvd.
Arlington, VA 22201-3000
Phone: (703) 243-7100
FAX: (703) 243-7177
E-mail: publicinfo@NSTA.org
Website: http://www.nsta.org
Publications: *The Science Teacher, Science and Children, Science Scope, Quantum*

National Association of Biology Teachers (NABT)
11250 Roger Bacon Dr. #19
Reston, VA 20190-5202
Phone: (703) 471-1134
(800) 406-0775
FAX: (703) 435-5582
E-mail: NABTer@aol.com
Website: http://www.nabt.org
Publications: *National Association of Biology Teachers—News and Views, The American Biology Teacher*

Social Studies

National Council for the Social Studies (NCSS)
3501 Newark St. N.W.
Washington, DC 20016-3167
Phone: (202) 966-7840
FAX: (202) 966-2061
E-mail: ncss@ncss.org
Website: http://www.ncss.org
Publications: *Social Education, The Social Studies Professional, Social Studies Middle School Journal, Theory & Research in Social Education*

Technology

Association for the Advancement of Computing in Education (AACE)
P.O. Box 2966
Charlottesville, VA 22902
Phone: (804) 973-3987
FAX: (804) 978-7449
Website: www.aace.org

Publications: *Journal of Computers in Mathematics and Science Teaching, Information Technology and Childhood Education Annual, Educational Technology Review, Journal of Interactive Learning Research*

International Society for Technology in Education (ISTE)
1787 Agate St.
Eugene, OR 97403-1923
Website: http://www.iste.org
Publications: *The Computing Teacher, Journal of Research on Computing in Education, Telecommunications in Education*

General Professional Organizations

Association for Supervision and Curriculum Development (ASCD)
1250 N. Pitt St.
Alexandria, VA 22314-1453
Phone: (703) 549-9110
(800) 933-2723
FAX: (703) 299-8631
Website: http://www.ascd.org
Publications: *Educational Leadership, Journal of Curriculum & Supervision*

Council for Exceptional Children (CEC)
1920 Association Dr.
Reston, VA 20191-1589
Phone: (703) 620-3660
FAX: (703) 264-9494
Website: http://www.cec.sped.org
Publications: *Teaching Exceptional Children, Exceptional Child Education Resources, Exceptional Children*

National Association for Gifted Children (NAGC)
1707 L St. N.W., Suite 550
Washington, DC 20036
Phone: (202) 785-4268
Website: http://www.nagc.org
Publication: *Gifted Child Quarterly*

National Middle School Association (NMSA)
2600 Corporate Exchange Dr., Suite 370
Columbus, OH 43231
Phone: (614) 895-4730
(800) 528-6672
FAX: (614) 895-4750
Website: http://www.nmsa.org
Publications: *Middle School Journal, High Strides, Middle Ground*

Notes and Favorite Strategies

APPENDIX B

ASSESSING TEXT DIFFICULTY USING READABILITY FORMULAS

Overview

Texts have varying degrees of difficulty. Consider the following sentence from a chemistry book: "An electron carries exactly one unit of negative charge and its mass is 1/1840 the mass of a hydrogen atom." Note the length of the sentence, the vocabulary, and the concepts. These are some of the factors that can have an impact on the difficulty of a text. Such factors are called text variables. In addition to text variables, students vary in their reading levels, motivation, and interests. These factors, called reader variables, can also influence the difficulty of a text for a particular student. Some text and reader variables are shown below.

Text Variables

- vocabulary difficulty
- sentence complexity
- format
- typography
- content
- literary form
- literary style
- concept load
- cohesiveness

Reader Variables

- reading level
- motivation
- background knowledge
- interests
- engagement
- intellectual abilities
- topic familiarity

Harris and Hodges (1995, p. 203) note that "text and reader variables interact in determining the readability of any piece of reading material for any individual reader." Readability refers to estimating the difficulty of understanding a particular text by using some of the text variables listed above. One way to estimate the difficulty of a text is to use a readability formula. It can provide one answer to the question "How difficult is this text or book?"

The first true readability formula was probably published in 1923 (Klare, 1963). Since that time, over 100 readability formulas have been published. A few of the more popular formulas include the Dale-Chall, Spache, Flesch, and Fry. Below is a step-by-step procedure for using the Fry readability graph to make a readability calculation by hand.

Procedure for Using the Fry Readability Formula

1. Randomly select three sample passages and count out exactly 100 words in each, starting with the beginning of a sentence. Count proper nouns, initialisms, and numerals.

2. Count the number of sentences in the 100 words, estimating the length of the fraction of the last sentence to the nearest one-tenth.

3. Count the total number of syllables in the 100-word passage. If you don't have a hand counter available, an easy way is to simply put a mark above every syllable over one in each word. When you get to the end of the passage, count the number of marks and add 100. Small calculators can also be used as counters by pushing numeral 1 and then pushing the + sign for each word or syllable when counting.

4. Enter the graph with *average* sentence length and *average* number of syllables; then plot a dot where the two lines intersect. The area where the dot is plotted will give you the approximate grade level.

5. If a great deal of variability is found in the syllable count or sentence count, putting more samples into the average is desirable.

6. A word is defined as a group of symbols with a space on either side; thus, *Joe, IRA, 1945,* and & are each one word.

7. A syllable is defined as a phonetic syllable. Generally, there are as many syllables as vowel sounds. For example, *stopped* is one syllable and *wanted* is two syllables. When counting syllables for numerals and initialisms, count one syllable for each symbol. For example, *1945* is four syllables. *IRA* is three syllables, and & is one syllable.

Fry's Graph for Estimating Readability

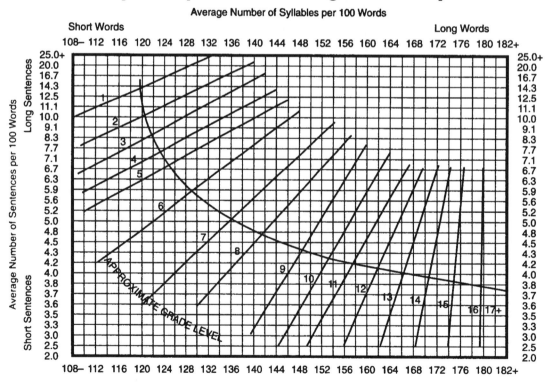

Adapted from Fry, E. (1968). A readability formula that saves time. *Journal of Reading, 11,* 513–516 and Fry, E. (1977). Fry's readability graph: Clarifications, validity, and extension to level 17. *Journal of Reading, 21,* 242–252. The Fry Readability Graph is not copyrighted. Reproduction is permitted. From Susan Davis Lenski, Mary Ann Wham, and Jerry L. Johns, *Reading & Learning Strategies: Middle Grades through High School,* 2nd Edition. Copyright © 2003 by Kendall/Hunt Publishing Company (1-800-247-3458, ext. 4 or 5). May be reproduced for noncommercial purposes.

A Few Notes on the Fry Readability Technique

1. It is recommended that a minimum of three samples from a book be evaluated for readability. The procedure is exemplified below.

	Sentences Per 100 Words	Syllables Per 100 Words
100-word sample, page 5	4.0	148
100-word sample, page 89	3.6	152
100-word sample, page 163	5.0	144
	12.6÷3=4.2	444÷3=148

By plotting the average sentence length (4.2) and the average number of syllables (148) on the graph, the readability is tenth grade. If great variability is encountered in either sentence length or in the syllable count for the three samples, randomly select several more passages and average them before plotting the results on the graph. Be certain to note that the book has uneven readability.

2. The readability estimate is probably accurate within a grade level.

3. The readability estimate is given in terms of a grade level. There are **no** fine distinctions such as 6.1, 7.4, or 11.2. Readability is given in terms of whole grade levels.

4. The Fry formula correlated highly with the Dale-Chall (r=.94) and the Flesch (r=.96) readability formulas.

Example of Applying the Fry Readability Formula

Below is one sample from an algebra text. At least two additional samples should be evaluated, but they are not included in the example.

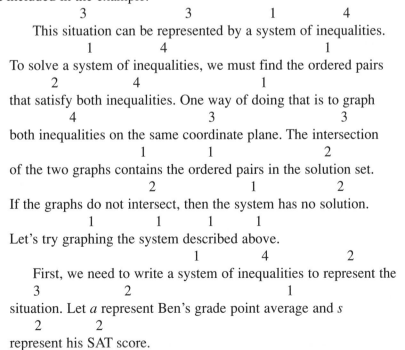

       3   3   1   4
This situation can be represented by a system of inequalities.
    1   4   1
To solve a system of inequalities, we must find the ordered pairs
   2   4   1
that satisfy both inequalities. One way of doing that is to graph
  4   3   3
both inequalities on the same coordinate plane. The intersection
      1   1   2
of the two graphs contains the ordered pairs in the solution set.
      2   1   2
If the graphs do not intersect, then the system has no solution.
    1   1   1   1
Let's try graphing the system described above.
        1   4   2
First, we need to write a system of inequalities to represent the
  3   2   1
situation. Let *a* represent Ben's grade point average and *s*
  2   2
represent his SAT score.

5. Count the number of sentences. The number of sentences is 8.

6. Count the number of syllables. Begin with 100 (the number of words) and then put numerals above each word for *every syllable over one*. The number of syllables is 164.

7. Enter the graph with the sentence length (8) and number of syllables (164). Place a dot where the two lines intersect. The area where the dot is plotted gives the approximate grade level. In this example, the approximate grade level is 10.

Using Personal Computers to Estimate Text Readability

With the growing use of personal computers, it is not necessary to go through the laborious process of doing the numerous calculations by hand to estimate the readability of a piece of writing. You can type in selections from the text or piece of writing, and the computer does the rest. Word-processing programs will often contain one or more readability formulas. In addition, separate readability programs can be purchased; these programs are usually available in Macintosh and Windows versions. Listed below are two readability programs that can be used with personal computers.

Readability Master 2000 (Brookline Books, P.O. Box 1047, Cambridge, MA 02238) 800-666-BOOK.

Macintosh and Windows versions of this program give scores based on the New Dale-Chall Readability Formula, the Spache Readability Formula, and the Fry Readability Formula.

Readability Calculations (Micro Power & Light Company, 8814 Sanshire Avenue, Dallas, TX 75231) 214-553-0105.

Macintosh and Windows versions of these programs provide scores for seven or eight readability formulas, depending on the particular program purchased. Among the readability formulas are Fry, Flesch, FOG, and Dale-Chall.

The same sample from the high school mathematics book was used with Readability Calculations. Below is the resulting printout (with numerals added on the left).

1. Sample Begins: This situation can be
   Sample Ends: and *s* represent his SAT score.

2. Words: 100
3. Syllables: 159
4. Syllables (Fry): 161
5. Monosyllabic Words: 75
6. Words of 3 or More Syllables: 21
7. Difficult Words (FOG): 18
8. Difficult Words (Dale-Chall): 31
9. Sentences: 8

10. Syllables/Word: 1.60
11. Syllables/100 Words: 159.01
12. Syllables/100 Words (Fry): 161.01
13. Monosyllabic Words/100 Words: 75.01
14. Polysyllabic Words/100 Words: 21.01
15. Sentences/100 Words: 8.01
16. Words/Sentence: 12.51

17. % of Words Not on the Dale-Chall List: 31.01
18. Dale-Chall Grade Level: 9.2
19. Flesch Reading Ease: 59.64
20. Flesch Grade Level: 8.0
21. FOG Grade Level: 12.2
22. Powers* Grade Level: 6.0
23. SMOG Grade Level: 11.9
24. FORCAST Grade Level: 8.8

Item 1 refers to the first and last phrases of the sample passage selected for the readability analysis. Items 2 through 17 refer to various aspects of the sample passage. These items are used in calculating the various readability formulas. For example, items 2, 4, and 8 are used in the Fry readability formula. The computer program automatically uses this information and plots the resulting grade level on a graph that can be viewed on the computer screen. In this case, the result is grade 10—the same level we obtained by doing the formula by hand. (The difference in the syllable count is due to the abbreviation SAT. The computer program apparently considered SAT one word; however, initialisms should be counted as one syllable for each symbol. In addition, *average* can be counted as two or three syllables.)

Items 18 through 24 present the resulting readabilities for the passage when six different readability formulas were used. Note that the results range from grade 6.0 to 12.2. It is not unusual for formulas to give different results for the same passage. Because readability formulas use information in different ways, the results should be expected to vary. Making sense of the results is the challenge.

The Powers-Sumner-Kearl Formula is used most often for the primary grades, and it seldom produces scores above the seventh-grade level. The FOG and SMOG results are often higher than other formulas because they estimate the reading level necessary to understand the material completely. Based on experience, we recommend that the results from the Fry and Dale-Chall formulas be given priority in estimating text difficulty. Both formulas are widely known and used. In addition, the Dale-Chall formula has been updated recently (Chall & Dale, 1995). If the results of these formulas applied to the mathematics textbook sample are considered, the grade levels are 9.2 and 10. Such results, when based on several samples from the text, suggest that the book may be suitable for students who read at the ninth-grade and tenth-grade levels.

Some Things to Remember about Readability Formulas

When using readability formulas, there are some general cautions to keep in mind. With regard to text variables, readability formulas do not consider graphic aids (charts, diagrams, photographs, etc.) that may help make the text more readable. Instead, the formulas rely heavily on word length and sentence length, thereby assuming that shorter words and sentences are easier to understand than longer words and sentences. There are times, however, when a longer sentence that links two thoughts may actually be more comprehensible than the same information in two shorter sentences. Remember that all readability formulas are only estimates of a book's difficulty, and the resulting grade-level score is not exact. Vacca and Vacca (1999, p. 155) use the term "rubber ruler" to describe readability formulas because the scores are estimates of text difficulty, not absolute levels. A Fry readability estimate, for example, is probably accurate within plus and minus one grade level.

Readability formulas can often be a useful beginning point for assessing text difficulty. The results of formulas should also be combined with qualitative judgments of the text's overall organization, other physical features of the text (e.g., photographs, illustrations, charts, headings, marginal notes), and your students' backgrounds.

Perhaps the most important reader variable to remember is that readability formulas do not directly consider the student who will read the book. A student's interests and motivation, for example, are generally not taken into account. All the reader variables listed above are important in determining the suitability of a book for a student or class.

Notes and Favorite Strategies

REFERENCES

Professional Material Cited in This Book

Afflerbach, P. (1996). Engaged assessment of engaged readers. In L. Baker, P. Afflerbach, & D. Reinking (Eds.), *Developing engaged readers in school and home communities* (pp. 191–214). Mahwah, NJ: Erlbaum.

Agnew, M.L. (2000). DRAW: A motivational reading comprehension strategy for disaffected readers. *Journal of Adolescent & Adult Literacy, 43*, 574–576.

Albright, L.K. (2002). Bringing the Ice Maiden to life: Engaging adolescents in learning through picture book read-alouds in content areas. *Journal of Adolescent & Adult Literacy, 45*, 418–428.

Alexander, P.A., & Murphy, P.K. (1998). Profiling the differences in students' knowledge, interest, and strategic processing. *Journal of Educational Psychology, 90*, 435–447.

Allen, C.A. (2001). *The multigenre research paper*. Portsmouth, NH: Heinemann.

Allen, J., Fabregas, V., Hankins, K.H., Hull, G., Labbo, L., Lawson, H.S., Michalove, B., Piazza, S., Piha, C., Sprague, L., Townsend, S., & Urdanivia-English, C. (2002). PhOLKS lore: Learning from photographs, families, and children. *Language Arts, 79*, 312–322.

Allington, R.L. (1994). The schools we have: The schools we need. *The Reading Teacher, 48*, 14–29.

Alvermann, D.E. (1991). The discussion web: A graphic aid for learning across the curriculum. *The Reading Teacher, 45*, 92–99.

Alvermann, D.E., & Hagood, M.C. (2000). Critical media literacy: Research, theory, and practice in "new times." *Journal of Educational Research, 93*, 193–205.

Anderson, T.H., & Armbruster, B.B. (1984). Studying. In P.D. Pearson (Ed.), *Handbook of reading research* (Vol. I) (pp. 657–679). New York: Longman.

Antes, R.L. (1989). *Preparing students for taking tests* (Fastback 291). Bloomington, IN: Phi Delta Kappa Educational Foundation.

Armbruster, B.B. (1984). The problem of inconsiderate text. In G. Duffy, L. Roehler, & J. Mason (Eds.), *Comprehension instruction* (pp. 128–143). New York: Longman.

Armbruster, B.B. (1986, December). *Using frames to organize expository text*. Paper presented at the annual meeting of the National Reading Conference, Austin, TX.

Artley, A.S. (1975). Teaching word meaning through context. *Elementary English Review, 20*, 68–74.

Au, K.H. (1993). *Literacy instruction in multicultural settings*. Fort Worth, TX: Harcourt Brace Jovanovich.

Au, K.H. (2001). What we know about multicultural education and students of diverse backgrounds. In R.F. Flippo (Ed.), *Reading researchers in search of common ground* (pp. 101–117). Newark, DE: International Reading Association.

Baker, L. (1991). Metacognition, reading, and science education. In C.M. Santa & D.E. Alvermann (Eds.), *Science learning: Processes and applications* (pp. 2–13). Newark, DE: International Reading Association.

Baker, L., & Brown, A. (1984). Metacognitive skills and reading. In P.D. Pearson (Ed.), *Handbook of reading research* (Vol. I) (pp. 353–394). New York: Longman.

Banks, J.A., & Banks, C.A.M. (2001). *Multicultural education: Issues and perspectives* (4th ed.). New York: John Wiley.

Baskin, B.H., & Harris, K. (1995). Heard any good books lately? The case for audiobooks in the secondary classroom. *Journal of Reading, 38,* 372–376.

Baumann, J.F., & Kame'enui, E.J. (1991). Research on vocabulary instruction: Ode to Voltaire. In J. Flood, J. Jensen, D. Lapp, & J. Squire (Eds.), *Handbook of research on teaching the English language arts* (pp. 604–632). New York: Macmillan.

Bean, T.W. (2000). Reading in the content areas: Social constructivist dimensions. In M.L. Kamil, P. B. Mosenthal, P. D. Pearson, & R. Barr (Eds.), *Handbook of reading research* (Vol. III) (pp. 629–644). Mahwah, NJ: Erlbaum.

Bean, T.W., Sorter, J., Singer, H., & Frazee, C. (1986). Teaching students how to make predictions about events in history with a graphic organizer plus options guide. *Journal of Reading, 29,* 739–745.

Beck, I.L., McKeown, M.G., Hamilton, R.L., & Kucan, L. (1997). *Questioning the author: An approach for enhancing student engagement with text.* Newark, DE: International Reading Association.

Berglund, R.L., & Johns, J.L. (1983). A primer on uninterrupted sustained silent reading. *The Reading Teacher, 36,* 534–539.

Blachowicz, C.L.Z. (1986). Making connections: Alternatives to the vocabulary notebook. *Journal of Reading, 29,* 643–649.

Blachowicz, C.L.Z., & Fisher, P. (2000). Vocabulary instruction. In M.L. Kamil, P.B. Mosenthal, P.D. Pearson, & R. Barr (Eds.), *Handbook of reading research* (Vol. III) (pp. 503–523). Mahwah, NJ: Erlbaum.

Blachowicz, C.L.Z., & Ogle, D. (2001). *Reading comprehension: Strategies for independent learners.* New York: Guilford.

Block, C.C., & Pressley, M. (Eds.). (2002). *Comprehension instruction: Research-based best practices.* New York: Guilford.

Bloome, D., & Egan-Robertson, A. (1993). The social construction of intertextuality in classroom reading and writing lessons. *Reading Research Quarterly, 28,* 304–333.

Bourdieu, P., & Passeron, J.C. (1977). *Reproduction in education, society and culture.* Los Angeles: Sage.

Braun, J.A., Fernlund, P., & White, C.S. (1998). *Technology tools in the social studies curriculum.* Wilsonville, OR: Franklin, Beedle.

Brechtel, T. (1992). *Bringing the whole together: An integrated whole-language approach for the multilingual classroom.* San Diego: Dominic Press.

Brophy, J. (1986). Teacher influences on student achievement. *American Psychologist, 41,* 1069–1077.

Brown, A.L. (1997). Transforming schools into communities of thinking and learning about serious matters. *American Psychologist, 52,* 399–414.

Brozo, W.G., & Simpson, M.L. (1995). *Readers, teachers, learners: Expanding literacy in secondary schools* (2nd ed.). Columbus, OH: Merrill.

Brozo, W.G., & Simpson, M.L. (1999). *Readers, teachers, learners: Expanding literacy across the content areas* (3rd ed.). Upper Saddle River, NJ: Prentice-Hall.

Buehl, D. (2001). *Classroom strategies for interactive learning* (2nd ed.). Newark, DE: International Reading Association.

Carr, K.S., Buchanan, D.L., Wentz, J.B., Weiss, M.L., & Grant, K.J. (2001). Not just for the primary grades: A bibliography of picture books for secondary content teachers. *Journal of Adolescent & Adult Literacy, 45*, 146–153.

Caverly, D.C., Mandeville, T.F., & Nicholson, S.A. (1995). PLAN: A study-reading strategy for informational text. *Journal of Adolescent & Adult Literacy, 39*, 190–199.

Cervetti, G., Pardales, M.J., & Damico, J.S. (2001, April). A tale of differences: Comparing the traditions, perspectives, and educational goals of critical reading and critical literacy. *Reading Online, 4*(9). Available: *http://www.readingonline.org/articles/art=index.asp?HREF=/articles/cervetti/index.html*

Chall, J.S., & Dale, E. (1995). *Readability revisited*. Cambridge, MA: Brookline Books.

Clewell, S., & Haidemeneous, J. (1982, April). *Organizational strategies to increase content area learning: Webbing, pyramiding, and think sheets*. Paper presented at the annual meeting of the International Reading Association, Chicago, IL.

Cline, Z. (1998). *Buscando su voz en dos culturas*—Finding your voice in two cultures. *Phi Delta Kappan, 79*, 699–702.

Collins, J.L. (1998). *Strategies for struggling writers*. New York: Guilford.

Comber, B. (2001). Classroom explorations in critical literacy. In H. Fehring & P. Green (Eds.), *Critical literacy* (pp. 90–102). Newark, DE, and South Australia, Australia: International Reading Association and Australian Literacy Educators' Association.

Countryman, J. (1992). *Writing to learn mathematics*. Portsmouth, NH: Heinemann.

Crawley, S.J., & Mountain, L. (1995). *Strategies for guiding content reading* (2nd ed.). Boston: Allyn and Bacon.

Cronin, D. (2000). *Click, clack, moo: Cows that type*. New York: Simon & Schuster.

Cummins, J. (1994). The acquisition of English as a second language. In K. Spangenberg-Urbschat & R. Pritchard (Eds.), *Kids come in all languages: Reading instruction for ESL students* (pp. 36–62). Newark, DE: International Reading Association.

Cunningham, J.W. (1982). Generating interactions between schemata and text. In J.A. Niles & L.A. Harris (Eds.). *New inquiries in reading research and instruction*. Thirty-First yearbook of the National Reading Conference (pp. 42–47). Rochester, NY: National Reading Conference.

Cunningham, P.M. (1978). Decoding polysyllabic words: An alternative strategy. *Journal of Reading, 21*, 608–614.

Cunningham, P.M. (2000a). Big words for big kids: The morphology link to meaning and decoding. In K.D. Wood & T.S. Dickinson (Eds.), *Promoting literacy in grades 4–9: A handbook for teachers and administrators* (pp. 282–294). Boston: Allyn and Bacon.

Cunningham, P.M. (2000b). *Phonics they use* (3rd ed.). New York: Longman.

Cunningham, P.M., & Hall, D.P. (1994). *Making big words: Multilevel, hands-on spelling and phonics activities*. Torrance, CA: Good Apple.

Cunningham, P.M., & Hall, D.P. (1997). *Making more big words: Multilevel, hands-on phonics and spelling activities*. Parsippany, NJ: Good Apple.

Curtin, S. (1984). Aging in the land of the young. In *Literature* (pp. 389–391). Evanston, IL: McDougal, Littell.

Dana, C., & Rodriguez, M. (1992). TOAST: A system to study vocabulary. *Reading Research and Instruction, 31*, 78–84.

Davis, S.J. (1990). Applying content study skills in co-listed reading classrooms. *Journal of Reading, 33*, 277–281.

Deighton, L.C. (1959). *Vocabulary development in the classroom.* New York: Teachers College Press.

Delpit, L. (1992). Education in a multicultural society: Our future's greatest challenge. *Journal of Negro Education, 61*, 237–249.

Delpit, L. (1995). *Other people's children: Cultural conflict in the classroom.* New York: New Press.

Denner, P.R., & McGinley, W.J. (1986). The effects of story-impressions as a prereading/writing activity on story comprehension. *Journal of Educational Research, 82*, 320–326.

Donahue, P.L., Voelkl, K.E., Campbell, J.R., & Mazzeo, J. (1999). *NAEP 1998 reading report card for the nation and states* (NCES 1999500). Washington, DC: National Center for Educational Statistics, U.S. Department of Education.

Dowhower, S. (1989). Repeated reading: Research into practice. *The Reading Teacher, 42,* 502–507.

Duffy, G.G. (2002). The case for direct explanation of strategies. In C.C. Block & M. Pressley (Eds.), *Comprehension instruction: Research-based best practices* (pp. 28–41). New York: Guilford.

Duke, N. (2000). 3–6 minutes per day: The scarcity of informational texts in first grade. *Reading Research Quarterly, 35*, 202–224.

Eanet, M., & Manzo, A.V. (1976). REAP—A strategy for improving reading/writing/study skills. *Journal of Reading, 19*, 647–652.

Ehrenreich, B. (2001). *Nickel and dimed: On (not) getting by in America.* New York: Metropolitan Books.

Fehring, H., & Green, P. (Eds.). (2001). *Critical literacy.* Newark, DE, and South Australia, Australia: International Reading Association and Australian Literacy Educators' Association.

Ferroli, L., Beaver, K., Hagan, R., & Moriarty, A. (2000, March). *Interventions for getting middle school readers caught up.* Presentation at the 32nd Illinois Reading Council Conference, Springfield, IL.

Ferroli, L., Cooper, L., & Zimmerman, L. (2001, March). *The compare-contrast procedure in word identification.* Presentation at the 33rd Illinois Reading Council Conference, Springfield, IL.

Fisher, J.B., Schumaker, J.B., & Deshler, D.D. (2002). Improving the reading comprehension of at-risk adolescents. In C.C. Block & M. Pressley (Eds.), *Comprehension instruction: Research-based best practices* (pp. 351–364). New York: Guilford.

Flavell, J.H. (1981). Cognitive monitoring. In W.P. Dickson (Ed.), *Children's oral communication skills* (pp. 35–60). New York: Academic.

Flood, J., & Lapp, D. (1995). Broadening the lens: Toward an expanded conceptualization of literacy. In K.A. Hinchman, D.J. Leu, & C.K. Kinzer (Eds.), *Perspectives on literacy research and practice* (pp. 1–16). Chicago: National Reading Conference.

Fractor, J.S., Woodruff, M.C., Martinez, M.G., & Teale, W. (1993). Let's not miss opportunities to promote voluntary reading: Classroom libraries in the elementary school. *The Reading Teacher, 46*, 476–484.

Frank, A. (1995). *Anne Frank: Diary of a young girl.* New York: Doubleday.

Freire, P. (1985). *The politics of education: Culture, power, and liberation.* New York: Bergin & Garvey.

Fry, E. (1968). A readability formula that saves time. *Journal of Reading, 11*, 513–516.

Fry, E. (1978). *Skimming and scanning*. Providence, RI: Jamestown.

Galica, G.S. (1991). *The blue book: A student's guide to essay examinations*. New York: Harcourt Brace Jovanovich.

García, G.E. (2000). Bilingual children's reading. In M.L. Kamil, P.B. Mosenthal, P.D. Pearson, & R. Barr (Eds.), *Handbook of reading research* (Vol. III) (pp. 813–834). Mahwah, NJ: Erlbaum.

Gay, G. (2000). *Culturally responsive teaching: Theory, research & practice*. New York: Teachers College Press.

Gee, J.P. (1993). What is literacy? In L.M. Cleary & M.D. Linn (Eds.), *Linguistics for teachers* (pp. 257–265). New York: McGraw-Hill.

Gere, A.R. (Ed.). (1985). *Roots in the sawdust: Writing to learn across the disciplines*. Urbana, IL: National Council of Teachers of English.

Gilbert, P. (2001). (Sub)versions: Using sexist language practices to explore critical literacy. In H. Fehring & P. Green (Eds.), *Critical literacy: A collection of articles from the Australian Literacy Educators' Association* (pp. 75–83). Newark, DE, and South Australia, Australia: International Reading Association and Australian Literacy Educators' Association.

Gillet, J., & Kita, M.J. (1979). Words, kids, and categories. *The Reading Teacher, 32*, 538–546.

Gipe, J.P. (1979). Investigating techniques for teaching word meanings. *Reading Research Quarterly, 14*, 624–644.

Grant, R. (1993). Strategic training for using text headings to improve students' processing of content. *Journal of Reading, 36*, 482–488.

Graves, M.F., & Prenn, M.C. (1986). Costs and benefits of various methods of teaching vocabulary. *Journal of Reading, 29*, 596–602.

Graves, M.F. (2000). A vocabulary program to complement and bolster a middle-grade comprehension program. In B.M. Taylor, M.F. Graves, & P. Van den Broek (Eds.), *Reading for meaning: Fostering comprehension in the middle grades* (pp. 116–135). Newark, DE: International Reading Association.

Graves, M.F., Juel, C., & Graves, B. (1998). *Teaching reading in the 21st century*. Boston: Allyn and Bacon.

Green, P. (2001). Critical literacy revisited. In H. Fehring & P. Green (Eds.), *Critical literacy: A collection of articles from the Australian Literacy Educators' Association* (pp. 7–14). Newark, DE: International Reading Association and Norwood, South Australia: International Reading Association and Australian Literacy Educators' Association.

Guthrie, J.T. (1996). Educational contexts for engagement in literacy. *The Reading Teacher, 49*, 432–445.

Guthrie, J.T., & Knowles, K.T. (2001). Promoting reading motivation. In L. Verhoeven & C.E. Snow (Eds.), *Literacy and motivation: Reading engagement in individuals and groups* (pp. 159–176). Mahwah, NJ: Erlbaum.

Guthrie, J.T., & Wigfield, A. (2000). Engagement and motivation in reading. In M.L. Kamil, P.B. Mosenthal, P.D. Pearson, & R. Barr (Eds.), *Handbook of reading research* (Vol. III) (pp. 403–422). Mahwah, NJ: Erlbaum.

Haddix, M.P. (2000). *Among the hidden*. New York: Simon & Schuster.

Haggard, M.R. (1986). The vocabulary self-collection strategy: Using student interest and world knowledge to enhance vocabulary growth. *Journal of Reading, 29*, 634–642.

Harmon, J.M., & Hedrick, W.B. (2001). Zooming in and zooming out for better vocabulary. *Middle School Journal, 32*, 26–29.

Harris, T.L., & Hodges, R.E. (1995). *The literacy dictionary: The vocabulary of reading and writing.* Newark, DE: International Reading Association.

Hartman, D.K. (1995). Eight readers reading: The intertextual links of proficient readers reading multiple passages. *Reading Research Quarterly, 30,* 520–561.

Harvey, S. (1998). *Nonfiction matters: Reading, writing, and research.* York, ME: Stenhouse.

Hayes, D.A. (1989). Helping students GRASP the knack of writing summaries. *Journal of Reading, 33,* 96–101.

Hemmrich, H., Lim, W., & Neel, K. (1994). *Primetime!* Portsmouth, NH: Heinemann.

Herber, H.L. (1978). *Teaching reading in content areas* (2nd ed.). Englewood Cliffs, NJ: Prentice-Hall.

Herrell, A., & Jordan, M. (2002). *50 active learning strategies for improving reading comprehension.* Columbus, OH: Merrill Prentice Hall.

Hidi, S., & Baird, W. (1988). Strategies for increasing text-based interest and students' recall of expository text. *Reading Research Quarterly, 23,* 465–483.

Hoffman, J.V. (1979). The intra-act procedure for critical reading. *Journal of Reading, 22,* 605–608.

Hoffman, J.V. (1992). Critical reading/thinking across the curriculum: Using I-Charts to support learning. *Language Arts, 69,* 121–127.

Holdaway, D. (1979). *The foundations of literacy.* New York: Ashton Scholastic.

Hunt, L.C., Jr. (1970). The effect of self-selection, interest, and motivation upon independent, instructional, and frustrational levels. *The Reading Teacher, 24,* 146–151, 158.

International Reading Association & National Council of Teachers of English. (1996). *Standards for the English language arts.* Newark, DE, and Urbana, IL: Author.

Irwin, J., & Baker, I. (1989). *Promoting active reading comprehension strategies.* Englewood Cliffs, NJ: Prentice-Hall.

Ivey, G. (1999). Reflections on teaching struggling middle school readers. *Journal of Adolescent & Adult Literacy, 42,* 372–381.

Ivey, G., & Broaddus, K. (2000). Tailoring the fit: Reading instruction and middle school readers. *The Reading Teacher, 54,* 68–78.

Ivey, G., & Broaddus, K. (2001). "Just plain reading": A survey of what makes students want to read in middle school classrooms. *Reading Research Quarterly, 36,* 350–377.

Jackson, A.W., & Davis, G.A. (2000). *Turning points 2000: Educating adolescents in the 21st century.* New York: Teachers College Press.

Jacobson, J.M. (1998). *Content area reading: Integration with the language arts.* New York: Delmar.

Johns, J.L., & Lenski, S.D. (2001). *Improving reading: Strategies and resources* (3rd ed.). Dubuque, IA: Kendall/Hunt.

Johnson, D.D., & Pearson, P.D. (1984). *Teaching reading vocabulary* (2nd ed.). New York: Holt.

Kame'enui, E.J., Dixon, S.W., & Carnine, R.C. (1987). Issues in the design of vocabulary instruction. In M.G. McKeown & M.C. Curtis (Eds.), *The nature of vocabulary acquisition* (pp. 129–145). Hillsdale, NJ: Erlbaum.

Kempe, A. (2001). No single meaning: Empowering students to construct socially critical readings of the text. In H. Fehring & P. Green (Eds.), *Critical literacy* (pp. 40–57). Newark, DE and South Australia, Australia: International Reading Association and Australian Literacy Educators' Association.

Klare, G.R. (1963). *The measurement of readability*. Ames, IA: Iowa State University Press.

Klemp, R.M. (1994). Word storm: Connecting vocabulary to the student's database. *The Reading Teacher, 48*, 282.

Klemp, R.M., Hon, J.E., & Short, A.A. (1993). Cooperative literacy in the middle school: An example of a learning-strategy based approach. *Middle School Journal, 24*, 19–27.

Koss, A.G. (2000). *The girls*. New York: Penguin Putman.

Laffey, D.G., & Laffey, J.L. (1986). Vocabulary teaching: An investment in literacy. *Journal of Reading, 29*, 650–656.

Langer, J.A. (1981). From theory to practice: A prereading plan. *Journal of Reading, 25*, 152–156.

Langer, J.A. (2001). Literature as an environment for engaged readers. In L. Verhoeven & C.E. Snow (Eds.), *Literacy and motivation: Reading engagement in individuals and groups* (pp. 177–194). Mahwah, NJ: Erlbaum.

Lenski, S.D. (2001). Intertextual connections during discussions about literature. *Reading Psychology, 22*, 313–335.

Lenski, S.D., & Johns, J.L. (1997). Patterns of reading-to-write. *Reading Research & Instruction, 37*, 15–38.

Lenski, S.D., & Nierstheimer, S.L. (2002). Strategy instruction from a sociocognitive perspective. *Reading Psychology, 23*, 127–143.

Lewkowicz, N.K. (2000). On the question of teaching decoding skills to older students. In D.W. Moore, D.E. Alvermann, & K.A. Hinchman (Eds.), *Struggling adolescent readers: A collection of teaching strategies* (pp. 189–196). Newark, DE: International Reading Association.

Luke, A., O'Brien, J., & Comber, B. (2001). Making community texts objects of study. In H. Fehring & P. Green (Eds.), *Critical literacy* (pp. 112–123). Newark, DE, and South Australia, Australia: International Reading Association and Australian Literacy Educators' Association.

Lyman, H.B. (1997). *Test scores and what they mean* (6th ed.). Boston: Allyn and Bacon.

Macrorie, K. (1984). *Searching writing*. Upper Montclair, NJ: Boynton/Cook.

Mannix, D. (1984). Woman without fear. In *Literature* (pp. 325–333). Evanston, IL: McDougal, Littell.

Manz, S.L. (2002). A strategy for previewing textbooks: Teaching readers to become THIEVES. *The Reading Teacher, 55*, 434–435.

Manzo, A.V. (1969). The ReQuest procedure. *Journal of Reading, 13*, 123–126, 163.

Manzo, A.V., & Manzo, U.C. (1990a). *Content area reading*. New York: Macmillan.

Manzo, A.V., & Manzo, U.C. (1990b). Note cue: A comprehension and participation training strategy. *Journal of Reading, 33*, 608–611.

Marzano, R.J. (1992). *A different kind of classroom: Teaching with dimensions of learning*. Washington, DC: Association for Supervision and Curriculum Development.

Mathison, C. (1989). Activating student interest in content area reading. *Journal of Reading, 33*, 170–176.

McCombs, B.L., & Barton, M.L. (2001). Motivating secondary school students to read their textbooks. In J.A. Rycik & J.L. Irvin (Eds.), *What adolescents deserve: A commitment to students' literacy learning* (pp. 72–81). Newark, DE: International Reading Association.

McKenna, M.C., & Robinson, R.D. (1990). Content literacy: A definition and implications. *Journal of Reading, 34*, 184–186.

McKenna, M.C., & Robinson, R.D. (1997). *Teaching through text: A content literacy approach to content area reading* (2nd ed.). New York: Longman.

McLaughlin, M. (2000). Inquiry: The key to critical and creative thinking in the content areas. In M. McLaughlin & M. Vogt (Eds.), *Creativity and innovation in content area teaching* (pp. 31–54). Norwood, MA: Christopher-Gordon.

McNamera, T., Miller, D., & Bransford, J. (1991). Mental models and reading comprehension. In R. Barr, M.L. Kamil, P. Mosenthal, & P.D. Pearson (Eds.), *Handbook of reading research* (Vol. II) (pp. 490–511). White Plains, NY: Longman.

Moffett, J. (1989). *Bridges: From personal writing to the formal essay*. Berkeley, CA: Center for the Study of Writing.

Moll, L.C., Amanti, D., Neff, D., & Gonzales, N. (1992). Funds of knowledge for teaching. *Theory into Practice, 31*, 132–141.

Moore, D.W., Bean, T.W., Birdyshaw, D., & Rycik, J.A. (1999). Adolescent literacy: A position statement. *Journal of Adolescent & Adult Literacy, 43*, 97–112.

Moore, D.W., & Moore, S.A. (1986). Possible sentences. In E.K. Dishner, T.W. Bean, J.E. Readence, & D.W. Moore (Eds.), *Reading in the content areas: Improving classroom intruction* (2nd ed.) (pp. 174–179). Dubuque, IA: Kendall/Hunt.

Moore, D.W., Moore, S.A., Cunningham, P.M., & Cunningham, J.W. (1994). *Developing readers and writers in the content areas K–12*. New York: Longman.

Morgan, R.F., Meeks, J.W., Schollaert, A., & Paul, J. (1986). *Critical reading/thinking skills for the college student*. Dubuque, IA: Kendall/Hunt.

Mueller, P.N. (2001). *Lifers: Learning from at-risk adolescents readers*. Portsmouth, NH: Heinemann.

Nagy, W.E., & Anderson, R.C. (1984). How many words are there in printed school English? *Reading Research Quarterly, 19,* 304–330.

Nagy, W.E., & Herman, P.A. (1987). Breadth and depth of vocabulary knowledge: Implications for acquisition and instruction. In M.G. McKeown & M.E. Curtis (Eds.), *The nature of vocabulary acquisition* (pp. 19–35). Hillsdale, NJ: Erlbaum.

Nagy, W.E., & Scott, J.A. (2000). Vocabulary processes. In M.L. Kamil, P.B. Mosenthal, P.D. Pearson, & R. Barr (Eds.)*, Handbook of reading research* (Vol. III) (pp. 269–284). Mahwah, NJ: Erlbaum.

National Assessment of Educational Progress. (1997). *Report in brief: NAEP 1996 trends in academic progress*. Washington, DC: Author.

National Reading Panel (NRP). (2000). *Teaching children to read: An evidence-based assessment of the scientific research literature on reading and its implications for reading instruction*. Washington, DC: National Institute of Child Health and Human Development.

Nist, S.L., & Simpson, M.L. (1989). PLAE, a validated study strategy. *Journal of Reading, 33*, 182–186.

Nourie, B.L., & Lenski, S.D. (1998). The (in)effectiveness of content area literacy instruction for secondary preservice teachers. *The Clearing House, 71*, 372–374.

Ogle, D.M. (1986). K-W-L: A teaching model that develops active reading of expository text. *The Reading Teacher, 39,* 564–570.

Ogle, D.M., & Blachowicz, C.L.Z. (2002). Beyond literature circles: Helping students comprehend informational texts. In C.C. Block & M. Pressley (Eds.), *Comprehension instruction: Research-based best practices* (pp. 259–274). New York: Guilford.

Ohanian, S. (2001). *Caught in the middle: Nonstandard kids and a killing curriculum.* Portsmouth, NH: Heinemann.

Oldfather, P., & Wigfield, A. (1996). Children's motivations for learning. In L. Baker, P. Afflerbach, & D. Reinking (Eds.), *Developing engaged readers in school and home communities* (pp. 89–113). Mahwah, NJ: Erlbaum.

Olson, M.W., & Gee, T.C. (1991). Content reading instruction in the primary grades: Perceptions and strategies. *The Reading Teacher, 45,* 298–307.

Pailliotet, A.W., Semali, L., Rodenberg, R.K., Giles, J.K., & Macaul, S.L. (2000). Intermediality: Bridge to critical media literacy. *The Reading Teacher, 54,* 208–219.

Parks, R., & Reed, G. (1994). *Quiet strength: The faith, the hope and the heart of a woman who changed the nation.* Michigan: Zondervon.

Pauk, W. (1974). *How to study in college.* Boston: Houghton Mifflin.

Paul, D.G. (2000). Rap and orality: Critical media literacy, pedagogy, and cultural synchronization. *Journal of Adolescent & Adult Literacy, 44,* 246–251.

Paul, R.W. (1993). *Critical thinking: How to prepare students for a rapidly changing world.* Santa Rosa, CA: Foundation for Critical Thinking.

Pearson, P.D., & Fielding, L. (1991). Comprehension instruction. In R. Barr, M.L. Kamil, P. Mosenthal, & P.D. Pearson (Eds.), *Handbook of reading research* (Vol. II) (pp. 815–860). New York: Longman.

Perkins, D.N. (1994). *Knowledge as design: A handbook for critical and creative discussion across the curriculum.* Pacific Grove, CA: Critical Thinking Press and Software.

Poe, E.A. (1974). The purloined letter. In *The American tradition in literature* (pp. 844–860). New York: Grosset & Dunlap.

Poe, E.A. (1979). The purloined letter. In *An Edgar Allan Poe reader: Adapted classic tales* (pp. 45–56). New York: Globe.

Poorman, L., & Wright, M. (2000). Middle school students learning to research: An inquiry-based approach. In M. McLaughlin & M. Vogt (Eds.), *Creativity and innovation in content area teaching* (pp. 259–280). Norwood, MA: Christopher-Gordon.

Powell, R., Cantrell, S.C., & Adams, S. (2001). Saving Black Mountain: The promise of critical literacy in a multicultural democracy. *The Reading Teacher, 54,* 772–781.

Power, B.M., & Hubbard, R.S. (2002). Oral histories as a research tool. *Language Arts, 79,* 309.

Pressley, M. (1995). More about the development of self-regulation: Complex, long-term, and thoroughly social. *Educational Psychologist, 30,* 207–212.

Pressley, M. (2000). What should comprehension instruction be the instruction of? In M.L.Kamil, P.B. Mosenthal, P.D. Pearson, & R. Barr (Eds.), *Handbook of reading research* (Vol. III) (pp. 545–561). Mahwah, NJ: Erlbaum.

Pressley, M. (2002). Comprehension strategies instruction: A turn-of-the-century status report. In C.C. Block & M. Pressley (Eds.), *Comprehension instruction: Research-based best practices* (pp. 11–27). New York: Guilford.

Pressley, M., El-Dinary, R.B., Gaskins, I., Schinder, T., Bergman, J.L., Almasi, J., & Brown, R. (1992). Beyond direct exploration: Transactional instruction of reading comprehension strategies. *Elementary School Journal, 92,* 513–535.

Purcell-Gates, V. (2001). What we know about readers who struggle. In R.F. Flippo (Ed.), *Reading researchers in search of common ground* (pp. 118–128). Newark, DE: International Reading Association.

Rand Study Group. (2002). *Reading for understanding: Toward an R&D program in reading comprehension*. Santa Monica, CA: Author.

Randall, S.N. (1996). Information charts: A strategy for organizing student research. *Journal of Adolescent & Adult Literacy*, *39*, 536–542.

Readence, J.E., Bean, T.W., & Baldwin, R.S. (2001). *Content area reading: An integrated approach* (7th ed.). Dubuque, IA: Kendall/Hunt.

Reasoner, C. (1976). *Releasing childen to literature* (Rev. ed.). New York: Dell.

Reinking, D. (2001). Multimedia and engaged reading in a digital world. In L. Verhoeven & C.E. Snow (Eds.), *Literacy and motivation: Reading engagement in individuals and groups* (pp. 195–221). Mahwah, NJ: Erlbaum.

Richardson, J. (2000). *Read it aloud*. Newark, DE: International Reading Association.

Risko, V.J., Fairbanks, M.M., & Alvarez, M.C. (1991). Internal factors that influence study. In R.F. Flippo & D.C. Caverly (Eds.), *Teaching reading & study strategies at the college level* (pp. 237–253). Newark, DE: International Reading Association.

Ritter, S., & Idol-Maestas, L. (1986). Teaching middle school students to use a test-taking strategy. *Journal of Educational Research Quarterly*, *79*, 350–357.

Robinson, H.A. (1975). *Teaching reading and study strategies: The content areas*. Boston: Allyn and Bacon.

Rogovin, P. (2001). *The research workshop: Bringing the world into your classroom*. Portsmouth, NH: Heinemann.

Rosenbaum, C. (2001). A word map for middle school: A tool for effective vocabulary instruction. *Journal of Adolescent & Adult Literacy, 45*, 44–49.

Rosenblatt, L. (1978). *The reader, the text, the poem: The transactional theory of the literacy work*. Carbondale, IL: Southern Illinois University Press.

Rosenblatt, L. (1994). The transactional theory of reading and writing. In R.B. Ruddell, M.R. Ruddell, & H. Singer (Eds.), *Theoretical models and processes of reading* (4th ed.) (pp. 1057–1092). Newark, DE: International Reading Association.

Rothstein, R. (1998). Bilingual education: The controversy. *Phi Delta Kappan*, *79*, 672–684.

Ruddell, R.B. (2002). *Teaching children to read and write: Becoming an influential teacher* (3rd ed.). Boston: Allyn and Bacon.

Ruiz, N.T., Vargas, E., & Betrán, A. (2002). Becoming a reader and writer in a bilingual special education classroom. *Language Arts*, *79*, 297–309.

Ryder, R.J. (1994). Using frames to promote critical writing. *Journal of Reading*, *38*, 210–218.

Ryder, R.J., & Graves, M.F. (1998). *Reading and learning in content areas* (2nd ed.). Upper Saddle River, NJ: Merrill.

Sadler, C.R. (2001). *Comprehension strategies for middle grade learners: A handbook for content area teachers*. Newark, DE: International Reading Association.

Sakta, C.G. (1998/1999). SQRC: A strategy for guiding reading and higher level thinking. *Journal of Adolescent & Adult Literacy*, *42*, 265–269.

Sampson, M.B., Sampson, M.R., & Linek, W. (1995). Circle of questions. *The Reading Teacher, 48,* 364–365.

Samuels, S.J. (1979). The method of repeated readings. *The Reading Teacher, 32,* 403–408.

Santa, C.M., Dailey, S.C., & Nelson, M. (1985). Free-response and opinion proof: A reading and writing strategy for middle grade and secondary teachers. *Journal of Reading, 28,* 346–352.

Scala, M.C. (2001). *Working together: Reading and writing in inclusive classrooms.* Newark, DE: International Reading Association.

Schon, I. (2002). From *Días de Pinta* to *Las Christmas*: Noteworthy books in Spanish for adolescents. *Journal of Adolescent & Adult Literacy, 45,* 410–414.

Schumm, J.S., & Mangrum, D.T. (1991). FLIP: A framework for content area reading. *Journal of Reading, 35,* 120–124.

Schwartz, R. (1988). Learning to learn vocabulary in content area textbooks. *Journal of Reading, 32,* 108–118.

Schwartz, R., & Raphael, T. (1985). Concept of definition: A key to improving students' vocabulary. *The Reading Teacher, 39,* 198–205.

Scieszka, J. (1995). *Math curse.* New York: Viking.

Sejnost, R., & Thiese, S. (2001). *Reading and writing across content areas.* Arlington Heights, IL: Skylight Professional Development.

Shearer, B.A. (2000). Student-directed written inquiry: Transferring ownership to students. In M. McLaughlin & M. Vogt (Eds.), *Creativity and innovation in content area teaching* (pp. 209–229). Norwood, MA: Christopher-Gordon.

Short, K., Harste, J., & Burke, C. (1996). *Creating classrooms for authors and inquirers.* Portsmouth, NH: Heinemann.

Siegel, M., & Fernandez, S.L. (2000). Critical approaches. In M.L. Kamil, R. Barr, P.D. Pearson, & P. Mosenthal (Eds.), *Handbook of reading research* (Vol. III) (pp. 141–151). Mahwah, NJ: Erlbaum.

Simpson, M.L. (1986). PORPE: A writing strategy for studying and learning in the content areas. *Journal of Reading, 29,* 407–414.

Simpson, M.L. (1993, December). *An examination of elaborative verbal rehearsals and their impact on college freshmen's cognitive and metacognitive performance.* Paper presented at the annual meeting of the National Reading Conference, Charleston, SC.

Simpson, M.L., & Nist, S.L. (2002). Encouraging active reading at the college level. In C.C. Block & M. Pressley (Eds.), *Comprehension instruction: Research-based best practices* (pp. 365–378). New York: Guilford.

Sinatra, G.M., Brown, K.J., & Reynolds, R.E. (2002). Implications of cognitive resource allocation for comprehension strategies instruction. In C.C. Block & M. Pressley (Eds.), *Comprehension instruction: Research-based best practices* (pp. 62–76). New York: Guilford.

Sis, P. (1996). *Starry messenger: Galileo Galilei.* New York: Farrar, Straus & Giroux.

Smith, D. (1992). Common ground: The connection between reader-response and textbook reading. *Journal of Reading, 35,* 630–634.

Spiegel, D.L. (1981). Six alternatives to the directed reading activity. *The Reading Teacher, 34,* 914–922.

Spinelli, J. (2000). *Stargirl.* New York: Knopf.

Spivey, N.N. (1997). *The constructivist metaphor.* San Diego: Academic Press.

Spor, M.W., & Schneider, B.K. (1999). Content reading strategies: What teachers know, use, and want to learn. *Reading Research and Instruction, 38,* 221–231.

Stahl, N.A., King, J.R., & Henk, W.A. (1991). Enhancing students' notetaking through training and evaluation. *Journal of Reading, 34,* 614–622.

Stahl, S.A. (1986). Three principles of effective vocabulary instruction. *Journal of Reading, 29,* 662–668.

Stahl, S.A., Hynd, C.R., Glynn, S.M., & Carr, M. (1996). Beyond reading to learn: Developing content and disciplinary knowledge through texts. In L. Baker, P. Afflerbach, & D. Reinking (Eds.), *Developing engaged readers in school and home communities* (pp. 139–163). Mahwah, NJ: Erlbaum.

Stauffer, R.G. (1969). *Directing reading maturity as a cognitive process.* New York: Harper and Row.

Stephens, E.C., & Brown, J.E. (1994). Discussion continuum. *The Journal of Reading, 37,* 680–681.

Stephens, E.C., & Brown, J.E. (2000). *A handbook of content literacy strategies: 75 practical reading and writing ideas.* Norwood, MA: Christopher-Gordon.

Stevens, L.P. (2001, December). *A critical discourse analysis of two science teachers' literacy practices.* Paper presented at the National Reading Conference, San Antonio, TX.

Taba, H. (1967). *Teacher's handbook for elementary social studies.* Reading, MS: Addison Wesley.

Tanner, M.L., & Casados, L. (1998). Promoting and studying discussions in math classes. *Journal of Adolescent & Adult Literacy, 41,* 342–350.

Taylor, B.M., & Beach, R.W. (1984). The effects of text structure instruction on middle-grade students' comprehension and production of expository text. *Reading Research Quarterly, 19,* 134–146.

Taylor, K., & Walton, S. (2002). Questioning the answers. *Instructor, 111,* 16.

Tiedt, I.M. (2000). *Teaching with picture books in the middle school.* Newark, DE: International Reading Association.

Tobias, M.C. (1988). Teaching strategic text review by computer and interaction with student characteristics. *Computers in Human Behavior, 4,* 299–310.

Tomlinson, L.M. (1995). Flag words for efficient thinking, active reading, comprehension, and test taking. *Journal of Reading, 38,* 387–388.

Trabasso, T., & Bouchard, E. (2002). Teaching readers how to comprehend text strategically. In C.C. Block & M. Pressley (Eds.), *Comprehension instruction: Research-based best practices* (pp. 176–200). New York: Guilford.

Trelease, J. (2001). *The read-aloud handbook* (5th ed.). New York: Penguin.

United States Bureau of the Census. (1998). *Statistical abstract of the United States* (118th ed.). Washington, DC: U.S. Government Printing Office.

Unrau, N.J. (1997). *Thoughtful teachers, thoughtful learners: A guide to helping adolescents think critically.* Scarborough, Ontario: Pippin.

Vacca, R.T., & Vacca, J.L. (1999). *Content area reading* (6th ed.). New York: Longman.

Vacca, R.T., & Vacca, J.L. (2002). *Content area reading* (7th ed.). Boston: Allyn and Bacon.

Verhoeven, L., & Snow, C.E. (2001). Literacy and motivation: Bridging cognitive and sociocultural viewpoints. In L. Verhoeven & C.E. Snow (Eds.), *Literacy and motivation: Reading engagement in individuals and groups* (pp. 1–20). Mahwah: NJ: Erlbaum.

Vygotsky, L.S. (1978). *Mind in society: The development of higher psychological processes.* Cambridge, MA: Harvard University Press.

Weaver, C.A. III, & Kintsch, W. (1991). Expository text. In R. Barr, M.L.Kamil, P. Mosenthal, & P.D. Pearson (Eds.), *Handbook of reading research* (Vol. II) (pp. 230–245). White Plains, NY: Longman.

Wertsch, J.V. (1991). *Voices of the mind: A sociocultural approach to mediated action.* Cambridge, MA: Harvard University Press.

Whitin, P. (2002). Leading into literature circles through the sketch-to-stretch strategy. *The Reading Teacher*, 55, 444–450.

Wilkinson, L., & Silliman, E. (1997). Alternative assessment, literacy education and school reform. In J. Flood & D. Lapp (Eds.), *Handbook for literacy educators* (pp. 6–76). Newark, DE/New York: International Reading Association and Macmillan.

Wink, J. (2001). *Critical pedagogy: Notes from the real world* (2nd ed.). New York: Longman.

Wood, K.D. (1984). Probable passages: A writing strategy. *The Reading Teacher, 37*, 496–499.

Wooten, D.A. (2000). *Valued voices: An interdisciplinary approach to teaching and learning.* Newark, DE: International Reading Association.

Yopp, R.H., & Yopp, H.K. (2001). *Literature-based reading activities* (3rd ed.). Boston: Allyn and Bacon.

Zemelman, S., Bearden, P., Simmons, Y., & Leki, P. (1999). *History comes home.* Portland, ME: Stenhouse.

Zorfass, J.M. (1998). *Teaching middle school students to be active researchers.* Alexandria, VA: Association for Supervision and Curriculum Development.

Content Area Texts

BSCS biology: An ecological approach. (1998). Dubuque, IA: Kendall/Hunt.

Biology. (1981). New York: Macmillan.

Exploring art. (1992). Mission Hills, CA: Macmillan/McGraw-Hill.

Exploring our world: Eastern hemisphere. (1980). Chicago: Follett.

Government in the United States. (1990). New York: Glencoe/McGraw-Hill.

History of England. (1974). London: Collins.

Literature and language. (1994). Evanston, IL: McDougal, Littell.

Science and technology: Changes we make. (1985). San Diego: Coronado.

Science interactions. (1995). New York: McGraw-Hill.

The pageant of world history. (1994). Needham, MA: Prentice-Hall.

Notes and Favorite Strategies

INDEX